Learning Activities for the Young Preschool Child

Learning Activities for the Young Preschool Child

Rita Watrin
Paul Hanly Furfey
The Catholic University of America

D. VAN NOSTRAND COMPANY
New York · Cincinnati · Toronto · London · Melbourne

D. Van Nostrand Company Regional Offices:
New York   Cincinnati

D. Van Nostrand Company International Offices:
London   Toronto   Melbourne

Copyright © 1978 by Litton Educational Publishing, Inc.
Library of Congress Catalog Card Number: 77–939–29

ISBN: 0–442–29227–9

Published by D. Van Nostrand Company
135 West 50th Street, New York, N.Y.   10020

10 9 8 7 6 5 4 3 2 1

Preface

The goal of a good day care center is to stimulate and support the growth of young children. By giving children the opportunity for play, both spontaneous and structured, in an active, secure, and loving environment, a good center contributes to the mental, social, emotional, and physical development of the child. Even though early development of a child's human potential does not guarantee satisfactory continued growth in later, less stimulating environments, it can prevent mental stagnation that can severely limit the child's capacity to learn in future years.

Learning is as natural for the normal infant as is physical growth and development. Two important elements in maintaining this natural capacity to learn are the physical and social environments. The physical environment should provide a wide range of objects and the freedom to explore them; the social environment should provide care and attention and appropriate learning opportunities in an atmosphere that makes learning enjoyable and satisfying for young children. In such an environment most children are eager to learn.

The primary task of the teacher in a day-care center is to provide a learning environment that allows the child to learn naturally. To do this successfully, the teacher must use materials and teaching strategies that match each child's level of development, each child's way of learning. What is interesting to, and within the learning capability of, one child may be outside the interest and capability of another child. The purpose of this book is to help teachers find activities suitable to the child's level of development.

Learning Activities for the Young Preschool Child is primarily a practical how-to book that provides preservice and inservice teachers with structured play activities in teaching toddlers from the ages of one to three. It makes available sound teaching and learning principles, appropriate and inexpensive materials, and a variety of teaching strategies which encourage specific kinds of learning by children at varied developmental levels. Equally practical are the guidelines for developing and maintaining an emotional climate that frees the child for learning and enjoying each new experience. In addition, recipes and directions for constructing simple teaching materials are included. Constructing these materials requires no special talents of the teacher and the child can often be an active participant.

The organization of the book also contributes to its practicality and ease of use. The first three sections lay a foundation for the 170 model activities that make up the remainder of the book. These sections present general principles of child development in early years, appropriate teaching principles and guidelines, and an explanation of the book's structure and use.

Following these introductory sections are 11 broad learning areas: sensory skills, motor skills, art, music, books, dramatic play and games, puzzles, sorting and ordering, mathematics, science, and trips. Each learning area is introduced with a brief exposition of the nature and purpose of the learning activities within the section, along with important teaching guidelines, strategies, and learning materials.

The activities share a common format of performance objectives, materials needed, the lesson proper (provided through sample language and specific teaching strategies), additional information on inexpensive materials and specific teaching tips, and suggested follow-up activities for repeating, reinforcing, and extending the learning. Within each activity section, the lessons are classified by the developmental levels of young children (which are defined in the text) and are arranged in a learning sequence from less difficult to more difficult.

Thus the entire book, through its content and organization, permits the student teacher to begin developing expertise in selecting and using appropriate learning experiences for individual children and in planning other play activities that incorporate sound teaching and learning strategies for young children. Through these efforts, the teacher will create an environment that will make learning enjoyable and exciting for both the young learner and the teacher.

SPECIAL ACKNOWLEDGEMENT

This book was written under the auspices of the Curriculum Development Center, School of Education, The Catholic University of America, Washington, D. C.

Introduction

The present book grew out of a large research undertaking, the Infant Education Research Project (IERP), which was financed by the National Institute of Mental Health, grant number MH09224, from September 1, 1965 to August 31, 1971, and carried out by the Bureau of Social Research of The Catholic University of America. The project was conceived by Earl Schaefer of the Center for Studies of Child and Family Mental Health, NIMH. This study has been adequately described elsewhere and no more need be said about it here.[1] The important point, however, is that the research involved devising methods for intellectually stimulating a group of 28 male, black, inner-city infants from the ages of 15 to 36 months. They were visited in their homes for one hour a day, five days a week, by staff members who were referred to as "tutors." Afterwards, up to the age of six years they were followed less intensely.

There was the obvious problem of devising specific techniques for mental stimulation. How does one teach a toddler to distinguish between soft and hard objects? To "read" a picture? Or to sort big and little buttons by size? Very little had been written about such specific questions. So the tutors tried out their own ideas. The first working hour of each day was devoted to a staff meeting at which the tutors described their efforts to interest the children and discussed the failure or success of these efforts. Thus, gradually, by trial and error, successful techniques were worked out. For the sake of uniformity, the agreed-upon techniques were written out and passed among the tutors. When particularly difficult problems arose, special meetings were called to which Earl Schaefer would invite colleagues from NIMH who had special competence in special fields. Out of all these cooperative efforts was built a collection of tested techniques for stimulating young children of various early ages in a wide variety of areas.

As the IERP began to near its end, the staff began to realize how valuable their well-tested methods might be to a wide readership, to the staffs of day-care centers and nursery schools, to parents, indeed, to anyone who had to deal with young children. So it was decided to publish the stimulation techniques in book form. This involved a good deal of revision in order to make

[1] Earl S. Schaefer and May Aaronson, "Infant Education Research Project: Implementation and Implications of a Home Tutoring Program," in *The Preschool in Action: Exploring Early Childhood Programs,* edited by Ronald K. Parker (Boston: Allyn and Bacon, Inc., 1972).

clear to outsiders things that were taken for granted within the staff. Background information was also supplied so that a reader could understand what specific techniques were appropriate for a particular child.

At this point, Brother John D. Olsen, then Assistant Dean of the School of Education at Catholic University, offered his cooperation. The school's Curriculum Development Center took over after the IERP grant expired in 1971. A preliminary edition of the text, then a manual, was published in 1972. After this, an enormous amount of revision and rewriting was undertaken by the Center. The present volume is the result.

The reader should bear in mind that the material in this text is prepared for use with young children of both sexes. The pronouns *he* and *his* are sometimes used to refer to the child, but this is done merely to avoid the awkwardness of such expressions as *he/she* and *his/her*. The lessons presented are deliberately planned for use with both young boys and girls.

This book is the result of the cooperation of a great many people. The bulk of the original work was done by the IERP staff: Beatrice Ashford, Lucille Banks, Jane Blais, Patricia Cernoff, Patricia Gentry, Bonita Jones, Betty Pair, Caroline Parnell, Lydia Thornton, Joicey White, and Carol Zucker. One male staff member, Belford Fisher, cooperated on special occasions. All these were supervised first by Maureen Nichols and then Lillie Davidson. The latter also worked for the Curriculum Development Center after the end of the IERP. Many of Earl Schaefer's colleagues at NIMH also helped, particularly, May Aaronson, Julie Forest, and Linda Waldman. Lois Bellin of New York University was called in for a short time as a special consultant. After the work was taken over by the Curriculum Development Center, one individual is particularly worthy of mention: special thanks are extended to Dorothy G. French, Special Consultant and Lecturer on Early Childhood Education, who provided extensive and valuable criticism and suggestions throughout the rewriting process. As the reader can see, this volume represents the combined experience and judgment of many persons.

Sincere thanks must also go to the staff and delightful youngsters of St. Joseph's Day Care Center, Washington, D.C. Observing and photographing the children in the happy process of learning was indeed a pleasure, one which we hope readers will share.

Paul Hanly Furfey
Rita Watrin

Contents

Part 2.   Motor Skills   79

Part 3.   Art   145

Part 4. Music   **189**

Part 5. Books   **227**

Part 9. Mathematics 367

Part 10. Science 403

Part 11. Trips   **439**

Index   **462**

EARLY YEARS: A PERIOD OF RAPID GROWTH

Although considerable controversy and debate focus on early childhood education, on what and how to teach the preschooler, general agreement does exist on the great amount of learning mastered by the normal child in the first three years of life. During this period most children learn to walk and to talk. They develop voluntary muscle control so that they are able to feed and toilet themselves, to manipulate objects, to run and jump, and to climb stairs. They develop emotionally, socially, and intellectually as they explore their surroundings and experience new relationships with objects and people.

The rapid development that takes place during this period becomes even more apparent when one compares children of 12 months to children of 36 months. At 12 months, most youngsters can stand; some can take a few steps without help. Left to themselves, they get around on all fours. Toddlers of 36 months have developed sufficient balance and coordination not only to run and jump but also to perform such feats as hopping, kicking a ball, and climbing stairs. One-year-olds may say "ma–ma" or "da–da" or "bye–bye." The same youngsters at age three will have acquired a good working vocabulary, will articulate more plainly, and will use short sentences which include the rudiments of grammatical form.

Between the first and the third birthday these children achieve a great deal in many other areas. They move gradually toward some degree of self-control as they begin to understand what *need* means. They become less demanding, willing more often to wait "until it is time" or to "take turns." A degree of independence develops which permits older youngsters to tolerate separation from their mothers and to play by themselves with objects and toys of high interest. During this period children usually pass through a highly possessive stage to one in which they are more willing to share their belongings. At this stage greater sensitivity to other people develops as is shown by their desire to please others. They learn to respond to simple commands and to attend to and exchange ideas with others. The attention span increases from a few minutes of concentrated play and learning to more extended periods of concentration. In other words, during this period the child is becoming more recognizably human in behavior.

The learning of these junior members of human society is even more remarkable when one realizes that during these same early years they are learning a whole way of life. Not only do young children learn a particular language and a particular dialect within that language, but they learn also the basic elements of a culture: the clothes, the food habits, the customs and values of the group to which they belong. The newborn is so adaptable that he can be made to adopt fully any life-style into which he is born. And an

1

important part of this adaptation is accomplished between the ages of one and three. Clearly, those around the child have a great responsibility, for to a surprising extent they make him what he is and what he will become.

Research findings in child development further emphasize the importance of the child's intellectual development in early years. Considerable evidence has been offered that a child's intelligence is highly flexible during his first three or four years. The theory is that intelligence can be stimulated and raised in these preschool years, but that, once set, greater forces are needed to bring about change in a child's social and intellectual competencies.[2]

Relevant to this theory and especially significant to this book is the Infant Education Research Project (IERP) described in the introduction. The purpose of the IERP was to study the effect of intellectual stimulation in a group of culturally deprived infants. The children, from the age of 15 months until they were 36 months old, were tutored in their homes for one hour a day, five days a week. The tutoring program provided a broad range of experiences and verbal interaction that typically occurs in a highly motivated middle-class family. The need met by the program was for varied materials, methods, and activities to create a high level of child interest and enthusiasm and, through these experiences, to maintain and promote the child's intellectual development. The activities of this text are adapted from the IERP activities.

The project was also concerned with the emotional factor in early learning. It confirmed that a good mother–child relationship, interest in the child's education, and verbal interactions with the child are related to early intellectual development. The same is probably true of the teacher–child relationship. Moreover, the relationship between a mother's acceptance of the child and her informal efforts to teach the child were paralleled by the relationship between the child's competence and his adjustment. From this evidence it was concluded that a good educational program can and should promote both competence (intellectual development) and adjustment (social and emotional development).

As recognized and confirmed by the IERP, a strikingly important factor in the young child's development is the emotional relationship between the child and his mother or mother-substitute. Progress toward emotional maturity is very much affected by this relationship. Emotional development, in turn, affects intellectual and social development. Children who were raised in hospitals or institutions without a mother or a mother-figure to show them love and affection have been found to remain emotionally immature, to relate poorly to others, to be apathetic and inaccessible, and even to be re-

[2] Benjamin S. Bloom, *Stability and Change in Human Characteristics* (New York: John Wiley and Sons, 1964); Burton L. White and Jean G. Watts, *Experience and Environment: Major Influences on the Development of Young Children* (Englewood Cliffs, N.J.: Prentice–Hall, 1971).

tarded intellectually. Evidence is not conclusive, but there is some reason to believe that a child thus emotionally retarded cannot be totally remediated by later treatment.

Whether such emotional damage is permanent or not, one certainly does not want it to occur. Love and affection are important in the education of young children. The educational process is not entirely intellectual. Emotional factors must be considered in any learning activities involving a child and an adult. Whether the child is acquiring sensory or motor skills or exploring new experiences in art or music or what-have-you, the instructor must show interest and give encouragement, praise learning successes (however small), and demonstrate affection and approval by a hug, a smile, a comforting pat. For then the child learns something else. He learns to relate positively to another human being, to acquire self-confidence and a sense of security—all of which make for emotional maturity and an emotional environment that is supportive of the youngster's intellectual growth.

Also relevant to this book are Piaget's research findings on the stages of intellectual development. Understanding the basic rudiments of the child's intellectual development from birth through his first years is important in understanding how young children learn and in planning effective educational activities for children in their first years.

According to Piaget, infants from birth to about two years of age learn by using their senses: looking, listening, smelling, tasting, and touching. They develop motor or action responses to their sensory experiences, including such movements as grasping, throwing, banging, and waving. They learn to recognize familiar objects which they experience frequently through their senses. They learn that a bottle is for drinking, a rattle is for shaking, a coat and cap are for going "bye–bye." They also begin to become aware of the permanency of objects in that they will look for a ball that has rolled away or for a toy when asked, for example, "Where's Teddy?" But in this first stage, children learn through their senses by interacting with the environment; that is, by interacting with the concrete or real objects and people that are part of their environment.

Sometime around two years of age, children move into a new stage of intellectual development and remain there usually until the age of six or seven. In this stage children are no longer completely confined to sensory–motor learning in dealing with their environment. They now begin to build mental pictures, or *concepts,* of objects and situations encountered frequently, and to use these concepts in their thought processes. And because they are learning to talk, they are able not only to learn the labels (names) of these concepts but also to use these concept words to communicate their thoughts to others without the actual presence of the real objects in their immediate environment.

Concept development at this second stage still depends largely on sensory–motor experiences with real objects and situations. The child, for example, will develop the rudiments of the concept *bus* by seeing and hearing various buses as they pass by on the street. This concept expands and becomes more accurate when the child experiences how it feels to ride a bus, watches someone drive the bus, and becomes aware that a bus takes him to a park with ''lots of swings and a big slide.'' Once a mental picture of a bus is formed in the child's mind, he can then think and talk about a bus without having one in view.

As a youngster's experiences with real objects and events and language competencies increase, he is also storing up many perceptions in his mind. Through these perceptions he begins to discover relationships which exist between objects and/or events—that, for instance, the little box will go inside the big box or that setting the table means it is time to eat. This new ability provides the child with a new way of interpreting the environment. He no longer sees it merely quantitatively, merely as a series of unrelated objects and situations. It now begins to take on qualitative aspects of size and color and shape, of relationships of likeness and difference, space and time. He becomes aware that some objects are red and some are blue; that one object is *on* the table and another is *under* the table; that eating breakfast comes *after* getting up in the morning; getting into pajamas, *before* going to bed at night.

In other words, as the young child progresses through this second stage of intellectual development, he is developing the ability to deal with objects and situations intellectually. He can think about real and experienced objects even when they are not physically present (recognition of the permanency of objects). He recognizes familiar objects even though viewed from different angles and distance (recognition of the constancy of objects). He develops the ability to organize his many perceptions to find relationships and to make finer discriminations among objects and events. Although the child still relies heavily upon his senses and firsthand experience for developing new concepts and for the store of perceptions from which an understanding of relationships grows, once these concepts and their relationships are grasped he is able to use them in his thought process. This is demonstrated by a mature three- or four-year-old who has had experiences in planting and watching a bean or tomato seed grow when he later says ruefully, ''I think my plant died because I forgot to water it.'' From his experiences with growing plants, he has grasped the relationship that exists between a plant and water, and has used this understanding in his thought process to find a reason for the unhappy demise of his plant.

An important point to remember is that the intellectual stage of the child, not his chronological age, determines what and how the child learns. In both of these early stages of intellectual development, the child's learning depends upon real objects and situations and upon the freedom to explore and manipulate the environment. Activity is vital if the child is to discover relationships that exist among objects and between himself and objects. Educational activities should center on building accurate though rudimentary concepts and on acquiring basic skills which will permit the youngster to acquire more complex competencies when he moves into the later stages of intellectual development.

The goal of education in the first years is to help the child to maximum development within each stage and thus to prepare him for the next stage. Providing activities beyond the child's intellectual, physical, social, or emotional development may not only cause frustrations but may also produce in the youngster negative feelings about learning in general, feelings he may well carry with him into his school years.

TEACHING THE TODDLER

Although the child's first years are a period of rapid growth and development, all children do not develop at the same rate. No specific time or schedule can be set for the mastery of skills by all children. One cannot say that a child *should* have learned to do this or to say that at a precise age. Each child is unique and develops at his own rate. Even though patterns or stages of growth, as well as general characteristics of youngsters at given age levels, have been identified, the individual child passes through these stages on his own timing. Moreover, within a particular child's growth pattern, that child may move at varied rates: sometimes rapidly, sometimes slowly.

A youngster will learn readily only when he is sufficiently matured and experienced for a particular learning task. Physical growth and muscular development can be dominant factors. A child, for example, cannot be taught to speak until nerves and muscles are so developed as to permit the complicated motions of the vocal organs involved in speech. Nor is the child ready to learn the skill of hopping on two feet until the balance and muscular control required in walking has been acquired with some degree of competence and confidence. Using a tool is another example of physical readiness. The toddler usually will be able to finger paint before he has acquired the muscular control and coordination needed for painting with a brush.

Readiness to learn also involves intellectual growth. The one-year-old who is in the sensory–motor stage of intellectual development cannot be expected to perform intellectual tasks which involve abstract qualities of objects (for example, color, shape) and use of perceptions to find relationships between objects. The ability to deal with objects and situations intellectually appears only in the child's second stage of intellectual development.[3] Put somewhat differently and more specifically, a youngster has to become aware of particular concrete objects through sensory and motor experiences before he is ready to organize his impressions and perceptions in such a way, for instance, to accomplish the more complicated intellectual task of sorting and ordering objects by gross differences of size, color, or shape.

Signs of readiness for learning·can often be seen in a child's behavior. An obvious interest in an activity is such a sign. Interest may be indicated by the child's watching intently while others perform a skill, by the questions the child asks, or by the attempts made to try some new activity on his own. The youngster who watches, fascinated, someone blowing bubbles, or who tries with gusty blows to produce the elusive bubbles, is probably ready to learn the art of bubble blowing. The child who asks questions about how a zipper works may well be willing to attend to a short, simple lesson on the manipulation of a zipper. Or the child who attempts to balance a large block on a small block, with some perserverance in his futile attempts, may be teling you that he is ready to be shown how to build a tall tower.

The principle of readiness does not necessarily mean that a teacher must simply wait for the child to give signs of readiness to learn. In fact, waiting may not be the problem. Indeed, the adult may find it difficult at times to keep up with a youngster's eagerness to try new skills and to learn new concepts. But readiness itself can often be taught in that the learner can be prepared for a complex learning task by activities that help him to master a single component of the complex task (for example, random scribbling with a crayon in preparation for using a crayon to draw objects—recognizable or unrecognizable). Activities to master a skill at its lowest level can also be considered readiness learning in preparation for mastering the skill at higher levels of competence (such as putting small objects in large wide-mouth containers in anticipation of putting even smaller objects in small-mouth containers).

Readiness can also be taught more informally in conversations with the child. To a youngster who is in the sensory–motor stage of intellectual development, you say casually, "Oh, you have your pretty *red* sweater on today." Or in an activity where the learning is focused on the skill of rolling a ball, you might direct the child to "Roll the *red* ball to me"—the red ball being the only one available to the child. By these and other similar instances, you are teaching readiness for the later task of distinguishing objects by color through familiarizing the toddler with the word *red* and with *red* objects, without expecting him to respond to the color *red* in any particular way.

---

[3] See pp. 3–4 for a discussion of these stages.

Often simply providing a youngster with materials fosters readiness. The child who is given a large box and blocks and is encouraged to put the blocks in the box as part of his play, or who discovers for himself that the blocks can go into the box, is being prepared or readied for the somewhat more complicated task of putting buttons in a coffee can. Suggesting without coercion, encouraging efforts begun but not completed, and simply helping the child over difficult spots are all ways to promote readiness for particular kinds of learning and to tempt the youngster into higher levels of learning.

Disinterest in a learning activity may be a sign of a lack of readiness. Insisting on the activity when a young child is not interested, for whatever reason, will produce little or no learning and may well cause frustrations and feelings which turn the youngster against the particular task. By the same token, a child's interest in a learning task is crucial to learning success, for only with interest will he give the needed attention to the task. Sustained attention depends also upon the degree of interest and curiosity manifested by the child.

Interest can be aroused through play, and play is the young child's way of learning. Through play, the child develops physically, emotionally, socially, and intellectually. Both spontaneous play initiated by the child and play which has been loosely structured by an adult provide avenues for the youngster to explore and discover the world and for the development of a great many skills. It is through play that the child's attention is captured and his imaginative and creative forces are unloosed. By manipulating objects in play, he practices a variety of skills, making them so much a part of himself (internalization) that they become the basis of his thought process. Not only does the young child learn little by quietly listening to an adult, but what he learns is not likely to be internalized and is soon forgotten.

The key to fostering a young child's total development is the provision of many opportunities and a large variety of concrete objects for spontaneous exploration, or play, in a secure, trusting climate. More formal learning can also be provided if it is introduced as play, as something exciting, something that is fun. "Let's play a game," or "Let's have fun with these boxes," may be all that is needed to get the child's attention and lead him into productive play. If the planned activity is of interest to the child and remains fun for him, learning is likely to take place.

From these basic ideas of varied learning rates, readiness for learning, play, and interest, flow several general principles of teaching and learning which are of importance in tutoring the toddler. They are discussed briefly below.

1. Provide the child with many opportunities for spontaneous play by furnishing him with interesting toys and objects that he is free, and safe, to explore and manipulate. Extend the climate of play and exploration into

your more structured learning activities so that they become a natural out-growth of play and part of the young child's play experiences.

A climate of play implies a certain degree of freedom for the child, freedom to express himself and to react to materials and objects in his own way. When a child's interest takes off in a direction different from that of your planned activity, follow the lead. You may be pleasantly surprised at how much of your planned lesson the youngster is able to discover on his own. And you can always bring him back to the planned activity or try it on another day.

2. Plan your learning activities around familiar real objects and situations in the child's world. Exotic objects and fancy, detailed toys are often of very little interest to young children. They are more apt to be interested in the box the toy came in than in the toy itself.

Moreover, because young children must rely on sensory–motor experiences for learning, the actual presence of objects on which learning is focused is vital for learning to take place. An activity based on, say, a flower seen last week or yesterday or even an hour ago usually has little or no learning value for one- or two-year-olds. Nor can you teach effectively about rain on a clear, sunny day. Yet how easily most children learn about flowers when they see, feel, and smell a flower, and about rain when they feel it on their hands and face, see it on a window pane, and walk (boots on, of course!) through tempting small rain puddles.

3. Planned learning activities for young children must be *doing* activities. Involve them whenever possible in all aspects of the activity. Let them help prepare and arrange materials for an activity when the tasks are simple. In a pasting activity, for example, not only should children be directly involved in the pasting, but they might also help make the paste and lay out other materials to be used. In other words, don't do anything yourself that the toddler can already do safely for himself. He is the one who needs the experience and the practice. And being overprotective and overhelpful encourages over-dependency.

4. Language should be made a tool, as well as an objective, of learning. In your activities often ask simple questions that you think the toddler can answer. You might ask, for example, in a tasting activity using fruit, "Where is the apple?" "Do you like apples?" "What color is the apple?" Or if the child cannot yet distinguish colors, "The apple is red, isn't it?" Such questions become a technique for keeping the child involved in the activity as well as a way to review and check on what the youngster has already learned about particular objects or situations or, as in the last question, to prepare him for future learning (distinguishing colors).

As language competencies grow, encourage the young child to talk about what he sees or experiences and how he feels about it. Not only do these conversations provide needed language practice, but also they contribute to the child's intellectual, social, and emotional development. The child uses language to help clarify his thoughts, to put his thinking into words. And an interested, accepting listener gives him good feelings about himself, feelings of worth and self-confidence.

These conversations, too, provide the adult with opportunities to note and correct, pleasantly and patiently, many misconceptions held by children. But in your talks with toddlers, use words they understand, keep your answers to questions short and simple but accurate, and avoid long explanations. If you fail to follow these rules, you force the child into the role of a passive listener who soon becomes disinterested in the subject.

5. A well-planned schedule of different kinds of activities will make the child's day—and yours—more pleasant, interesting, and profitable. Observe the child frequently in his spontaneous play to help you make decisions about readiness and interest, and select and plan your activities accordingly.

Work on quiet attention-demanding activities, when the child is alert and well rested. Start, for instance, with book, puzzle, or sorting tasks and then move on to games, music, art, or any other activity requiring less concentrated effort or more noisy, romping participation.

Changing pace in keeping with the child's attention span and interest is an important part of a workable schedule. If the child becomes absorbed in an activity which is not particularly fatiguing, do not insist on switching to another one simply because your schedule calls for a change. Absorption is a sign of interest and learning.

6. Small children like to play with familiar toys and materials. They often develop a strong attachment to certain toys. Capitalize whenever possible on the toddler's preference. A favorite teddy bear or blocks can be used over and over again in a variety of activities. Teddy, for example, can be given rides to practice the motor skills of pushing and pulling or can be included in the child's dramatic play or in listening to a story. The blocks can be used for filling containers and building towers and in a variety of sorting and counting activities.

Familiarity with a song, story, or puzzle often makes it more enjoyable for the child. The familiar and the enjoyable can be reused as long as the youngster remains interested. A good balance, however, between old, familiar objects and new ones is best. Introduce new toys and materials while keeping the old and familiar ones around. Your goal is to provide the child with an ever-widening world of objects and experiences, but always at a pace that is comfortable for the child. Cramming too many new things too rapidly into the youngster's play will only bewilder him.

7. Reinforcement and assimilation of learning are key factors in the education of the very young. Youngsters need to hear words over and over again. They need to meet the same object often and in different settings and situations. They need to experience many examples of a class of objects to form

the rudiments of accurate concepts. They need to practice a newly acquired skill to gain proficiency, gradually enlarging and extending it to include somewhat more complex aspects of the skill.

An example of this principle in action can be drawn from the skill of sorting. A youngster usually requires many experiences in sorting objects to acquire the concepts *like* and *different*. He sorts blocks/balls, spoons/forks, mittens/socks, and many other household objects with a focus on their important similarities and differences. Once these concepts are grasped, he then needs time to assimilate what has been learned. So continuing to practice sorting skills is important. Interest in sorting tasks can be maintained by changing the kinds of objects to be sorted. Or the task can be made more difficult, and interesting, by increasing the number of kinds of objects (spoons/forks/knives) or by looking for finer distinctions among the objects (little spoons/big spoons).

This approach to learning is far more valuable to the child than one in which the child is introduced to a great many skills for shorter periods of time. In the latter, the youngster will probably never really assimilate or internalize the learning to make it a permanent part of himself and a stepping stone to more complex related learning.

8.   Don't expect instant learning every time from toddlers; they will not always succeed at an activity on the first try. Even when a youngster is ready and interested, the activity may have to be repeated several, or many, times before the learning is mastered or even partially mastered. This is particularly true when the learning is focused on abstract concepts such as colors and relationships of space (*on, off*) or time (*before, after*).

Repetition of activities for mastery of learning will not become a problem if you keep the activity fun for the youngster. Adapt the activity to include questions he can answer and things he can do while trying to lure him to go beyond to the new learning task. Because the child gains some satisfaction in knowing and doing, and has fun, he will probably be willing to repeat the activity at later times.

You may find, too, that some of the activities in this text need to be broken into two or more activities for a child—either because his attention spar. will not carry him through the entire activity in a single session or because he needs time and repetition to assimilate the learning of one part before he is ready to tackle the next learning step. Do not force the issue of continuing in these instances. Praise the youngster's initial success, and repeat the first step. Plan activities around the additional learning steps for use on other days.

9.   Emotional reinforcement is also important for the small child's learning. Good feelings come from being accepted and loved by others, from enjoying comfortable, trusting relationships with teachers and other adults, and from being able to do things. Acceptance, approval, and praise are all part

of a good relationship between the child and the teacher. They are also part of the climate for learning.

The emphasis in learning must be on the positive, not on the negative. Tell the toddler what he is doing right to encourage continued effort and to make him feel that he can do it. Compliment him on things done well. Let your voice and gestures indicate acceptance and approval. When possible, and especially in music and art activities, copy some of the child's acceptable behaviors, for young children generally view such emulation as a high form of praise and approval. Simply stopping and listening to what a child has to say and showing interest in what he is doing indicate acceptance and caring.

Patience, of course, is a necessary virtue for the tutor of small children. One way to practice it is to ignore mistakes whenever you can. When you feel that you should make a correction, don't make too much of it. To a youngster who points to a green balloon and says, "Red," say only, "Green," and continue with the activity or your conversation with the child. If the error involves some form of motor skill, you might say calmly, "Let me help you," or, "Let me show you again," and encourage the youngster to try once more.

Try always to prevent complete failure by the child. When a task becomes frustrating or the child loses interest, move on to a task the child is able and likes to do. Help him over difficult spots so that he can again continue with confidence restored. But don't be overprotective. Don't be too quick with the answer or with physical help. By stepping in too soon you may restrict the child's efforts and limit imagination and creativity. The youngster needs some challenge and time to meet the challenge, time to discover some things for himself. What he doesn't need is frustration and total failure.

If you are working with toddlers in an infant education program, some additional teaching–learning principles are relevant and important.

10. It is important for small children to like and trust the grown-ups around them. Children who are fearful or unhappy will not be able to play and talk with you in a free and easy manner. Building a warm and friendly feeling between you and the child may not always be easy. But the best learning and teaching will take place only when you and the child have a good feeling for each other. Thus, the first days of an infant education program should be used primarily to help the youngster become more comfortable and at ease with the adults and other children in the program.

The new youngster may be experiencing for the first time a prolonged separation from his parents or parent-figure. To make the separation easier a few strategies are suggested. (a) Invite the mother or father to stay and participate with the child in his first activities. (b) A special part of a room could be selected as the place for the new child to become acquainted with his teacher. If several attractive toys are available on low shelves, the child can be encouraged to select one and play with it. If the child is very shy and withdrawn, the parent could select a toy and play with him, but the teacher should also join in the play. (c) Showing the child around his new environment can be comforting to a new child and can speed up his feeling of being at ease. To make him feel that he belongs, show him things he will be using and talk about them. "This is your very own coat hook. We'll put your coat here each day. Watch while I write your name to show that this is Tom's coat hook." Or you might say, "This is the table where we will eat lunch. I think you are going to like your lunch today." Show an older child the bathroom and how to use things in it. Demonstrate as you say such things as, "This is a bar of soap to wash your hands. / Put it back in the soap dish when you finish. / Dry your hands on one of these paper towels, like this. / When your hands are dry, throw the towel in this basket." (d) On subsequent days, continue building up a warm friendship by welcoming the youngster when he arrives, making him feel wanted and special. Help him put his coat in his very own place. Also help him to find a toy and space to play with it so that his day starts off enjoyably. (e) Use the child's first name when speaking to him. Talk *and* listen to him as much and as often as possible. And show him affection. Small children enjoy being held, even though often they may not wish to be held very long. (f) During the youngster's first week, use learning activities that you think will be especially appealing. Blowing bubbles and balloons are activities few children can resist. Even the youngster who has not as yet learned the skill of blowing can have fun trying to catch a bubble or batting a balloon with his hands. Musical activities can also be used to break the ice. Most children will enjoy clapping, marching, singing, or just watching and listening while an adult sings a short song or plays a happy tune on an instrument. Getting involved in housekeeping tasks can be fun and satisfying for a new youngster. He might help pour juice, wipe up spilled milk with a sponge, or pick up and put paper in a trash basket to feel a sense of belonging and sharing in the care of "his" room.

11.   Small children need a lot of individual attention. Infants especially notice every movement and sound around them. If you want a child to listen and to look at what you are doing, you will have to work with him individually. Working with one child at a time will not only help you to get acquainted but will also help to develop a warm, trusting relationship.

12.   When children are older and have been together for some time, some activities can and should be carried on in small groups. Keep the group small enough to permit each youngster to talk quite often and to participate actively in the activity. Activities such as singing, dancing, games, trips, dramatic play, reading books, and telling stories are suitable for a group of three or four children.

In your small-group activities place some emphasis on social learnings: sharing, taking turns, listening to others, helping. Learning to play with others, however, is not always easy for all children. Putting in the same group those children who play well together may help, but do not force an unwilling child to participate. Leave the door open for his joining the group on his own timing, perhaps when he sees how much fun the others are having or when he feels that he can do whatever is involved in the group play.

13. Parents can help and should be encouraged to do so. Keep parents or parent-substitutes informed of the child's progress and learning successes, and suggest, if necessary, that their interest in and praise of the youngster's learning achievements can be an important motivating force.

If a child wishes to take home certain learning materials and is permitted to do so, use the opportunity to involve the parents in the learning. When the material involves an activity on which the teacher and child have worked successfully, send a written description of the activity along with the material. Children will enjoy sharing with parents their new competencies. Parents will enjoy and appreciate being a part of the child's learning. Materials which are especially suited for use at home with parents are books, puzzles, sorting objects, games, and art materials of the non-messy variety.

Other learning-teaching principles and guidelines which are especially relevant to a particular kind of learning have been included in the introductory chapter of each section of this book. Still more specific kinds of help are given in the "Helpful Hints" section of each of the activities. We hope that all these notes on principles, strategies, and techniques will help you to bring to the toddlers you teach higher levels of learning success and the joys of learning.

THE TEXT AND ITS USE

Taken as a whole, the text provides a wide range of learning activities to help young children develop physically, mentally, and socially. The activities have been selected for their value in promoting simple concept and skill learning in ways compatible with the way small children learn. They attempt to stimulate the intellectual development of children in their first years, preparing them for the successful mastery of more complex learning in later developmental stages. Many of the competencies acquired through these activities will be useful in the child's preschool and school learning experiences.

Although the emphasis is on stimulating the intellectual development of the child, emotional development is not ignored. The education of children in their first years is not entirely an intellectual process but an interplay of affection and intellectual stimulation. A concern for this dual nature of the education process is apparent in the strategies and guidelines suggested. They focus frequently on ways to help build a secure emotional climate for learning and a trusting tutor–child relationship that is supportive of the child's intellectual growth.

The materials and toys suggested in the activities have been chosen for their high interest to small children. They tend to arouse the child's natural curiosity and lure him into active involvement in structured play designed to bring about particular kinds of learning. Suggested tutoring strategies and language examples, too, emphasize play and enjoyment so that the activities become, simply, ways for an adult to play with, and at the same time teach, the young child.

More succinctly then, the primary goal of this book is the development of sensory and motor skills to further concept, skill, and language learning and, ultimately, the intellectual development of young children. In the achievement of this goal, the activities should foster also a positive self-image and self-confidence as well as feelings of satisfaction and pleasure resulting from successful learning. They should excite interest, curiosity, and creativeness in the learners as they explore their immediate world and ways to cope with it. These goals will be realized by individual children to the extent that the suggested activities are selected and used judiciously to match the child's stage of development.

Flexible Use of the Text

Judicious use of the activities implies that the text is not a blueprint for the education of toddlers. Its flexible use appropriate to the developmental stage and interests of individual children is very important. Perhaps the only inflexible rule to be followed is to make each learning–play activity enjoyable for the youngster. This rule, too, is a call for flexibility, for the selection and adaptation of activities that will enhance the child's enjoyment and, in turn, the resultant learning.

Selecting activities to match the individual child's growth pattern is the first consideration in using this material flexibly. Because children develop physically, mentally, and socially at different rates, the appropriateness of activities will vary from child to child. Some children, through spontaneous play and informal language experiences, may have already acquired certain skills and concepts so that they will not need some of the suggested activities. Other activities may have to be delayed because a youngster is not developmentally ready for them. Some may have to be delayed until after a child's third year because certain kinds of learning develop slowly and may not emerge until then.

Within stages of development, too, rates of learning vary, and the amount of repetition needed for mastering learning tasks will vary accordingly. One child may require many experiences to master a particular task while another child does so with fewer experiences.

The rule of flexibility extends also to adaptations within activities. Using your own language and language the child understands, substituting favorite toys and materials, reducing lesson length in keeping with a youngster's attention span, and modifying motor and social skills to a child's level of competency are ways of adjusting an activity to meet an individual child's needs, to catch and hold his interest, and to quicken his enjoyment of an activity.

The activities provided in the text should be thought of primarily as *models*. A model is very much like a recipe, something to be followed closely by a new, inexperienced cook. But as most master cooks know, recipes often need adjustments to suit individual tastes—an extra pinch of this, a little more of that, a substitute flavor, or additional trimmings to please the eye and palate of the eater. What recipes insure is that the cook does not omit a necessary ingredient and that he follows important sequences in combining ingredients. So too the value of model lessons. As you become more experienced in using the models, you will quickly learn which ingredients and sequences are essential to the learning and what adjustments and added trimmings can and should be used to meet the learning needs and interests of individual children.

The Activities

The activities have been divided into eleven groups: (1) sensory, (2) motor, (3) art, (4) music, (5) books, (6) dramatic play and games, (7) puzzles, (8) sorting and ordering, (9) mathematics, (10) science, and (11) trips. Each of these sections of the text is introduced by a brief discussion of the nature of the learning fostered by the particular group of activities and of important teaching strategies for bringing about the desired learning. Additional information on inexpensive materials appropriate for use in the suggested activities are often included in these introductions and/or immediately following them.

The activities within each section of the manual are arranged in approximate order from simple to more complex. This means that later activities often build on skills and understandings taught in the earlier activities of the section or in early activities of other sections. An example of the latter can be found in the section on dramatic play and games, where the child's success in role-playing concepts will depend on his having already acquired particular concepts and motor skills through sensory–motor activities in other sections. The "Helpful Hints" section of particular activities will sometimes identify such prerequisite learning, but your own analysis of an activity will also uncover those concepts and skills the child must have already mastered for success in the new activity.

The activities follow a common overall pattern. The components are described below.

LEVELS OF DIFFICULTY: In addition to the approximate sectional sequencing of activities from simple to more complex, each activity is classified by level of difficulty. Since the age period from one to three years is one of rapid development, a considerable gap often exists between the interests of the younger and older children in this age group. Activities which interest the former may well bore the latter. Moreover, the level of physical and intellectual development of the one-year-old may preclude success in activities which older children can handle with great enjoyment.

For these reasons the curriculum items of each section are divided into three levels which are identified as Levels A, B, and C. The letter classification of an activity appears in the upper, righthand corner of the first page of the activity.

Level A   The activities classified at Level A are apt to be interesting and challenging to children who are just beginning to develop language and motor skills. These activities involve very young children in sensory, motor, and manipulative experiences. They help them to build simple, accurate concepts of common everyday objects and actions, to label these concepts with the correct words, and to use their newly acquired language to express themselves meaningfully. Through these activities, children grow in awareness of their senses and body functions. They are encouraged to develop gross motor skills such as walking, pushing, pulling, and clapping and to perform simple tasks like stacking blocks and nesting objects in order to develop fine motor skills and hand–eye coordination. At the A level the activities take into consideration the child's short attention span and the need for more individual attention than can be given in a group-learning situation.

Although Level A cannot be equated with any specific age period, it frequently begins when children are about 12 months old.

Level B   Level B activities can be thought of as transitional or facilitating activities which help children who have been successful in Level A learning to move gradually into the more complex learning and thinking of Level C activities. It is, however, an important level for children who have developed some language skill and who are still thinking in terms of concrete and real objects which they experience in their environment. These children can begin to form, through firsthand sensory experiences, concepts like *hot/cold, soft/hard, little/big,* and *red/blue.* They can also follow simple one-step directions. And because their motor skills have improved, they can now learn to manipulate smaller objects and simple tools and, with greater balance and coordination, they can learn to jump and hop. They are apt to profit from motor experiences which focus on particular positional relationships between two objects and between an object and themselves (*on/off, up/down,* and so on).

Interests of children at the B level can also be expanded beyond the immediate surroundings of the school to animals, common objects, and people in the immediate neighborhood, and also beyond concrete objects to pictures of objects. Attention spans still remain relatively short for the child at this level, but he may be willing to include the presence of other children in his play. If so, the ideas of sharing and taking turns can be introduced through cooperative play and learning with one or two other children for short periods of time.

A child may be ready for B level activities at about 18 months of age. But perhaps a more realistic yardstick of readiness for this level is simply the child's ability to perform well at Level A. Readiness, however, may vary with kinds of learning. For example, a child may be ready to move to the B level of sensory skills but needs additional time with motor skills at the A level.

Level C   Children entering Level C, as defined for this book, are entering a developmental stage of learning which will probably extend through their preschool years and even into their formal learning years within a school. The C level activities are designed for children in the earliest period of this development stage. They build on and extend A and B level learning. They also introduce youngsters to more complex language patterns and concepts and help them deal with their environment with less reliance on the physical presence of the familiar real objects. In other words, the Level C activities encourage children not only to broaden and deepen sensory–motor learning begun at the earlier levels but also to use learned concepts (internalized mental pictures) in their thought processes and to use language to express that which they have internalized.

Children who are ready for Level C activities are those who have acquired some degree of competency with words and short sentences. Their language learning has become rapid. They talk more and learn new words easily. They are able to follow a simple oral direction. In motor skills, too, their advancement, especially in balance and hand–eye coordination, permits them to try more complex and precise movements. And because of these growing competencies in language and motor skills, they are probably ready to learn ways to organize their accumulated store of concepts and perceptions. Such tasks as sorting and ordering objects by size, color, and shape, recognizing an object by its parts, following two- and three-part oral directions, and discovering simple properties of water and air are now possible.

The C level child has also matured socially and emotionally so that he is

more able and willing to work and play with other children, to share and
take turns. His attention span has increased a bit, especially if an activity is
of high interest. Interests, too, are expanding to include familiar objects
(man-made and natural) in the larger community. Learning media such as
art, music, books, and puzzles can be given greater emphasis to provide exciting and enjoyable learning experiences.

Again, no specific age period can be equated with Level C. Between the
ages of 24 and 36 months a child will often be ready for Level C activities.
The best guide to a child's readiness for this level is the ability of the youngster to perform successfully on Level B activities.

WHY: The specific learning objectives of each activity are given under the
heading "Why" at the top left of the first page of each activity. These objectives are stated in terms of what the youngster can be expected to be able
to do as a result of the activity. Their simplicity is matched with the young
child's capabilities, but each objective is important to the child's progressive
development.

Each activity is limited to one or two objectives. The learning is accordingly strongly focused on one or two tasks rather than on multiple tasks
which tend to obscure just what the youngster is expected to accomplish.

WHAT YOU NEED: Under the heading "What You Need" at the top
right of the first page of each activity is listed the materials needed for the
activity. The materials are drawn frequently from common household articles. Substitutions can often be easily made, and suggested substitutions
and/or directions for make-it-yourself items are sometimes included in the
"Helpful Hints" column of the activity. Note, too, that some materials can
be used over and over again in various kinds of activities. Colored beads for
stringing, for example, can be used not only in the stringing activity but also
for filling containers, for teaching colors and positional relationships (such
as *on* or *in* or *under* a box), for dramatic play, for matching and sorting and
patterning objects by size or color, and for other activities which call for
small or colored objects.

TALK ABOUT WHAT YOU DO: Language is basic to the lesson
model. Each lesson uses language to focus directly upon the specified objectives. Each attempts through language to keep the child involved in the
learning throughout the activity. Lengthy teacher explanations and demonstrations are avoided so that the youngster is encouraged to play an active
role in the learning. When a child is willing to try new things without
coaching by the teacher, explanations and demonstrations can often be
further reduced, permitting the child to learn simply by doing. The more
the teacher's role becomes one of facilitating and guiding, rather than one of
telling and showing, the more likely it is that the small child is learning.

You are encouraged to use your own language in presenting the lessons. However, the sequence of tasks and the kinds of questions asked are often important in helping the child to accomplish the objective(s) of the activity. Notice also the opening and closing language of the lessons. Openings suggest a variety of ways to gain the small child's attention and arouse interest and curiosity—an important first step for learning success. Closure of the lessons includes language to elicit responses from the child, not always verbal, which can be used to judge whether or not the youngster has mastered the objective(s). (Don't expect too much of small children on the first use of an activity. They may well need repetition of learning tasks to attain an objective. And once attained, they need more repetition to reinforce the learning and to internalize it.)

Within the lessons, diagonals (/) are used to indicate points at which some kind of response (words or action or, perhaps, body language) is expected of the child or some action is required by you. If the youngster fails to give the expected response at these points, you should usually simply supply it and continue. When the desired response is given, some sign of your approval is important. An encouraging nod or smile will often be enough.

Specific directions are included within the lessons as needed. They are enclosed in parentheses. These directions are often important in helping the youngster isolate exactly what it is that he is to attend to; or they suggest other techniques which will help maximize learning by small children.

HELPFUL HINTS: Below the lesson model is a section of "Helpful Hints," which include additional specific guidelines and reminders for the teacher. Notes on materials may be included in this section.

THINGS TO DO ANOTHER TIME: Last on the activity page are suggestions for varying ways to repeat and extend the learning promoted by the model lesson. Usually the first suggestions given provide variations of materials or learning situations for repeating and adapting the particular lesson at approximately the same level of difficulty as that of the model lesson. Later suggestions may provide ways to extend the learning to include closely related but somewhat more complex learning. These tasks may well be at higher levels of difficulty. When this is true, the child should master the lower-level learning before being presented with the more advanced tasks.

Using the Text: Brief Guidelines

1. Start by familiarizing yourself with the book: the initial chapters, the introductory chapters for each of the manual's sections, and the activities.
2. Consider the individual child in selecting your activities. The child's stage of development, acquired language and motor skills, attention span,

favorite toys and materials, and social skills are all important considerations in selecting an activity for a particular youngster.

3. Prepare for presenting an activity by reading the model lesson carefully to decide what the essential sequence and techniques are that you will need to use in your presentation. Keep your focus on the specified objectives in the plan you make. Include an opening that will arouse the child's interest and gain his attention and a closing that will help you evaluate the learning results. Check the "Helpful Hints" section of the activity to help you in making your adaptations of the lesson.

4. Collect and/or prepare the necessary materials for the activity.

5. Remember that the most important rule to follow in carrying out your plan is to make the lesson enjoyable for the child—and for yourself. So relax and enjoy the time spent in playing and talking with the youngster as you follow your planned lessons. Don't be upset if the child's interests lead you off in a different direction. Just try your planned activity at a later time. Also, don't force the child to continue if he becomes tired or disinterested. Again, try the activity another day.

The more you work with a youngster, the more attuned you will become to his likes and dislikes, to what he can and cannot do, and the better you will become in capitalizing on these factors to promote the child's learning. And soon, like the master cook, you will be creating your own recipes to tempt the learning appetite of the toddler.

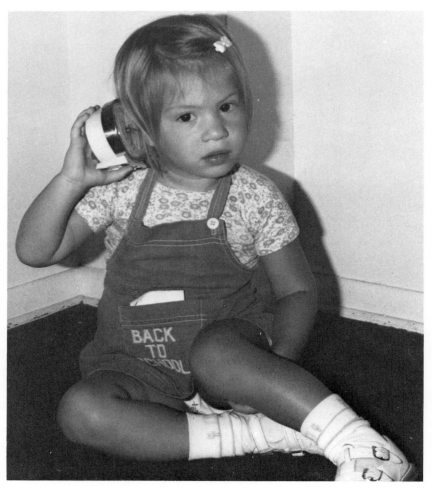

Young children learn through the senses. Here a youngster explores a clock by using her sense of hearing as well as those of sight and touch.

Part 1

Sensory Skills

SENSORY SKILLS

Young children develop sensory skills through daily contact with objects. They learn to use their senses—to see, hear, feel, smell, and taste—to distinguish the different qualities of different objects. They learn that objects come in different shapes, sizes, and colors; that things may be soft or hard, scratchy or rubbery, and may have different smells and tastes or make different sounds.

Unstructured play and exploring activities involving a variety of objects and sensations are important in the early development of sensory skills. These kinds of activities, often initiated by the child, should be encouraged. But in addition, other simple, structured activities can be planned and used to stimulate the senses. Everyday objects should be called to the toddler's attention. "See what I have," you might say. "It is a pink cup. / You drink out of a cup, don't you? / I'll put some juice in the cup, and you can use the cup to drink the juice." Common sounds should be isolated and explored: "Hear that sound? / What do you think it is? / Could it be someone knocking at the door? /Let's see who it is." Awareness of common smells and tastes and the way things feel is also important: the smell of soap, the taste of an apple, the softness of a blanket. Such experiences arouse the child's curiosity as he explores his immediate surroundings and expands his world into the larger community in which he lives.

As a youngster engages in sensory experiences, the language you use is important. Words can be used to call attention to a particular object and to encourage exploration and enjoyment of new objects. By words of praise, you make the child feel good about himself and the things he can do or tries to do. Language combined with sensory experience is the key to helping young children make sense of their world and thus makes an important contribution to early and continued intellectual development.

The activities of this first section are examples of simple ways to combine particular kinds of sensory experiences and language to help youngsters acquire particular kinds of learning. They are structured to provide a step-by-step approach to learning so that small learners are led through a series of small steps to accomplish what is, for them, a complex learning task.

An example of such a structure can be seen in the task of learning the names of objects and identifying objects by name. This is a three-step task. The first step includes two small tasks: (a) being able to point to an object when named and (b) repeating the name of the object. In this step you must isolate the object for the child's attention, describe it briefly and/or let the child explore it, and name the object. As a result, you hope the child will be able to point to or touch the object when you again name it and will be able to repeat the name of the object. What you say in this first step might go like this: "See what I have. (Hold up ball.) It is a ball. It's round and it rolls. See it roll. / Where is the ball? / That's right! Can you say *ball?*"

When the first step has been accomplished, the youngster may be ready to try the next: to pick out the object from among several objects. "Look at all those toys," you might say. "Which one is the ball?" And when he is able to perform this task, you try moving into the third step: to recall a little later the name of the object and to identify it by name. "What is this I have in my hand? / Oh, you remembered! It *is* a ball."

Activities 1, 2, 3, 8, and 9 are structured around the three basic steps described above. They are meant to serve as models of lessons to teach the names of a variety of objects encountered by very young children.

Going beyond learning the names of specific objects in this section is concept learning through sensory experiences. Concepts are not just words, although words are used to express concepts. Examples of concept words or labels are *ball, spoon, cup, baby, dog, toy,* and *flower.* Each of these words—and many, many more like them—represents a class or group of objects which share certain essential qualities and may be used to identify any object belonging to that group. When the mind forms the concept *ball,* the word *ball* is no longer the name for just one specific ball, but it becomes the name of all objects that are round (or roundish) playthings that can be rolled and bounced.

No one can form a concept for another person. It results only from the individual's internal mental process called *conceptualizing.* Although the process of conceptualizing is not entirely clear, we know that it is a natural aptitude of the human mind. The mind forms concepts given the proper stimuli. Concepts of concrete objects, such as *ball* and *spoon,* are usually formed readily by young children through firsthand experiences with various examples of a class of objects. For example, a youngster experiences several spoons of different sizes and shapes as well as their uses (eating, stirring) and becomes aware through language that each of these objects is a *spoon.* If later, when he sees for the first time a large ladle-like spoon, he says *spoon* without prompting, he has formed at least a rudimentary concept of *spoon.* His mind has abstracted some essential qualities shared by all the spoons he encountered and has put them together to form a mental picture of a spoon. And once the mental picture is formed, the mind is able to use it to recognize other new examples of the class of objects we call *spoons.*

Although we cannot "give" concepts to a child, concept development can be stimulated and augmented through informal and structured activities that encourage the child to use his innate ability to conceptualize. Such activities can be especially important in helping youngsters grasp more abstract concepts such as colors, *hot/cold,* and *soft/hard.* These concepts are qualities of objects, not the objects themselves. The color *red,* for instance, may be a quality of such diverse objects as a ball, a fire engine, and a piece of paper. "Teaching" *redness,* then, must focus on helping youngsters abstract the particular quality from concrete objects.

This is done by using as examples several familiar but very different objects which share the one quality that is to be learned. A *red* ball, a *red* block, and a *red* piece of paper, for instance, will help the child realize that the color *red* is something other than the objects themselves. Non-examples of the concept can also be helpful in isolating the concept. Good non-examples in teaching *redness* are objects which are similar to those used as examples but are *not red:* a blue ball, a blue block, a blue piece of paper. Through language, such as that used in Activity 18 of this section, the child is led to compare the examples to find the quality common to all but missing in the non-examples.

Concept learning also takes place in this section as children use their senses to develop sensory skills related to tasting, smelling, listening, and touching. They form such concepts as *sweet* and *sour* through experiences in tasting, and *pointed* and *rubbery* through touching particular objects. They learn to associate objects with distinguishing sounds, smells, tastes, and touch sensations. In so doing they are not only forming abstract concepts of sounds, smells, tastes, and textures, but they are also forming or enlarging concepts of the objects themselves: bells ring, perfumes smell nice, lemons are sour, and sandpaper is scratchy. In fact, all the activities in this section, and in the entire text, will contribute in some way to a young child's development of concepts.

Forming concepts is often a slow process. This is especially true of abstract concepts which may require many experiences with appropriate objects or events for a child to grasp the basic idea. Once basic concepts are formed, he will through new experiences with objects and events continue to enlarge and deepen those concepts, the process extending well beyond early preschool years into school years and into adulthood.

In using the activities in this section, several rules of thumb may be helpful to you in working with an individual child or a small group of children. Some of these guidelines are given below; others are included under the "Helpful Hints" provided in each of the activities.

1. *Try always to select your activities to match the child's (or children's) developmental level.* The A, B, or C classification of an activity will be helpful since these classifications are based on the developmental level of children matched with the learning complexity of activities. Not only is the learning of the A activities less complex than that of the B and C activities, but it often must be mastered first if the child is to be successful in the B and C activities. The same is true of the B activities in their relation to the more complex learning of the C activities. In other words, B and C activities build on and require previous learning by the youngster. A lack of success in these

activities may mean that the child needs to spend more time at a lower classification level. (See pages 16–18 for fuller explanation of the classification of activities by developmental levels.)

2. *Adapt the lesson you select to your own teaching style and the interests of the youngster.* Determine, first, the important learning steps and their sequence in the model lesson. Follow this sequence in planning your lesson, but use your own language to present the lesson. Materials may also be substituted whenever you have other objects that you feel will be of particular interest to the youngster.

3. *Vary your activities so that the child learns by using each of the five senses.* This is important for the development of all the sensory skills and for maintaining a high level of interest in the learning. And whenever appropriate, have the child use more than one sense to explore an object. Let him, for instance, see, feel, taste, and smell a banana even though the learning may be focused on a tasting experience.

4. *An important rule of thumb for all learning is to keep the child actively involved in the learning.* Let him touch and examine an object, try to make it "work," discover its sounds or smells or tastes, and talk about it. In the banana example used above, let the youngster help peel the banana and, using a blunt knife, to cut himself a piece to taste. Do not do things for the child that he can safely do (or help to do) for himself. Keep in mind that everything a young child does is a learning experience. And what he does and says will often provide you with the cues you need for making a learning activity fit the particular learning needs and interests of the individual child.

5. *Remember to encourage and to be accepting of the child.* Praise appropriate responses and efforts. Make him feel good, make him want to try again. If the child is not successful, do not scold or push too hard. Make each activity enjoyable for both him and yourself. As long as you keep the activities "fun," learning is probably taking place. When they are no longer fun, not only is learning not apt to take place but the child may be developing a dislike for learning that may well be carried into school years and throughout life.

ACTIVITY 1: Locating and Naming Common Objects

WHY

To repeat names of familiar objects.
To locate an object when named.

WHAT YOU NEED

Cup; spoon; ball.

TALK ABOUT WHAT YOU DO

(Use your own language. This is an example.)

"Oh, look at these things! What are they? / What can you do with them?" (Give the child time to explore each object.)

"Which one is something you use to drink your orange juice? / Right! It is a cup, a pretty yellow cup. Can you say *cup?* / Very good! Now put the cup on the chair. (The chair should be nearby.) That's right. Can you point to the cup? / Say, you're a good pointer!"

"Do you see something here that you use to eat? / Yes, it's called a spoon. Show me how you eat with a spoon. / Very good. Can you say *spoon?* / Try again: *spoon.* / Good! Can you put the spoon on the chair with the cup? / That's good!"

"What is this last thing? (Put the ball in the child's hand.) It's a ball, a pretty blue ball. Can you say *ball?* / That's right. What can a ball do? / Can it roll? / Let me show you. Like this. / Oh, where's the ball? / Can you bring me the ball? / Oh, you brought me the ball. That's good!"

"Do you remember where the cup is? / Yes, on the chair. Can you bring me the cup? / No, that's the spoon. Bring me the cup. / Thank you. Can you say *cup?* / Very good!" (Repeat for spoon).

(Place the three objects on the rug directly in front of the child.) "Now, point to each thing when I name it. Which is the ball? / The spoon? / The cup? / Oh, that was good."

"Can you tell me what this is called? (Hold up cup.) / Right!" (Repeat for ball and spoon.)

HELPFUL HINTS

Don't forget to touch or point to the object you are teaching so that the child knows which object to observe.

If the child cannot or is unwilling to repeat the name of an object, don't insist. Come back to it another time.

Don't scold the child for mistakes, and don't forget to praise successes.

Don't let the child fail. If, for example, he is unable to locate the objects you name (toward the end of the lesson when you ask "Which is the ball?"), quickly build in success by saying "Give me one of those things. / Oh, you gave me the ball! Very good!" Repeat until he has given you all three objects. The child will feel good because he is able to do what you ask.

If a child has difficulty with the lesson, try a lesson using a single object. Work, for instance, just on a ball, having the youngster repeat the name after you and point to or give you the ball when you name it. Plan similar lessons for each of the other objects.

The purpose of this activity is to guide the child through the first step in learning the names of objects. (See pp. 25–26 for a description of the three-step process.) It may require several experiences with an object (especially if the child is not familiar with it) for mastery of this first step. Note, however, that the last question in the activity ("Can you tell me what this is called?") goes beyond the first step. Although it is a good idea to check on the child's ability to name the objects at this point, do not be disturbed if he is unable to do so. It simply means that he needs additional experiences with the objects and their names to prepare him for the second and third steps.

If the child is able to name one or more of the objects at this point, his ability to do so may be greatly reduced after a longer lapse of time. Activity 8, which takes the youngster through Steps 2 and 3 of identifying objects by name, allows for such a lapse of time. It assumes that between Activity 1 and 8 the child has had several experiences in repeating the name and locating a given object when named. So continue to reinforce the Step 1 learning whenever you can by having the child repeat the names of the objects and find the objects when you name them. Only after he has mastered this task should you try Activity 8.

THINGS TO DO ANOTHER TIME

Use two, three, or four different small, familiar objects and repeat the activity: various kinds of dishes, utensils, tools, toys, clothing, and so on.

Adapt the activity to a few larger objects such as furniture and furnishings. Walk around the room with the child, touching or pointing to table, chair, window. Name and talk about each. Have the child repeat each name. Then see if the child can locate each item when you name it.

Repeat the activity using some new objects and some objects used in a previous activity. See if the child can remember the names of the old objects. If he cannot, give him the name again and continue as though the object were new. But include the object in later activities and ask the child to recall its name.

ACTIVITY 2: Locating and Naming Parts of the Body

SENSORY
A

WHY

To repeat names for hair, eyes, nose, and mouth.
To locate hair, eyes, nose, and mouth.

WHAT YOU NEED

No materials needed.

TALK ABOUT WHAT YOU DO

(Use your own language. This is an example.)

"Look at this. (Touch your hair.) It's my hair. It's on top of my head. (Pat top of head.) Show me where your hair is. / That's very good! It's pretty hair, too. Can you say *hair?* / Good!"

"These are my eyes. (Point.) I have two eyes—one, two. (Point to each eye as you count.) Can you find your eyes? / That's good. We use our eyes to see. Can you say *eyes?* / Very good!"

"Here is my nose. (Touch it.) Can you touch your nose? (If child doesn't touch his nose, playfully tweak it and say, "Here it is!") Do you have two noses? / No, only one nose. We would look pretty funny with two noses, wouldn't we? / Can you say *nose?* / That's right! Show me where your nose is again." (Repeat similar language and gestures for mouth.)

"Let's play a game. See if you can find each thing as I name it. Ready? / Where are your eyes? / Good! (Repeat for hair, mouth, and nose.) That's very good! You're so smart!"

HELPFUL HINTS

Teach the child one feature at a time, and isolate it for his attention by touching or pointing to it.

If the child has difficulty with the activity, repeat it another time rather than push him the first time.

Praise the child for correct responses. Correct errors in a way that the child still feels good about himself.

THINGS TO DO ANOTHER TIME

Use the activity for other parts of the body: head, face, tongue, teeth, chin, cheeks, neck, shoulders, back, chest, stomach, arms, wrists, elbows, hands, fingers, legs, knees, ankles, feet, toes.

Try the activity in front of a large mirror. The mirror may be confusing to a small child, so continue only if the mirror adds something to the learning and to the child's enjoyment of it.

Have the child point to the parts of a doll's body as you name them. Ask the child to repeat the name for each part.

Ask the child to find your hair, your eyes, etc. See if he can recall the names when you point to your hair, eyes, and so on.

ACTIVITY 3:   Observing and Naming Objects

SENSORY
A

WHY

To observe common objects in surroundings.
To repeat names of the objects seen.

WHAT YOU NEED

No materials needed.

TALK ABOUT WHAT YOU DO

(Use your own language. This is an example.)

"Let's look out the window. What do you see? / A car. That's right. It's a red car. Have you been in a car?"

"I see a lady over there. (Point to be sure the child sees her.) She has on a blue sweater. See her? / What is she carrying? / It is a bag, a big brown bag like the ones we get at the grocery store. I bet she's been to the grocery store. What do you think she has in the bag? / I bet you're right. The lady probably has cookies in the bag. Can you say *lady?* / That's pretty good. Say it again: *la-dy.* / That's better."

"What else do you see? / Yes, I see the dog too. It's a little white dog. He's running on the sidewalk. Where do you think he's going? / Yes, he's

probably going home. What do you think he'll say when he gets home? /
He'll probably say 'bow-wow.' That is the way a little dog says 'Hello. I'm
home.' "

"Oh, look at the big truck coming down the street. What do you think it
is hauling? / It's hauling sand. Remember the sand you played in at the
playground? / That's what the truck is hauling. Can you say *truck?* / Very
good. Can you say *sand?* / That's good too."

"We saw a lot of things, didn't we? / Can you tell me some of the things
you saw? / Yes, a truck. What else? / Remember the lady with the big
brown bag? / And the little dog running on the sidewalk?"

"Did you have fun looking out the window? / I had fun too."

HELPFUL HINTS

Encourage the child to identify things he sees and to talk about them.
Point out a few other things so that he extends his observation skills.

Do not include too many names at one time. Three or four is probably a
good number. And be sure to talk about each object: its size, color, what it
is doing, what sounds it makes, and so forth. If the child has already experienced the object, help him recall the previous experience.

Reinforce the learning by calling the child's attention to the objects when
seen again: "Look! What is that? / It's a truck. A truck can carry sand, can't
it? / Can you say *truck?*"

THINGS TO DO ANOTHER TIME

Repeat the activity, observing and naming different things. Talk about
each object. See also if the child remembers the names of objects seen
before (lady, truck). If not, have him repeat the names and try his recall of
the names another time.

Repeat the activity on a rainy/snowy day. Observe, talk about, and name
objects associated with such a day: rain/snow on the windowpanes, boots,
umbrella, puddles.

Try the activity on the playground or a walk.

ACTIVITY 4: Listening to Common Sounds

SENSORY
A

WHY

To listen to sounds made by an alarm clock.
To be aware of the act of listening.

WHAT YOU NEED

An alarm clock set for the time of the activity.

TALK ABOUT WHAT YOU DO

(Use your own language. This is an example.)

"Look what I have. It's a clock. A clock tells us it's time to eat or time to go to school. Can you say *clock?* / Pretty good. Try it again: *clock.* / Good!" (Let the child handle and explore the clock before continuing.)

"Let's listen to the clock. What do we use to listen? / We use our ears. Where are your ears? / Here's one. (Touch one ear.) And here's the other ear. (Touch other ear.) Can you find your ears? / Very good!"

"We have to be very quiet for our ears to hear the clock. Ready to listen? (Help child hold the clock to his ear.) What do you hear? / The clock is saying 'tick, tick, tick.' Listen again. / What is it saying? / That's right! Tick, tick, tick."

"This clock can tell you it's time to get up. Do you know how? / I'll show you. Watch. (Pull out the alarm button.) Now listen. (Let it ring for a moment.) What kind of noise was that? / It sure was a loud noise. It tells you when to wake up."

"Is it saying 'Get up! Get up!' now? / No, it's not ringing now. But listen again. (Repeat alarm.) Did you hear that? / What did the clock say?"

"Do you want to listen again? / What is it saying?"

HELPFUL HINTS

It is a good idea to start an activity by doing or saying something that is attention-getting and places the focus on what you want the child to give at-. tention to. Saying, "Look!" or, "Watch!" or doing something mysterious (like hiding the object of attention behind your back and saying "Guess what I have.") usually works well.

Don't push the child too hard. The important thing is for the child to show interest in the particular sounds and enjoy them. So don't worry if the child can't say *clock* or doesn't know where his ears are. Make it fun for him.

Reinforce the learning. Later, let the child re-experience the sounds of the clock. If you have a toy clock, ask him what it says. Or have him make believe he is a clock and make clock sounds.

THINGS TO DO ANOTHER TIME

Adapt the activity to teach other common sounds heard in the school: footsteps in the hall, the door closing, the bell ringing.

Adapt the activity to listen to and be aware of sounds made by toys: a rattle, a talking doll, a bell or whistle on a fire engine.

Take a walk and call attention to things that make sounds: car horns, a truck going by, a dog barking, birds chirping, children laughing/screaming in play, a fire or police siren.

ACTIVITY 5:   Tasting Sweet Foods

SENSORY
A

WHY

To be aware of the act of tasting.
To recognize sweet tastes.

WHAT YOU NEED

Tray; small quantities of sugar and jelly; a lemon; small glass of water; spoon and knife.

TALK ABOUT WHAT YOU DO

(Use your own language. This is an example.)

"What are all these things on this tray? / That's right, food. What is this? (Point to jelly.) Yes, it's jelly. Jelly is sweet. Here is some sugar. (Point.) It tastes sweet too. This is a lemon. (Let child hold and feel it.) The lemon is a fruit. It is yellow. Can you say *lemon?* / Good!"

"Now let's have some fun tasting these things. What do you use to taste with? / Where is your mouth? / Very good! We use our mouths to taste food and we use our tongues, too. Where is your tongue? / Oh, that's a very nice tongue!"

"Let's start with the sugar. Taste the sugar. It is sweet. / Sugar makes other things taste sweet. You put a little of the sugar in this glass of water and stir it. / Oh, what happened to the sugar? It disappeared, didn't it? / I wonder if the water tastes sweet. (Taste it.) Oh, that's good. The sugar made the water sweet. Would you like to taste it? / Was it sweet? / Can you say *sweet?* / Very good!"

"Try the jelly now. (Help the child only if necessary.) Was that good? / Was the jelly sweet? / Yes, jelly is very sweet. Sugar and jelly are sweet."

"I wonder how the lemon tastes. Let's cut a small piece of lemon and taste it. / Oh, it tastes different. You try it. / That wasn't sweet at all, was it? / The lemon tastes sour."

"Would you like to taste something sweet again? / What would you like? / Okay, jelly it is. / How does it taste? / Very good! Jelly is sweet."

"Let's make some lemonade with this lemon. We'll use some sugar too to make it taste sweet."

(Let the child help you make the lemonade. Before adding the sugar, continue.)

"Try a small sip of the lemonade. / Is it sweet? / No, it is still sour like the lemon. Now let's add some sweet sugar and stir it. / Taste the lemonade again. / Is it sweet now?"

HELPFUL HINTS

Remember to first identify the foods on your tray so that the child becomes aware that sweetness is not a name for the food itself but for a kind of taste associated with some foods.

Be sure to make tasting activities fun so that the child is willing to taste new foods and is less apt to take a dislike to some foods. Also, use small quantities for tastes that the child may find "unpleasant." And follow such tastes by one that is "good."

Reinforce the learning at meal or snack time: "How does the ice cream taste? / Is it sweet like sugar or sour like the lemon?"

THINGS TO DO ANOTHER TIME

For the child having difficulty understanding *sweetness,* try similar activities at snack time. Focus on food that is definitely sweet (jello, pudding, cookie) contrasted with a definitely non-sweet food (pickle, catsup, few drops of salad dressing).

Adapt the activity to teach the concepts *sour* and *salty.* For *sour* you might use small amounts of lemon, pickle, and vinegar water. For *salty,* have the child taste a few grains of salt and a few drops of salty water, then a vegetable or soup before and after adding salt to get across the idea that salt makes some foods taste good.

ACTIVITY 6:   Exploring Smells

SENSORY
A

WHY

To be aware of the act of smelling. To experience several different smells.

WHAT YOU NEED

Perfume or cologne; onion; vanilla; three cotton balls; knife.

TALK ABOUT WHAT YOU DO

(Use your own language. This is an example.)

"Guess what! Today we are going to use our noses to do some smelling. Where's your nose? / Right! Can you say *nose?* / Very good!"

"This is a cotton ball. It doesn't have any smell. (Demonstrate smelling by holding the ball under your nose and sniffing.) You try it. / Can you smell anything?"

(If the child has difficulty duplicating the act of smelling, you may have to help him: "First, close your mouth. Now, breathe in through your nose. Like this." Demonstrate sniffing again. "Now, you've got the idea!")

"This is perfume. I'll put a little bit on the cotton ball. Now I'll smell it. (Sniff audibly.) Oh, that's nice. Here, you smell it. / Did you like that?"

"This is an onion. Let's cut it in half. / Let's rub some onion on another cotton ball. / Would you like to smell it? / How did that smell? / Was it a nice smell?''

"This is vanilla. We put vanilla in ice cream and other foods to make them taste good. Let's put some vanilla on a ball. / Do you want to be first to smell it? / Did you like that smell? / Was it different from the perfume? / Was it different from the onion?''

"Wasn't that fun? / What did we do? / Can you show me how you smell things?''

HELPFUL HINTS

If the child has difficulty learning the act of smelling, you may have to repeat the activity several times before he catches on. In the meantime, make the activity enjoyable for both of you. And don't push too hard. If the activity isn't fun any more, drop it and come back to it when the child is a little older.

Do not expect the child to name objects by their smells in this activity. The idea is simply to introduce the child to several different smells.

THINGS TO DO ANOTHER TIME

Repeat the activity using such other distinctive odors as those produced by spices, scented soap, vinegar, detergent, and peanut butter.

Smell and talk about real or artificial flowers sprinkled with perfume or cologne.

Call attention to and talk about particularly noticeable smells as they occur in or outside of the school: wet wool or fur, recently cut grass, a food served as a snack or for lunch, shrubbery such as boxwood, or a flowering bush or plant.

ACTIVITY 7:   Exploring Objects by Touching

SENSORY
A

WHY

To experience various touching sensations.
To be aware of the act of touching.

WHAT YOU NEED

Teddy bear; plastic animal; wood block (or objects of similar contrasting textures).

TALK ABOUT WHAT YOU DO

(Use your own language. This is an example.)

"Look what we have to play with! Which one would you like to play with first? / Teddy? Okay. Can you give Teddy a big hug? / That's right. He's soft and cuddly, isn't he? / Can you pet his head like this? (Demonstrate) Oh, he feels so soft and kind of furry. Does he feel that way too when he touches your cheek?''

"Here's a horse. Can you pet him? / Does he feel soft and cuddly like Teddy? / No, he feels different. How does he feel when you pet him? / He feels hard. Does he feel hard when he touches your cheek?''

"Where's a block? / Oh, you found it. Feel the block. It's made of wood. / Look, here's a corner. See, it's got a point. Can you feel the point? / Can you find another point on the block? / Can you pet the block? / Does it feel like Teddy or the horse?''

"You felt a lot of things, didn't you? / What did you use to feel with? / Yes, you used your hands. Show me how you use your hands to feel things. / That's right.''

HELPFUL HINTS

For this activity be sure the objects provide different kinds of tactile sensations: *soft/hard, rough/smooth, angular/rounded.* Although the child will not be able to identify such particular sensations, he will be aware of a variety of different touching sensations.

Reinforce the learning by additional, varied touching experiences in the child's everyday routine and free play: the softness of a blanket, the bumpiness of a bean bag, the sponginess of a soft ball, the hardness of his plate and spoon, the feeling of smoothness and roughness of clothing, the warmth or coldness of a cup filled with warm/cold liquid.

THINGS TO DO ANOTHER TIME

Repeat the activity using other objects that feel different: a feather, a soft sweater, suede shoes, a newspaper, corrugated cardboard.

Use the activity outdoors, having the child explore how such things as sand, pebbles, leaves, twigs, and cement feel. Name the objects he feels and talk about the tactile sensations.

ACTIVITY 8:   Naming Common Objects from Memory

SENSORY
A

WHY

To locate common objects when named.
To identify common objects by name.

WHAT YOU NEED

Plate; bowl; cup; glass.

TALK ABOUT WHAT YOU DO

(Use your own language. This is an example.)

"Look at all these dishes! Which one is the cup? / That's right. What do you drink out of a cup? / Milk. Very good! Now point to the dish that is a plate. / No, that's a bowl. Try again. / You're right this time. Can you say *plate?* / Good. You eat your dinner off a plate, don't you?" (Continue in similar fashion for glass and bowl, adding comments on what they are used for. Also repeat plate to give the child a second chance to locate it.)

"We'll play a game now. You tell me the name of each dish when I touch it. Ready? / What is this? (Touch the plate.) Very good!"

(Use the same idea for cup, glass, and bowl. If the child misses one, supply the name and have him repeat it. Then touch the same dish later to see if he can recall the name.)

"That was fun, wasn't it? You really know your dishes."

HELPFUL HINTS

This activity builds on the learning of Activity 1. Be sure the objects you use here are not new to the child and that he has already experienced them and heard and repeated their names.

Note that the first task of the activity takes the child through Step 2 of learning to identify objects by name: locating the named object from among other objects. The game task requires taking the third step in the process: naming the object from memory. Use the game by itself to check on the child's ability to recall the names without first hearing them as he does in the Step 2 task.

If the child has difficulty remembering the name of an object, simply say the name and have him repeat it. But let him try again later in the activity.

It may be important when a name is missed to give the child additional experiences with the object and its name. This can be done informally: "Look at what I am washing. Do you know its name? / It is a bowl. Did you eat cereal out of a bowl this morning?" And later: "Look at what I am drying. What is it called? / That's right! It is a bowl."

THINGS TO DO ANOTHER TIME

Use this activity with other common objects, such as furniture and furnishings (chair, table, desk, wastebasket, coat hook), eating utensils (spoon, fork, knife), toys (ball, car, doll, block), tools (hammer, saw, screwdriver).

Put several small common objects in a large paper bag. Be sure they are objects the child has already worked with. Take out one object at a time. Say something like this: "Oh, isn't this pretty. Do you know what it is called?" If the child cannot remember the name, tell him and have him repeat it. Return the object to the bag for another go-around.

Adapt the game to a double set of the same objects: for example, two plates, two cups, etc. The objects can vary somewhat in size and/or color. The objectives of this activity are (1) to identify the objects by name (from memory) and (2) to develop an awareness that names can apply to more than one specific object, to a class of objects (concept).

ACTIVITY 9: Naming Parts of the Body from Memory

SENSORY
A

WHY

To locate hair, eyes, nose, and mouth.
To name from memory hair, eyes, nose, and mouth.

WHAT YOU NEED

A full-length mirror or individual hand mirror(s).

TALK ABOUT WHAT YOU DO

(Use your own language. This is an example.)

"Look what I have! Do you know what it is called? / It is a mirror. What can we do with it? / Right. We can see how we look in it." (Let the child explore the mirror and himself in it.)

"Let's play a game. We'll both stand so we can see ourselves in the mirror. I'll ask you if you can find something, and you show me where it is by pointing to it or touching it. Okay?"

"Can you find your hair? / Good! Where is your nose? / Is that your nose? I thought this was your nose. (Touch the child's nose.) Can you say *nose?* / Very good! Can you touch your nose?" (Continue "Can you find . . . ?" for *eyes* and *mouth* and repeat *nose* to give the child another chance to locate his nose.)

"Now, let's play a different game, a remembering game. You tell me the name of each thing I point to. Watch me in the mirror. Here goes!"

"What is this called? (Point to open mouth.) Oh, you remembered. That's very good!"

"What is this? (Touch your nose.) (If the child cannot remember the name, playfully cover the child's nose with your hand.) Oh, you lost your nose. Where is your nose? / Oh, there it is. (Take hand away.) Can you say *nose?* / Very good!" (Continue game for *hair* and *eyes* and then try *nose* again to see if the child remembers the second time around.)

HELPFUL HINTS

This activity, which builds on Activity 2, takes the child through Step 2 (first game) and Step 3 (second game) in learning to identify objects by name. Use the second game by itself to check on the child's ability to recall the names of body parts without first hearing them as he does in the first game.

If using a mirror seems to confuse the child in performing the tasks, forget the mirror. Play the games without it.

If the child is unable to respond or makes a mistake, help him. And make a joke of it. Don't make him feel bad. Then later repeat the missed task. If

46   SENSORY SKILLS

he still has difficulty, you may want to play the game often until he is successful. Or you may need to go back to more basic tasks (Activity 2) and
then try this activity again.

Be sure to praise the child for correct responses, especially on the second
or third try.

THINGS TO DO ANOTHER TIME

Play the games again using other parts of the body for which the child has
heard and repeated names (see Activity 2). Increase the number of parts of
the body you include in the games as the child's awareness of the parts and
their names grows.

Adapt the second game by giving a function of a part of the body or
something associated with it and asking the child to name the part: "What
do we see with? / What goes into the sleeve of your coat?" This game may
be more difficult for the child not only because he has to match a name with
a function or an association, but also because the game is not preceded by a
review of the names as is provided by the first game in the activity above.
So keep the activity enjoyable for the child by playfully supplying missed
names and later repeating the function or association missed to give him a
second or even a third chance.

ACTIVITY 10:   Light and Dark

SENSORY
B

WHY

To recognize qualities *light* and
 dark.
To use words *light* and *dark* to
 identify each quality.

WHAT YOU NEED

Large box with lid and about a
two-inch hole punched in one
end; toy (Teddy bear.)

TALK ABOUT WHAT YOU DO

(Use your own language. This is an example.)

"Look what I have! It is a box. See, it has a lid. (Touch or point.) Can you take the lid off the box? / Let's put Teddy in the box. / Can you put the lid back on the box? / Let me help you. / Very good!"

"Oh, look! Here is a hole in the box. (Point.) I wonder if we can see Teddy through the hole. (Demonstrate looking through hole.) I can't see anything. It is dark in the box. Here, you try. / Do you see Teddy? / No, you can't see Teddy when it is dark. Can you say *dark?* / Right. The box is dark when the lid is on.'

"Let's take the lid off the box again. / Now it's not dark inside the box. It is light. Look through the hole. / Can you see Teddy now? / That's because it is light in the box. Can you say *light?* / Good!"

"Help me put the lid on the box now. / Let's look through the hole to see if it is dark or light inside. / Is it dark? / Can you see Teddy? / No, because it is dark in the box. You keep looking and I'll take off the lid. / What happened? / Yes, it got light and you could see Teddy."

"Let's play a game. Each time you look in the box, tell me if it is light or dark. Okay?" (Alternate taking the lid off and putting it on the box several times. Each time ask if it is dark or light in the box. Then keep the lid on or off twice in a row to check the child's concept of *light* and *dark*.)

"Was that fun? / We can play 'light and dark' again sometime if you would like to."

HELPFUL HINTS

In teaching the concepts *light* and *dark* be careful not to frighten the child by the dark. That's why the box idea above is a good way to start. If the child does become frightened in the other suggested activities, stop the activity and try it again later.

If the child needs help in putting the lid on or taking it off the box, stop and demonstrate how to do it. Continue to help if he has difficulty.

If saying *light* and *dark* in the game does not work out, change the response simply to telling you whether or not the child sees Teddy. To a response that he sees Teddy, you might say, "You can see Teddy because it is light in the box." To a response that he cannot see Teddy, you might say, "That's because it is dark. You can't see in the dark."

THINGS TO DO ANOTHER TIME

Darken the room. Have a toy available. Say something like this: "Let's make the room light and then dark." Use the light switch to turn the lights on and off, each time saying: "Oh, it is light now. / Now it is dark." Next focus on being able or not able to see the toy: "It's light now. Can you see Teddy? / Now it is dark. Where is Teddy? / You can't see Teddy in the dark." Then alternate light and dark. Ask whether it is light or dark or if the child can see or not see Teddy. Also lift the child so he can work the switch to make it light/dark.

Play the "Hide–and–Seek" game with a blanket or cloth. Start by throwing the cover over both of you and talk about it being dark, that you can't see the child: "Where is Johnny? I can't see him in the dark. / Oh, there you are. I can feel you." Then throw off the cover. Be surprised to see the youngster. Tell him that because it is light you can see him. Ask, when he can see you, whether it is light or dark. Repeat as often as the child continues to enjoy the game.

ACTIVITY 11:   Cold and Hot

SENSORY
B

WHY

To recognize qualities *cold* and *hot* in objects.
To use the words *cold* and *hot* to identify each quality in objects.

WHAT YOU NEED

Two pans of water, one with ice cubes and the other with fairly warm water (but not too hot to touch); refrigerator and stove (if available).

TALK ABOUT WHAT YOU DO

(Use your own language. This is an example.)

"Look at what I have: two pans of water—one, two. (Point to each pan as you count.) See the water in this pan? / I wonder how it feels. Let's find out. (Put your finger in the cold water; encourage the child to do the same.) It feels cold, doesn't it? / That's because there are ice cubes in the water and ice is very cold. Do you want to hold one of the ice cubes? (Let the child pick up one of the cubes.) How does it feel? / Right. Ice is very cold, like ice cream."

"Let's see how this other pan of water feels. Does it feel cold? / No, it feels nice and hot like your bath water, doesn't it?"

"Let's feel the outside of these pans. Put one hand on this pan and the other on that one. Let me help you. / Which one feels cold? / How does the other one feel? / Very good! You know, you're pretty smart!"

(Point to the refrigerator.) "This is a refrigerator. Do you know what it does? / It keeps our food cold so it won't spoil. Let's see how the things in the refrigerator feel. (Let the child feel several refrigerated foods.) Is that hot or cold?"

(Point to the stove.) "Do you know what this is? / Right! It is a stove. Here is the oven. (Open oven door.) Remember when we baked cookies in the oven? / The oven got very hot then. It was too hot to touch because it would burn and hurt you. The stove makes food hot. Maybe we'll have soup for lunch. You like hot soup, don't you?"

HELPFUL HINTS

Be sure the difference between cold and hot objects is great enough to be distinguishable without causing the child pain or shock. The "hot" objects should be fairly warm rather than hot.

If you use the stove idea as suggested in the activity, be sure to teach safety. Impress the child that the oven and stove are "no-noes" when they are being used.

If you are working with a small group of children give each child a turn feeling each cold and hot object.

Reinforce the learning at snack or meal time by asking if the foods the child is eating are hot or cold.

THINGS TO DO ANOTHER TIME

Expand the concepts to include *warm*. Have the child feel and identify water when it is cold, warm, and fairly hot (but touchable). Show him also that the water can be *very* hot and explain that when it is, it too can burn and hurt.

Use a heating pad to let the child experience the feeling of something growing warm or hot. Let the child feel the pad before it is turned on. Then let him continue to feel it as it warms up. Have him tell you when he thinks the pad is hot.

ACTIVITY 12: Soft and Hard

SENSORY
B

WHY

To recognize qualities *soft* and *hard* in objects.
To use words *soft* and *hard* to identify each quality in objects.

WHAT YOU NEED

Cotton ball; piece of soft sponge; small pile of colored yarn; pebble; key; coin (or similar small soft/hard objects).

TALK ABOUT WHAT YOU DO

(Use your own language. This is an example.)

(Place the objects in front of the child. Allow time to explore each object. Talk about each one so that he recognizes it. For example: "This is a sponge. You can use a sponge to wipe up things. See, like this./ This is a stone. We found it on the playground. Remember when we picked up stones on the playground?'')

"We're going to have fun feeling these things now. Let's start with the cotton ball. Put it in your hand and squeeze it. Like this. / It feels very soft. I'll touch my cheek with it. / Oh, that feels soft and nice. Here, you try it, too."

"See if you can squeeze the sponge. See if it's soft, too. / How does it feel? / Yes, it's soft. Very good!"

"Guess what I've got in my hand this time. / It's the little stone. Here, you squeeze it. /Does it feel soft like the cotton ball? / No, the stone is hard. You can't squeeze it."

"Touch your cheek with the cotton ball again. / That's soft, isn't it? / Now touch your cheek with the stone. Does it feel soft like the cotton ball? / How does it feel? / It feels hard. Can you say *hard?* / Good!"

"Take the key and squeeze it. / That's right. How does it feel, soft or hard? / Right! It feels hard, just like the little stone does."

"We're going to play a game. You close your eyes and hold out your hand. I'll put one of these things in your hand. You try squeezing it and then tell me if it is hard or soft. Okay? (Put the cotton ball in child's hand.) There, squeeze it now. / Is it hard or soft? / Oh, that's right. It's soft. You're so smart!" (Continue playing the game, using all your objects.)

HELPFUL HINTS

Be sure to identify each object first so that the child is less apt to associate the object itself with the qualities of *soft* and *hard*.

Start the game with the object with which he is most apt to be successful (e.g., cotton ball) so that he is encouraged to continue playing the game.

Save several of your objects to use the first time in the game. If the child is able to identify these new objects correctly as soft or hard, he probably has formed the concepts.

Reinforce the learning by later asking the child if other objects around him are soft or hard.

THINGS TO DO ANOTHER TIME

Expose a marshmallow to the air until it hardens. Use a soft and a hard marshmallow and let the child feel each. Ask him which one is *soft,* which one is *hard.* Give him the soft marshmallow to eat as a reward for "being so smart."

Play a game of "Can you find something that is soft (hard)?" Set the room up with objects that are soft (pillow, sweater, spongy ball) and some · that are hard (block, pencil, plastic or metal toys). Keep them easily within child's reach. Tell the child how to play the game: feel an object (try to squeeze it) and if soft (hard), bring the object to you. Help the child when he makes a mistake so that he does not become frustrated.

ACTIVITY 13:   Distinguishing Tastes

SENSORY
B

WHY

To recognize familiar foods by tasting.
To name the foods tasted.

WHAT YOU NEED

Tray; small pieces each of apple, carrot, cheese, and banana.

TALK ABOUT WHAT YOU DO

(Use your own language. This is an example.)

"Look at what I have on this tray! What do you see? / That's right, some food. What's this? (Point to apple.) Very good! What's that? (Point to banana.) That's a banana. Can you say *ba-na-na?* / Good! The apple and banana are fruit."

"Have you ever eaten one of these? (Point to carrot.) Do you know what it's called? / It's a carrot. A carrot is a vegetable. Can you say *carrot*? / That's very good!"

"This is cheese. (Point.) Do you know where we get cheese? / Cheese is made from milk. Can you say *cheese*? Try again: *cheese*. / That's good!"

"Now let's have a tasting party. Take a piece of the apple. / That's right. Now, take a bite. / Was that good? / It tastes sweet and juicy, doesn't it? / What did you just taste? / Right, an apple." (Repeat for each food.)

"Let's play a game now. Close your eyes. I'll put a piece of food in your hand, and you eat it without opening your eyes. Are your eyes closed? / Here's a piece. Don't peek. Pop it in your mouth. / What do you think it is? / No, guess again. / That's right. It was the carrot." (Repeat for other three foods.)

"What did we do today? / What kinds of food did you taste? (If the child cannot remember, point to each piece still on the tray, one at a time, and, when necessary, give him the name and have him repeat it.)

"Did they taste good? / Which one did you like best? / Would you like another piece of it?"

HELPFUL HINTS

Use foods that taste quite different and are easily distinguished.

When you are using a food that you think the child can already name, start your activity with it. If he remembers, praise him. His success sets him up for the task of learning the names of new foods.

If a child has difficulty distinguishing between four foods, reduce the number to two (or three) for the game.

Reinforce the learning at snack or meal time. Place, for example, small pieces of cheese and apple on a plate and ask the child to identify each piece. Then have him close his eyes and pop one of the pieces in his mouth. Ask him to tell you what it was.

THINGS TO DO ANOTHER TIME

Repeat the activity with different kinds of drinks: milk, water, a soda, orange juice.

Use three or four foods the child has already tasted several times: jelly, peanut butter, cheese, orange, celery, apple, etc. Show him the food, see if he can name each food (or repeat the names after you), and talk about them—but without his tasting them again. Play the guessing game to see if he can identify each food by its taste.

Repeat the activity using all fruit (apple, banana, orange, grapes) and talk about their all being *fruit*. Or use all vegetables and talk about their all being *vegetables*. *Fruit* and *vegetables* are more abstract concept words than are words representing a particular kind of fruit or vegetable. The idea that vegetables are an important part of dinner (and lunch) while fruits are often eaten after dinner (dessert) or for snacks, may help the child form rudimentary concepts of these two kinds of foods.

ACTIVITY 14:   Distinguishing Sounds

SENSORY
B

WHY

To recognize differences in sounds.
To be aware of the act of hearing.

WHAT YOU NEED

Small metal can with lid; dry beans; large metal pan or can; wooden spoon.

TALK ABOUT WHAT YOU DO

(Use your own language. This is an example.)

"Listen! (Strike the "drum" to make a loud bong.) What did I do? / Did it make a noise? / Do you want to hear it again? (Repeat.) Can you make a bong? / Very good! That sounded like Bong! Bong! Bong!"

"Now let's make a different sound. Can you take some of those beans and put them in this little can? / Good. Now put the lid on. / Can you make a sound with the can? / That's right. Shake it hard./ What kind of sound was that? Was it a big bong? / Do it again. / It's a rattling sound, isn't it?"

"What did we hear those sounds with? (If the child can't answer, touch your ears and ask, "What are these?") That's right. We hear with our ears. Where are your ears? / Very good! You've got two ears—one, two. (Touch an ear on each count.) You hear with your ears."

"I'm going to cover your ears like this. (Put your hands over child's ears.) When I do this, you shake the can. Ready? / Remember, shake the can. (Cover child's ears during the rattle; then remove your hands.) Could you hear the rattle? / Not very well. That was because your ears were covered. Let's try it again. (Repeat) This time I won't cover your ears. Now shake the can again. / Your ears could hear it better that time, couldn't they?"

"Can you make a big bong? / Show me. / Oh, that was good. What would you use to make a rattle?" (Let the child continue to explore the sounds if he's interested.)

HELPFUL HINTS

Adhesive bandage and small spice cans with tight lids and such things as dry beans, acorn, and pebbles are good to make your rattle. A large metal coffee can makes a good drum. By padding a spoon or a stick a bit, you will have a good drum stick. (See also Part 4 for other ideas.)

For the demonstration of not being able to hear with the ears covered, you will want to experiment before the activity to see how well the sound is eliminated when the ears are covered. As a result, you may prefer to use your own voice (instead of the rattle) for the last part of the activity. Or use a radio, TV, or record player in order to be able to soften the sound while

the child's ears are covered. If you do, have the child listen to the sound
before covering his ears, then to the sound with his ears covered.

THINGS TO DO ANOTHER TIME

Add a bell and/or a whistle (or toys that make sounds: a doll, squeaking
duck) to the activity. After listening to and talking about each sound, have
the child cover his eyes while you make sounds and tell you if the sounds he
hears are bongs, rattles, bells, or whistles (or are made by the doll, the
duck, and so on).

With the child's help, make several rattles by using materials that produce different sounds (see Part 4 for suggested materials for making
rattles). Let the child explore the sounds and enjoy making them. The child
may not be able to verbalize the differences in the sounds, but if he enjoys
making the different sounds, he is probably recognizing their differences.

ACTIVITY 15:   Distinguishing Smells

SENSORY
B

WHY

To be aware of the act of smelling.
To distinguish among smells.

WHAT YOU NEED

Four cotton balls; perfume (cologne); an onion; knife.

TALK ABOUT WHAT YOU DO

(Use your own language. This is an example.)

(Tweak the child's nose, pretending you have captured it.) "Oh, I've got
Judy's nose. Does Judy need her nose? / What is a nose for? / You smell
with your nose, don't you? / I had better give Judy's nose back to her

because we are going to play a smelling game and she will need to use her nose to smell."

"What is this? (Hold up perfume bottle.) It is some perfume. It smells nice. Would you like to smell it? (Demonstrate by audible sniffs if the child has difficulty with the act of smelling.) The perfume smells pretty and sweet, doesn't it? / I am going to sprinkle a little perfume on these two cotton balls so they will smell pretty and sweet too. / Smell the perfume on each of these balls."

"Do you know what this is? (Hold up onion.) / Right! It is an onion. I'll cut it in half. / Smell this half. / That's a different smell, isn't it? / It's a nice strong onion smell. Let's rub these other two cotton balls on the onion so they will smell like the onion. (Let the child help you prepare the balls but be sure they pick up a good onion scent.) Now see if you can smell the onion on each of these balls."

"Now I'm going to put two cotton balls here (one perfume and one onion ball directly in front of the child) and the other two balls over here (a little to one side). You pick one of these balls (point in front of the child) and give it a big smell. / Is it a good smell? / Can I smell it too? / Oh, that's a sweet smell. Can you guess what we used to make the ball smell so pretty? / We used the perfume. Remember?"

"See if you can find the same pretty smell in these two other balls. / You will have to smell each ball to find the one that has the same pretty smell. / You found it? Let me smell it too. / You are right! Oh, you're so smart."

(Replace the perfume ball in the *second* set and repeat for the onion balls.) "Wasn't that fun? / We'll play the smelling game again soon."

HELPFUL HINTS

The two smells you use for this activity must be distinctly different or the child may have difficulty distinguishing between them.

Prepare the balls in front of the child and let him help you. This will help the child understand the true sources of the smells and avoid the idea that the cotton balls of themselves have particular smells.

Although you want to identify each of the smells (perfume, onion), do not make this the important task for the child. His learning task is to match the two balls that smell the same.

THINGS TO DO ANOTHER TIME

Play the game again, using two different smells: vinegar/vanilla, an aromatic spice/perfumed talcum powder, and so on.

Increase the number of smells in the set of balls to three. You might repeat some of the smells used in previous activities so that the matching will not become too difficult for the child. Be sure, also, to use three smells that are distinctly different from each other.

Use a blindfold and two or three items with different smells: peanut butter, onion, perfumed soap. Have the blindfolded child smell one item. Then ask him to smell a second item and tell you if it smells the same as or different from the first. Repeat the first item and ask again if it is the same smell. Remove the blindfold so he can see what he smelled and talk about the item and the way it smells. Repeat for each item.

ACTIVITITY 16:   Smooth and Rough

SENSORY
B

WHY

To recognize the qualities *smooth* and *rough* in objects.
To use the words *smooth* and *rough* to identify each quality in objects.

WHAT YOU NEED

Sandpaper; nail file; corrugated cardboard; small mirror; small plate; smooth piece of cardboard.

TALK ABOUT WHAT YOU DO

(Use your own language. This is an example.)

"Look what I have here on the floor. They are all things that are fun to feel. How do you feel something? / That's right. You use your fingers like this." (Demonstrate and give the child time to explore and feel the various objects on his own.)

"Do you know what this is? / It's sandpaper. Feel it. / It's bumpy and scratchy, isn't it? / It's rough. Can you say *rough?* / Very good!"

"Here's something else that feels rough. It's a nail file. See, I can file my nails with it, like this. (Demonstrate.) Feel the file with your fingers. / How does it feel? / It's rough like the sandpaper, isn't it?"

"What's this? / Right. It's a mirror. Feel it. / It's not rough like the sandpaper, is it? / The mirror is smooth, so *smooth*. Can you say *smooth?* / That's good!"

"What's this thing? / Right. It's a plate that we can use when we eat. How does it feel? / Is it smooth like the mirror?"

"Feel the sandpaper again. / Now feel the mirror again. Can you feel the difference? / Which one is bumpy and rough? / Which one is oh-so-smooth? / Right! You're oh-so-smart!"

"Here are two pieces of cardboard—one, two. (Touch the pieces, one on each count.) Feel each piece. / Can you point to the one that is smooth? / Very good! Now point to the one that is rough. / Right again. It's full of little bumps, isn't it?"

HELPFUL HINTS

Be sure to first identify each object to help the child realize that *rough* and *smooth* are not the names for the objects but a quality of the object, a quality one can feel.

Remember, too, that the child may be able to recognize the difference between rough and smooth but may have difficulty saying the words (he might only say, for example, "wuf" for rough). Accept anything that sounds like the words and praise him for it. He has formed the concepts, and better pronunciation will come with time and practice.

If the child has difficulty distinguishing between rough and smooth objects, make the activity an enjoyable "feeling" experience. And repeat as often as needed for recognition of the two different qualities.

THINGS TO DO ANOTHER TIME

Put the same smooth/rough objects in a paper bag or box with a cover. Have the child insert his hand, find an object, feel it, and tell you if it's smooth or rough. Have him remove the object so that you can check his answer. If he's wrong, have him feel the object again, talk about its roughness or smoothness, and return it to the bag or box for another try with the same object.

Feel and talk about the textures of different kinds of materials: smooth silk and satin and soft velvet contrasted with coarse, rough wools and other knobby materials.

Adapt the activity to feeling smooth/rough objects outdoors: the smoothness of a playground slide, of a metal railing, of a green leaf; and the roughness of a brick, of the bark of a tree, of a dried leaf.

ACTIVITY 17: Distinguishing Objects by Touch

SENSORY
B

WHY

To experience familiar objects through touching.
To identify familiar objects by touch.

WHAT YOU NEED

Large paper bag; common small objects such as comb, pencil with eraser, spongy ball, rubber band.

TALK ABOUT WHAT YOU DO

(Use your own language. This is an example.)

"Look what I have! A bag! Do you want to see what's in the bag?"

"What's this? / Yes, it's a comb. Feel it with your fingers. / Rub your fingers along the edge of the comb, like this. / It has lots of points, doesn't it? / Now shut your eyes and feel the comb. How does it feel? / It's hard, isn't it? / Can you feel the end that has the points?"

"I've got something else in the bag. What's this? / It's a pencil. Can you say *pencil?* / Very good! Can you feel the sharp end? / That's right. Now feel the other end. / That's an eraser. It feels rubbery. / Look, I can mark with the sharp end and erase it with the rubbery end. / Do you want to try that? / Now close your eyes and feel the pencil again. / Can you find the sharp end? Good! Now feel the rubbery end."

"What's this? / Right! It's a ball. Close your eyes and feel it. / It's round and smooth. Is it soft? / It feels different from the comb and the pencil, doesn't it?"

"Oh, here's something that is very different. Do you know what it is? / It's a rubber band. Look what I can do with it. I can stretch it. (Demonstrate). You try to stretch it. / Let me help you. Whee! / Close your eyes again and feel the rubber band. Scrunch it all up. / Can you say *rubber band?* / Good!"

"Let's put all these things in the bag again, and we'll play a game. You put your hand in the bag and find one thing. Then feel it good without peeking and tell me what it is. Ready, set, go! / Have you found something? / Feel it good. / What do you think it is? / Take it out and see if you are right. / Yes, it is the pencil. Very good! Which end of the pencil is sharp? / Which end is rubbery?"

(Continue playing the game until all objects are identified. If the child misses an object, have him feel it again and talk some more about how it feels. Return it to the bag, and let him try again.)

HELPFUL HINTS

Be sure that the objects you use are quite different in the way they feel: different shapes, hard/soft, rough/smooth.

If the child has difficulty identifying the object, make the activity easier by having him identify a quality of each object: soft or hard, rough or smooth. Then try this activity again when the child is a little older and has experienced other touching activities.

THINGS TO DO ANOTHER TIME

Repeat the activity with different objects: small toy, block, nail file, small hair brush, small mirror, spoon, piece of material.

Put more objects in the bag to make the game harder.

Have the child feel and talk about different objects in the room (cap, chair, paint brush, book). Then blindfold the child, lead him to a particular object, and ask him to feel and identify the object. If you are working with several children, have them take turns. Also, one child might select the object to be felt by another child.

ACTIVITY 18: A Color Game

SENSORY
B

WHY

To recognize the color *red*.
To use the word *red* to identify red
    objects.

WHAT YOU NEED

Tray; four or five red objects (ball, crayon, block, button, toy car); three non-red objects (ball, crayon, block); white paper; several red objects in room (pillow, book, sweater, toy).

TALK ABOUT WHAT YOU DO

(Use your own language. This is an example.)

(Place the red and non-red objects on the tray.) "Look at this! Did you ever see so many things on a tray? / Can you tell me what some of them are?" (Help the child identify the various objects.)

(Take the red ball from the tray and place before child.) "What did you say this was? / Right! It is a ball. A red ball. Can you say *red?* / Good! (Place red crayon in front of child.) And here is a *red* crayon. We can make *red* marks with this crayon. Watch. (Make several marks on the white paper.) See the red marks? (Hold red ball close to marks.) The ball and the marks are both red. Now you make a red mark with the crayon."

"See if you can find another ball on the tray? / Good! (Place balls together.) One ball is red (point) and one ball is not red (point). Which is the red ball? / Right you are. Now see if you can find something else on the tray that is red just like the ball. / Say, that's good. You picked the red block."

"Keep looking at the things on the tray. See if you can find some more things that are red." (Continue until the child has identified all the red objects on the tray. If he makes a mistake, say, "No, that's not red. It has to be red like this ball. Try again.")

"Now let's play a 'red' game. Can you find something in this room that is red? / Look all around. When you find something that is red, go over and touch it. / Oh, you're so smart! You found the red pillow." (Continue the game until the child identifies several red objects.)

HELPFUL HINTS

Always identify the objects you use to help the child understand that a color is not an object itself but something *about* an object.

Teach one color at a time. Do not introduce a second color until the child shows mastery of the first.

Reinforce the learning by asking the child the color of red things he encounters: red pants or sweater he is wearing, a red toy he is playing with, a red hen he sees in a picture, a red apple he is eating.

THINGS TO DO ANOTHER TIME

Make up a "mystery bag" of articles of clothing, some of which are red. Have the child put his hand in the bag and remove one item. Have him identify the item (or give him its name) and tell you if it is *red* or *not red*. Include other colors as the child learns them.

Repeat the activity for mastery of each of the other common colors: blue, yellow, green, black, white, purple, orange, and brown.

When the child has learned several colors, play the game in the activity above with two or more colors. For example, use red and blue objects placed earlier around the room and ask the child to find first a red object and then a blue one.

ACTIVITY 19:   A Matching Game in Touching

SENSORY
C

WHY

To identify objects as *soft/hard* and *smooth/rough*.
To match objects that feel the same.

WHAT YOU NEED

Box; two pieces of sandpaper; two small mirrors; two balls of cotton; two pebbles (about the same size and shape); other single objects that are soft/hard and rough/smooth (ball of yarn, nail file, small glass).

TALK ABOUT WHAT YOU DO

(Use your own language. This is an example.)

(Put one of each of your duplicated objects on the floor and the other in a box. Place your single objects on a table or chair elsewhere in the room.) "Come, look at these things on the floor. Would you like to feel them? / That's right. What are you using to feel them? / Yes, your hand—and your fingers too."

"What's that you are feeling now? / It's sandpaper. How does it feel? / It feels rough, sort of scratchy. Feel it again. / Can you say *rough?* / Very good!"

"Now close your eyes and put your hand in the box. See if you can find something that feels just like the sandpaper. / Feel all around. Don't peek. / Oh, you found it. Now you have two pieces of sandpaper—one, two." (Touch one piece at each count.)

"Let's try that again with something else on the floor. / Okay, try the cotton ball. Feel it. / Does it feel soft? / It feels very soft. / Close your eyes now and see if you can find in the box another ball that feels just as soft. / Oh, you did it again! You matched the cotton balls!" (Repeat for other two objects.)

"Let's see what is over here on the table. Can you find something that is both hard and smooth? / You have to feel each thing. / That's very good." (Repeat for an object that is soft and one that is hard and rough.)

HELPFUL HINTS

Be sure to identify each object used so that the child realizes he is looking for something *about* the object rather than the object itself.

If an object is new to the child, you may want him to repeat the name of the object. But don't place major emphasis on remembering the name. Keep the focus on the "touching" activity.

If some of your objects have more than one quality (hard and smooth or hard and rough), be sure to accept either answer. If you don't, the child will probably become very confused.

THINGS TO DO ANOTHER TIME

Repeat the activity using three of four kinds of fabric which feel very different: denim, corduroy, velvet, fake (or real) fur, coarsely woven wool, silk or satin, lace. Use two pieces of each fabric in different colors (or the child may match by colors rather than by touch). Have the child feel one set of the fabrics and talk about how each piece feels. Then put the duplicate set in your hand and ask: "Which piece in my hand feels like the one you have?" If either you or the child has on clothing made from similar materials, have the child match these also. If you are working with a group of children, have them feel each other's clothing to find matches.

Repeat the activity, using small, hard objects that are different in shape: nails, plastic or metal caps, square blocks, marbles, or pebbles, etc. Have the child feel each object in one set and talk about its shape. Then have him close his eyes and match the objects by feeling those in the box.

ACTIVITY 20:   Recognizing Objects by Smelling

SENSORY
C

WHY

To be aware of objects that smell. To identify the objects by their smell.

WHAT YOU NEED

Three (or four) things that have distinct smells, such as a spoonful of peanut butter, bar of soap, piece of onion, banana; tray.

TALK ABOUT WHAT YOU DO

(Use your own language. This is an example.)

"Look at what I have on the tray. Which one do you want to smell first? / Okay, let's try the peanut butter. Smell it, like this. (Demonstrate, sniffing audibly.) Now, you smell it. / Doesn't the peanut butter smell good? / It tastes good too, doesn't it?''

"Shall we try this bar of soap next? / It has a nice smell too, but it's different from the peanut butter. / Do you like that smell?''

"Let's see now if you can guess if you are smelling the peanut butter or the bar of soap. You have to close your eyes and no peeking. / Okay, smell. Does it smell like the peanut butter or the bar of soap? / Open your eyes and see if you guessed right. / You were right! It was the peanut butter.''

"Let's do the same thing with the onion and the banana. First you'll smell them with your eyes open and then with your eyes closed. Which one do you want to smell first?'' (Follow procedures similar to those used above for the peanut butter and soap.)

"What did we do today? / Can you tell me some of the things we smelled? / What did you use when you smelled all these things? / Would you like a taste of the peanut butter or of the banana?''

HELPFUL HINTS

Be sure the objects used in this activity have distinct and different odors to make the child's tasks less difficult.

Be sure also that the objects used and their smells are not ''new'' to the child. He should have previous experiences with naming and smelling them so that his major task in this activity is to distinguish objects by their smells.

The act of smelling and recognizing particular smells may be difficult for the young child. If so, make the activity enjoyable so that he will want to repeat it.

This activity and other smelling activities may be used with small groups of children. Just be sure that each child has a turn at smelling each object.

THINGS TO DO ANOTHER TIME

Repeat the activity using other things with distinctive smells: a flower, lotion, vanilla, spices, leather.

In the activity above, the child works on two objects in an effort to distinguish between their smells. When he is successful in this task, try him with three or four objects. Have the child smell all the objects with his eyes open and talk about the way each smells. Then with eyes closed, have him smell each object and try to identify what he is smelling.

Play a ''sniffing game,'' using objects with distinctive smells that the child is familiar with. Have him look at and identify the objects you plan to use, but do *not* have him smell them. With his eyes closed or blindfolded, have the child smell one object at a time and ask him what he thinks the object is. Set some kind of a winning standard: if he gets two objects right, he has won the game.

ACTIVITY 21:   Recognizing Foods by Tasting

SENSORY
C

WHY

To identify foods by tasting.
To identify different kinds of tastes: *sweet/sour/salty.*

WHAT YOU NEED

Tray; a few raisins; pretzels or saltines; small pickles.

TALK ABOUT WHAT YOU DO

(Use your own language. This is an example.)

''Let's have a tasting party today! See all the things to eat on the tray? They're all things you probably like. Can you name each one?''

''Now close your eyes and hold out your hand. I'm going to put one of these foods in your hand. Ready? / Okay. Put it in your mouth and eat it. / What do you think it is? / Right! It was a raisin. How did it taste? / Was it sweet or sour?''

(Repeat for other foods. For foods like the pretzel and pickle, use a small piece for the child to taste.)

"There is still some of each food on the tray. Can you tell me which one tasted salty? / Which one was sour? / Which one was sweet? / Was one more juicy than the others?"

"That was a nice party, wasn't it? / And you are really a good taster!"

HELPFUL HINTS

To help the child name each food in the beginning, use a whole pretzel and pickle. But for the tasting activity, give the child small parts of these foods so that he is less apt to recognize the food by touching rather than by tasting.

In the answer to the question of which food tasted salty (in last set of questions of the activity), be prepared to accept either of two possible responses. The child may think of both the pickle and the pretzel (or saltine) as being salty.

Reinforce the learning at snack or meal time. Ask him to close his eyes and give him a small piece of some familiar food you are serving. See if he can guess what it is and tell you if it is sweet, sour, juicy, and so on.

THINGS TO DO ANOTHER TIME

Repeat the activity using other familiar foods, but use foods that have distinctive and different tastes: nuts, lifesavers, chocolate cookies, carrots, lettuce.

Repeat the activity using drinks: soda, milk, chocolate milk, water, orange juice, grape juice.

Try the activity using all fruits or all vegetables with a secondary focus on the development of the concepts *fruit* and *vegetable*.

ACTIVITY 22: Recognizing Objects by Sounds

SENSORY
C

WHY

To be aware of objects that make sounds.
To identify the objects by their sounds.

WHAT YOU NEED

Whistle; bell; hammer; board (or other hard object for pounding).

TALK ABOUT WHAT YOU DO

(Use your own language. This is an example.)

"Look at all these things. They can all make sounds. Can you tell me the names of these things?" (Supply names of any object missed by child).

"Do you know how to make a sound with the bell? / Oh, do it again. / That's the sound the bell of the fire truck makes, isn't it? / It goes 'ding, ding, ding-a-ling.' "

"A hammer makes a sound when you pound something with it. Can you pound this board with the hammer? / Did you hear the sound the hammer made? / Pound the board again and listen. / That was a 'bang, bang, bang' sound. It is different from the sound made by the bell. Listen again while I ring the bell. / Now you pound with the hammer. / What kind of sound does the hammer make?"

"See if you can make a sound with the whistle. / You have to blow hard into this end of the whistle. / That's hard to do. Do you want me to blow the whistle? / Okay, listen. / Oh, that is a loud sound. It sounds like 'whee-e-e' to me."

"Let's listen again to each sound. You ring the bell. / I'll blow the whistle. / You pound the hammer."

"Now shut your eyes. I'll make a sound and you tell me whether it was the bell or the whistle or the hammer. Eyes closed? / Here is the first one. / Very good! That was the hammer's 'bang, bang, bang.' / Here is another sound. Are your eyes closed?" (Continue in similar fashion, making each sound several times.)

HELPFUL HINTS

The bell you use may be one on a toy fire truck or other toy; you could use a few jingle bells (found in a dimestore) sewn on a ribbon.

If the child offers a different sound in imitation of an object, accept his sound and use it throughout the activity.

If you are working with a small group of children, give each child a chance to make the sounds with the object, to imitate the sounds, and to guess the objects being imitated.

THINGS TO DO ANOTHER TIME

Listen to and talk about sounds made by several (three or four) other objects: the ringing of a class bell or alarm clock, the "tick tick" of a clock, the buzz of a saw, the rumble of a truck, the gurgle of water. Then play a "pretending" game. Pretend to be an object and make a sound like it makes. Have the child guess what you are by the sound you make. Let the child be the object and make the sound, and you be the guesser. If you are working with a small group of children, give each child a turn in pretending to be an object and have all the other children guess what object the child is.

Play the "Pretending Game" by having the children be various animals and make appropriate sounds: cat/meow, dog/bow-wow, pig/oink, duck/quack, bird/tweet, bee/buzz, etc. Use animals the child has experienced firsthand (including their sounds) or in picture books. Talk about the sound each makes before playing the game.

ACTIVITY 23:   Observing Details in Objects

SENSORY
C

WHY

To observe details of objects.
To recall objects and details seen.

WHAT YOU NEED

A magnifying glass; small box or tray; several small, interesting objects: penny, veined or multicolored leaf, feather, postage stamp; pencil for pointing.

TALK ABOUT WHAT YOU DO

(Use your own language. This is an example.)

"Look at what I have. It's something very special. It's a magnifying glass. It makes things look very big. See how my fingernail looks through the magnifying glass. / It's big, isn't it? / And it looks different. See those lines? (Use pencil to point.) Do you want to look at your fingernails? (Let the child use the magnifying glass to explore his nails and hands.)

"I've got some tiny things in this box. Can you tell me the names of any of them? / Right! That's a penny. Let's look at it through the magnifying glass. / What do you see? / A man. Can you see his hair? / Where's his nose?"

"What should we look at next? / Okay, the leaf. / Look at all those lines. (Point) They are called veins. See all those little points at the side of the leaf? (Point.) What colors do you see in the leaf?"

(Continue with the other objects, pointing out detail the child will understand.)

"What did we do today? / That's right. Can you tell me some of the things we looked at? / Can you tell me some special things you could see using the magnifying glass?"

HELPFUL HINTS

Encourage the child to talk about what he sees. Let him use his imagination in describing what he sees.

Use the pencil to point so that the child is aware of the detail you are talking about.

Reinforce the learning in some of his everyday activities: "Can you find a flower on your plate?" "Where is the duck on your shirt?" "I see a raisin in your cookie. Can you find the raisin?"

THINGS TO DO ANOTHER TIME

Find an interesting picture in a book or magazine and ask the child to find and point to some details in the picture: in a picture of a man, for example, his ears, his moustache, his tie, a button on his coat. Give cues when the child has difficulty: "The tie is yellow. Can you find something yellow? / It's under his chin." Let the child talk about other things he sees in the picture.

Take a magnifying glass outside on a nature walk. Look at a bug or ants, a flower, a colorful pebble, an acorn. Point out interesting details and let the child talk about what he sees through the glass.

ACTIVITY 24:   Observing Parts of Objects

SENSORY
C

WHY

To be aware of parts of objects.
To identify parts of objects.

WHAT YOU NEED

Tubes from paper towel rolls or similar tubes; fairly large objects with several observable parts such as a Kiddie Cart and a potted plant.

TALK ABOUT WHAT YOU DO

(Use your own language. This is an example.)

"Let's play a seeing game. What do we need to see? / Right! Eyes. Where are your eyes? / Very good! We're going to use a make-believe telescope in our seeing game."

(Give child a tube.) "Here is your 'telescope.' You look through it like this. (Demonstrate) Now you try. / Close one eye and look with the other. / That's right. What do you see? / Oh, that's good. What color is it? / People use real telescopes to help them see things that are far, far away."

"The Kiddie Cart is over there. (Point) Can you see it through your 'telescope'? / Keep looking. A little lower. / You found it. Good. Now tell me which part of the Kiddie Cart do you see? / The wheels. Good. Can you find the seat where you sit? / What color is it? / Right! It is red. Now see if you can find the handles, what you hold onto with your hands. / Keep looking. (Help the child adjust his aim if necessary.) What color are the handles? / Yes, they are red too."

"Now look over at the table. Can you see the plant on it? / Look up a little higher. / Does it have leaves? / What color are they? / What is the plant growing in? / What color is the pot? / Does the plant have a flower?"

"Let's go to the window and look at the sky. / Look up high. Do you see clouds? / What color is the sky? / What color are the clouds? / What do the clouds look like? / They look like big marshmallows, don't they? / Can you find a star? / No, you can see stars only at night when it is dark."

"You saw a lot of things, didn't you? / What were some of the things you saw that were part of the Kiddie Cart? / When you looked at the plant, what things did you see?"

HELPFUL HINTS

If you use this activity with a small group of children, have a "telescope" for each child. Give each child a turn in telling what he sees and answering questions about various parts of objects.

By this time, the child will probably learn the names of objects without your going through the steps of having him repeat the name after you and recalling the name at a later time. But if an object is new to him and its name is difficult to pronounce, you may wish to use the formula to help him add the word to his vocabulary.

THINGS TO DO ANOTHER TIME

Repeat the activity using different large objects: a pull toy, a lamp, a chair, a shelf with items on it, car parked on the street, etc.

ACTIVITY 25:   Recognizing an Object from a Part

SENSORY
C

WHY

To identify parts of an object.
To recognize the object from only
   a part of it.

WHAT YOU NEED

A scarf; several small objects already familiar to the child (toy car, airplane, and horse).

TALK ABOUT WHAT YOU DO

(Use your own language. This is an example.)

"Bet you can't guess what is under this scarf. (After a moment or a guess or two, swish the scarf away.) Oh, it's some toys. Which ones are they?"

"Now let's look at the car. Can you tell me about it? / Yes, I see the wheels. Where is the engine? / And where does the driver sit? / Which way does the car go when it's going down the road? / Oh, then this is the front? Where is the back? / Very good!"

(Talk in similar fashion about the other toys. Help the child identify their essential parts: for the airplane, its wings, where the pilot sits, its front and back; for the horse, its tail, head, body, legs, and where a person sits when he rides the horse.)

"Close your eyes now. Don't peek until I tell you to. (Hide the toys under the scarf but allow the front half of the car to show.) Okay, you can look now. What's that thing sticking out there? / No fair peeking under the scarf. Just look. What's that a part of? / You're right! (Lift scarf.) See, it is the car.''

"Close your eyes again. Are they tight?'' (Repeat the process for another two toys.)

HELPFUL HINTS

Don't make the task too hard. Be sure that the part not covered shows some distinctive feature of the object.

If the child has difficulty with the activity, uncover more of the object. If he is good at it, cover more of the object. For example, show the child only one wing of the airplane.

THINGS TO DO ANOTHER TIME

Repeat the activity with other familiar toys and objects: for example, a spoon, knife, and fork. Be sure to talk about the handle end of each utensil and the shape and use of the other end before starting the "hiding" game.

Use pictures of familiar objects found in books and magazines. Cover part of the picture and ask the child to identify what the object is. For example, show the child half of a bed, the upper half of a chair (seat showing), or the upper half of an animal. It may be important to talk first about the parts of the object in order to get the child to observe carefully that part of the object he will eventually use to recognize the whole object.

Learning what muscles can do and how to control them is important learning for the young child. These children are learning balance and what it feels like to walk straight and wavy chalk lines.

Part 2

Motor Skills

MOTOR SKILLS

Motor skills refer to motion and the use of muscles in a controlled and efficient way to produce movement. They are classified as *gross* and *fine*. Gross motor skills involve large muscle movement and include such activities as walking, running, climbing, pushing, and pulling. The fine or small muscle skills require a greater degree of precision than do gross motor skills. Buttoning, lacing, pouring, using a crayon, manipulating puzzle pieces, and using a spoon are some examples of fine motor skills which require small muscle coordination.

Both kinds of motor skills are important in the physical and mental development of children. The most obvious need for motor skill development is in the performance of the daily tasks of eating, dressing, and carrying on other routine activities requiring the controlled use of muscles. Perhaps somewhat less obvious is the importance of motor skills in helping the very young to learn about themselves and their surroundings. Young children are often in motion during their waking hours. They climb over and under things, pull themselves up on whatever will steady and support them, and manipulate anything that is movable and within their reach. Through these and other actions they become aware of what they can do with their bodies and with objects. They discover relationships that exist between themselves and the movement of objects and between objects and motion. In other words, they are becoming comfortable with their world by mastering those skills that permit them, through action, to cope with a variety of situations and things, and to make sense out of these experiences.

As children grow, they continue to use motor skills to acquire concepts and language that have to do with actions and positions. Through their own actions they understand what it means and feels like to walk, to run, to climb, to jump, to swing. A youngster learns what such positions as *off* and *on, inside* and *outside, behind* and *in front of* mean as they apply to himself in relation to an object (he is *on* the chair or getting *off* the chair; he is *inside* or *outside* the house) and as they apply to the position of one object in relation to another object (the ball is *behind* or *in front of* the chair). By manipulating objects, the youngster becomes aware of sizes and shapes. As he tries to place one object inside another, he discovers differences in size: some objects are little and some are big. And in trying to fit puzzle pieces together, he discovers, too, a variety of shapes.

Another area of importance for motor skill development is the child's self-concept. As the toddler gains control of muscles, self-confidence increases. He enjoys being able to do things. He is often willing to try new actions and will find new ways to use newly acquired motor skills. By the same token, lack of motor skills can frustrate and discourage the toddler, especially when playing with others who are able to do something he cannot do. A teacher can try to offset such feelings by supplying the physical and psychological support the child needs: a steadying hand or a boost, praise for each accomplishment, encouragement to try again, assurance that he, with a little more time, will be able to do what older children do.

Motor skills can be used to promote still other areas of learning. The child will learn to follow directions by using motor skills: "Walk to the tree and then run back to me." He is developing writing readiness skills when he learns to hold a pencil or crayon and to make marks with it. Reading readiness skills are involved when from memory (visual memory) he is able to reproduce a structure or a design that you made for him with blocks the day before. Motor skill experiences can also be used to teach self-control and self-direction, an important part of happy group work and group play. For instance, you might use an experience with the playground equipment for this purpose: "You'll have to get in line for the slide and take your turn. See how other children are waiting in turn. Can you do that too?"

The rate of development of motor skills varies with children. No specific time can be set for the performance of a particular activity by all children. The individual characteristics of each child—physical strength and structure—largely determine when a new skill is learned and how much time will be needed to perfect it. It is generally agreed, however, that many developmental activities appear during the child's first six years. During these years certain skills are acquired by many children at an approximate age level, give or take several months. For example, some competences that you may expect to appear before or about the age of two years include walking without support, self-feeding, building a tower of four or five blocks, putting pellets in a bottle, climbing stairs, turning pages in a book, lugging, pulling, pounding, hurling a ball (and other objects!), manipulating a cup or glass for drinking, unzipping, taking off shoes and socks, jumping, and running—all with varying degrees of skill. By the time the child is three, he may be expected to have grown considerably in competency in all these things and will have added a long list of new skills, such as dressing and undressing with help on buttons, catching a large ball, hopping a few steps, descending steps, holding a pencil or crayon and making scribbles with it.

When using these age-level guides in selecting appropriate motor skill activities for a particular child, the teacher must be guided also by signs of readiness for the learning. Interest in a skill is often a sign. A child's interest can be shown in various ways: by attempting to try a skill on his own, by his close attention to others performing a skill, or by talking about a particular skill. Negative clues (indicating non-readiness) may be frustration and unhappiness accompanying an unsuccessful attempt to perform a skill or inattention or disinterest in an activity.

Although a youngster can be encouraged and stimulated to try a new experience, he should not be forced to do so. A learning activity for which the child is not ready, for one reason or another, will probably end in failure and may, then, build up an aversion to the activity. One simple way to further and/or determine readiness is to "ask" the child about an activity in such a way as to entice him into it: "Look at this pretty blue ball! Here, I'll bounce it to you. / Now you bounce it back to me." Take your cue to continue or stop from the child's reaction.

A basic rule in helping children develop motor skills is to provide them with many opportunities to develop all their muscles. Young children need many opportunities for active, unstructured play in which both large and small muscles are used in a safe, protected environment. They need freedom to romp, run, and climb, and to explore and manipulate a variety of objects. They need encouragement and practice in doing things for themselves and for others—like self-feeding, taking off cap and mittens, shoes and socks; helping with small chores around the school; and getting out and putting away their own toys.

Simple, structured learning activities are also valuable in helping toddlers develop gross motor skills and small muscle coordination, and to acquire other appropriate kinds of learning through the use of these skills. This section of the text provides samples or models of such activities. Activities elsewhere in the book (especially sections on music, art, games, and puzzles) suggest additional ways to promote motor skill development in young children. In fact, any activity that involves the child in learning by actively doing contributes in some way to motor skill development.

Specific guidelines to promote maximum learning of a particular motor skill or related concept are included in the "Helpful Hints" of each activity in this section. Other more general guidelines that are applicable to motor skill activities in general follow below.

1. *Select your motor skill activities based on the child's stage of development, interests, and needs.* The extent to which competency in a motor skill is acquired by a particular child is related to his physical development and maturity. Although the sequencing of the activities in this section and their A, B, and C classifications follow the anticipated general rate of development of most children, each child has his own growth and developmental pattern. (See pages 16–18 for an explanation of the A, B, and C classifications.)

2. *Vary your activities to ensure the child's use of many different muscles and the development of many different kinds of coordination.* Mix opportunities for exercising and developing large muscles in more active, strenuous play with those that require small muscle coordination and concentration.

3. *The language you use in motor skill activities remains important.* Words that focus the child's attention on what is to be learned, words that

arouse curiosity and help to maintain interest, words that put fun into the activity and make it enjoyable regardless of the child's degree of success, words that praise and encourage—all tend to reinforce learning and the development of self-confidence.

4. *If an activity does not work for a child* (*and you decide to discontinue it*), *see if you can find the reason.* Could the materials be made more interesting for him? Does the learning need to be presented differently for this particular child? Was a basic skill or concept needed for the successful accomplishment of the new task missing? Or was it just the wrong time of day, a time when the child was already fatigued and unable to give full attention to the activity? If you can find answers to these and other similar questions, you may be able to replan the activity accordingly and try it another day. Or if you decide that there is a developmental problem, that the youngster is not ready for the learning, you will have to wait several weeks or several months before trying the activity again.

5. *Helping a child form abstract concepts through motor skills* (*in/out, up/down, etc.*) *requires isolating the concept for the child.* This is done by (a) identifying the objects to be used so that the child becomes aware that the concept is not the object but has something to do with what is being done to the object, (b) providing action examples (and non-examples) of the concept you are teaching, and (c) repeating frequently the concept word as the proper action or a positional relationship is demonstrated. Activity 28 provides an example of this three-part rule applied to a lesson structure.

6. *Competency in a skill comes with repeated practice of the skill.* So repeat an activity or variations of it to help the child acquire increased competency in a particular skill. A youngster can, however, be encouraged to practice a skill on his own, especially once he had been introduced to it. After an appropriate and successful activity, give him blocks for building towers or beads for stringing, and he may well take over from there.

7. *Take all safety precautions necessary to prevent the child from harming himself in learning new motor skills, but don't be overprotective.* He needs to find out what he can do by himself. Foreseeing and eliminating dangers, a watchful eye, and controlling excesses are important in the more strenuous activities.

Remember, too, that if your motor skill activities seem to do nothing more than make the child healthier and happier, they are a success. For the healthy, happy child has also a great potential for all kinds of learning.

ACTIVITY 26: Pulling and Pushing

MOTOR SKILLS
A

WHY

To develop arm and leg muscles.
To distinguish *pulling* and *pushing*

WHAT YOU NEED

A medium-sized carton with hole punched in center of one side; sturdy cord; several smaller, light objects to go in box.

TALK ABOUT WHAT YOU DO

(Use your own language. This is an example.)

"Oh, look at this big box! You know what? We're going to make the box into a toy. Won't that be nice?"

"First I'll make a big knot at the end of this rope. / The other end goes through this hole in the box. / There. You pull the rope all the way through. / Now you have a toy that you can pull all around. / That's right. Pull it with the rope."

"Let's put all these things in the box. In goes a block. / Put Teddy in too. / That's right, in goes the plastic bottle / and in goes another one. / Can you pull the box with all those things in it to the chair way over there? (Point.) Oh, that was terrific!"

"Now I'll help you take the box back to the table. I'll push and you pull with the rope. / Go ahead. / You're pulling and I'm pushing."

"You push this time and I'll pull. / Say, you're as good at pushing as you are at pulling."

"Can you pull the box all by yourself? / Pull it over here to me. / No, *pull* it—with the rope. / Now *push* it back to the chair. / Very good!" (Repeat the pulling and pushing task if the child remains interested.)

"What did you do today? / Yes, you pulled the box. Show me how you pull the box. / Did you push the box too? / How did you push the box?"

HELPFUL HINTS

Cover the box with bright Contact paper and use it also for other activities that require a box.

Use the words *pull* and *push* frequently as the child performs each action so that he will associate the word with the proper action.

If the child wants to load and unload the box with the objects, simply incorporate these actions in the lesson. Talk about putting the objects *in* the box and taking them *out* as he does so.

Reinforce the learning by giving the child the pull box to use in his unstructured play. Encourage him to both pull and push.

THINGS TO DO ANOTHER TIME

Adapt the activity to other pull toys. You might, for instance, attach a cord to a toy car or truck (not too small) for pulling as well as pushing.

When the child has acquired the concept *wagon,* pretend the box is a wagon and use it to haul objects, by pulling and pushing, from one place to another.

ACTIVITY 27:   Rolling a Ball

MOTOR SKILLS
A

WHY

To develop arm–hand muscle control.
To roll a ball.

WHAT YOU NEED

Small, soft ball (about the size of a tennis ball); large, soft ball (beach ball about size of a volley ball or larger.)

TALK ABOUT WHAT YOU DO

(Use your own language. This is an example.)

"What's this? (Hold up big ball.) / Yes, it's a ball. It's a *big* ball. Let's sit on the floor and roll it. / Spread your legs like this. / That's good. Now the ball can't get away. I'll roll the big ball to you."

"Can you roll the ball back to me? / That's pretty good. Here it comes again. / Roll it back to me. / That's much better." (Repeat several times.)

"Here is another ball. / It's a little ball. (Place it beside the other ball.) See how little it is beside the big ball? / The big ball is big like this (make large circle with your arms) and the little ball is little like this." (Make small circle with your thumbs and index fingers.)

"Let's try rolling the little ball. / Wheee! That's fun." (Repeat rolling little ball several times.)

"Can you find the little ball? / Very good! Can you roll it to me? / Where is the big ball? / Can you roll it to me one more time? / Oh, you are a good ball roller!"

HELPFUL HINTS

The activity is focused on developing the muscle control needed to roll a ball. By using two balls, you are also helping the child build the concept *ball*. By using two balls easily distinguishable by size, you are likewise providing readiness learning for forming the concepts *big* and *little*. But consider both kinds of concept learning as incidental. Your prime purpose is to have fun rolling a ball to help the youngster achieve the stated objectives of the activity.

A child usually learns to roll a ball before he learns to throw, catch, bounce, or kick it. Keep the distance to roll the ball short at first. Increase the distance as skill increases.

Start the activity with the *big* ball, as rolling it requires less skill than does the little ball.

To develop the skill of rolling a ball will probably require practice so don't be disturbed by a child's limited success at first. Praise whatever success occurs to encourage willingness to try again.

THINGS TO DO ANOTHER TIME

Line up two or three chairs and have the child roll the balls under their legs. Talk about the big and little balls. Ask which ball he is rolling, the big or little one.

Make a ramp by placing a board (the ironing board will work nicely) on a slant (raise one end by placing it on a sturdy box or chair.) Have the child roll the ball down the "big hill." You stand or sit at the bottom of the ramp to stop the ball and return it to the child for another roll. If the child wants to exchange places with you, do so and continue the fun. At some point, change balls (from big to little) and talk about the size of the ball: "The little ball fell off the side of the hill. Stay on the hill, little ball," or "Let's roll the big ball down the hill again."

Have the child help you make a road between two rows of blocks or strips of wood. Have him roll the balls down the road. Again, talk about the size of the balls and ask him which ball he is rolling.

ACTIVITY 28:   Building with Blocks

MOTOR SKILLS
A

WHY

To develop hand–eye coordination. To build a two- or three-block tower.

WHAT YOU NEED

Three blocks (cubes).

TALK ABOUT WHAT YOU DO

(Use your own language. This is an example.)

"Let's play with these blocks and see what we can build. I'll build a tower. You watch so that you can build a tower too."

"I'll take this block for the bottom of my tower. / Now I'll put this other block carefully *on top* of the bottom block. / See, there's my tower. Now, you build a tower the same way. / Oh, that's a nice tower!"

"Do you think you could build a bigger tower? / Let's try. Take this block and put it on top of the tower. / Oh, the tower went 'boom.' Towers do that sometimes. Let's try again. I'll help you. / That's right. Now put this last block on top of the other blocks. / You did it! You made a really big tower!" (Repeat if the child is interested.)

"What did you use to make your tower? / Can you tell me what you did?"

HELPFUL HINTS

Be sure to work on a flat, steady surface.

If the child cannot manage a three-block structure, settle for two. But increase the number of blocks as the child shows readiness to build taller structures.

If the child has difficulty building with the blocks, start him with boxes (lids taped on or covered with Contact) which are somewhat larger than the blocks. Then later try the blocks again.

Although your main focus in this activity is on the stated motor skill development, you are also teaching the concepts *on* or *on top of*. Thus, to the last question you asked, you are hoping the child will say, in some fashion, that he placed one block *on* another block. If the child cannot so respond, ask him to show you what he did. He may understand the concept without being able to express it.

Do *not* confine the child's building activities to duplicating structures first built by you. The activity above is offered as a way to start a youngster on building very simple structures and to introduce the concept *on* or *on top of*

The child should be encouraged to build many structures on his own and will probably do so if the materials are made available in free play.

THINGS TO DO ANOTHER TIME

Repeat the activity increasing the number of blocks to four, then five, and up to seven or eight as the child's skill in building towers increases.

Use blocks that are of different shapes (cubes, rectangles, triangles) and sizes. Have the child build various structures, such as a house, church, fire station, or any building he is aware of. Start by building a very simple structure: two cubes together for the base of the building and a triangular or rectangular block on top of these for the roof. Then have the child build the same structure, directing him, if necessary, to put one block *on top of* another. Encourage him to design his own structures and tell you about them.

ACTIVITY 29:   Nesting Objects

MOTOR SKILLS
A

WHY

To fit smaller object into larger object (eye–hand coordination).
To recognize differences in size: *little/big*.

WHAT YOU NEED

Two cans (without lids) of different size so that the smaller one fits easily into the larger one; Contact paper (optional).

TALK ABOUT WHAT YOU DO

(Use your own language. This is an example.)

"Look at these pretty cans. What can you do with them?" (Let the child play with the cans. If while playing he places one inside the other, praise him and pick up the activity from there.)

"This is a *big* can. (Touch it.) This is a *little* can. (Touch it.) See, I can put the little can inside the big one. (Demonstrate.) Can you do that?"

"Oh, where is the little can? / Can you find the little can? / Can you take the little can out of the big can? / Very good! Let's do that again." (Repeat.)

"Which can is the little one? / Which can is the big can? / Can you put the big can in the little one? / No, that doesn't work, does it? Try to put the little can in the big can. / That works, doesn't it?" (Repeat nesting several more times if the child enjoys it.)

HELPFUL HINTS

Cover the cans with Contact paper if you wish to make them more eye-catching.

Sizes are relative. An object is little or big only when compared with other objects. A child under two years of age will probably not fully grasp the concepts *little* and *big* and their dependence on comparing objects. But if the child recognizes that one can will fit into a larger can, he has the beginning of the concepts. Later, by using a third can of still a different size, the child will be able to grasp the ideas more fully. He may, however, need repeated activities involving the ideas of *little* and *big* and *littler* and *bigger*.

To reinforce the learning, let the child use several various sized cans, boxes, plastic bowls, or other unbreakable containers in his unstructured play. You may be surprised at how fast he discovers which sizes will fit in the larger sizes.

THINGS TO DO ANOTHER TIME

Repeat the activity using two lidless boxes, bowls, or other containers, one of which fits easily into the other.

When the child has mastered nesting two objects, try three different sizes. The differences in size of cans or other objects should be easily distinguishable by the youngster. Start the activity by lining up the three cans according to size (little to biggest) in front of the child. Then say something like this: "Will this little can (point) go into the bigger can (point)? / You try it and see if it goes in. / Oh, it went in! I wonder if both of these cans (point to nest of two cans) will go into the big can. See if you can put them in the big can. / Say, that is something! Look, all the cans are in the big can. / Can you take them out?" From then on let the child experiment with nesting the various sized cans. Comment on his successes and note combinations that do not work ("That big can won't go in the little can, will it?").

See also Activities 126, 130, and 132, which focus on the concepts *little/big*.

ACTIVITY 30:   Putting Small Objects in a Jar

MOTOR SKILLS
A

WHY

To put small objects in a larger object and take them out (hand–eye coordination).
To recognize positions of one object as *in* or *out* in relation to a second object.

WHAT YOU NEED

Wide-mouth plastic jar or a box; buttons of various sizes.

TALK ABOUT WHAT YOU DO

(Use your own language. This is an example.)

"Look at the pretty buttons. Some are little and some are big. Can you find a big button? / That's right. Now find a little button. / Very good!" (Let the child examine the buttons if he is interested.)

"This is a plastic jar. See, it has a round opening at the top. (Run your finger around the opening.) You can put your little hand in the big opening, if you like."

"I can put a button in the jar. (Demonstrate.) Can you pick up one of the buttons and put it in the jar too? / Oh, you put a little button in the jar. See it? / Can you put your hand in the jar and take *out* the button? / That's right. / The button is out of the jar now."

"Let's do that again. / In goes the button! / Out comes the button! / Can you say *in?* / Good! That means you can put a button in the jar. / Can you say *out?* / Okay. When you say *out,* you can take a button out of the jar. / Let's play an 'in and out' game. You have to put a button in the jar and then you have to take it out. Ready? / In! / Out! / In! / Out!" (Encourage the child to say the words *in* and *out* along with you. Continue the game as long as the child enjoys it.)

"Now put all the buttons in the jar. / Can you dump all of them out? / Just turn the jar over. / See, they all came out. / Where are the buttons now? Are they in or out of the jar?"

HELPFUL HINTS

The size of the opening of the jar must allow the child to insert his hand easily. A large cold cream jar or an oatmeal box is a good example.

Use fairly large buttons so that the child can handle them with ease. But be sure that at least a few are decidedly smaller (or larger) than the others to help the child recognize the *little/big* concepts as they apply to the buttons.

The opening suggested for this activity reviews and extends the learning of Activity 29, the *little/big* concepts. Such a review of previous learning is a good idea whenever appropriate. In this instance, the concepts are also extended since they are applied to new objects (*buttons* and *hand* compared to mouth of jar).

To encourage the child to put smaller objects in larger ones during spontaneous play, use a box or plastic bowl for the large container, and blocks or large beads for the smaller objects. Glass bottles or jars than can be broken and small objects that can be swallowed should be avoided, especially in unsupervised play.

THINGS TO DO ANOTHER TIME

Use a plastic container or a box with a somewhat smaller opening (about two inches wide) and somewhat smaller objects (dried beans or beads). Have the child put the small objects in the container. This task will require finer eye–hand coordination than that required in the activity above. Have the child say *in* each time he puts an object in the container. At the end of the task, ask him to pour *out* the objects into a bowl or box.

Repeat this activity using a plastic bottle with an opening of about one or one-half inch. This will require still finer coordination. Be sure the small objects will go through the opening of the bottle easily.

ACTIVITY 31:   A Game of "On Again, Off Again"

WHY

To develop large muscle coordination.
To recognize positions *on* and *off*.

WHAT YOU NEED

Chairs or low stools.

TALK ABOUT WHAT YOU DO

(Use your own language. This is an example.)

"See what I have? (Point to your chair.) It is a chair. I am going to put the chair right here (next to you on the floor) so we can play a game. The game is called 'On Again, Off Again, Gone Again, Finnegan.' I'll show you how to play it."

"When we say 'On again,' you have to sit on the chair like this. (Demonstrate sitting on the chair.) When we say 'Off again,' you have to get off the chair like this. (Get up.) And when we say 'Gone again, Finnegan,' you have to hide so I can't see you. See, I'll hide behind the chair. (Demonstrate.) You be Finnegan now, and we'll play the game."

"On again! / That means you sit on the chair. / That's right. You are *on* the chair. Off again! / You have to get off the chair now. / Good! Now you are *off* the chair. Gone again, Finnegan! / You hide, remember? I'll close my eyes. / Oh, where has Finnegan gone? (Pretend to look for the child.) There he is. I see Finnegan behind the chair."

"Let's play the game again." (Repeat the game, helping the child to remember what he must do when you say the words "On again," and so on. When he is familiar with the words and actions, just say the words and have fun. Encourage the child to say the words of the game also.)

"That was fun, wasn't it? / Are you on or off the chair now? / Are you 'Gone again, Finnegan'? / No, you are right here where I can give you a big hug."

HELPFUL HINTS

Since the game can be fairly strenuous, watch for signs of fatigue in the child. Stop the game, with a promise to play it again soon, before the child becomes overtired.

THINGS TO DO ANOTHER TIME

Repeat the game using varied objects for the *on* and *off* task: small rug, newspaper, step.

Play the game outdoors. Use a low step or a section of marked-off sidewalk or ground for the child to stand *on* and *off* when he plays the game. Let him hide behind a tree, bushes, corner of a house, or any other nearby larger object.

Transfer the idea of *on* and *off* to positional relationships between two objects. For example, let Teddy be "Finnegan." Have the child place Teddy *on* a chair, *off* a chair, and hide Teddy for you to find. Take a turn at playing the game to give the child a chance to "find Teddy."

ACTIVITY 32: Climbing Steps

MOTOR SKILLS
B

WHY

To develop leg muscles and balance.
To distinguish between *up* and *down*.

WHAT YOU NEED

Steps.

TALK ABOUT WHAT YOU DO

(Use your own language. This is an example.)

"We are going to play a game. It is called 'Up, 1, 2, 3, 4—Down 1, 2, 3, 4.' That's a funny name for a game, isn't it? / These are steps. (Touch two or three steps.) Where is the wall? / This is the wall." (Touch it.)

"First, we'll do the 'up' part of the game. We'll walk up the steps using our feet like this. (Demonstrate, using alternate feet.) When we walk up the steps, you hold my hand. Ready? / Hold my hand now."

"Here we go! Up, 1 step / 2 steps / 3 steps / 4 steps. (Count slowly, giving child all the time he needs.) Look how far up we came. We climbed up four whole steps."

"Now we are going to play 'Down 1, 2, 3, 4.' Hold my hand again and I'll help you. You can put your other hand against the wall if you like. / Down 1 step / 2 steps / 3 steps / 4 steps. / That was very good! You are a big boy (girl)! First you went *up* the steps; then you went *down* the steps."

"Let's play the game again. Should we play 'up' or 'down' first? / All right. First we'll play 'Up, 1, 2, 3, 4.' "

"Would you like to try going up the steps all by yourself? / You can put your hand against the wall to help you. And I'll be right here to help you too."

HELPFUL HINTS

The child may not use the "alternative-feet" method in climbing the steps. He may put both feet on a step before proceeding to the next step. Play the game his way until he catches on the alternate-feet method. Or try only two steps alternate-feet style.

Also, do not insist that the child try the steps by himself if he doesn't wish to do so. Repeat. the activity at later times to help him build confidence to try by himself.

If the child tries the steps by himself, stand close behind him as he ascends and in front of him as he descends so that you can easily catch him should be lose his balance.

THINGS TO DO ANOTHER TIME

When the child has improved his balance, increase the number of steps to six and then to larger numbers until the child is able to manage an entire flight of stairs.

ACTIVITY 33:   Zipping and Unzipping

MOTOR SKILLS
B

WHY

To open and close a zipper.
To distinguish between directions of *up* and *down*.

WHAT YOU NEED

A zipper frame or a short zipper on a garment.

TALK ABOUT WHAT YOU DO

(Use your own language. This is an example.)

"We are really going to have fun today. You are going to learn to zip and unzip a zipper. / What do you wear that has a zipper? / Right. Your pants (jacket) have (has) a zipper. Well, here is another zipper. This is the one we will use."

"See this little piece of metal? / It is called the zipper fly. We use the fly to pull a zipper up or down. Feel it. / Feel the zipper too. / It feels sort of rough, doesn't it?"

"Watch carefully. I hold the fly tight with my fingers. / Then I pull it *down* like this. I am zipping it down, down, down, down. / I'll pull it up again: up, up, up, up."

"Now you try it. Hold the fly tight. / Now pull hard. / Let me help you get started. / There it goes: down, down, down. / Can you zip it up? / Up, up, up, up. / Very good! Let's do that again. / Down, down, down, down. / Up, up, up, up. / That was good. You made the zipper go down and up." (Repeat if the child is interested.)

"Are you pulling the zipper up or down now? / Down, yes. Show me how you pull it up. / That was fun, wasn't it?"

HELPFUL HINTS

The zipper you use should work easily. A drop of machine oil may help to make it work smoothly.

If you are using a zipper in a piece of clothing, use one that will lie flat. A short neck zipper is good. Lay it flat first. For the child's later tries, hold the article in front of the child so that the ideas of *up* and *down* become more accurate for him.

Reinforce the learning by letting the child try to manipulate the zippers on his own clothing. Always help him as needed: start the zipper when it is difficult to move but let the child finish closing or opening it.

THINGS TO DO ANOTHER TIME

Play a "Surprise!" game. Use a traveling bag, briefcase, pocketbook or similar container that has a zipper. Put several small, wrapped "surprises" (cookies, balloon, small toys) in the container and zip it closed. Have the child unzip the container, select a surprise, and open it. Then have him close the zipper again. Repeat until the "surprises" are all opened. Emphasize the concepts *open* and *closed* in this activity. For example, say: "The bag (or case) is *open* now. See, you can see inside. / Can you *close* the bag with the zipper? / Good. It is *closed* now. You can't see inside the bag. / *Open* your surprise. / Oh, it's open. You can see the surprise. What is it?"

ACTIVITY 34:   Pounding with a Hammer

MOTOR SKILLS
B

WHY

To develop wrist and finger muscles.
To develop eye–hand coordination.

WHAT YOU NEED

Hammer; board with large nails or pegs started in it.

TALK ABOUT WHAT YOU DO

(Use your own language. This is an example.)

"Look at what I have! / This is a hammer. Do you know what you can do with a hammer? / You can pound nails with it. This is the handle (touch or point) that you hold when you pound the nails. / See this other end. This flat part (touch or point) does the pounding on the nails." (Let the child touch and examine the hammer.)

"This other thing is a piece of board that has nails in it. See the nails. (Touch several of the nails.) We are going to use the hammer to pound these nails all the way into the board. Watch, I'll show you. (Demonstrate, using slow motion.) See, the nail is going into the board.''

"Now you try pounding the nails. Hold the hammer here by its handle. / That's right. Now pick one of the nails and pound it. / Oh, you missed. Try again. / You hit the nail right on the head that time. Try some more. / Can you hit a little harder? / Very good! That nail is all the way down into the board. / Can you pound another nail into the board?''

(Let the child pound in all the nails if he remains interested.)

"What did you do today? / Be sure to tell your daddy (or some other adult) about it tonight. He'll be proud of you.''

HELPFUL HINTS

A peg board with large pegs may be purchased and used for this activity, but you may make your own "peg board." Use roofing nails or similar nails (about 1″ long with large, flat heads). Pound them half-way into a board of soft wood about three inches apart (see Fig. 34.1).

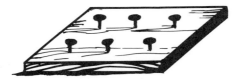

Fig. 34.1

Place the board on a flat, hard surface that is at a comfortable height for pounding by the child.

The child will probably be able to aim better at the nails if he holds the hammer fairly close to its head. But if this doesn't work for the child, allow him to find his own most comfortable grasp of the handle.

If pounding pegs or nails proves too difficult for the child, adapt the activity to simply pounding on a bench or board with a hammer.

THINGS TO DO ANOTHER TIME

Fasten three or four empty spools to a board by pounding a long nail through their center holes. Place the spools about three inches apart. Have the child pound on the spools with a wooden mallet, pretending he is a carpenter putting a new roof on the house. Be sure to explain first (and show pictures of) what a carpenter does and what part of the house is called the *roof*.

Let the child build something simple with hammer and nails. For example, take two small pieces of wood (2 or 3 inches long) and partially nail them together to form an airplane (see Fig. 34.2). Let the child complete the hammering. Praise what he made.

Fig. 34.2

ACTIVITY 35: Kicking a Ball

MOTOR SKILLS
B

WHY

To develop leg muscles and eye–foot coordination.
To kick a ball.

WHAT YOU NEED

Large, soft ball.

TALK ABOUT WHAT YOU DO

(Use your own language. This is an example.)

(Hold the ball back of you.) "Can you guess what I have behind my back? / No fair peeking. (Show ball.) What is this? / Yes, it is a ball. We are going to have fun kicking the ball today."

"I'll put the ball on the ground here in front of us. Now watch. (Demonstrate kicking the ball gently.) Can you do that? / You have to stand closer to the ball. / Say, that was a good kick. Run over to the ball and kick it back toward me."

"Let's see if you can kick the ball over toward the tree. (Point.) Oh, it went the other way, but that was a good kick. I'll kick it back to you and then you try again. / You kicked the ball right toward the tree that time."

(Continue the kicking activity until the child loses interest, but stop it before he becomes overtired.)

"Let's rest now. Tell me what you learned today. / Was it fun?"

HELPFUL HINTS

This activity is best suited to the outdoors. Use a nearby park if no playground is available to you. If you do use the activity indoors, clear away all breakable objects and make as much open space as possible.

A large beach ball is good for the child's first kicking lessons. When his kicking skills improve, smaller balls can be introduced.

Keep the activity informal and relaxed. The child will probably not be able to kick the ball in any particular direction and may miss it as often as he kicks it. The important thing is simply to provide the child with enjoyable practice (and exercise) in the basic motion of kicking.

THINGS TO DO ANOTHER TIME

Repeat the activity with variations, such as: kicking the ball back and forth between you and the child; kicking the ball to hit another object (tree or wall or you); kicking the ball down and up a small hill or slope; kicking the ball over another small object (rock, box). But keep the activity fun inspite of the misses or where the kicks carry the ball.

Repeat the activity using a somewhat smaller ball (volleyball size).

ACTIVITY 36: Slow and Fast

MOTOR SKILLS
B

WHY

To develop controlled use of leg muscles.
To distinguish between *slow* and *fast*.

WHAT YOU NEED

No materials needed.

TALK ABOUT WHAT YOU DO

(Use your own language. This is an example.)

"Let's have some fun walking different ways. First, I am going to walk slowly. Ver-ry slow-ly. (Walk very slowly for a distance of about six feet.) Let's see if we can do a slow walk together. Take my hand. / We want to walk ver-ry slow-ly. / Slow. / Slow. / Slow. / (Walk as you repeat the word slow.) That was really slow, wasn't it?"

"Now I'll show you my fast walk. / This is my fast hurry-up walk. / Can you walk as fast as I can? / No, don't run. Just walk. Take my hand and we'll walk fast together. / My, we walked fast, didn't we?"

"This time you walk fast and I'll walk slowly. We'll walk over to the door. (Point.) We'll see who gets to the door first. Ready? / Remember, walk fast but don't run. / Oh, you got to the door first. That's because you walked fast."

"This time let's see who can get to the door *last*. That means you have to walk very slowly. Remember, you win if you get to the door *after* I do. So walk ver-ry slowly. Ready? / Let's walk slowly." (In the last few steps walk a little faster than the child does so that he wins.)

"Oh, you won the game again! You got here after I did. That's because you walked more slowly than I did." (Repeat the game if the child remains interested.)

"Can you show me how you walk fast? / Am I walking fast now? (Walk very slowly.) / No, I wasn't walking fast. How was I walking? / Right. I was being a slowpoke."

HELPFUL HINTS

Use a walking distance of about six feet so as not to overtire the child.

The child will probably have the tendency to run rather than to walk fast. Holding his hand will be restraining influence without needing to repeat "Don't run." Holding his hand will also help him to slow his walk. But after he senses the idea of walking fast and walking slowly, let the child walk freely on his own.

Reinforce the learning by calling the child's attention to other things and animals that are moving at *fast* or *slow* paces: a dog, a car, a bicycle, a running child, a creeping bug, a hovering or fast-flying bird.

THINGS TO DO ANOTHER TIME

Adapt the "Slow/Fast" game to running outdoors in the playground or park. Demonstrate first running slowly and running fast. Then use a tree or other object to set a goal for the game. Alternate running fast with running slowly by changing the rules of the game from "getting there first" to "getting there last."

Demonstrate a *fast* and a *slow* moving object by using two similar objects such as two toy cars or two small balls. Make one car or ball move fast on a hard surface toward a wall (or box) while making the other car or ball move slowly toward the wall. Talk about the fast one and how it got there first. Then talk about the slow one and how it got there last. Repeat the race and ask the child which was the fast one and which was the slow one.

ACTIVITY 37: Sweeping

MOTOR SKILLS
B

WHY

To develop arm, back, and leg muscles.

To develop balance and coordination.

To sweep up small objects.

WHAT YOU NEED

Toy broom; large broom; dustpan; small pieces of newspaper.

TALK ABOUT WHAT YOU DO

(Use your own language. This is an example.)

"Today we are going to have fun sweeping with a broom. First we have to crumple up these pieces of paper like this. (Demonstrate.) And then we'll scatter the crumpled paper on the floor. Come on. Help me with the paper. / Oh, look at the mess on the floor. We are going to have to sweep up all that paper."

"Do you know how to sweep? / No? Well, I bet you can learn. What are these? (Touch or point to the brooms.) They are brooms. We sweep with a broom. Can you say *broom?* / Good!"

"This little broom is for you and this big broom is for me. Watch carefully and I'll sweep with mine. (Demonstrate.) Now you sweep with your little broom. / Very good!"

"Let's sweep up all the paper with our brooms. We have to get the paper all in one big pile. / Don't sweep too hard or we'll scatter the paper all over the floor again. / Look at the big pile of paper we swept up."

"Now we have to pick the paper up with a dustpan. Can you find the dustpan? / Right you are! I'll hold the dustpan while you sweep the paper onto it. / Sweep nice and easy or you'll miss the dustpan. / Say, that was good. All the paper is on the dustpan."

"Where should we empty the dustpan? / That's a good idea. Can you empty it carefully in the trash basket? / My, look how clean the floor is now."

"What did you learn to do today? / What did you use to sweep? / What else did you use? / Remember what you used to pick up the trash?"

HELPFUL HINTS

If the child has difficulty with the sweeping motion, demonstrate the process in more detail: "Stand sideways like this. / Let the broom touch the floor. / That's right. A little farther back. / Good. Now bring the broom over to the piece of paper and push the paper with the broom."

If you are working with a small group of children and do not have a toy broom for each child, have them take turns sweeping and holding the dustpan.

Reinforce the learning by having the child sweep up small bits of trash to help you clean up after snack time.

THINGS TO DO ANOTHER TIME

If you have a sandbox or access to one, have the child use a toy shovel (or large spoon) to fill a small bucket or other container with sand. Have him build a "big mountain" by emptying the bucket in another area of the sandbox.

Cover a large mirror (that the child can reach) with a thick film of cleansing powder (or glass wax) and let it dry. Demonstrate *wiping* (or rubbing) by using a cloth to wipe a small area of the mirror clean. Let the child get a peek of himself in the clean area. Then let the child wipe off the larger areas, encouraging him to tell you more things he can see in the mirror as he wipes.

ACTIVITY 38:   Pouring Water

MOTOR SKILLS
B

WHY

To develop eye–hand coordination.
To pour from a pitcher to a bowl
and to a cup.

WHAT YOU NEED

Plastic pitcher with water; large,
deep bowl, basin, or tub; child-
size table or bench.

TALK ABOUT WHAT YOU DO

(Use your own language. This is an example.)

(Place the three utensils on a low table or bench.) "You are going to
learn to do something new this morning. You are going to learn to pour
water. First, let's look at these things you are going to use."

"Do you know the names of any of these things? / Right! That's a cup.
What do you drink from a cup: / Very good! What is this? (Touch bowl.)
What is a big bowl like this used for? / Well, I can mix cookies in this bowl.
Or frosting for a cake. Have you ever licked the frosting left in a bowl? /
What is this called? (Touch pitcher.) It is a pitcher. Can you say *pitcher?* /
Good! Can you think of something we use a pitcher for? / Sometimes we
pour milk from a pitcher into a cup. Or we pour orange juice from a pitcher
into a glass."

"There is water in this pitcher. See? (Hold pitcher so child can see the
water.) I am going to pour some of the water into this bowl. (Demonstrate,
using exaggerated movements of raising, centering, and pouring as you continue to talk.) I have to raise the pitcher up over the side of the bowl. Then I

have to tip it *slowly* toward the bowl. There goes the water! / Now I tip the pitcher back to stop the water.''

"Now you try that. / Slowly. Very good!'' (Let the child repeat the act of pouring into the bowl several times.)

(Empty bowl and refill pitcher if necessary.) "We'll put this cup in the bowl and fill the cup with water. You have to be more careful because the cup is little. / Tip the pitcher v-e-r-y slowly over the cup. / Pour just a little water into the cup. / Good! Let's empty the cup and do that again.''

"What did you learn to do today? / What did you use? / What did you do with the pitcher?''

HELPFUL HINTS

Children love to play with water so make this activity fun. Use unbreakable utensils and protect the child's clothing with an apron. Newspapers or an old rug under the table may help make clean-up easy.

Do not use such a big pitcher or fill it so full of water that the child has difficulty handling it.

Reinforce the learning by letting the child help you at snack time. He can fill his own cup or glass with milk from a milk carton (this job will require two hands).

THINGS TO DO ANOTHER TIME

Have the child pour water as slowly as he can, and play a "counting" game. The purpose of the game is to encourage the child to pour more slowly each time so you can count higher. When the child begins to pour, you begin to count. Tell the child to see if he can pour even more slowly the next time so that you can count more numbers before the pitcher or cup runs out of water.

In a sandbox have the child fill a small container (cup) with sand. Then, using a funnel, have the child pour the sand into a small-mouth bottle. Teach him to stop pouring when the funnel fills up and to start again when it empties.

ACTIVITY 39: Blowing Bubbles

MOTOR SKILLS
B

WHY

To use mouth muscles for blowing.

WHAT YOU NEED

Plastic bowl or large glass; soapy water; bubble blowers or drinking straws.

TALK ABOUT WHAT YOU DO

(Use your own language. This is an example.)

"Have you ever seen bubbles? / Well, we are going to blow some bubbles today. We need soapy water and blowers to blow bubbles. The soapy water is in this bowl. (Stir the water.) See the suds. Those are little bubbles. / These are little paddles or bubble blowers. Here is one for you."

"Watch now. (Demonstrate as you talk.) I put the little paddle all the way in the bowl to get some of the soapy water on it. / Then I take it out carefully and hold it in front of my mouth. / Now I blow very gently. / See the big bubble? / Oh, it burst." (Act disappointed.)

"You try to blow a bubble. Put your paddle in the bowl and take it out carefully. / Now blow it ever so gently. / You blew too hard. You want to make your lips round, like when you say 'Oh.' Like this. (Demonstrate, saying "Oh.") Can you say 'Oh'? / Good. Now make your lips round again and blow. / That's good. Now let's try the bubbles again."

"Put your paddle in the bowl. / Make an 'O' and blow. / Oh, you blew lots of bubbles! I knew you could do it." (Continue as long as the child enjoys blowing bubbles.)

"Can you blow one more bubble? / See if you can catch it. / Oh, it got away. That was lots of fun, wasn't it?"

HELPFUL HINTS

Bubble mixture and blowers can be purchased, but your own soapy water and a drinking straw works just as well. If the child is using a straw, warn him not to "blow in" or he will get a mouthful of the soapy water.

This is a good activity for outdoors.

The act of blowing is difficult for some children. You may have to work on the "O" formation of the mouth first. If the child continues to have difficulty blowing bubbles and becomes frustrated, switch the activity to trying to catch a bubble. You do the blowing and let the child try to catch the bubbles. Before coming back to learning to blow bubbles, try some of the other "blowing" activities (given below). The child may be more successful in blowing bubbles after these additional experiences in blowing.

THINGS TO DO ANOTHER TIME

Place soapy water in a plastic cup. Insert a drinking straw and blow up a batch of bubbles or suds. Let the child do the same.

With the child watching, try to keep a small feather in the air by blowing. Have the child try. He probably won't be very successful but will enjoy the game.

Have a feather race. Using small feathers, see who can blow his feather first from one side of the table to another without blowing it off the table.

Light a couple of candles and give the child three chances to blow them out. If he is not successful, give him three more chances, and another three, and so on.

ACTIVITY 40: Opening and Closing a Bottle with a Screw Lid

MOTOR SKILLS
B

WHY

To unscrew lid and screw it on bottle.
To recognize positions *open* and *closed*.

WHAT YOU NEED

An empty plastic bottle or jar with a small screw lid.

TALK ABOUT WHAT YOU DO

(Use your own language. This is an example.)

"Do you know what this is? (Hold up bottle.) It is an empty plastic bottle. Detergent to wash clothes came in it. See the lid at the top of the bottle? (Point.) It unscrews and comes off. Watch. (Hold bottle so child can observe closely as you unscrew lid.) See the lid is off. The bottle is open. You can put your finger in the little hole at the top."

"I'll close up the bottle again. (Demonstrate.) Can you stick your finger in the top of the bottle now? / No, it's closed. The lid is back on."

"You open the bottle now. Put your hand around the lid, like this. (Demonstrate grasp.) Okay, now turn it this way. (Make counter-clockwise motion.) Keep turning. There, it's off. Is the bottle open now? / Can you put your finger into the top of the bottle? / Then it is open."

"Let's close the bottle. Take the lid and put it on the top of the bottle. / See if you can put it on straight. I'll help you. / The lid has to be straight or it won't close right. / Now turn the lid the other way, that way. (Make a clockwise motion.) There it goes! / Is the bottle all closed up tight? / Where is the hole for your finger? / It's gone. The lid is on and the bottle is closed.''

"Let's do the whole thing over again. / Is the bottle open now ? / How can you tell? / What do you have to do to close the bottle? / Right! We have to put the lid on. I'll help you get started."

HELPFUL HINTS

Unscrewing the lid will be considerably easier for the child than screwing it on. You may at first have to start the latter process by fitting the lid properly on the bottle or jar.

Be sure to screw the lid on very loosely so the child will have no difficulty unscrewing it.

Reinforce the learning by asking the child to help you open and close food jars or cosmetic jars that have screw lids.

THINGS TO DO ANOTHER TIME

Repeat the activity using other bottles/jars with different sized lids.

Put something small and attractive to the child in several jars. Tell him he can have what is in the jars if he can unscrew the lids. Encourage him to find the right lid for each jar and to screw them back on the right jars.

ACTIVITY 41: Stringing Beads

MOTOR SKILLS
B

WHY

To develop eye–hand coordination.
To distinguish between *on* and *off*
positions.

WHAT YOU NEED

Wooden beads with large holes;
sturdy cord or shoelace with a
knot on one end (see possible
substitutes in "Helpful Hints"
section).

TALK ABOUT WHAT YOU DO

(Use your own language. This is an example.)

(String beads on shoe lace before activity.) "See what I have! (Hold up
string of beads.) It's a long string with lots of pretty beads on it. / Can you
take the beads *off* the string? / Off comes one bead. / Off comes another
bead. / Boy, the beads come off easily, don't they? / Are they all off?"

"Let's see if the beads go back *on* the string. I'll show you how to put
them back on. First, take a bead. / Look for the little hole in the bead. See
it? (Point.) Now take the string in your other hand. Can you feel the stiff
end of the string? / Push the stiff end through the hole. / Good! Pull it out at
the other end of the bead. / Say, it worked. The bead is back *on* the string."

"Pick out another bead and put it on the string. / Can you put all the
beads *on* the string? / That's good!"

"Let's count each bead as you take it *off*. / One / two / three / . . ."

"What did you do today? / Are the beads *on* or *off* the string now?"

HELPFUL HINTS

Beads for stringing are available in toy stores, but you can also use substitutes. Small wooden spools can be dyed with vegetable coloring or Easter egg dye. Or nuts and washers (fairly large) are also good for stringing.

Be sure the cord you use goes easily through the holes of your beads. If a shoelace is too thick, use a thinner cord. Stiffen the stringing end by dipping it in glue and letting it dry.

Let the child play with the large beads in his unstructured play. In addition to stringing them, he will probably find other uses for them, such as filling a truck or sorting them in various ways. All such activities promote the development of eye–hand coordination and should be encouraged.

THINGS TO DO ANOTHER TIME

Provide the child with other materials for stringing: cereal loops, large straws cut in pieces, large macaroni rings. Continue stressing the *on* and *off* positions.

Color empty wooden spools with red and/or green vegetable coloring or, better yet, have the child color the spools. Then have him string the spools on picture wire. Make a wreath and hang it in the window or on the wall as *his* Christmas decoration.

The same idea of a wreath can be used to make an Easter wreath. Use blue and yellow vegetable coloring or Easter egg dyes.

Encourage the child to string beads to make a color pattern: all reds, all blues, for example, or some combination of colors.

Bend out a little the outer loops of 10–20 paper clips so that it is easy to slip one paper clip onto another. Have the child put the paper clips together to make a bracelet or a necklace.

ACTIVITY 42: Hopping on Two Feet

MOTOR SKILLS
B

WHY

To hop forward and backward on two feet.
To recognize *forward* and *backward* directions.

WHAT YOU NEED

No materials needed.

TALK ABOUT WHAT YOU DO

(Use your own language. This is an example.)

"Let's pretend we are bunnies. Remember how a bunny goes hop, hop, hop? / Well, we are going to learn to hop just like a bunny."

"First you have to put your feet together like this. / Then you hop forward like this. (Demonstrate a hop.) Feet together? / Okay, hop like a bunny. / Pretty good for your first bunny hop. Try it again. / Can you do two hops forward like this? (Hop two times.) Oh, that was good. Just like a bunny." (Repeat hopping forward several more times.)

"Let's see if you can hop backward like this. (Demonstrate one hop backward.) I'll hold your hand and you hop backward with me. Remember, keep your feet together. / Let's try that again. / That was good. Let's try one more hop backward. / You know, you're better than a bunny. A bunny can't hop backward like you can."

"Ready for a hopping game? / All right, take my hand and I'll show you. / First we hop forward three hops: hop, hop, hop. / Now we hop backward one big hop. / Let's play the game again: forward, hop, hop, hop; backward, one big hop. / Do you want to play the game again?''

"Was it fun being a bunny? / Show me which way you hop when you hop backward. / Show me which way you hop when you hop forward."

HELPFUL HINTS

You may have to work only on forward hopping in your first hopping activity, especially if the child has difficulty keeping his feet together when he hops. If so, modify the game to a series of two or three hops forward, and start the child on hopping backward at a later time.

You probably will be able to increase gradually the number of forward hops as you repeat the activity. By the time the child is three years old, he often can manage seven to ten consecutive hops. Backward hopping, however, will probably remain at one or two hops.

Give the child all the time he needs to make his hops, especially in the game.

THINGS TO DO ANOTHER TIME

Vary the "Hopping" game by using different patterns of hops; for example, one hop forward, one hop backward, one hop forward; or two hops forward, one hop backward, two hops forward.

Place a small, soft object (handkerchief) on the floor and demonstrate hopping *over* it. Have the child practice hopping over the object several times. Then play the game "Hop, Hop, Hop Over." On the third hop, the child tries to hop over the object on the floor.

ACTIVITY 43: Jumping

MOTOR SKILLS
B

WHY

To jump from an eight-inch step.
To recognize the direction *down*.

WHAT YOU NEED

A step (or block) about eight inches high.

TALK ABOUT WHAT YOU DO

(Use your own language. This is an example.)

"Come stand with me on this step. Up you go! / We are going to jump down from the step. First we have to put our two feet together like this. (Demonstrate.) Watch me. I am going to jump down. (Demonstrate.) That was fun."

"Now it is your turn. Are your two feet together? I'll hold your hand and we'll jump down together if you like. / Okay, you try it all by yourself. / Say, that was good! You jumped down better than I did." (Continue to practice jumping several more times.)

"Now let's play a game. First we will jump down from the step and then we will hop like a bunny. Do you remember how to hop like a bunny? / Show me how a bunny hops. / That's right."

"The game is 'Jump Down, Hop, Hop, Hop.' Ready? / Jump down, hop, hop, hop. (Say the words slowly so as not to hurry the child.) Very good! Let's play the game again." (Repeat the game several more times if the child enjoys it.)

"What did we do today? / Show me where you jumped down from. / Show me the place where you landed when you jumped down from the step."

HELPFUL HINTS

Be sure the child has already learned to hop before introducing the game (see Activity 42). If the child has difficulty jumping, limit the activity simply to practicing jumping and save the game for a later time.

If the child hesitates to try jumping from the step, encourage him by holding his hand the first time so that you are able to practically lift him down the step. As courage grows, let him try jumping by himself.

By increasing the height of the step or block an inch or two at a time, the child, by the age of about three can often make an 18-inch jump. Be sure, however, if you increase the height of his jump that you provide a soft surface for the jumping. A rug is a good idea even for the eight-inch jump. A mattress or heavy pad can be used for higher jumps.

THINGS TO DO ANOTHER TIME

Play varying versions of the "Jumping" game. For example, have the child jump down from the step or block, hop several times, and then climb up on the step and jump again. Be careful not to hurry the child's actions and to stay close in case you need to give help.

Plan jumping activities for outdoors on surfaces that are relatively soft: jumping up and down on the grass, jumping into a pile of leaves, or jumping down from any small elevation to the ground below.

ACTIVITY 44: Positions *Over* and *Under*

MOTOR SKILLS
C

WHY

To develop coordination.
To distinguish between positions *over* and *under*.

WHAT YOU NEED

Small block and ball (or similar small objects); chair; other furniture.

TALK ABOUT WHAT YOU DO

(Use your own language. This is an example.)

"Can you tell me what these things are? What is this? (Point to chair.) What is this? (Touch or point to block.) And this? (Touch or point to ball.) Very good! You got all of them right."

"Look. I am holding the ball *over* the chair. / The ball is over the chair. Can you take the block and hold it *over* the chair like this? / The ball and the block are *over* the chair. Where is your block? / Right. The block is *over* the chair."

"Now watch. I am going to put the ball *under* the chair. / The ball is under the chair. Put your block *under* the chair too. / Now the ball and the block are *under* the chair. Where is the ball? / Yes, the ball is *under* the chair."

(Remove toys from under the chair.) "Watch carefully now. (Place the block under the chair.) Where is the block? / It is *under* the chair. See the chair is here (touch chair seat) and the block (point) is under the chair. (Leave block under the chair and hold ball over the chair.) Where is the ball? / The ball is *over* the chair. The chair is here (touch chair seat). The ball is *over* (point *up* to ball) the chair, but the block is *under* (point *down* to block) the chair.''

"Can you take the block and hold it *over* the chair? / Now put it *under* the chair. / Oh, that's very good!''

"We are going to play the game of 'Over and Under.' Which toy do you want? / Okay. You take the ball and put it wherever I tell you. Ready? / Hold the ball *over* the chair. / Good! Now put the ball *under* the table. / *Under*. Where is *under* the table? / Right. Now hold the ball *over* the table.'' (Continue the game, using other readily available furniture.)

HELPFUL HINTS

Over and *under* are concept words denoting both stationary positions (an object is located *over* or *under* another object) and motion (an object is moving *over* or *under* another object) of one object in relation to another object. The activity above teaches the *stationary* positions. After the child masters these ideas, then teach the idea of moving an object over and under another object (see ''Things To Do Another Time'').

The small objects to be placed over and under other objects should be ones that the child can easily handle. The furniture used in the game should permit the youngster to place a small object over and under it without great effort—not too high and with space between it and the floor.

When teaching such concepts as *over* and *under,* be sure to use the concept words often and to emphasize them each time used. The repetition and the stressing of the words provide the child with important clues to the focus of the learning.

THINGS TO DO ANOTHER TIME

Play the ''Over and Under'' game using different objects.

String a fairly heavy cord from one chair to another so that the cord is about a foot off the floor. Pretend the cord is a fence. Roll a small, soft ball (tennis size) under the cord to the child seated on the other side of the cord. Say: ''The ball is rolling *under* the fence. / Roll the ball back to me *under* the fence.'' Repeat several times, each time repeating ''under the fence.''

Then toss the ball gently to the child, saying: "The ball is going *over* the fence." Repeat their motion several times. Next, play a game, alternating the ball under and over the cord. Encourage the child to say "over the fence" and "under the fence" with the appropriate action.

ACTIVITY 45: Positions *Behind* and *In Front Of*

MOTOR SKILLS
C

WHY

To develop coordination.
To distinguish between positions *behind* and *in front of*.

WHAT YOU NEED

A large box; Teddy bear and toy car or other small objects.

TALK ABOUT WHAT YOU DO

(Use your own language. This is an example.)

"Look at what I have. (Point to box.) What is it? / Yes, it's a box. What else is here? (Point to the two toys.) Right. Let's start by playing a game with Teddy. Come over beside me. (The box should be in front of you and the child.) Watch now."

"I am going to put Teddy *behind* the box. / Where is Teddy? / He is behind the box. See. (Hold Teddy up.) He was behind the box. That's why we couldn't see him. I'll put him behind the box again. / See if you can find Teddy behind the box. / Oh, you found him. Was he hiding behind the box?"

"Here is your car. Can you put it *behind* the box? / No, put it all the way behind the box. / Good! Put Teddy behind the box too. / Very good!"

"I am going to take Teddy from behind the box and put him *in front of* the box. / Teddy now is in front of the box. I'll put the car in front of the box with Teddy. / Where are Teddy and the car? / Can you say *in front of the box?* / Try saying *front.* / That's good."

(Collect both toys and return to original position.) "Now you take Teddy. Put him *behind* the box. / Now take the car and put it *in front of* the box. / Good! You're very smart."

"Can you hide behind the box with Teddy? / Oh, where is Karen? (Use child's name.) She must be behind the box. Come out, Karen, and stand in front of the box so I can see you. / I still can't see all of you. You have to stand in front of the box. / Good! Now I see all of you."

HELPFUL HINTS

At the beginning of the activity, establish both your position and the child's so that you both have the same view of the box. This is important since *behind* and *in front of* the box must be from a particular position.

If you are working with a small group of children, have them all stay on one side of the box with you, since they must all view the box from the same direction. Have each child take a turn at placing an object behind and in front of the box and getting behind and in front of the box.

If the child has difficulty understanding the meaning of *behind* and *in front of,* repeat the activity using different objects.

THINGS TO DO ANOTHER TIME

Position yourself at one end of a room with 4–6 blocks in front of you. Tell the child you are going to play a "Hide and Find" game. Direct the child to hide each block in a *behind* or an *in front of* position in relation to another object in the room (behind the red chair, in front of the table) until all the blocks are hidden. Then ask the child to find the blocks and tell you where he found each one. If he has difficulty, help him by saying such things as "Look behind the red chair," and "Was this block in front of the table or behind the door?"

Play "Hide and Find" using four positions: *on, under, behind,* and *in front of.* Be sure the child has already learned all four positions when you try this variation of the game.

ACTIVITY 46: Position of *Between*

MOTOR SKILLS
C

WHY

To develop eye–hand coordination.
To recognize the position *between*.

WHAT YOU NEED

Two small blocks and a larger block; a toy car or other small toy.

TALK ABOUT WHAT YOU DO

(Use your own language. This is an example.)

"What do we have here? (Point to blocks.) Yes, they are blocks. Is one bigger than the others? / Which block is bigger? / What is this? (Point to or touch car.) What color is the car? / Where is the front of the car? / Very good!"

"Let's put the two little blocks like this. (Place them about a foot apart, opposite each other.) Now, I'll put the big block *between* the two little blocks." (Touch each block and draw an imaginary line from one little block to the other as you continue.) See, this big block is between this little block and this other little block."

"You pick up one of the little blocks. / Okay. I'll put the big block where your little block was. / Now you put your little block *between* the big block and the other little block. (Point to a spot directly in a line *between* the two blocks if the child is unsure of what is expected of him.) Look! This little block is now between this big block and this other little block." (Touch blocks and draw your imaginary line again.)

"Let's try something different. Put one little block here. / Put the other little block there. / Now let's put the car between the two blocks. Can you do that? / Very good!"

"Do you know that the car can move *between* the two blocks too? / See." (Push the car between the blocks.)

"Let's pretend this is a road. (Use your hand to show that the road runs parallel to and between the two blocks.) Pretend the blocks are houses. This one is your house and that one is Jerry's house across the street. Can you drive your car down the road between your house and Jerry's house? / Oh, that's very good. I saw Jerry wave at you as you went by his house."

HELPFUL HINTS

Remember that the position *between* always relates one object to *two* other objects. If the child has difficulty grasping this idea, try several additional examples: spoon between two forks, glass between two cups.

If the activity is difficult or cannot hold the child's interest, save the idea of *moving between* two objects for another time.

Reinforce the learning of the concept *between* by helping the child make a sandwich ("See, the meat is *between* this slice of bread and that slice of bread").

THINGS TO DO ANOTHER TIME

Play a game of "Between" using a variety of objects. Ask the child to find an object that is between two other objects: "Can you find something that is between the two big boxes? / Can you find something that is between the desk and the little table?" You may want to set up the room before the game, placing small objects between the furniture you specify or between such other small objects as two books, two toys, and so on.

Give the child a small object (block, book) and play a game that requires the child to place the object between two other objects: "Put the block between the door and the window. / Put the block between my two feet."

Outdoors, play a running or walking game that calls for the child to move between two specified objects: "Can you run between the wagon and the sidewalk? / Can you walk between the two chalk lines?"

ACTIVITY 47: Open and Closed Positions

MOTOR SKILLS
C

WHY

To develop eye–hand coordination.
To distinguish between *open* and *closed*.

WHAT YOU NEED

Things that open and close: door, window, jar with lid, box with lid, coin purse with snap closing.

TALK ABOUT WHAT YOU DO

(Use your own language. This is an example.)

"We are going to play a game called 'Opening and Closing.' You are going to see how many things you can *open* and *close*."

"Let's start with our eyes. *Open* them wide. / What are some of the things you see with your eyes open? / Now *close* your eyes. / What do you see with your eyes closed? / Are your eyes closed when you are asleep?"

"Open your hands like this. (Demonstrate, palms up.) Both hands are open now. (Touch each of the child's hands as you count.) One, two. Now close your two hands like this. (Demonstrate making a fist.) Are your hands closed tight? / Very good. Your hands are closed. I can't see if you have anything in your hands when they are closed."

"Where is the door? / Is it open? / No, the door is closed. (Open the door.) See, now the door is open. We can see into the hall. / What can you see?"

"What about the windows? Are they open or closed? / Right! They are closed. Help me, and we'll try to open this window. Take hold here (point) and push up. / There, the window is open. Can you feel the air coming in through the open window? / Let's close it again.''

(Place the purse, jar, and box in front of the child, purse open, jar and box closed.) "What are these things? / Very good! Now tell me if each thing is open or closed. Is the purse open or closed? / Is the box open? / Is the jar closed? / Oh, you are so smart! You were right each time. Would you like to open and close all these things?''

HELPFUL HINTS

The focus of this activity is on a variety of opening and closing experiences to help the child grasp the concepts *open* and *closed*. If the child attempts to open and close a particular object himself and has difficulty with the mechanics of opening and closing it, help him. Go back to the object another time and teach the mechanics, step by step. Keep the focus here on the concepts.

If you are working with a small group of children, have enough jars and boxes (or similar objects) for each child to experience opening and closing them. For objects more difficult to come by, have the children take turns opening and closing them.

THINGS TO DO ANOTHER TIME

Give the child other things to open and close: other jars and boxes, can with a flip lid (Band-Aid can), bottle with a cork (not way in and not too tight). Put a "treat" or a "surprise" inside one of the containers and tell the child to open all of them to find the surprise.

Have the child open and close a drawer. Say, "Open the drawer," "Close the drawer" as he goes through the motions. Repeat, using different drawers if the child enjoys the game.

Have the child practice opening and closing a door. Take him through each step: both hands on the door knob, turning the knob, and pulling (or pushing) with the knob turned. To close the door, have him push (or pull) the door closed, using the knob to control the door and prevent slamming it. "Let's see how quietly you can close the door. See if you can make no noise at all.''

ACTIVITY 48: Walking a Straight and a Wavy Line

MOTOR SKILLS
C

WHY

To develop balance.
To distinguish between a *straight* and a *wavy* line.

WHAT YOU NEED

Chalk; a one-inch-wide straight chalk line about three feet long.

TALK ABOUT WHAT YOU DO

(Use your own language. This is an example.)

"What is this on the pavement (floor)? / It is a straight line. It doesn't have any wiggles (make wavy motion with hand) in it. / See how straight it is? (Trace the line with your finger.) Let's make believe we are circus clowns and the line is a rope high in the air. Let's see if we can walk on the rope without falling off." (Let the child try. Then give him some additional help if he needs it.)

"Let's see if I can walk on the tightrope. / Oh, I slipped off. (Do so deliberately, waving arms as if losing your balance.) You try again. / Sometimes it helps to hold your arms like this (spread arms out) to give you better balance. / That's very good."

"I'll count the steps you make on the rope. You walk and I'll count. / 1 step on / 2 steps on / Oh, that step was off. / That's right. Keep going. / 3 steps on / 4 steps on / Ooops, that one was off."

"Turn around and walk back on the straight line toward me. Help me count this time. / 1 step on / 2 steps on / . . . ."

"Let's try a wavy line. (Make a chalk line with several long curves.) See how a wavy line is not like a straight line? It goes in and out. (Use hand motion to demonstrate a wavy line.) Can you walk this line?" (Repeat walking on wavy line and counting steps.)

"Was that fun? / You walked on a straight line and on a wavy line. (Use chalk to make a short straight line and a wavy line.) Which of these lines is straight? / That's the one we pretended we walked on high up in the air, wasn't it?"

HELPFUL HINTS

Don't be surprised at the number of times the child steps off a straight or wavy line the first time he tries. With practice, he will improve but expect some "off" steps whenever you try the activity or some variation of it.

Pretending to be circus clowns on a tightrope assumes that the child has seen such an act (on TV or a story-book picture of it). If not, bring the play within the child's experience: walking on a very narrow road or sidewalk or bridge.

THINGS TO DO ANOTHER TIME

Locate straight lines on sidewalks or use the edge of the sidewalk for the child to practice walking on a straight line. Or use a stick to make straight and wavy lines on the ground (or in sand) for repeating the activity.

Make a chalk circle one inch wide and about four feet in diameter. Talk about going around the circle as the child walks the circle. The child may enjoy chanting, "Around and around and around he (she) goes and where he (she) will stop no one knows."

Adapt the activity to walking a chalk square, each side about three feet long. By having the child walk the square in clockwise direction and counter-clockwise direction, the child will be developing the skill of making both right and left turns.

ACTIVITY 49:   Walking, Running, Jumping

MOTOR SKILLS
C

WHY

To develop leg muscles and coordination.
To remember and follow two- and three-part directions.
To distinguish between such directions as *to, back, forward, backward,* and *around.*

WHAT YOU NEED

Small area outdoors with a landmark (tree) or marker (stone, stick).

TALK ABOUT WHAT YOU DO

(Use your own language. This is an example.)

"We are going to play a lively game. It's called 'Following Directions.' I am going to call out different things to do. You've got to remember what I say and do it. Okay?"

"See the tree right there? (Point.) Run over to the tree. / Now touch the tree. / Now run back to me here. / You are a good runner."

"This time we'll both walk to the tree and then we will walk around the tree. Let's go. / Remember, walk; don't run. / Here we are. Now what else were we to do? / We have to walk around the tree. That means doing this. (Demonstrate.) See. I walked all around the tree. Can you do that? / Good. You went *around* the tree."

"Now let's walk backwards five whole steps. Like this. (Demonstrate a few steps.) Let's count together so that we will know when we have taken five steps. / 1 step / 2 steps / . . . .''

"Now turn around and run forward to the tree and around the tree. Don't forget to run *around* the tree. / You remembered. That's good!"

"Take three big steps forward, toward me. / One / two / three. / Take one big jump backwards. / No, don't turn around. Jump backwards. / Oh, that was a good one."

"Now listen carefully. I am going to tell you three things to do. First, run to the tree. Second, walk around the tree. Then take *one big jump forward.* Can you remember all that? / Run to tree; walk around it; then take a jump forward."

(If the child enjoys the game, continue giving him two- and three-part directions that involve going *to, back,* and *around* something and moving *backward* and *forward.*)

"Let's sit on the grass and rest. You can tell me all the things you just did."

HELPFUL HINTS

Start with one-part directions and gradually build to two- and three-part directions.

If the child does not understand a direction (*around, backward*), demonstrate it, have him repeat it, and then repeat the direction a little later to see if he remembers what it means.

If you are working with a small group, have all the children follow each direction. They will probably learn a lot from each other.

Alternate the most strenuous activity (running) with less strenuous ones (walking) so that the child does not get over-tired.

THINGS TO DO ANOTHER TIME

The "Follow Directions" game is good for indoors on rainy or cold days if you exclude the running activity and give two- and three-part directions involving walking, climbing (steps), jumping, swinging arms or a leg. Continue developing comprehension of the direction concepts. Others you might add are: *over/under* (step over the book, walk under the light), *up/down* (go up two steps, go down two steps), *in/out* (go in the closet, jump out of the closet), *through/in front of/behind/between* (walk through the door, jump in front of the chair, walk behind the chair, walk between the two chairs).

ACTIVITY 50:   Building Short and Long Structures

MOTOR SKILLS
C

WHY

To build short and long structures (eye–hand coordination).
To distinguish between *short* and *long*.

WHAT YOU NEED

Blocks of two lengths, one length decidedly longer than the other.

TALK ABOUT WHAT YOU DO

(Use your own language. This is an example.)

"Let's see what we can make with these blocks. Oh, look. Some of the blocks are short. (Place one of the short blocks in front of the child.) And some of the blocks are long. (Place a long block on the floor parallel to the short block.) This block is *short*. (Point and indicate how short with your thumb and index finger.) This block is *long*. (Point and indicate how long with your thumb and index finger.)

"Can you find some more *short* blocks like this one? (Point.) No, that's long like this long block. (Lay it next to long block.) See, they are both long. Find another block that is short like this short block. / That's right. Put it beside the other short block. See if you can find some more short blocks."

"You found a lot of short blocks. Now see if you can find some *long* blocks. / Very good! Put it with your other long blocks. / Keep looking for some more long blocks."

"Let's use these short blocks to make a short sidewalk. / Put another block here (point) beside that short block. (When child has made a sidewalk of three short blocks, continue talking.) Oh, that's a nice short sidewalk. Now use the long blocks to make a long, long sidewalk right here beside your short sidewalk." (Build a second sidewalk parallel to and at least twice as long as the first.)

"Look at the long sidewalk you made! (Use hands to indicate length.) See, your *short* sidewalk goes from here to here. Your long sidewalk goes all the way from here to here."

"Watch. These two fingers (index and middle finger) are Mr. Finger. He is going for a *short* walk on your *short* sidewalk. (Walk your fingers down the short sidewalk.) Can you walk your Mr. Finger along your short sidewalk like I did? / Oh, that was a nice short walk. Now take Mr. Finger for a *long* walk on your *long* sidewalk. / Say, Mr. Finger had to take many more steps on his long walk than he did on his short walk, didn't he?"

"What would you like to build now with your short and long blocks? / That's a good idea. Show me how you do it."

HELPFUL HINTS

If you do not have blocks of two lengths, you can make them from styrofoam (or wood). Make some blocks considerably longer than your short blocks.

Remember that the concept *tall* refers to objects in a *vertical* or upright position and the concept *long* refers to objects in a *horizontal* position. The child may grasp this distinction by your talking about a *tall* tower that "goes up, up, up" and a *long* road that "goes from here to way over here" on the floor (see "Things To Do Another Time"). If not, demonstrate and explain the difference when the youngster is somewhat older.

THINGS TO DO ANOTHER TIME

Build other *short* and *long* structures. For example, have the child build a long road with houses (one block) on each side of it. Then suggest building a short road from the long road to each house. Also have the child build a tall tower beside the road, a tall tower that "goes up, up, up." Ask him to tell you about something *long,* something *short,* and something *tall* that he built.

Cut a short (2 feet) and a long (8 feet) piece of string. Extend them on the floor. Have the child walk from one end of each string to the other. Talk about how much farther he walked to reach the end of the long string. Try the walking again and count the steps taken to reach the end of each string.

ACTIVITY 51: Building Structures from Models

MOTOR SKILLS
C

WHY

To develop eye–hand coordination.
To build a structure from a visible model.
To build a structure from memory (visual memory).

WHAT YOU NEED

Blocks of various shapes and colors, each block with at least one duplicate (same shape, size, and color).

TALK ABOUT WHAT YOU DO

(Use your own language. This is an example.)

(Place the blocks in front of the child on a flat surface.) "Look at all these blocks! Let's play a game. I'll make something, and then you make exactly the same thing. Okay?"

"I think I'll make a house. This big red block will be good for the bottom of the house. I'll put it right here. / The house needs a roof. A block that is a triangle would make a good roof. Here is a blue triangle. / See, it has three sides. (Trace each side with your finger, counting the sides as you trace.) One—two—three. Can you show me the three sides of the triangle? / Good! I am going to put the blue triangle on top of the red block. And there's my house! / Can you point to the roof? / That's right. A roof is always on the top of the house.''

"Can you make a house just like mine? (If the child can do so without coaching, let him; if he has difficulty, use words to coach him.) First you need a red block just like the one I have there. (Point.) / That's right. / Now what do you need for a roof on your house? / Can you find a blue block that is a triangle? / Very good. Now where does the roof go? / Right you are. Now your house is exactly like mine.''

"Let's knock down both of our houses. / Now see if you can build another house just like the one you built before. / Do you remember which block you used first? / Good! Which block did you use for the roof? / Say, that's very good. You remembered just how to build the house.''

"This time you make something, and I'll see if I can make one just like it.''

HELPFUL HINTS

A parquetry set usually has the kind of blocks you need for this activity. You can, however, make your own blocks out of styrofoam or bits of wood and spools, painting them various colors. Be sure that you have duplicates (shape, size, color) so the child can find and use the same kind of blocks as those used in the model.

The idea of a *model,* as used in this activity, refers both to your showing the child how to build a particular structure and to the completed structure. The first task for the child is to duplicate the steps you used to build the same structure while it is still visible to him.

The second task is more difficult: to rebuild the same structure from memory *after* the model has been scrambled. If the child cannot perform this second task, rebuild the house again and have him duplicate it from the visible model.

Note that in using a model in this activity your end goal is the development of the child's visual memory, a reading readiness goal. The use of the model for this purpose in no way implies that the child's play with blocks should be restricted to duplicating models. On the contrary, asking young children to duplicate what an adult can do, often at difficulty levels far beyond them, can be frustrating, tedious experiences, and should be avoided. The general emphasis should be on free play with building blocks and similar materials.

THINGS TO DO ANOTHER TIME

Repeat the activity by building other simple two-block structures: chair (square block for seat, long block for back), road (two long blocks laid end to end), or any other structure with which the child is familiar.

When mastery of building two-block structures from memory is satisfactory, increase the number of blocks in your model to three. For example, build a car or wagon using a rectangular block for the body and two round blocks (circles) for wheels. Or simply use different shapes and colors: a large blue rectangle, a yellow square on top of it, and a red circular block (cylinder) on top of the square.

ACTIVITY 52: Unbuttoning and Buttoning

MOTOR SKILLS
C

WHY

To unbutton a button.
To button a button.
To recognize the postion *through*.

WHAT YOU NEED

An article of clothing with fairly large buttons and buttonholes, or a button frame.

TALK ABOUT WHAT YOU DO

(Use your own language. This is an example.)

"What is this? (Hold up buttoned garment.) Right! It is a blue sweater. Does it have any buttons? / Let's count the buttons (touch each button): one button / two buttons / three buttons / four buttons. It has four pretty buttons. Watch. I will show you how to unbutton one of the buttons. (Demonstrate in slow motion.) Now I wonder if you can unbutton one of the buttons.''

(Let the child try on his own. If he succeeds, don't forget to praise. And have him try another button if he is interested. Then pick up the activity at the second paragraph below, which is on buttoning. If the child is not successful in unbuttoning, continue with the next paragraph.)

''Let me show you again. See this hole behind the button? (Unbutton a button.) See it? / It's called a buttonhole. Stick your finger through the buttonhole. / When you unbutton a button, the button has to go through that hole. (Then rebutton and continue.) To unbutton, you have to push the button through the buttonhole like this. (Demonstrate.) Can you do that with one of the other buttons? (Give whatever help is necessary for success.) Oh, you did it! You unbuttoned a button!''

''Let's button up the sweater again. (Demonstrate as you continue.) Hold the button with one hand and push it right through the buttonhole from this side (underside). Now you try it. I'll hold the sweater and you push the button. / There it went—right through the hole! See. The button is buttoned again.''

(Have the child repeat unbuttoning and buttoning another button if he remains interested.)

''That was fun, wasn't it? / Show me where a buttonhole is? / Can you put your finger *through* it?''

HELPFUL HINTS

Be sure the buttonholes you use are sufficiently large that the buttons go through them easily.

If you use a button frame, adapt the activity accordingly. Include identifying the button and the buttonhole, the demonstrations, and the emphasis on the concept *through*.

The child will probably be able to unbutton a button before buttoning one. Don't continue with the buttoning if the child becomes frustrated. Come back to it later.

THINGS TO DO ANOTHER TIME

Repeat the activity using different articles of clothing with larger/smaller buttons.

When the child masters the skills of unbuttoning and buttoning buttons on clothing he is *not* wearing, encourage him to unbutton and button something he is wearing. Use a garment on which the buttons are fairly large and start him with the unbuttoning task. When he is ready to try buttoning his own clothing, again have him work with fairly large buttons, limit the first try to a single button, and be prepared to help him if he finds the task difficult.

ACTIVITY 53: Untieing and Unlacing

MOTOR SKILLS
C

WHY

To untie a bowknot.
To unlace a shoe.

WHAT YOU NEED

A loosely laced large shoe, with shoestring tied in a bowknot.

TALK ABOUT WHAT YOU DO

(Use your own language. This is an example.)

"Look at this big shoe! Is it your shoe? / Would you like to try it on? / Oh, your foot goes in, shoe and all. This is a big shoe for a little foot, isn't it?"

"Does the big shoe have a shoestring? / This is the shoestring. (Touch it.) Do your shoes have shoestrings? / Show them to me. / Very good! / The shoestring on the big shoe is tied in a bow. See the bow? (Point.) Are your shoestrings tied in bows too? / Where are your bows? (Point to bows if child is unable to identify them.)

"Let's untie the bow on the big shoe. You pull this end (point) and I'll pull this other end. / Pull hard. / There goes the bow! / The bow is all gone. We untied it. Only the knot is left. See the knot. (Point.) Let's untie the knot too. You have to put your finger under here. (Put your index finger under knot.) That's right. All the way under. Good. Now pull the string up with your finger. / Now the knot is gone too."

"Look at how the shoestring is laced. It goes through the holes (point) and crisscrosses from side to side. (Trace crisscrossing back and forth with your finger.) That's why we say the shoestring is *laced*. Let's *unlace* the shoestring. Let's take it out of the holes. I'll show you how."

(Demonstrate in slow motion as you continue.) "First I have to put my finger under the lace here in the middle, like this. / Then I pull up hard. See the shoestring is moving through the holes. / There. The string is out of the top holes." (Point to each hole.)

"Now you unlace the next crisscross / No, use that finger. (Point to index finger.) It goes right under there. (Point.) Okay. Now pull up hard with your finger. / See, the lace is moving. Keep pulling. / Oh, the string is out of two more holes. See? (Point to holes.) That's very good. Unlace another crisscross. / See if you can unlace the whole shoestring."

"That's very good! The shoestring is completely unlaced. It is out of the shoe. Would you like to unlace the shoe again all by yourself?"

(If the child wants to repeat the unlacing, relace the shoe with the child watching you, but do not attempt to teach the steps of lacing in this activity. Retie the bowknot too and let the child untie it. This time have him use both hands and pull both ends of the shoestring to release the bow.)

HELPFUL HINTS

A large shoe with large holes is easier for the child to work with than his own smaller shoe. Move to the smaller shoe once he can unlace the larger shoe by himself.

Or start the child on a lacing/tieing frame. You can make one yourself from a paper plate (or two paper plates pasted together) and a shoestring. Punch two rows of parallel holes (about ½ inch wide) in the plate, and lace the shoestring through the holes. The frame is especially good for the child's unstructured play.

Tieing a bowknot and lacing a shoe are complex tasks for the young child. Complete mastery of lacing may be attained by the child in his fourth year; mastery of tieing a bowknot may come a year or two later.

If, however, after the child has mastered the skills of untieing and unlacing a shoe you would like to start him on the tieing and lacing processes, it is important that you break down each process into its smaller steps and teach one step at a time. The best way to identify the steps is to perform each task yourself in slow motion, noting every movement your hands make. Then plan your activities around a few related hand movements.

Be patient with the child if he finds these advanced activities difficult. And stop the activity if he finds it frustrating. Wait until the child is older and try again.

Suggested steps for lacing:

1.   Thread the shoestring through a hole from the underside of the shoe flap upward; pull the string through until it is tight. (Note: Shoe is partially laced for this first step.)
2.   Cross the same end of the shoestring to a hole on the other side of the flap; thread and tighten the string in the same way as in the first step.
3.   Thread holes alternately on both flaps (crisscrossing), working with both ends of the shoestring; tighten lace by pulling both ends.

Suggested step for tieing a bowknot:

1.   Make the first knot of a bowknot by crossing the two ends of a string and bringing one end of the string under the other; pull both ends of the string to tighten the knot.
2.   Make the *second* loop of the bowknot by pulling the string through the hole made by crossing one end of the string over the first loop. (Note: You make the bowknot up to this point; the child merely pulls the string through the hole to make the second loop.)
3.   When both loops are made, pull both loops at the same time to tighten the bowknot. (Note: This may be as far as the child will be able to go in the process until he is older.)
4.   Make the first loop; cross the other end of the string over the first loop; pull the piece of string through the hole to make the second loop; pull both loops at the same time to tighten the bowknot.

THINGS TO DO ANOTHER TIME

Have the child untie and unlace the shoestrings of his own shoes—both off and on his feet. Show him how to loosen the lace and remove the shoes without completely unlacing the shoestring.

Place a surprise (cookie, balloon) in a box and tie the box with a pretty colored ribbon. Make a bowknot that is not too tight. Have the child untie the ribbon to get the surprise.

Art activities can be exciting experiences. Young artists enjoy discovering what they can do with crayons.

Part 3

Art

ART

Most children are naturally curious and exploring. They are also potentially creative. Fostering and developing these qualities through a variety of art experiences is an important part of their early education; for through such development other means of growth are stimulated. The youngster who experiments with paints, clay, or other art media is not only satisfying curiosity and being creative, but he is also developing intellectual, sensory, and motor skills. At the same time, he is finding an outlet for emotions, new ways to express feelings and experience satisfaction, and enjoyment in making something. Thus, art activities contribute to building self-confidence and to social development.

The preschooler's first pictures are usually merely paint blobs or crayon scribbles. Their value lies in the child's exposure to the processes used to produce the blobs and scribbles. As the child continues to experience and experiment with the processes, he becomes increasingly aware of colors, textures, lines, and shapes. And as skills develop, he learns to manipulate the materials and tools in a controlled way so that he can more effectively use them to express ideas and feelings. The resulting product often has great meaning for the child. It is something that expresses his individuality, that he enjoyed making, that brings him satisfaction.

What preschoolers need, then, is a variety of art experiences in which they explore and experiment with varied materials and processes. They need to find out what they can do with different kinds of paper. They need to tear, cut, and arrange shapes to make designs and pictures. They need to use their fingers to discover how paint feels and what it will do; to use a brush to make blobs, drips, lines, and to fill space with color. They need to feel the stickiness of clay and discover what happens when they punch, roll, or squeeze it. They need to manipulate a pencil, crayon, and chalk to learn that these things can be used to make lines and circular scribbles, and to fill in empty spaces. And they need to work with objects of many different shapes and textures—flowers, sand, macaroni, seeds, twigs, and feathers, to name a few—in order to become aware of textures, shapes, a third dimension (depth), and simple beauty in common objects all around them.

Calling the child's attention to a colorful sunset, the blueness of the sky, sparkles of dew on the grass, a velvety flower, the pleasing colors of a dress or shirt helps the child find and appreciate beauty in his life, a basic goal of early art education. Providing youngsters with simple art activities in which they have freedom to explore and experiment with a variety of art media is another important goal.

The activities in this section of the text attempt to do just that. They suggest a wide assortment of materials and processes to introduce the child to the world of art. In addition to the art processes of arranging, painting, modeling, constructing, coloring, and drawing, they include such basic skills as tearing, cutting with scissors, pasting, and folding. Prewriting skills, too, are developed through the use of pencil, crayon, and chalk.

The objectives of the activities focus directly on learning skills that will help the youngster to develop creative potential as well as to attain the goals already mentioned. The activities are arranged in sequence from simple to more complex and in accord with the developmental levels of young children. They have been coded A, B, and C (see pages 16–18 for a fuller explanation of the coding system) to assist in planning activities for a particular child. It is important to remember that B and C activities often build on skills and experiences provided through one or more of the previous activities. Since, however, no one pattern fits all children, you will want to consider the particular child's interests and his overall readiness for each learning experience.

Additional assistance in putting activities in a sequence that will help a child improve and extend a particular skill can also be found in the sections "Things To Do Another Time." The first suggestions in these sections are usually variations of the activities just above them. They can be used to reinforce the basic learning without losing the interest of the youngster. Later suggestions often offer ways to build on and extend the learning and should be used only after the child has mastered the basic learning. In other words, some of the additional later suggestions in an A activity, for instance, may be appropriate for a child who is at a B or C developmental level, provided he has already acquired the basic skills involved in the original activity.

The example of language provided in the activities follow several general principles or guidelines which are important for the attainment of the goals of art education. In adapting the activities to your own language style, you need to be aware and make use of these guidelines. They are:

1. *Give the youngster the freedom needed to be creative.* He will not learn to be creative if an adult makes all the decisions for him: "Use the red color. / Make this area red. / Now use the blue, and color this area blue." Such language will stifle rather than promote creativity. Let the child decide what color to use and where to use it. Let him select colors, shapes, and/or materials for a collage and decide where to paste them. If, however, the youngster seems to need a nudge in the creative process, fall back on questions: "What color could you use there?" or "Look at all this space over here. What could you paste in it?" Then leave the decision to the child, even if the decision is that the space should remain empty. For only by having this kind of freedom in art activities will art become for the child a form of self-expression.

2. *Keep your demonstrations short, simple, and basic.* Then let the child take over. He needs, first, to find out what *he* can do with the material. In an activity with clay, for instance, start by letting him find out what the clay feels like and what happens to it when he squeezes or pounds it. If the child needs encouragement to handle the clay or if he loses interest after only a brief and limited handling of it, then become a participant in the activity, *doing what you think the child will also be able to do.* Pound the clay, poke it, pinch it. Begin rolling it between your hands to make a big fat worm. Sentences like "I'm going to break off a small piece and try rolling it between my hands. / My goodness! See the fat worm I made. / What do you think you could do with the clay?" will be more helpful than "Watch. I'm going to make a cup. After you see how I do it, you can make a cup too." Such direct imitation may well be too difficult for the youngster. If he tries at all, he may quickly become discouraged and frustrated, retreating to a spectator's role rather than taking an active, creative part in the activity.

3. *Do not require one technique, one way of doing something.* Techniques may be too difficult for the preschooler. He may need time to do things his own way as a lead into what you consider the proper way of doing something. If he prefers to use fingers rather than a paste brush, let him. If he can make a pencil or crayon work only by holding it in his fist, let him experiment with it that way. The child may find his way better than your way, and, with time, he may discover your way for himself.

4. *Avoid scolding for messiness in messy art activities.* Messiness in such activities as finger painting, using wet chalk techniques, and pasting is to be expected. Cover working and drying areas with newspaper or easily washed coverings (plastic). Use large aprons or old shirts to cover clothing during the activity. Nothing is more discouraging to the new artist than to be told repeatedly "be careful," "don't drip," "don't get that on your shirt." When necessary precautions are taken, you and the child can both enjoy the experience.

Freedom to create and to be messy does not exclude rules. Set your limits and keep the activity within those limits. Also have the youngster participate in the clean-up chores. Most children enjoy washing paintbrushes or molding the clay back into balls for storing.

5. *Praise the results of the child's artistic efforts.* As in all the preschooler's early learning efforts, praise is important in art activities. Comment on the choice of color or the arrangement of shapes in a positive manner. Perhaps the best form of praise is to display the art work to show how important it is. Display it on a wall or a bulletin board. Print the child's name on the picture to give it a personal touch. If you are working with a small group of children, be sure that each child's work is displayed. Change displays often to maintain the child's or children's interest in art activities.

More specific guidelines related to particular art media are given in "Helpful Hints" sections. Included, also, are recipes and directions for making some of your own art materials. These suggestions are given to make you aware of other materials which you can use to structure art activities for the enjoyment and creative development of the young child.

ACTIVITY 54: Coloring with a Crayon

ART
A

WHY

To be aware that crayons produce color.
To produce color with a crayon.

WHAT YOU NEED

One crayon (blue, red, or yellow); several sheets of paper.

TALK ABOUT WHAT YOU DO

(Use your own language. This is an example.)

"Look at this crayon! (Hold it up.) Do you know what it can do? / A crayon can make a pretty color. See? (Scribble with crayon on paper in front of the child.) Here is a piece of paper for you. Can you color it with a crayon? / What color is that? / It's blue. Your crayon is blue. You made blue marks on the paper."

"Here is another piece of paper. Would you like to color with the crayon? / What color is on the paper? / That's right, blue. What are you using to make it blue? / You are using a crayon. Can you say *crayon?* / Very good."

"Have you finished coloring? / My, it's pretty. I'll write your name on the paper with the blue crayon so everyone will know you colored it. (Say each letter as you print the name.) J / A / N / E. There, that's your name: Jane. Let's hang it on the wall so that everyone can look at your *blue* picture."

HELPFUL HINTS

Large, fat crayons are easier for the young child to handle. Start with just one color.

The child's first attempts to color will be random scribbling. He will need repeated coloring experiences before he will be able to go beyond this scribbling stage.

The child will probably start to color with the crayon clutched in his fist. Do not attempt in this early stage to teach him the proper way to hold it. Let him experiment and find a way that is comfortable for him. Modeling the correct way can come later.

Remember, too, that for the child, coloring requires considerable physical effort and mental concentration. If the child tires of the activity, do not prolong it. Instead, repeat the activity often for short periods of time.

THINGS TO DO ANOTHER TIME

Repeat the activity, each time using a different colored crayon. Start with the primary colors: blue, red, yellow. Then introduce the secondary colors: orange, green, and purple.

Have the child select two or three crayons to use to make a picture. If he needs ideas for his picture, become a participant in the activity by saying, "I think I'll make a tree with lots of leaves and a trunk." Then using scribbling/circular strokes, make a simple tree (see Fig. 54.1).

 **Fig. 54.1**

The youngster may try to imitate you or he may come up with his own ideas. But do not expect realism in his picture. To the child it may look like the real thing even though to you it has little similarity.

ACTIVITY 55: Finger Painting with One Color

ART
A

WHY

To be aware that paint produces color.

To paint with fingers.

WHAT YOU NEED

Red (or blue or yellow) finger paint; large sheets of glossy shelf paper; wet sponges, aprons. (See page 152 for additional information on materials.)

TALK ABOUT WHAT YOU DO

(Use your own language. This is an example.)

"We are going to paint with our fingers today. So the first thing we must do is put on our aprons. / There, now if you get some paint on the apron, it won't matter."

"Here is the paper you are going to paint on. What is this? (Point to sponge.) It is a sponge and it is wet. See, we can wet the paper with it. (Demonstrate.) Here, you take the sponge and finish wetting all the paper. / Get this part too. / Good! It's all wet."

"This is your paint. It is red paint. Let's use our fingers to paint on the paper. (Dip your fingers in the paint.) Oh, the paint feels nice. (Do one or two good sweeps of the paint on the paper.) Look at that pretty color! What is that color? / Right! It's red. Look at those swirls. (Make a swirling motion with your hand.) Now you go ahead and paint with your fingers."

"Oh, that is beautiful! / You can use your whole hand if you like. / What else can you make with the paint?"

"Is your painting done? / Let's lay it here on the newspapers to dry. / When it is dry, we'll put it on the wall. You are a good painter."

"Now we have to clean up. I would like you to help."

HELPFUL HINTS

Most children will enjoy finger painting. If, however, the child is reluctant to use the paint, do not force him. Encourage him by showing the fun you are having while finger painting. If he is still reluctant, try sponge painting (see Activity 60).

Encourage the child to use his knuckles, fingernails, and even his elbows to paint. Do not make learning colors your focus of learning in this activity, although such learning may well result from it. Keep the focus on enjoying the painting and on the colored designs as they occur in these first painting experiences.

FINGERPAINTS: Fingerpaints can be purchased in toy and art stores or can be made. Here are two recipes for home fingerpaints:

Small Quantity (single color)

¼ cup liquid starch
coloring (see below)
Stir coloring into starch.

Larger Quantity (several colors)

2 cups laundry starch
1 cup soap flakes (not detergent)
water
coloring (see below)

Add sufficient water to starch and soap flakes and mix well to make a smooth, thick, slippery consistency. Pour small amounts (½ cup) of the uncolored mixture into small, wide-mouth jars (with tight lids for storage). Add a different color to each jar, enough to make the paint bright and deep in color. Stir well.

COLORING: Food coloring (from grocery stores), powdered poster paint (from toy or art stores), or powdered tempera paint (from toy or art stores) may be used in the recipes.

PAPER: The paper must be of a glossy type such as glossy shelf paper. Pages from a glossy magazine may also be used. Use as large a piece as you can (18″ x 18″ or larger) as the child will enjoy using large movements to make large designs.

DRYING SPACE: If the painting is quite wet, you will need a flat surface for drying it. Cover the area with newspaper. If the painting is not drippy, you can use a clothes drying rack, hanging the paintings over the rungs. A line and clothespins can also be used for drying.

THINGS TO DO ANOTHER TIME

Repeat the activity to introduce the child to each of the primary colors: red, yellow, and blue.

If you have a Formica or porcelain table top or other non-porous surface, adapt the activity to finger painting directly on the surface. The table should be of a height that the child is comfortable painting in a standing position or kneeling on a chair. Wet the surface of the table for finger painting. When the child has completed his picture, let him remove it with a wet sponge or an old, wet cloth. Call attention to the transfer of color onto the sponge or cloth.

Use a heavy piece of plastic or a non-porous tray for the child's painting surface. Wet the surface. When the child is finished painting, let him watch (and help) as you run water in the sink over the plastic or tray. Talk about how the water becomes colored from the paint.

ACTIVITY 56: Using a Flannel Board To Make a Picture

ART
A

WHY

To develop awareness of colors and shapes.
To experiment with arranging shapes.

WHAT YOU NEED

Flannel board; precut felt shapes (see "Helpful Hints" for directions).

TALK ABOUT WHAT YOU DO

(Use your own language. This is an example.)

"Look at what I have! It's called a flannel board. Feel it. / It feels smooth and soft like winter pajamas, doesn't it?"

"Look at all these colored pieces. They are all different shapes and colors. Would you like to feel them? / They are made from felt. They feel nice and smooth too. / Can you tell me some of the colors you see?" (Let the child manipulate the pieces if he is interested.)

"Let's stand the flannel board up against this chair. / What do you suppose will happen if you put one of the pieces of felt on the flannel board? / My goodness! It sticks. It doesn't fall off. Why, you can make a design on the flannel board by putting the felt pieces on it. Would you like to do that? / Oh, that's a nice design. Tell me about it."

"Would you like to make another design? / You can take off all the felt shapes and start all over again."

HELPFUL HINTS

To make a flannel board, use a piece of sturdy cardboard about 18″ x 24″. Cover the cardboard with a larger piece of flannel by folding the flannel over the edge of the cardboard. Glue it to the back of the cardboard. Let it dry thoroughly.

Make the felt shapes from small rectangles or swatches of felt, which can be purchased in a variety of colors in department or dime stores. Use several colors and cut them into shapes (not too small, about two inches) such as circles, squares, triangles, diamonds, stars, hearts.

Encourage the child to talk about his arrangement. For example, you might say: "Is that star up in the sky?" or "'Is this a house?" But do not insist that his design must mean something. He may simply enjoy the colors and the shapes.

THINGS TO DO ANOTHER TIME

Repeat the activity. For variation, cut simple outlines of animals, flowers, trees, houses. Cut some long, narrow and some wider block-like pieces that the child can use to build such things as a road or a house. This may become a picture! Have the child tell you about his picture.

ACTIVITY 57:   Forming Shapes by Tearing

ART
A

WHY

To make shapes by tearing.

WHAT YOU NEED

Several half-sheets of old newspaper (use the want-ad section for uniformity in background print).

TALK ABOUT WHAT YOU DO

(Use your own language. This is an example.)

"We have some sheets of newspaper. We are going to tear different shapes. (To demonstrate the act of tearing, start by tearing one of the half-sheets into several long strips and large squares.) See if you can tear these into different shapes. / Very good!"

"What else can you make? / Say, that's a nice piece. It has lots of bumps. See, all the bumps along this side? (Trace with your hand.) What does it look like? / Maybe it is a cloud, a nice big, bumpy cloud. / Let's put this cloud on the floor and see what other shapes we can make."

(Continue to encourage the child to tear a variety of shapes and sizes. Lay the pieces on the floor so that each shape can be easily seen.)

"Look at all these shapes! Here is a little one (point) and there's a big, fat one (point). / Which shape do you like best? / Should we save that one? / We can put it on the bulletin board so we can admire it for a couple of days."

HELPFUL HINTS

Children usually enjoy tearing paper and need little prompting in this activity. But if you wish to encourage the child to tear a larger variety of shapes and sizes, join the fun. Tear a few *simple,* varied shapes without making a "demonstration" out of it. Don't make the shapes too complex, or the child may become just a spectator watching you.

The child probably will not yet be able to distinguish colors, geometric shapes, and sizes. Call his attention to a little piece and a big one, to one that is sort of round or sort of square. Through such language and motions, you are preparing the child for later learning of shapes and sizes; you are providing readiness learning.

THINGS TO DO ANOTHER TIME

Look at white clouds in the sky and talk about them. Then give the child several sheets of white tissue paper and suggest you make clouds by tearing the paper into different large shapes. Use something blue (scarf, blanket) as a background of sky and have the child arrange his clouds on it. If the child discovers he can make fluffy clouds by crushing the tissue paper, let him arrange these also on the blue background.

Make a picture using shelf paper or brown wrapping paper as a background. Have the child tear colored paper (or old magazine pages that have colored pictures on them) into different shapes. Have the child make a picture by pasting the colored pieces on the larger piece of paper. Put the picture on display.

ACTIVITY 58:   Finger Painting with Two Colors

ART
B

WHY

To produce designs of more than one color.

To be aware that two (primary) colors can make a different (secondary) color.

WHAT YOU NEED

Finger paint in two primary colors; large sheets of glossy shelf paper; wet sponge; aprons. (See pages 152–153 for additional information.)

TALK ABOUT WHAT YOU DO

(Use your own language. This is an example.)

"Look at these things I have all ready for you. I bet you can guess what we are going to do today. / That's right. We are going to finger paint again. What do we have to do first? / First we have to put on our aprons so we won't have to worry about our clothes. / What else do we have to do? / We have to wet the paper with the sponge. Remember? / That's your job."

"We are going to paint with two colors (touch each jar as you count), one, two. What color is this? / Very good! What is this other color? / It's yellow, yellow like a banana. You can use red and yellow to do finger painting.''

"You are mixing the red and yellow as you paint. Goodness gracious, look at that! You are making another color. You just made orange. When the red and yellow paint gets mixed up, you make a new color. It's orange. See, it's the same color as the oranges we eat."

"Those are interesting designs. What colors are in your painting? / Red, yes. Where is the red? / What color is this? (Point.) / Right, yel-low. / What's this new color called? (Point.) / It's orange. Remember? Just like oranges we eat."

"Is your painting finished? / It is ready for drying then. Help me lay these newspapers on the floor. / Now take those ends (point) of your picture and help me place it on the newspapers. / You are a great little painter!"

HELPFUL HINTS

In introducing the activity, encourage the child to recall the steps in the finger painting process. But be ready to supply the answers yourself if he cannot remember.

Although learning the names of various colors may well be the result of this activity, do not make it your primary focus. Keep the focus on enjoyment and experimenting with the colors to make different color designs.

If you are working with a small group of children, do *not* compare work; the children should not feel that they are in competition with each other.

THINGS TO DO ANOTHER TIME

Repeat the activity, using two different primary colors to introduce the child to the remaining secondary colors: red and yellow will make orange; blue and yellow, green; and red and blue, purple.

Repeat the activity using all three primary colors for the child to make a multicolored picture. Don't be disturbed if in experimenting with the colors, the child ends up with muddy colors. That, too, is a part of learning about colors.

Demonstrate a folding technique: have the child put a few drops of the colors on a piece of wet shelf paper; fold the paper; rub your hand over the new surface; then unfold the paper. Have the child use the technique to produce his own designs.

ACTIVITY 59: Arranging and Pasting Precut Shapes

ART
B

WHY

To experiment with arranging shapes.

To paste precut shapes on a background.

WHAT YOU NEED

Large piece of shelf paper or brown wrapping paper; four or five precut colored pieces of paper two inches or larger, in different shapes; a shallow dish of paste.

TALK ABOUT WHAT YOU DO

(Use your own language. This is an example.)

(Place the materials on a flat surface in easy reach of the child.) "Look at this big piece of paper. And look at all these colored pieces of paper. (Let the child examine them.) Do you know what is in this dish? / It is paste. Paste is sticky. Feel it. / Does it feel sticky? / We will use the paste to make the little pieces stick on the big piece of paper."

"We are going to use all these things to make a picture. We'll paste these shapes on the big piece of paper to make a picture. Which color and shape will you start with? / Oh, that's a red square. Put some paste on the back of it. (You may want to demonstrate applying the paste.) Now where will you put the square on the big piece of paper? / Right there? Okay. Turn it over and put it right there. / Pat it a little to be sure that it sticks."

"Which piece are you going to use now? / The pretty blue piece. It has a round shape. Remember, you have to put some paste on it. / That's right. Use a little more paste. / Where is it going to go? / Pat it a little. / Oh, that looks so pretty there."

(Let the child continue until all the shapes are used or he decides the picture is finished.)

"Look at what you have made with shapes. (Hold it up to admire.) I think we should put it on the wall so everyone can enjoy it. Where should we put it?"

HELPFUL HINTS

Your precut shapes may be circles, squares, rectangles, diamonds, stars, hearts. Keep them large enough that the child will have no difficulty handling them. Construction paper is good for the precut shapes but you may also use a fairly sturdy type of white paper and color the shapes with crayons.

You can make your own paste from flour and water. Add the water gradually until you have a nice, thick, sticky consistency.

Keep a damp washcloth or sponge handy to remove paste from hands as child is working.

Remember that creativity is not developed by telling the child exactly what to do. Demonstrate the pasting process, then let him choose shapes and decide where to paste them. If encouragement to continue pasting is needed, make suggestions in the form of questions: "Do you plan to put something in this space?" or "Do you want to use this pretty yellow diamond?"

THINGS TO DO ANOTHER TIME

Repeat the activity using different precut shapes: simple outlines of animals, flowers, trees, leaves, fruit. Talk about each shape and its color as the child pastes it on the background. But keep this kind of learning incidental; keep the focus on arranging the shapes on the background.

Cut out a large outline of a butterfly, worm, or some animal the child recognizes. Use small bits of colored paper for the child to paste on the animal to make it "beautiful."

ACTIVITY 60:   Painting with a Tool: *Sponge*

ART
B

WHY

To paint with a sponge.
To make designs.

WHAT YOU NEED

Finger paint (red, yellow, or blue); large pieces of shelf paper; small pieces of sponge (about two inches square and one inch thick); wet sponges.

TALK ABOUT WHAT YOU DO

(Use your own language. This is an example.)

"We are going to do a different kind of painting today. We are going to paint with a sponge. Can you point to the sponge? / Right. Where is the paint? / What color is it? / It is yellow, just like a banana."

"First we have to wet this big piece of paper. Can you do that with this big sponge? / Oh, you did a good job. Now use this small piece of sponge. Dip it into the paint. / Is there paint on the sponge? / Good. Next you pat the paper with the sponge. (Demonstrate if necessary.) Pat the sponge on the paper a lot to make a design. / Now pat the paper some more with the sponge."

"Look at all the pretty yellow shapes you painted. / Are you going to make some more on this side of the paper? / No? Is your picture ready for drying then? / Let's put it over here on this newspaper."

"Would you like to try this again? / Let's use another color."

HELPFUL HINTS

The materials used for this activity are the same as those used for finger painting, with the addition of a piece of sponge for applying the paint. See pages 152–153 for additional helpful hints on the materials.

If the child remembers finger painting from a past experience, he should be able to wet the shelf paper and identify the paint. If he has not had a previous experience in finger painting, you will have to demonstrate wetting the paper with the large sponge and you may want to talk about and have the child feel the paint with his fingers.

THINGS TO DO ANOTHER TIME

Repeat the activity for each primary color: red, yellow, and blue.

After one of the chiid's sponge paintings is dry, have the child sponge paint with a different primary color on the same painting. Interesting designs and color contrasts will develop as the child uses the second color on top of or beside the first.

Adapt the activity to sponge painting with two primary colors. Provide a small piece of sponge to apply each color (but don't be surprised or upset if the child forgets and uses the same piece for both colors). In using two primary colors, the child will, of course, produce a secondary color. Talk about the change in color on the paper (and on the sponge if he uses it for both colors).

Thin the paint and put several drops of paint on paper. Have the child use a straw to blow the paint in different directions, making a design. Use the same process with two colors of paint.

ACTIVITY 61:   Glass Wax Painting

ART
B

WHY

To experiment with color and design on glass.

WHAT YOU NEED

Small amount of glass wax in wide-
mouth container; food coloring;
damp sponge; a fairly large mirror (or window); dry cloth.

TALK ABOUT WHAT YOU DO

(Use your own language. This is an example.)

"I bet you can't guess what we are going to use to paint today? / We are
going to paint right on this mirror. First we have to make our paint. We put
a few drops of this red color in this glass wax. / What happened? / The glass
wax turned red. Now we can use this paint on the mirror."

"I'll dip the sponge in the red paint, like this. / Then I'll rub the sponge
on the mirror. (Make a big swirl.) Look. It's getting redder and redder as it
dries. Now it's your turn to paint on the mirror."

"Oh, that's interesting. Can you still see yourself in the mirror? / I can
see a bit of you here (point) and over here (point)."

"Your mirror has a painting on it. Would you like to clean off the mirror
and paint again? / You can wipe off your dry painting with this cloth. / Rub
it all off. / There, now you can make another mirror picture."

HELPFUL HINTS

Use a strong, vivid color for the child's first experience with glass painting. If you use a mirror, lay it on newspaper on the floor, or place newspaper under a stationary wall mirror. Take precautions against spilt paint by setting your container in a small box.

If you use a window, take similar precautions against spillage. The window should be at a height that is comfortable for the child to reach.

The glass wax has to be dry for easy removal from the glass. Help the child wipe off the wax if he has difficulty.

THINGS TO DO ANOTHER TIME

Repeat the activity using a different color of food coloring.

Have the child use two different colors of paint. He will discover that the glass-wax paint will not blend with another color but that one erases the other. He may also discover that he can paint part of the mirror (or window) with one color and use another part for the other color. If he doesn't discover this solution for himself, ask: "Do you suppose you could use this side for your red paint and this other side for your green paint?"

Have the child decorate a window (or mirror) for a special occasion: green / red for Christmas, red / white (clear glass wax) for Valentine's day, blue / green for Easter.

ACTIVITY 62:   Coloring with Crayons

ART
B

WHY

To make two-color designs.
To use crayon to fill in an area
   with color.

WHAT YOU NEED

Crayons, red and blue; paper.

TALK ABOUT WHAT YOU DO

(Use your own language. This is an example.)

"Let's have fun today coloring with these crayons. Which color do you want? / This one? / What color is it? / Blue, that's right. I'll color with the red one. Here is a piece of paper for each of us."

"You color whatever you want to on your piece of paper. I'll color on my paper. / Oh, you are making big circles. I think I'll do that, too."

"Let's play a game. It's called 'Finish Coloring the Design.' First you color some on the paper. Then give it to me and I'll finish it with my crayon. / Is the design ready for me? / Oh, you made lots and lots of circles. I think I'll try to make some red lines. / I finished our design. Do you like it?"

"Should we play the game again? / Would you like to color with the red crayon this time? / I'll start the design and you finish it this time. Okay? (Make several fairly large box-like outlines and color inside one of them.) Now you finish the design."

"Oh, that's a great idea. You are filling in one of the boxes with your red crayon. / Would you like to use the blue crayon, too?"

"That is a really interesting design. Where do you think we should hang it? / I bet someone is going to ask who did that design. I am going to put your name on it so they will know."

HELPFUL HINTS

Work on a hard surface or the child may have difficulty bringing out the colors. The large, fat crayons will be easier for him to manage.

If the child does not complete the second design by filling in (in some fashion) one of the box-like outlines, try a third design, using the same approach. He may get the idea this time. If not, complete the activity and try it another time with more emphasis on filling in the boxes or circles.

This is a good activity to use if you are working with a small group of children because it teaches cooperation and group effort. Give each child a different colored crayon. Rotate turns so that each child can finish the design.

THINGS TO DO ANOTHER TIME

Repeat the activity using different colored crayons.

Repeat the activity, allowing the child to choose his crayons from a larger variety of colors.

Have the child experiment with designs made by putting paper on top of other flat objects of uneven texture and coloring the paper with the side of the crayon (paper wrapping removed). You may have to show the child how to hold the crayon and shove it back and forth over the paper's surface. Materials with uneven textures will work well: lace or a lace doily, straw mat, corrugated paper, strip of wide braid.

ACTIVITY 63:   Sand Painting

ART
B

WHY

To experiment with design.
To use texture in a design.

WHAT YOU NEED

Shaker with large holes; sand; paper; glue (or paste); large box without lid.

TALK ABOUT WHAT YOU DO

(Use your own language. This is an example.)

"What do you think is in this shaker? / Hold out your hand, and I'll shake some of it into your hand. / Now can you tell what it is? / Yes, it is sand. Have you ever played in sand? / Well, this time we are going to use the sand to make a design."

"This is a bottle of glue. Watch. If I press the bottle like this on the paper, glue comes out on the paper. (Demonstrate, making several irregular lines with the glue.) Feel the glue. / How does it feel? / Right, glue is very sticky."

"I am going to make streaks of glue on my paper. / Now you try to make streaks of glue on your paper. / That is right. Make some more any way you want to."

"We'll use the sand now. Shake this shaker (demonstrate) so that sand comes out on the paper. / Good! Shake it all over your paper."

"Now shake the paper carefully over this box so that the extra sand falls off. / Look at that! You made a sand design."

"When the design dries, we'll hang it up."

"Would you like to make another sand design all by yourself?"

HELPFUL HINTS

Seasoning bottles (onion or garlic salts, for example) make good shakers because they have fairly large holes. If the sand pours out too freely, try a bottle with smaller holes. This activity may be done outside to eliminate any clean-up problems. If done indoors, cover the entire painting area with newspaper and place the open box for catching extra sand on the newspaper.

Elmer's glue is good for this activity. Help the child manipulate the glue bottle if necessary, or use paste and a brush applicator if he finds it easier to handle. But once he gets the idea, let the rest of the painting be his.

THINGS TO DO ANOTHER TIME

Repeat the activity with colored sand. Mix sand with moist paint. Let dry.

Adapt the activity by using colored confetti (or colored paper cut in very small pieces), glitter (or foil cut in very small pieces), small seeds (bird seed), or any small objects that will adhere to the sticky paper. Put whatever you use in a small, shallow container from which the child may take small quantities and sprinkle them by hand over the paper.

ACTIVITY 64:   Making Shapes with Pipe Cleaners

ART
B

WHY

To experiment in creating shapes.
To make three-dimensional shapes.

WHAT YOU NEED

Colored pipe cleaners (some cut in half).

TALK ABOUT WHAT YOU DO

(Use your own language. This is an example.)

"Look at these pretty colored pipe cleaners. Look, you can bend them. (Demonstrate.) What can we make out of them? / I think I'll make a wiggly worm out of this blue one. / See the wiggly worm? / That's his head. (Point.) Oh, you're going to make a wiggly worm, too. / Say, that's a great big wiggly, wiggly worm!"

"What else can we make?" (If the child has an idea, let him carry it out. Help him only if necessary. If the child offers no suggestions, continue with another idea.)

"I know. Would you like to make a car wheel? / What shape is a wheel? / Good! Can you make one of the pipe cleaners into a circle? / Can you twist the ends together? / Let me show you. (Demonstrate as you talk.) You cross the two ends and you twist them around each other, like this. / Look at the red circle you made! It's like a car wheel."

"What are you making now? / Another circle. Very good! What are you going to do with your circle? / My, you made a lollipop. Very good!"

"Would you like to make a cane? / You know, like the candy canes at Christmas. / What color will you use? / That looks just like a candy cane. It looks good enough to eat."

"Look at all the different shapes you made. Can you tell me what they are?"

HELPFUL HINTS

Keep the ideas you suggest very simple so that the child can successfully make the shapes. If they are too complex, he may become disinterested or merely watch what you do.

Do not tell the child to make a particular shape. Make your suggestions in the form of questions: "Would you like to make . . . ?" Or simply go ahead as a participant in the activity and make a simple design. He may or may not copy you. Your idea may give him a new idea of something to make.

Encourage creativity by going along with the child's ideas. Praise the results.

THINGS TO DO ANOTHER TIME

Make decorations for special occasions out of pipe cleaners: outlines of eggs mounted on paper for display at Easter, chains of circles linked together to decorate for a birthday (or to use as a belt or bracelet), ornaments to be hung on the Christmas tree.

Collect pictures that show clearly the shape of various kinds of fruit: orange, lemon, cherry, banana. Let the child decide what he would like to make with the pipe cleaners, using the pictures to give him ideas.

Use drinking straws (cut in different lengths) for the same learning objectives as those given for this activity. Let the child use the straws to make various shapes and designs on the floor or table (covered so the straws do not roll easily). If the child needs help thinking of things to make, say something like this: "Would you like to make a long road for your car?" "I wonder if we could make a tall chimney." Or, "I think I'll make a little box (square)."

ACTIVITY 65:   Making Art Objects for Special Occasions

ART
B

WHY

To share art products with others.

WHAT YOU NEED

Colored paper; small, precut pictures; paste; Magic Markers or crayons.

TALK ABOUT WHAT YOU DO

(Use your own language. This is an example.)

"Guess whose birthday is next week. / It is Jimmy's birthday. Do you have a birthday? / Yes, everyone has a birthday. Do you know what we say to people on their birthday? / We say 'Happy Birthday!' And we can send them Happy Birthday cards too. Let's make a Happy Birthday card for Jimmy."

"You will need a piece of paper. Pick out any color you like. / What color did you pick? / Right! Here are some pictures and some paste. You can paste some pictures on your card. Make the card any way you like."

"Oh, that is a lovely birthday card. Would you like me to write something on it so Jimmy will know it is a Happy Birthday card from you? / What should I write on it?"

HELPFUL HINTS

If you use construction paper for the card, fold the piece in half for pasting on the top half and your birthday message on the inside. Other kinds of paper should be reduced to about 12″ × 15″ and folded the same way.

Most children will view acceptance of their works of art as a form of praise. A negative response by the recipient of a card (or picture) will be a big disappointment for the child. If there is any danger of this, prepare the receiver of the gift to give a positive response.

THINGS TO DO ANOTHER TIME

Make cards for other special occasions, varying your colors and materials to fit the occasion: small pictures and designs or glitter cut from old Christmas cards to paste on a precut green tree for Christmas; precut pictures or outlines of a turkey and fall leaves for Thanksgiving; precut small, colored hearts to paste on a larger red heart for Valentine's day; precut orange pumpkins to paste on black paper for Halloween. Talk a little about the meaning of the occasion or even better, read a story about what makes it a special day. Then suggest the appropriate art activity.

Let the child try his hand at decorating cookies or cupcakes or doughnuts for special occasions. Use colored icing and/or colored sugars. Use other small objects for decoration: a small candle for a birthday, a small flag for the Fourth of July, pastel jelly beans for Easter. Have the child decide for whom he is making the special ''goodie.''

ACTIVITY 66:   Using a Pencil

ART
C

WHY

To draw with a pencil.

WHAT YOU NEED

Pencil with soft lead; paper.

TALK ABOUT WHAT YOU DO

(Use your own language. This is an example.)

"Do you know what this is? (Hold up pencil.) Yes, it is a pencil. See this sharp end? / You can draw with it. Watch. (Demonstrate drawing by making marks up and down, sideways, and circular on the paper.) Here. You try drawing with the pencil."

"Oh, you made some nice lines on the paper. Let me show you another way to hold the pencil. Put it between these two fingers. (Point or touch thumb and index finger.) Let me help you. / There. Now see if you can draw with the pencil. / That's good. Draw some more."

"Here is a nice clean piece of paper. Why don't you draw a whole lot of things on it?"

HELPFUL HINTS

The child may have difficulty holding the pencil properly. So make the activity a short one as his concentration will be intense. Or he may revert to holding the pencil in his fist. Try gently to encourage using the proper grasp, but do not insist. Let him scribble at random and try another time to teach the proper grasp. If the child favors holding the pencil in his left hand, do not object.

The child's first drawing will be random or uncontrolled scribbling and will probably have no particular meaning for him. But if, for example, he shows you a page of scribbling and tells you he made trees, encourage his imagination by going along with the idea and praise his trees.

THINGS TO DO ANOTHER TIME

Repeat the activity using colored pencils and/or colored paper.

In later activities encourage the child to make lines and circular shapes. This is called "controlled scribbling." This scribbling may also begin to take on meaning for the youngster, even though the drawings in no way resemble the real thing. About this time, he may be able to copy (roughly) a circle or square that you make. Encourage these ideas in your later drawing activities, but don't persist if the child continues random scribbling. He simply needs more time at the earlier stage before moving into the controlled stage.

ACTIVITY 67:   Playing with Play Dough

ART
C

WHY

To manipulate Play Dough or clay.
To experiment with making forms.

WHAT YOU NEED

Several small balls of Play Dough or clay; a non-porous table surface or a board (12″ x 12″ or larger) on a table.

TALK ABOUT WHAT YOU DO

(Use your own language. This is an example.)

(Sit at a table with the child.) "What do you suppose we can do with this Play Dough? (Give the child a small, soft ball of dough.) It feels nice, doesn't it? (Begin working with another ball yourself.) I bet we can do all kinds of things with it."

(If the child begins to work with the dough, follow his leads by doing some of the same things he does and talking about them.) "Say, you made a pie. Or is it a pancake? / What kind of pie is it? / I think I'll make a pie, too."

(If the child needs encouragement and ideas, work with the dough, doing things the child also will be able to do.) "Look what happened when I poked my finger in the dough. It made all kinds of holes. How can we get rid of the holes again? / Oh, that's a good idea. We can pound the holes out with our hand."

"I wonder if we can roll the dough. (Roll a piece of dough back and forth between your hands or between the palm of your hand and the table surface.) Look what happened! I made a worm, a long wiggly worm. / Oh, you're going to make a wiggly worm too. I bet your worm will be a long, long wiggly worm."

"Do you think we could break this ball into two pieces and make two little balls? / Let's try. / Here's your piece. I'm going to roll mine between my hands to see if I can make a little ball. / Oh, you made a nice little ball. Now we have two balls (touch each as you count)—one, two."

"That was fun. Help me put the dough back in this container. / Now we'll put the lid on tight. / We'll save the dough and make some more things with it another day."

HELPFUL HINTS

Clay, available in toy stores, is easier for the child to work with, but it is also messier.To store the clay, place it in a tightly covered jar with some wet paper toweling in the lid.

Play Dough can be purchased in a toy store, but you can also make a substitute. For a small amount:

> Mix: 1 cup flour
> ⅔ cup salt
> ⅓ cup water

One teaspoon of alum can also be added for increased pliability.
Food coloring or powdered poster or tempera paint can be added for color.

The dough should be readily pliable without being sticky. If wrapped in a plastic bag or put in a tightly covered jar and placed in the refrigerator, it can be reused. The forms made by the child can also be painted with tempera paint when dry.

Before starting the activity, work the dough well so that it is soft and easily manipulated by the child.

Some of the things a young child will be able to do with the dough are kneading it, pounding it, squeezing it, pinching it, poking it, and rolling it. Do not be too concerned about making things, especially in first experiences with the dough.

THINGS TO DO ANOTHER TIME

Place a ball of Play Dough or clay in a paper bag. Have the child work with the dough through the bag. Then open the bag and take out the clay. Talk about the different forms that were made and any objects they may resemble. Emphasize the element of surprise. "Oh, look at that! What does it look like? / I think it looks like a tower. Can you make it stand? / Doesn't it look like a wobbly tower?"

After watching and perhaps helping you make cookies, the child will probably enjoy making cookies with the Play Dough. He will need a rolling pin (or long narrow bottle) to roll the dough, cookie cutters (or a lid from a jar), a spatula to lift them onto a cookie sheet, and a cookie sheet (or piece of sturdy cardboard).

Have a bread-making activity, using the Play Dough. If the child has had no opportunity to see how bread is made, you will have to demonstrate kneading the dough, shaping it into a loaf, and placing the loaf in a small bread pan (box). Keep your demonstrations brief, and let the child do most of the work.

ACTIVITY 68:   Marking with Chalk

ART
C

WHY

To use chalk as an art form.
To "draw" with chalk.

WHAT YOU NEED

Chalk; chalkboard (see directions below); damp sponge.

TALK ABOUT WHAT YOU DO

(Use your own language. This is an example.)

"Do you know what this is? (Hold up or point to chalkboard.) It is a chalkboard. You can draw on it with chalk. Here is a piece of chalk. / See if you can make some lines and shapes on the chalkboard with it."

"Oh, that's good. But you don't have to push so hard. / That's right. See the different kinds of lines you made? / Make some more."

"'You know what else you can do with chalk? / You can wipe your lines away with a swish of this sponge. It's called erasing. Do you want to erase your lines? / Wipe it good. / There, now you have a clean chalkboard and you can make some more lines and shapes."

HELPFUL HINTS

Regular white chalk can be used but the pastel chalks found in toy stores are especially good for young children. They are thick and long and come in a variety of colors.

A chalkboard can be made by painting a board (plywood) or heavy cardboard with blackboard paint, which comes in black and other colors.

Like the child's first experiences with pencil and crayon, his first chalk experience will probably be one primarily of discovering how to use chalk. Control and direction will come with more experience in using chalk.

THINGS TO DO ANOTHER TIME

Repeat the activity. To vary it, use light colors of chalk on dark colors of non-glossy paper (construction paper). Or use darker colors of chalk on newsprint (even old newspapers) or wrapping paper.

Wet chalk drawings can be made with the pastel chalks by dipping wrapping paper in water and laying the paper on old newspapers. The child draws on the wet paper with the chalk. Because the chalk rubs off easily, the activity may become messy. So cover the child with an apron or old shirt. If the picture is to be saved, set it aside in a drying area covered with newspapers.

ACTIVITY 69:   Making a Collage

ART
C

WHY

To make a collage.
To apply paste with a brush.

WHAT YOU NEED

Piece of shelf or wrapping paper (about 12″ x 15″); paste; small brush for pasting; various small pieces of odds and ends (see "Helpful Hints" for ideas); small box to hold the odds and ends.

TALK ABOUT WHAT YOU DO

(Use your own language. This is an example.)

"Look at all these pretty pieces." (Empty the box of odds and ends on the floor or table. Let the child examine them if he likes and talk about what some of them are.)

"You know what we are going to do with all these pretty pieces? / Well, we are going to make the most beautiful picture you ever saw. We are going to paste them on this big sheet of paper. Here is your paste. And here is a brush you use to put paste on the paper."

"Which piece do you want to paste on your picture first? / Where do you want to put it on the paper? Right here. Okay, I'll put some paste right there. / Now put the yarn on top of the paste. / Good! Pat it down a little so that it is sure to stick. / My, doesn't that look pretty already?"

"Now what do you want to paste on your picture next? / Where are you going to put it? / Use a brush to put a little paste there on the paper. / Put your piece right on top of the paste. / Pat it down well. / You did that piece all by yourself."

(Let the child continue selecting pieces and pasting them on the paper. Help him only when necessary and praise his work.)

"What are you going to put over here? / (Point to empty space.) Oh, that's a good idea. I would like something red there."

"Is your picture finished? / What a beautiful picture. We will have to save it. Where should we put it to dry?"

HELPFUL HINTS

Use a variety of odds and ends such as bits of fluffy cotton, small pieces of colored yarn and ribbon, pieces of colored paper in irregular shapes, bits of cellophane and foil, pieces of glitter (from Christmas cards), small pictures of animals or objects cut from magazines. Do not make the pieces *too* small or the child may have difficulty handling them.

Note in the first part of the activity you are teaching the child the process of making a collage (fragments of materials pasted on a picture surface). Turn over the process to the child as soon as possible. But if he needs help, continue helping with the pasting but not with choosing the pieces or the place to paste them.

If after pasting only a few pieces the child tells you the picture is "finished," encourage him to continue by saying: "Look at all this empty space. Something especially pretty could go there. Can you find something you would like to paste there?" But don't push too hard. If the child insists the collage is finished, accept it and praise the picture.

THINGS TO DO ANOTHER TIME

Make other collages using a variety of different kinds of materials: other kinds and colors of paper for the background and other kinds of small odds and ends for pasting on the background.

Introduce the child to a third-dimensional effect by using such things as cereals, dried beans/peas, macaroni, dry noddles/spaghetti, eggshells, plain or colored toothpicks, light-weight buttons, pieces of colored drinking straws. For background use paper of fairly heavy weight (construction or thin cardboard). Apply thick paste in small globs. And be sure to let paste dry before attempting to display the collage in an upright position.

Make an outdoor collage. Use such materials as leaves, flowers, acorns, twigs, seeds, small flat stones, feathers. Again, use fairly heavy paper for the background and apply the paste in small globs. Let the collage dry before handling or standing it upright.

ACTIVITY 70: Free Cutting with Scissors

ART
C

WHY

To hold and cut with a scissors.
To practice free cutting with a scissors.

WHAT YOU NEED

Blunt scissors; pieces of thin paper (such as newspaper).

TALK ABOUT WHAT YOU DO

(Use your own language. This is an example.)

"Do you know what this is? (Hold up scissors.) Yes, it is a pair of scissors. See the two blades. (Touch each blade as you count.) One, two. You can make the blades move back and forth, like this. (Demonstrate the blade movement slowly several times.) The blades will cut paper when you do that. See?" (Demonstrate cutting a piece of paper.)

"Now you try that. First, hold the scissors for cutting. Let me help you. / Put your thumb in this hole. / Now put your fingers in that hole. / Try to make the blades move back and forth. /Very good! Try again." (Have the child move the blades back and forth several times.)

"Let's try now to cut a piece of paper. Hold the paper in your other hand. / The paper has to go between the blades. / That's right. Make the blades move. / Oh, see the nice cut you made in the paper. Can you do it again?"

(Allow the child to experiment with ways to hold the scissors and give him time to become comfortable with the cutting movement. In other words, let him practice cutting paper on his own.)

"Here is another piece of paper. Can you cut out something with your scissors? / Oh, that's a nice small piece. / Very good! What else can you make with the scissors?"

HELPFUL HINTS

Free cutting means that the child cuts the paper with no particular design in mind. He simply enjoys cutting. Your purpose is to help him develop the skill of cutting with scissors, which in turn develops hand and finger muscles. His first attempts may be awkward and frustrating for him. If so, keep the activity short, repeating it at frequent intervals.

Controlled cutting, cutting with an idea in mind, is the next stage in the development of cutting skills. In this stage, the child decides he wants to cut something and does so without a pattern or outline. This stage requires considerable hand–eye coordination and control of the scissors, as does the third stage, that of cutting along lines (straight, curved).

Use thin, firm paper for the child's first attempt at cutting and keep the pieces of a size that the child can easily handle (4″ x 6″).

Although the scissors used by the child should be blunt, they should also cut easily. Have left-handed scissors for children who tend to use their left hands.

THINGS TO DO ANOTHER TIME

Repeat free cutting activities until the child becomes fairly comfortable using the scissors. Ways to vary the activities might be: (a) have the child cut out pieces and paste them on shelf or wrapping paper to make a picture (see Activity 69); (b) use the pieces he cuts out to decorate a wall, curtain, and so forth; (c) vary the colors of the paper to be cut.

When the child becomes more adept at free cutting, try moving him into the next stage, that of using scissors to express an idea. Select *a very simple object* that is familiar to the child. Say, for example: "I'd like to cut out a hose like the one a fire fighter uses," or "I think I'll make a leaf." Then proceed to cut out a very simple shape, talking about it as you cut: "The fire fighter's hose is sort of wavy, like this. / It's sort of skinny too. / There, does that look like a hose?" The child may decide to follow your example or may come up with a different idea of something to make. In any case, praise the results.

ACTIVITY 71: Making Designs by Folding and Cutting Paper

ART
C

WHY

To experiment with designs.

WHAT YOU NEED

Pieces of thin paper; blunt scissors.

TALK ABOUT WHAT YOU DO

(Use your own language. This is an example.)

"I know something that is fun to do. All we need are pieces of paper and scissors. Now watch carefully and I'll show you a new way to make a design."

"First I fold the paper in half, right down the middle, like this. / Next, I'll fold it again right down the middle. / And I press the folds down. / Now we'll cut off each corner. I'll cut the first one. Off goes the corner. / You cut off the next corner. Cut right across there. (Indicate direction with finger.) Now it's my turn again. Snip, snip. Off goes the corner. / You cut off the last corner."

"We are all ready now to open up the paper again. Here, you open it. / Hold it up. / Why, look at that! It is a beautiful design, isn't it? / Wasn't that fun?"

"You want to do another one? / Okay. This time you fold the paper. I'll help you. Fold it down the middle. / Good. Press it down hard. / Now fold it again. / No, the other way. / That's right. Here comes the big old giant thumb again to press it down."

"How should we cut it this time? / All right. You cut off all the corners this time. / That was a good job. Can I have a turn now? / I'll cut out a piece between the corners. / See? I cut out a triangle. / Do you want to cut a piece out between these corners? / That's right. You have to cut a little more so that the piece falls out. / Do you want to cut any more pieces out?"

"Ready for the big opening? / Tra-la! Look at that! You made another beautiful design."

HELPFUL HINTS

Use thin paper (newspaper or similar weight) so that the child will be able to cut through the several folds.

Keep the designs simple. If they are too complex, the child will become an onlooker and not be able to participate in creating the designs.

THINGS TO DO ANOTHER TIME

Repeat the activity, folding the paper in half a third time. Use tissue paper so that it does not become so thick that the child cannot cut it. Help the child with the folding if necessary, but let him decide where to cut and do his own cutting.

Have the child make designs by folding and cutting thin but fairly substantial white paper. Then let him decorate the designs with crayons.

ACTIVITY 72:   Painting on an Easel

ART
C

WHY

To paint with a brush.
To use colors, shapes, and space.

WHAT YOU NEED

Easel; one primary color in tempera paint; paintbrush; large sheet of paper to fit the easel; aprons; newspaper to cover the painting area (see page 184 for additional information on the materials needed).

TALK ABOUT WHAT YOU DO

(Use your own language. This is an example.)

"We are going to be artists today and paint with a brush and an easel. This is an easel. See the paper on it? / That is what you will paint on. Here is your paintbrush." (Let the child hold and examine the brush.)

"Let's make believe we are painting, first. See, I am pretending I am painting on the paper. (Make strokes as if making lines and circles.) Can you make believe you are painting? / Very good!"

"Your paint is in this jar. What color is it? / Right! I'll show you what to do. Watch. First I dip the brush in the paint. / See all the paint on the brush? / Then I squeeze the brush like this against the side of the jar. (Demonstrate.) This way the paint won't drip over everything. Now I'll paint on the paper. / Oh, look at that!"

"It is your turn now. Dip the brush in the paint. / That's right. You have a lot of paint on the brush. Squeeze it against the side of the jar. / Like this. / There. You are ready to paint. / Oh, that's good! Paint some more."

(Continue with gentle reminders of dipping and squeezing if necessary but don't be too concerned about drips and spatters since you covered the area well with newspaper.)

"You painted a lot of interesting things. What else can you do on your paper? / That is different from what you did before."

"You painted a lot of different things, didn't you? / I'll print your name at the top of the paper so that everyone will know who the artist was. / See, there's your name. (Point.) Now everyone will know this is your painting."

HELPFUL HINTS

The child will learn to adjust the amount of paint he takes on the brush, but until he does, drips and spatters are a part of painting. Cover the floor, the child, and yourself well so that keeping clean does not become a prime factor in the activity.

Do not expect the child to paint objects and express ideas. This will come later. He will at first simply enjoy painting the colors. Keep the focus of the activity on enjoyment and on trying a variety of lines and shapes.

EASEL: Children's easels are available in toy and art stores, but you can also make an easel by following the directions given below. Be sure the easel (on floor, table, or wall) is at a comfortable height for the child to paint.

To make a *table easel,* use a sturdy cardboard box with two sides that are at least 18" x 16". Remove top of box. Consider this open end to be the *bottom* of your easel. Cut four inches from the bottom (open end) of one of the long sides of the box. Then cut the bottom of the two adjoining sides on a diagonal (see Fig. 72.1). When the easel is placed on a table (open end at bottom and large, uncut side facing you), it will have an appropriate angle or slant for painting.

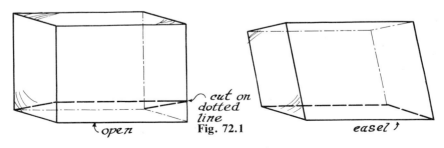

cut on dotted line

open

Fig. 72.1

easel

To make a *wall easel,* use a thin board (plywood) that is at least 18″ x 16″. Attach to the bottom of the back side of the longest side a narrow strip of 4″ board (piece of 2″ x 4″). When the easel is hung on a wall, the wedge at the bottom will provide an appropriate slant for painting. Two small-headed nails can be placed at the top (one near each end) of the board, left extending partially, to hold paper that has been pre-punctured to match the nails.

PAINTS: Tempera paint can be purchased in toy or art stores. It is available in liquid or powdered form. Place a small amount of the paint in a wide-mouthed jar. Place the jar in a small box or other similar container to reduce the danger of tipping and spilling.

PAINTBRUSHES: A wide brush with stiff bristles and a 12″ handle is best for the young child. Wash and dry the brushes carefully to make them reusable. Let the brushes dry by placing them, handles down, in a jar or similar container.

PAPER: Use large sheets of non-glossy paper that fits your easel. Pads of cheap paper in large sizes can be purchased, but non-glossy wrapping paper (or brown grocery bags slit and opened up) can be cut to appropriate size and used.

Fasten the paper securely to the easel with large tack pins, thumbtacks, clothespins, or some similar method.

PAINTING SPACE: Cover the floor under the easel (or the table if you are using a table easel) with several layers of newspaper, a large piece of heavy plastic, or a good-sized washable throw rug to catch the drippings.

DRYING SPACE: If you wish to save the paintings, prepare drying space by covering a flat surface (floor, table) with newspaper. Or hang the paintings on a drying rack or clothesline under which you have placed newspaper to catch any drippings.

THINGS TO DO ANOTHER TIME

Let the child paint with a different primary color.

Have the child paint with two primary colors. Let the child explore the use of the two colors and overlay them to produce a secondary color. It is a good idea to have a paintbrush for each color, but do not scold if the child

forgets to change brushes when changing colors (and he will). This is part of
learning about colors and mixing them.

Provide dark paper (black, deep red, or green) and white paint for a painting
session. Talk about painting snowflakes or piles of snow or big, big marshmallows or piles of ice cream.

ACTIVITY 73:   Making Three-Dimensional Objects

ART
C

WHY

To use many kinds of materials.
To make a three-dimensional object (puppet).

WHAT YOU NEED

Socks; scraps of felt precut for facial features (two circles for
eyes, a triangle for nose, a semi-
circle for mouth); glue (Elmer's).

TALK ABOUT WHAT YOU DO

(Use your own language. This is an example.)

"What is this? (Hold up sock.) Yes, it's a sock. (Put your hand in sock
and wiggle it.) See it wiggle? / Have you ever seen a puppet? / Well, a puppet is a kind of doll. We can make a puppet out of this sock. Then you can
put it on your hand and make it move like this." (Wiggle hand again.)

"We have to give our puppet a face. We can use these pieces of felt to
make a face. Can you find two pieces we can use for eyes? / Now where is
the mouth? / We need a nose, too, you know. / Very good. Now we are
ready to make our puppet."

"Can you place the felt on the sock to make a puppet face? (Lay sock on flat surface so that bottom of sock will be the face.) Where are your eyes on your face? / Then the puppet's eyes have to go toward the top of his face. / That's better. Where will you put the nose? / Where does the mouth go? / Very good. The puppet has a face now."

"We have to glue all the pieces to the sock so that they will stay on the puppet's face. Here is the glue. Put some on one of the eyes. / That's enough. Now put the eye back on the sock where the eye belongs. Be sure the glue side is down on the sock. / Press it down hard. / Good! Do the same with the other eye." (Continue until all the felt pieces are glued to the sock.)

"We'll put this heavy telephone book on the sock to hold the pieces until the glue dries. / When the puppet is dry, you can put it on your hand and we can have a puppet show."

HELPFUL HINTS

Let the child do as much of the work as he is able. Help only when necessary to prevent frustration or failure.

THINGS TO DO ANOTHER TIME

Help the child make a pinwheel, explaining that a pinwheel is a toy that turns round and round in the wind. (1) Start with a six-inch square of stiff paper. Have the child decorate the paper with crayons in any way he pleases. (2) Cut the paper from each corner to about one inch from the center to make four triangles which remain joined at center. (3) Bring one point of each triangle to center and glue. Each point is glued over the previous point. (4) Let glue dry. (5) Insert pin through center, enlarging hole slightly to permit easy spinning of wheel on the pin. (6) Insert pin in eraser of a pencil (see Fig. 73.1). You will have to do some of the steps yourself, but let the child help whenever possible.

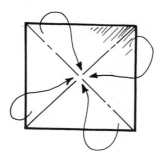

Fig. 73.1

These children are having fun marching. They are using rhythm sticks to help them become more aware of the rhythmic pattern of march music.

Part 4

Music

MUSIC

Enjoyment is the most important reason for introducing the child to music at an early age. As preschoolers listen to and enjoy music, they learn to distinguish between noise and musical sounds, between soft and loud music, fast and slow tempo, and high and low pitch. They become aware, too, that music communicates feelings—feelings that can be expressed by spontaneous chants, songs, and body movements.

And because of the natural appeal of·music to children, it can be used to further other kinds of learning: vocabulary building, concept reinforcement, the development of various motor and social skills, and memorizing. These secondary uses of music, however, should always remain secondary in your music activities. Enjoyment is the primary goal. The secondary goals should never be so emphasized as to destroy the natural enjoyment a child derives from music.

The musical education of the preschooler starts with opportunities to listen to music and, through enjoyment of it, to build basic music-related understanding and skills which will help him find increasing joy in music. Important to this goal is providing the child with many different kinds of music both in informal and in structured activities. Although the preschooler usually will not be able to distinguish between the specific kinds of music (spirituals, country, classical), he will become aware of changes in sounds and rhythms. And although he may not be able to keep perfect time to music or learn specific dance patterns, he will begin to respond in his own way to the feelings aroused by the various kinds of music. It is important for small children to hear simple melodies and songs over and over again. For through such repetition they learn the words and melodies of songs and are able to sing them.

Structured music activities can be used to promote enjoyment while at the same time promoting particular kinds of musical learning. The key to success in this dual endeavor is flexibility in the teacher. You should be able to accept more than one kind of response to the music and adapt your activity accordingly. If, for example, the child in a planned clapping activity chooses to pat the rug or his leg, accept the response and imitate it as you continue the activity. In fact, the youngster may interpret your imitation of his response as a form of praise, thus making the enjoyment of what he is doing even greater. Or, if the child is more interested in just listening to music than in dancing to it, accept that too. Try to catch him for your dancing activity at another time when he is in a dancing mood. In other words, take your cues from the child and build enjoyment and learning on what he already finds enjoyable.

The musical activities in this section of the text suggest ways to use music for the preschooler's enjoyment while at the same time promoting particular kinds of appropriate musical learning. Among the learning they seek to promote are the development of a sense of rhythm, an awareness of different sounds and rhythms, and such abilities as expressing feelings through singing and dancing, distinguishing between sounds made by simple rhythm instruments, and recognizing loud and soft sounds, fast and slow tempo, and high and low pitch.

In addition to these sample activities, you are encouraged to plan others for the kind of musical experiences you yourself enjoy. By so communicating to the youngster your own enjoyment of music, his enjoyment will continue to grow.

Some general guidelines which will be helpful to you in using these activities and the ones you design are:

1. *Within your total music program (free and structured activities), provide short selections of a variety of kinds of music for the child's listening pleasure.* Include both simple children's music and more complex adult music. You will find music suitable for and enjoyable to the young child in many categories: spirituals, folk and country, popular contemporary songs, classical and semi-classical, etc. Although the young child will probably not be able to distinguish among the specific kinds of music, he will become aware that sounds and rhythms vary.

2. *When you are selecting music for a structured activity, try to use music that you enjoy.* Your enjoyment is apt to be caught by the child.

3. *Schedule musical activities carefully.* Intersperse free or spontaneous music activities with your structured ones. Remember, too, that the structured sessions demand careful and concentrated attention by the child. Too much, too long may create an aversion to music rather than enjoyment of it. Avoid musical activities requiring concentration when the child is tired, and stop such activities at the first sign of fatigue. By the same token, follow strenuous musical activities with a quiet time, such as listening to restful music or to a relaxing story.

4. *Encourage musical creativity by the child.* Let him make up chants, let him suggest and use new words for a song or new actions to go with a musical story. Let him create dances and use rhythm in other things he does, like walking and jumping, pounding and swinging.

5. *Teach new songs and nursery rhymes in units rather than line-by-line.* Select short songs with simple melodies and with repetitive words or lines. Sing the song through and then repeat it as often as the child's interest permits. The youngster will learn both the words and the melody by hearing the song over and over again.

6. *Emphasize improvised body movement (creative or free dancing) in your dancing activities.* Patterned dancing or so-called dance steps are too

difficult for the preschooler. The goal is to have the youngster listen to the music and then express his feelings in his own way. One way to help him get started is for you to improvise when you dance. He may watch and imitate you, or he may improvise his own dance. In any case, praise his efforts and imitate some of his creations as a sign of approval and encouragement.

7. *Allow plenty of space for activities involving movement.* Nothing is so inhibiting as being told to be careful.

8. *Do not be concerned about the quality of your singing voice or your gracefulness when dancing.* Here is your chance to enjoy being a star. After all, you have a captive, uncritical audience who will think you are great!

9. *Make musical activities a shared experience.* Through music you can often teach such social skills as sharing, taking turns, and enjoying the company of others. Participate in the activities yourself whenever you can.

10. *If you are working with a small group of children, do not expect or insist on full or the same kind of participation by all the children.* Some may respond immediately to your plans. Others may need time to listen and observe before deciding to join the group, and still others may not be ready for the activity and will join the group only at some later time.

Reminders of these guidelines as well as other more specific guidelines are included in the "Helpful Hints" of the activities.

Every effort has been made in the activity samples of the text to keep expensive materials at a minimum. The songs used are generally well known. When you do not know a melody, you are encouraged to make up your own, or you may use another song that you do know. Substitutions for designated materials and equipment are suggested. In activities that call for a record player, a radio often makes a good substitute. Directions for making homemade rhythm instruments are also given on pages 193–195. On pages 195–196 you will find titles of songbooks and records which have been found suitable for young children.

If you do not have a record player, you may find an inexpensive child's record player and a few carefully selected records especially helpful. Of course, a piano, other musical instruments, toy instruments, and a collection of songbooks and records are all assets to a music program; but they are not essential to it.

HOW TO MAKE YOUR OWN RHYTHM INSTRUMENTS

Toy instruments (or the real thing) may, of course, be used to produce rhythm, but children will probably enjoy homemade instruments just as much. A few ideas for making them are given below. To add color and drama, bright Contact paper or paint can often be added. Or gay streamers can be attached to the instrument.

BELLS: Wrist and ankle bells are almost a necessity for youngsters as they dance and prance. Make them from flat elastic, with the ends sewn together to form a ring about the size of the child's wrist or ankle. Sew four or five bells to the elastic strip. These little bells are available at dimestores, especially about Christmas time. Or sew the bells on strips of colored ribbon for the child to hold and shake.

CYMBALS: Use two pot lids with knobs. Or punch holes in two pie pans and attach knobs to the top side of each pie pan. Knobs can be purchased in a hardware or dimestore.

DRUM: Large cartons (ice cream, potato chips), large coffee cans with plastic reseal lids, and other similar containers make good drums that can be used as tom-toms or wooden or metal spoons can be used as drum sticks. By punching a hole on opposite sides of the container and attaching a cord of suitable length for a shoulder strap, it becomes a good marching drum.

Metal containers, such as metal pails and pots turned upside down, can also be used as drums, but you will probably want to modify the drum stick to deaden the sound somewhat. To do this, wrap the bowl of the spoon or one end of your stick with cotton batting, cover the cotton with a piece of cloth, and fasten all securely with a rubber band stretched tightly around the edge of the cloth where it meets the spoon handle or stick. Or simply wrap several layers of cloth around one end of your drum stick and fasten securely with a rubber band.

GUITAR: A sturdy box (shoebox size) with an open top makes a guitar if several rubber bands are stretched lengthwise around the box. Rubber bands of different widths will produce different tones when plucked. Rubber bands stretched around the back of a chair make a good viola.

HORN: To make horn-like sounds, blow across the open mouth of empty soda bottles of various sizes.

MARACAS: These are made from dry gourds. Pierce and fill the gourd with such things as dried beans or small pebbles. Seal the hole with adhesive or plastic tape. The young child will use this type of maraca very much like a large rattle held in both hands. Or if you are ambitious, you might make two maracas by inserting sticks in the gourds. Make your holes the same size as your sticks and secure the sticks with Elmer's glue. These maracas are shaken separately (not hit together), one held in each hand.

RATTLES: You can make rattles from any small can or box and some small hard objects. Spice cans and adhesive bandage cans are good, but wood and cardboard boxes can also be used to make deeper sounding rattles. Dried beans, peas, pebbles, acorns, screws, small nails, or plastic or metal caps are a few of the small objects which can be used as fillers. Each will produce somewhat different sounds. Be sure to tape the lids of the cans or boxes securely to prevent spillage or any danger of the child's getting at any small, sharp objects.

RHYTHM STICKS: Two sticks, eight to ten inches long, will do. Dowel sticks made from old broom or other rounded wooden handles work well. Rhythm sticks are played by hitting the sticks together in the middle. Older children may play them by moving one arm up and the other down to bring the sticks together in the middle.

TAMBOURINE: Use two paper plates and staple or sew them together, top sides facing each other. Sew little bells (purchased in dimestores) around edge of plates. Or string a few metal buttons loosely on loops of heavy thread and attach four or five sets of these at intervals to the edge of the plates.

TRIANGLE: Bend a metal rod to the shape of a triangle and attach a string at one corner. The child holds the string in one hand and hits the triangle with another piece of metal—a spoon, for example. An old metal horseshoe also makes a good triangle. Or simply use a metal spoon with a string attached just below its bowl and another metal spoon for a striker. It will make a chime similar to that of a triangle.

SELECTED SONG BOOKS AND RECORDS

The song books and record albums listed below have been selected on the basis of their general appeal to small children and/or their appropriateness for use in the musical activities of this book. You may, however, find many additional songs and records which will prove equally enjoyable and satisfying to the very young musician.

Song Books

The Fireside Book of Children's Songs (Simon and Shuster)
More Songs to Grow On (William Morrow and Co.)
The New Golden Song Book (Western Publishing Co.)
Songs To Grow On (William Sloane Assoc.)

Record Albums

American Games and Activity Songs for Children (Folkways)
The Baby Sitters (Vanguard)
Bert's Blockbusters (Sesame Street)
A Child's Garden of Verses (Disneyland)
The Do–Re–Mi Children's Chorus: Playing Games and Having Fun (Coral)
Getting It Together and Other Nursery Songs (Folkways)
More Mother Goose (Disneyland), with the play-along rhythm band
Mother Goose Nursery Rhymes (Disneyland), with illustrated booklet
Mother Goose Nursery Rhymes and Their Stories (Disneyland)
Music for Ones and Twos (CMS)
Nursery Children's Songs (Folkways)
Nursery Rhymes: Rhythmic and Remembering (Folkways)
A Treasury of Mother Goose (Columbia)

ACTIVITY 74: Clapping to Music

MUSIC
A

WHY

To clap hands.
To clap to rhythm.

WHAT YOU NEED

No materials needed.

TALK ABOUT WHAT YOU DO

(Use your own language. This is an example.)

"I know something we can do that is fun. Can you clap your hands like this? / Oh, you missed! Try again. / That's good."

"I'm going to sing a song and clap my hands. You can clap along with me if you like."

Patty cake, patty cake, baker's man.	*(Clap in time)*
Bake me a cake as fast as you can.	
Roll it, pat it, mark it with a C.	*(Use child's initial)*
Put it in the oven for Charles and me.	*(Use child's name)*

"Oh, you clapped very well. Let's do it again, shall we?"

HELPFUL HINTS

If you do not know the melody for "Patty Cake," make up your own tune or chant the words.

Insert the child's initial and name in the third and fourth line of the song.

Don't expect perfect clapping or perfect timing at first. Both skills will improve with repetition.

THINGS TO DO ANOTHER TIME

Children love songs they know, so don't hesitate to repeat the activity. Encourage the child to sing along with you, at least a line or a few words. The words will be learned by such repetition.

Add additional actions for the third line of the song: "Roll it (imitate using a rolling pin), pat it (pat, pat), and mark it with a C (trace the initial in the air)."

Sing other songs or play a record of music that has a strong beat for the child to clap in rhythm.

Make up a "clapping" chant. Some examples are:

> This is the way we clap, clap, clap.
> Clap, clap, clap; clap, clap, clap.
> This is the way we clap, clap, clap
> When we are happy.

> I wish I were a clapper,
> A clapper, a clapper.
> I wish I were a clapper.
> I know what I would do.
> I'd clap, clap, clap.
> I'd clap, clap, clap.
> That's what I would do.

ACTIVITY 75:   Rhythmic Movement

MUSIC
A

WHY

To use body in rhythmic movement.
To be aware of chant.

WHAT YOU NEED

No materials needed.

TALK ABOUT WHAT YOU DO

(Use your own language. This is an example.)

"I am going to sing a song. Give me your hands and I'll sing it to you."

(Chant the lines clearly and use body movements as indicated.)

Ring around the rosy.	*(Swing arms gently in rhythm and sway with*
A pocket full of posies.	*body)*
Ashes, ashes,	*(Swing arms higher on each word)*
We all fall down!	*(Fall down)*

"Let's do that again."

"Would you like to sing with me this time?" (Chant each line slowly. If the child tends to repeat lines after you, allow time for him to do so.)

"Oh, you are a good singer and a good faller-downer! Let's rest now. I'm tired. I'll sing you a resting song if you like."

HELPFUL HINTS

To chant means simply to recite the words in a rhythmic, singsong tone.

Allow plenty of space for movement in this activity. A rug underfoot is also a good idea.

Holding the child's hands will help him sense the rhythm of the chant. But if after the first try or two the child would like more freedom of movement, do not insist on holding his hands.

Don't make an issue of learning the words as the child will learn them with repetition. Place your emphasis on enjoyment. Smile while you chant to show that you are enjoying yourself.

Be sure to stop the activity before fatigue sets in or at the first sign of fatigue.

THINGS TO DO ANOTHER TIME

If the child enjoys the activity, repeat it often. It may take several sessions before the child learns the words.

Encourage spontaneous chant that picks up the rhythm of movements. For example, hold the child on your lap in a rocking chair and rock while you chant: "We're rocking, we're rocking, we're rocking in a rocking boat." Encourage the child to chant along with you and to try the rocking movement and chant on his own.

Make up your own chants. Some other examples are: "I'm sweeping, I'm sweeping, I'm sweeping up the dirty dirt" (to accompany swinging arms in a sweeping motion); "I'm stirring, I'm stirring, I'm stirring up a cake for John (to accompany a circling movement of hand and arm); "I'm pounding, I'm pounding, I'm pounding down a big, fat pillow" (to accompany a slapping movement). Don't be surprised if the child begins to make up his own chants to go with movements.

ACTIVITY 76:   A Song To Learn Names

MUSIC
B

WHY

To identify name of child.
To identify names of other children.

WHAT YOU NEED

No materials needed.

TALK ABOUT WHAT YOU DO

(Use your own language. This is an example.)

"I've got a surprise for you. What's your name? / Okay, Jennie, would you like to hear a song about yourself? / Good! Listen!"

Oh, do you know the little girl, the little girl, the little girl,
Oh, do you know the little girl whose name is Jennie Brown?

Oh yes, I know the little girl, the little girl, the little girl,
  (*Point to child*)
Oh yes, I know the little girl whose name is Jennie Brown.

"Are you really Jennie Brown? / All right, Jennie Brown, let's sing it again."

(Repeat first verse.)

"Listen now. This is the part of the song you should sing."

(Sing second verse.)

"Let's try singing that together." (Sing slowly, cueing the child as needed.)

(Repeat the song again if the child is willing. Encourage the child to sing the second verse with you.)

HELPFUL HINTS

The song is sung to the tune of "The Muffin Man."

This is a good activity to use with a small group of children to help them learn each other's names. In the second verse have all the children point to the child being named. And repeat the song often enough that no one is left out.

It may take many repeats of the song for the child to learn it entirely. So don't push too hard on the first try.

THINGS TO DO ANOTHER TIME

Once the child has learned the song, substitute other people or animals that the child is familiar with. Here are some examples:

> Oh, do you know your Uncle Joe, . . .
> . . . who has a bright red car.

> Oh, do you know the bus driver, . . .
> . . . who drives a big blue bus.

> Oh, do you know the grocery man, . . .
> . . . who sells us fruit and candy.

ACTIVITY 77:   Running to Music

MUSIC
B

WHY

To be aware of music with fast
  tempo.
To respond to music through body
  movement.

WHAT YOU NEED

Record player; record of music
with strong rhythm and fast
tempo, such as "Comin'
'Round the Mountain''; pictures
of horse or pony.

TALK ABOUT WHAT YOU DO

(Use your own language. This is an example.)

"Look at what I have! It's the picture book of animals we looked at the
other day. Let's look at the picture of a horse again. / Which of these
animals is a horse? / Can a horse run very fast? / Oh, my, horses can run
very fast. Do you know what a little horse is called? / It's called a *pony.* Can
you say *pony?* / Good! A little pony can run very fast too."

"You know what? We are going to pretend we are little ponies and do
some dancing and prancing and running. I have just the music for ponies.
(Put on record.) Listen to that lively music. (Listen for a few moments.)
The music makes me feel like running. It makes me want to do a pony
dance. / Show me how you would dance if you were a pony."

(Run in a circle or run bringing knees up high so that you are practically
running in place.)

"Oh, are you a pony, too? / You are a real fancy-dancy pony!"

"Let's rest for a few minutes. Then we can play the fast, running music again and do some more pony dancing."

HELPFUL HINTS

"Comin' 'Round the Mountain" is a good piece for running but any music with a strong, fast beat will do. If you do not have a record player, try to find a radio station that tends to play music with a fast tempo.

The youngster should have some idea of what a pony is. A picture story about a horse or pony read prior to the activity will be helpful, along with a quick review of the pictures to introduce the activity. Or substitute the name of another fast moving animal with which the child is already familiar.

Do not limit the child's movements to running if he finds other movements equally or more satisfying. He may walk, hop, whirl, or just plain clown to the music. Whenever you can, pick up your cue from the child, imitate some of his movements, and enjoy the activity with him.

THINGS TO DO ANOTHER TIME

Use the record again or other music with strong rhythm and fast tempo (for example, "Pop Goes the Weasel" or "Yankee Doodle") to encourage the child to respond to the music with body movements. You might pretend to be a hopping frog or bunny, a running dog, a flying bird, or other animals which the child has seen first-hand or in pictures or on TV.

ACTIVITY 78:   Singing about Everyday Tasks

MUSIC
B

WHY

To participate in singing.
To respond to music through body
   movements.

WHAT YOU NEED

No materials needed.

TALK ABOUT WHAT YOU DO

(Use your own language. This is an example.)

"Let's pretend we've just gotten up this morning. Let's give a big stretch and a yawn. / Now, listen to what else we do in the morning."

This is the way we wash our face,   *(Scrubbing motion as though washing*
Wash our face, wash our face.   *face)*
This is the way we wash our face,
Early in the morning.

"Did you do a good job on your face? / Let's sing it again. You sing along with me."

(Repeat.)

"Oh, you want to do it one more time? / All right. Once more."

HELPFUL HINTS

The song is sung to the tune of "The Mulberry Bush."

Remember to teach the song through repetition rather than trying to have the child learn it a line at a time. Songs, such as this one, which repeat words, will be learned quickly if the child enjoys it.

THINGS TO DO ANOTHER TIME

Add other verses: "This is the way we comb our hair. . . ."; "This is the way we brush our teeth. . . ."; "This is the way we jump out of bed . . ."; etc. Use appropriate motions with each verse.

Make up verses and use them to encourage the child to do little chores: "This is the way we pick up toys . . . when we're finished playing" or "This is the way we set the table . . . when it's time to eat." Have the child suggest his own verses.

ACTIVITY 79:   Free Dancing to Music

MUSIC
B

WHY

To be aware of rhythm in music.
To respond to music with body
movement.

WHAT YOU NEED

Record player; record of music that
suggests swaying and swirling
(waltz);   square,   chiffon-like
scarfs.

TALK ABOUT WHAT YOU DO

(Use your own language. This is an example.)

"I am going to play a record for you. We can dance to the music." (Start record.)

"Oh, listen to the music. (Listen for a few moments.) It makes me want to sway and swing. I want to dance to the music." (Sway and swirl to the music. Hold a scarf in one hand, making it float gracefully as you dance.)

"Here is a pretty scarf for you. Would you like to dance to the music too?"

(Let the child do what he wants to do. Imitate him whenever possible to encourage him.)

"Would you like to take my hand? / We'll dance together." (Holding child's hand, continue moving to the music.)

"That was a beautiful dance. You are a great little dancer. / Let's just sit and rest for a few minutes. I'll sing you a "resting song." (Sing or hum a quiet song or play a quiet record, such as a lullaby or a ballad.)

HELPFUL HINTS

If you do not have a record player, try a radio. You should be able to find a station that offers "swaying and swirling" music.

A Strauss or any waltz is good for this activity because of the swaying, swirling movement it suggests.

Remember that the preschooler perceives dancing as any form of movement: walking, whirling, jumping, galloping. Accept whatever he does. By repeating the activity often, he may become more aware of the swaying rhythm of the music and begin to adapt his movements to it. The scarf is used to promote this awareness.

Holding the child's hand may also help to bring about an awareness of the swaying rhythm. But if he prefers to dance alone, let him.

THINGS TO DO ANOTHER TIME

Repeat and adapt the activity to music with different rhythms: folk music, lullabies, spirituals, polkas, jazz. Each time, improvise dance movements appropriate for the music and encourage the child to imitate you or to improvise his own movements. With repetition the child will begin to demonstrate an awareness of differences in rhythms.

ACTIVITY 80:   Marching to Music

MUSIC
B

WHY

To be aware of marching rhythms.
To march to music.

WHAT YOU NEED

Record player; marching record.

TALK ABOUT WHAT YOU DO

(Use your own language. This is an example.)

"Remember the parade we saw on TV? / Remember the band and all the people marching in the parade? / I have a parading record. Listen." (Start record and listen to the music for a few moments.)

"Do you hear that beat? / It says 'Step. Step. Step. Step.' (March in place as you repeat the word *step*.) Come on. Let's march in the parade." (March to the music, arms swinging.)

"I'll clap as we march. Okay?" (Clap and march.)

"Oh, that was fun. We had a parade all by ourselves and you marched in it!"

HELPFUL HINTS

If you do not have a record player, try the drum or chant activity suggested in the suggestions "Things To Do Another Time."

Do not expect the toddler to keep step to the music the first time you try this activity. And, if he does not, ignore it. Let him simply prance and enjoy himself.

Clapping in time or using the words *step, step,* repeated in march time may help the child find the beat of the music and keep step to it.

If possible, introduce the activity by recalling some recent experience the child has had related to marching or parading. If this is not possible, talk about and demonstrate marching before playing the record and demonstrate marching again to the music.

THINGS TO DO ANOTHER TIME

Repeat your parade to other marching music. Vary the activity by letting the child wear a "parade" hat or some other form of dress-up.

Add a toy drum (see our directions for making one) to the "parade." March to the beat of the drum. Let the child be the drummer too, but don't expect him to provide a perfect marching beat.

Make up a marching chant and march to it. Here is an example:

> Left, right, left, right.
> Here we go in line!
> Left, right, left, right.
> Aren't we doing fine!

ACTIVITY 81:   Rhythm and Hand Movements

MUSIC
B

WHY

To listen and respond to a song.
To make rolling movements with
  hands.

WHAT YOU NEED

Toy bus or car.

TALK ABOUT WHAT YOU DO

(Use your own language. This is an example.)

"Remember that big bus we saw (rode in) yesterday? / Can you tell me
about it? / Did the bus have wheels? / Right! The big bus has big wheels.
Where are the wheels of your little toy bus? / That's right. It has four
wheels—one, two, three, four."

"Let's pretend we are on the big bus and sing a song about it. Listen."

(Sing the song, using hand actions.)

> The wheels on the bus (car)
> Go round and round,   *(Roll each hand around the other.)*
> Round and round,   *(Roll hands.)*

Round and round,	(*Roll hands.*)
The wheels on the bus	
Go round and round	(*Roll hands.*)
All over town.	

"That was a good ride, wasn't it? / Show me how the wheels of the bus go. / Very good. Let's take another ride and you help me make the wheels go round and round."

(Repeat song with hand movements.)

"This time you help me sing too. Can you sing the part 'Round and round'? / Okay. I'll tell you when to sing it."

(Repeat with the child filling in the refrain "round and round." Clue him in at the proper time if necessary.)

"We'll take another singing bus ride tomorrow. Would you like that?"

HELPFUL HINTS

"The Wheels of the Bus" is sung to the tune of "The Mulberry Bush."

This activity is good to prepare the child or children for a bus trip (see Activity 167) or as a follow-up activity after a ride on the bus. Adapt your language to the occasion.

You may wish to use the word *car* instead of *bus* if the child has had no experience with a bus and none is anticipated.

Do not expect perfect rolling actions by the child. You can also reverse the action, alternating between a forward roll and backward roll. The child may enjoy the confusion that will probably result.

THINGS TO DO ANOTHER TIME

The child will learn the entire song if you repeat the activity frequently.

Vary the words and the actions. For example, sing "The wipers on the bus go back and forth . . ." Use a hand motion toward self on word *back* and away from self on word *forth*. Or, "The people in the bus go in and out

. . ." Pretend an open box is the bus and have the child put his hand *in* and *out* of the box at the proper words.

Change the words of the song to "The steps in the store go up and down . . ." and sing the song after a visit to a department store and ride on the escalator (see Activity 170). Have the child use the proper hand movements for *up* and *down*.

ACTIVITY 82:   Listening to Music

MUSIC
B

WHY

To be aware of the act of listening.
To listen to music.

WHAT YOU NEED

Record player; record of marching music or some other lively music.

TALK ABOUT WHAT YOU DO

(Use your own language. This is an example.)

"Where are your ears? / That's right. Can you find two ears? / One ear, two ears. (Touch or point to child's ears as you count.) What do we do with our ears? / Yes, we can hear all kinds of noises and sounds with our ears."

"Let's use our ears to listen to some music. (Start record.) Do you hear the music? (Listen for a few moments and then stop the record.) Do you hear the music now? / No, the music is all gone. Our ears can't hear it."

"Let's play a listening game. When you hear the music, march around the room. When you can't hear the music, sit down quick. Ready? / Remember, sit down as soon as you can't hear the music."

(Start music and march with child for a short time. Then turn off the record and sit down on the floor.) "Oh, you forgot to sit down when you couldn't hear the music. Let's try again. See if you can sit down before I do when the music stops."

(Continue with game as long as the child shows interest.)

HELPFUL HINTS

A radio or a musical instrument (or even singing or chanting) can also be used in this activity. Simply adapt your language to whatever you use.

Participate in the game if you are working with one child. If you are working with a small group of children, participate until they get the idea of the game. Then let them have fun while you take care of the music.

If you use marching music, march in time to it, but do not insist the child do the same. He may imitate you, but if not, accept any movements he decides to use.

If the game includes seeing who sits down first when the music stops, be sure to let the child win.

THINGS TO DO ANOTHER TIME

Play the listening game using various rhythm instruments to introduce the child to the sounds made by each instrument. A drum, bell, tambourine, and rattles work well for this activity. And let the child examine the instrument and try it out. See pages 193–195 for directions for making your own instruments.

Play or sing short selections of songs that require the child to listen carefully and react at a particular point in the song. For example, after the child is familiar with "Pop Goes the Weasel," have the youngster listen carefully for the point at which he says "pop" in the song. Or sing 'She'll Be Comin' 'Round the Mountain" with the youngster listening carefully to supply "chug, chug, chug" after each refrain.

ACTIVITY 83:   Nursery Rhymes

MUSIC
B

WHY

To sing nursery rhymes for enjoyment.

WHAT YOU NEED

Book of nursery rhymes that illustrates "Little Boy Blue," or
other pictures of farm animals.

TALK ABOUT WHAT YOU DO

(Use your own language. This is an example.)

"Look at this pretty picture! (Show picture illustrating "Little Boy
Blue.") What are all those things? / Yes, it's a boy. He's called Little Boy
Blue. What color is his suit? / Blue, that's right. Do you have on something
that is blue?"

"What else do you see in the picture? / Some sheep. Good! What color
are the sheep? / Sheep are white. Would you like to pat a little white sheep?
/ No? I think you would like it. A sheep feels nice and soft. / What's this?
(Point to haystack.) That's the farmer's haystack. It's a big pile of hay for
the farmer's cows and horses. Can you say *haystack?* / Very good!"

"I know a song about Little Boy Blue and the sheep and the haystack.
Listen."

> Little Boy Blue, come blow your horn.
> The sheep's in the meadow, the cow's in the corn.
> Where is the boy who looks after the sheep?
> He's under the haystack fast asleep.

"What happened in the song? / Where was Little Boy Blue? / Show me in the picture where he was when he was *under* the haystack. / No, that's on top of the haystack. He was down here when he was *under* the haystack. / Why do you think he went to sleep?"

"Shall I sing the song again?"

HELPFUL HINTS

If you do not know and cannot locate the song "Little Boy Blue," make up your own tune or chant for the rhyme.

Using the picture helps the child visualize the story of the rhyme. It can also be used to teach names of new objects and to reinforce concepts.

But don't yield just plain enjoying the music and the rhymes to these kinds of learning. Make enjoyment your focal point.

If you use a picture, start with an open question like, "What are all those things?" or "What do you see?" Such questions encourage the child to take the lead in talking about the picture. Use more specific questions only to expand his observation.

THINGS TO DO ANOTHER TIME

Repeat the song and/or recite the nursery rhyme frequently so that the child learns the words and can sing along with you or by himself.

Add simple actions to the words and encourage the child to act out the story of "Little Boy Blue." For example, pretend to blow a horn, shade your eyes with one hand and pretend to look for Little Boy Blue, and, on the last line, cradle your cheek against your hands as if asleep.

Plan similar activities around other nursery rhymes. Some that have been set to music are: "Hey, Diddle, Diddle"; "Polly, Put The Kettle On"; "Little Jack Horner"; "Little Bo-Peep"; and "Hickory, Dickory, Dock." Encourage the child to sing along with you and to act out the story with simple hand or body motions.

ACTIVITY 84:   Singing about Your Feelings

MUSIC
C

WHY

To be aware of happy and sad songs.
To clap to rhythm.

WHAT YOU NEED

No materials needed.

TALK ABOUT WHAT YOU DO

(Use your own language. This is an example.)

"Look at me. Do you think I'm happy or sad? (Give a big smile.) Yes, a big smile or grin tells you I'm happy. Can you show me you are happy? / Oh, that was a big smile."

"Do you think I'm happy when I do this? (Make a sad face.) No, I'm sad. What else do we do sometimes when we're sad? / Right. We cry."

"Do you think I'm happy or sad when I do this? (Bounce up and down and clap your hands.) / Yes, I'm very happy."

"Well, we're very happy today, aren't we? / So let's sing a happy song and show how happy we are. Listen to the song and clap your hands like this when I clap. Can you do that? / Very good!"

(Fast tempo.)   If you're happy and you know it,
Clap your hands.   *(Clap clap)*
If you're happy and you know it,
Clap your hands.   *(Clap clap)*

If you're happy and you know it,
Then your smile will surely show it.   (*Smile*)
If you're happy and you know it,
Clap your hands.   (*Clap clap*)

"That was very, very good! Let's see if we can sing a sad song now. Instead of clapping, we'll pretend we are crying. We'll say 'boo–hoo.' Can you say 'boo–hoo'? / Oh, that's sad. Ready for a sad song?"

(*Slow tempo.*)   If you're sad and you know it,
Shed a tear.   (*"Boo–hoo"*)
If you're sad and you know it,
Shed a tear.   (*"Boo–hoo"*)
If you're sad and you know it,   (*Look sad*)
Then your face will surely show it. (*"Boo–hoo"*)
If you're sad and you know it,
Shed a tear.   (*"Boo–hoo"*)

"Which song do you like best? / Let's sing that one again."

HELPFUL HINTS

If you do not know and cannot locate the song "If You're Happy And You Know It," make up your own tune or chant for the words.

To get across feelings of happiness and sadness, sing the first version with gusto, a relatively fast tempo, and obvious enjoyment. When you sing the second version, slow down the tempo somewhat and use facial expressions of sadness.

THINGS TO DO ANOTHER TIME

Use different versions of the song: happy verses:

Pull your ear   (*Tug tug*)
Pat your tummy   (*Pat pat*)
Toot your horn   (*Toot toot*)

sad versions:

Slap your wrist   (*Slap slap*)
Hide your eyes   (*Cover eyes with both hands*)

Sing (or play) other happy and sad songs and talk about the feelings each evokes. "Pop! Goes the Weasel" and "My Bonnie Lies Over the Ocean" are two well-known songs that bring out contrasting feelings. If you substitute the child's name in the latter and sing the song with pathos, the child will probably relate more readily to the sadness involved in his absence from home. Many spirituals are also good to use to bring out feelings of happiness and sadness.

ACTIVITY 85:   Exploring Pitch of Sounds

MUSIC
C

WHY

To be aware of difference in pitch. To distinguish between high and low pitch of sounds.

WHAT YOU NEED

A sturdy box (shoe-box size) with open top; several rubber bands ranging from wide to narrow.

TALK ABOUT WHAT YOU DO

(Use your own language. This is an example.)

"Lookie, lookie, lookie! (Hold up box.) What is this? / Yes, it's a box, a box that shoes came in. (Point to rubber bands.) What are these? / They are rubber hands. We can stretch rubber bands. Can you stretch one of the bands like this? (Demonstrate.) Oh, you made the rubber band good and long."

"Let's stretch the rubber bands around the box and make a make-believe guitar. (Help as necessary.). There, we have a guitar that you can play and make music."

"See this wide rubber band? Pluck it with your finger. / Oh, that was a low, deep sound (use low-pitched voice). Now pluck that one. (Point to finest rubber band.) Say, it made a different sound. It made a high, squeaky sound'' (use high-pitched voice).

"Play your guitar some more and listen to the sounds. / Was that a low (low voice) sound or a high (high voice) sound? / It sounded pretty high to me. Play that rubber band again. (Point to widest rubber band.) Was that a low (low voice) or high (high voice) sound? / Very good!''

(Give the chiid time to play and enjoy the guitar if he is interested.)

"Which rubber band made a low, deep sound? / See if you can find it. / That's right. That's the one. Now see if you can find the one that made a high sound. / Oh, very good. You are a very smart guitar player!''

HELPFUL HINTS

See also page 194 for additional directions for making a guitar.

Experiment with the guitar before the activity to be sure the rubber bands you plan to use will make sounds of distinctly different pitch. To secure a high pitch the rubber band must be very taut.

Place the emphasis of the lesson on distinguishing between high and low pitch. Do not talk about the sounds that are somewhere between the two, or you may confuse the child.

THINGS TO DO ANOTHER TIME

Explore pitch of tones made by other kinds of musical instruments. Use several different sounding pot lids with handles to make and compare sounds similar to those made by percussion instruments. Do the same with several drums that have readily distinguishable sounds. Use whistles to introduce the child to sounds related to woodwind instruments and horns. In each activity talk about the tones being high or low in pitch.

ACTIVITY 86:   Listening to Loud and Soft Music

MUSIC
C

WHY

To distinguish between loud and soft music.
To enjoy different kinds of music.

WHAT YOU NEED

A radio or a record player; record of your choice.

TALK ABOUT WHAT YOU DO

(Use your own language. This is an example.)

"I've got a secret. Do you want to hear my secret? / I'll whisper it softly in your ear. (Whisper.) I can play some music that's very loud and then make it very soft. / Listen. I'll show you."

(Turn the volume up on the radio or record player and listen to the music for a minute.)

(Cover your ears with your hands.) "Oh, that hurts my ears. It's so loud."

"Listen again. Tell me when the music is loud and when it is soft."

(Change the volume several times, each time asking the child if the music is loud or soft. If he makes a mistake, correct him and try him again on the same volume level.)

"Now you have the same secret that I have. You know when the music is loud and when it is soft. / Let's just listen to the music now. It's not too loud or too soft, is it? / No. It's just right."

HELPFUL HINTS

If you do not have a record player or radio, you can adapt the activity to a song by singing it first very loud and then softly.

Make the difference in volume easily distinguishable in the first demonstrations: very loud and very soft. Later, you may want to reduce or increase levels somewhat, although a distinct difference in volume should remain easily noticeable.

THINGS TO DO ANOTHER TIME

Sing a song loudly and then softly, talking about its loudness or softness each time you sing it. You might use the following verses sung to "The Muffin Man" (see Activity 76 for the rest of the words):

> Oh, do you know the great big dog . . .
> . . . Whose bark is very loud. (*Bark loudly*)

> Oh, do you know the little dog . . .
> . . . Whose bark is very soft. (*Bark softly*)

When the child learns the song, have him sing it first softly, and then loudly or vice versa.

Play other records or sing other songs that by intent are loud or soft (march or lullabye). Talk about the music being "booming" and "jumping" or "quiet" and "sleepy."

ACTIVITY 87:   Listening to Fast and Slow Music

MUSIC
C

WHY

To be aware of difference in tempo.
To distinguish between fast and slow tempo.

WHAT YOU NEED

No materials needed but use songs which the child already knows.

TALK ABOUT WHAT YOU DO

(Use your own language. This is an example.)

"Remember the song we learned about what we do in the morning? / Well, I am going to sing it for you, but I am going to pretend I'm very tired. I am going to sing the song ver-ry slo-ow-ly."

(See Activity 78 for words of song "This Is The Way We Wash Our Face." Sing it slowly and use very slow scrubbing motions.)

"That was really slow, wasn't it? / Now, let's pretend I'm wide awake and full of pep. This time I'll sing the song very fast. Listen to a fast song."

(Repeat the song at a fast tempo, using brisk, quick scrubbing motions.)

"That was a wide-awake, fast song. Let's sing the song together now. First we'll sing it slowly. Remember, you are very tired."

(Repeat song and motions at slow tempo.)

"That was a good slow song. Now let's see if we can sing it fast."

(Repeat song and motions at fast tempo.)

"Very good! Now I am going to sing another song and you tell me if it is fast or slow. Okay? / Listen."

(Sing "The Wheels Of The Bus Go Round And Round" at fast tempo and with fast actions. See Activity 81 for words.)

"Was that a fast or slow song? / Very good! Those were really fast wheels on that bus. Would you like to sing the bus song too? / Should we sing it slowly or fast? / Okay. Remember, this is going to be a slow bus, one that almost gets stuck."

HELPFUL HINTS

Use songs in this activity that the child is already familiar with. This will permit the child to experience for himself how it feels to sing both slow and fast.

If the child experiences any confusion in making the fast motions, make it part of the fun. The important learning is simply to distinguish between fast and slow tempo.

THINGS TO DO ANOTHER TIME

Sing or listen to other music sung or played normally at slow or fast tempo. For example, sing a lullaby, then "Pop! Goes the Weasel," and then talk about the tempo. Or play a lullaby and a rousing, fast-tempo march and talk about the slow, sleepy music and the fast, peppy music.

ACTIVITY 88:   Finger Play to Music

WHY

To listen and respond to song.
To iden*ify thumb and fingers.

WHAT YOU NEED

No materials needed.

TALK ABOUT WHAT YOU DO

(Use your own language. This is an example.)

(Have the child sit on the floor in front of you, facing you. Place your hands behind your back.) "I bet you can't guess where my hands are. / Let's see if you are right."

(Sing "Where Is Thumbkin" with actions as given.)

Where is Thumbkin?	*(Hands behind back)*
Where is Thumbkin?	
Here I am.	*(Right hand from behind back, thumb up)*
Here I am.	*(Left hand from behind back, thumb up)*
How are you today, Sir?	*(Right thumb "bows")*
Very well, I thank you.	*(Left thumb "bows")*
Run away.	*(Right hand behind back)*
Run away.	*(Left hand behind back)*

"Where are your hands? / Do you have more than one hand? / Right. / You have two—one, two. How about wiggling your fingers like this? (Demonstrate.) Very good!"

"Now, where are your thumbs? / Can you make them into Thumbkins by pointing them up like this? / Good. Let's sing the song again. This time, you be Thumbkins, too. Listen to the song and make Thumbkins do what I do. Okay?"

(Repeat song and actions, allowing a little time for the child to act out the song with his thumbs.)

HELPFUL HINTS

"Thumbkins" is sung to the tune of "Frère Jacques" or "Are You Sleeping?"

Don't stress the precise thumb and hand movements. The child will enjoy the play, and that's what is important. And with a few more tries, he will probably become very adept.

This activity is good for a small group of children also. Have them all seated in front of you, facing you, so they can see your movements.

THINGS TO DO ANOTHER TIME

Repeat the activity for "Handkins" (all four fingers up) and for each finger, using the names Pointer, Middle Man, Ring Man, and Little Man. The child will have difficulty extending the last two fingers, but let him have fun trying. When the child is ready, let him sing along with you.

Chant the verse below accompanied by the finger-play as noted:

Here are grandma's glasses.	(*Make round shape with thumb and index fingers and hold over eyes*)
Here is grandma's hat.	(*Make pointed hat with index fingers and hold over head*)
Here's the way she folds her hands.	(*Fold hands*)
And lays them in her lap.	(*Lay hands in lap*)

Through repetition, encourage the child to learn both the verse and the motions.

ACTIVITY 89:   Play Rhythm Instruments

MUSIC
C

WHY

To produce rhythm with a rhythm
instrument.
To enjoy a rhythmic experience.

WHAT YOU NEED

Record player and record of music
with a strong beat; tambourines.

TALK ABOUT WHAT YOU DO

(Use your own language. This is an example.)

(Start the record on the record player.) "Listen! Let's clap our hands to
the music. / Can you hear that beat? / The music is pretty fast, isn't it?"

"Let's do something different now. I've got a tambourine for each of us.
(Give the child a tambourine to examine.) What kind of music do you suppose we can make with a tambourine? / That's right. You can shake it and
the bells tinkle. Or you can hit it against your knuckles, like this." /
"Say, that's good!"

"Let's play the record again. This time we'll keep time to the music with
our tambourines."

"Was that fun? / Would you like to dance to the music now?" (Improvise a simple dance that includes shaking the tambourine in time with the
music. The child may imitate you or may improvise his own dance with or
without the tambourine.)

HELPFUL HINTS

See page 195 for directions to make your own tambourines as well as other kinds of rhythm instruments.

A radio can be substituted for a record player. Or adapt the activity to a song that you sing. "Pop! Goes The Weasel!" and "Jingle Bells" are two examples of songs that will work for this activity.

Do not expect the child to keep perfect time with the music at first. In fact, his response may be very hit-and-miss. But as he becomes familiar with a piece of music, his sense of timing will improve. So repeat the same music from time to time, as well as varying the activity with other kinds of music.

THINGS TO DO ANOTHER TIME

Adapt the activity to introduce the child to a variety of rhythm instruments: bells, triangles, drums, clappers, cymbals, rattles, maracas, and rhythm sticks. (See pages 193–195 for directions for making your own rhythm instruments.) Use a variety of kinds of music: different beats, loud and soft, fast and slow, happy and solemn. The child may or may not pick up the beat, so keep the focus on enjoyment. Talk about whether the music is fast or slow, loud or soft, happy or sad, so that he becomes aware of different tempos and different feelings evoked by music.

If you are working with a small group of children, form a rhythm band by giving each child an instrument to use to keep time with the music. Give each child a turn with each instrument by switching instruments among the children each time the band plays.

Make several sizes or use different materials to make variations of the same instrument. The child will enjoy trying out each model and comparing the sounds they make.

An early love for books can grow into a lifetime of enriching and pleasurable experiences.

Part 5

Books

BOOKS

An important goal in the education of the preschool youngster is the development of a love for books. Not only does the child who catches an enthusiasm for books at an early age have many moments of enjoyable and exciting learning in store for him, but he often develops a strong desire to learn to read. This desire becomes a valuable learning incentive. For when he is a little older, it will help make the difficult task of learning to read easier for him. An early love of books can also grow into a lifetime of enriching and pleasurable experiences.

Related closely to this overall goal is the use of picture "reading" and story telling to meet the emotional needs of toddlers. Sitting close to share a book with another person provides the child with feelings of security and of belonging. Appropriate books about family relationships and friendships and the importance of the child in these relationships further enhance these feelings. Other immediate educational objectives to be attained through books include concept reinforcement, language practice and vocabulary building, an awareness of simple story sequence, the development of listening and observing skills, and the ability to turn pages singly. These objectives, however, should not be so emphasized that the enjoyment of the pictures and stories is lost and the child's budding love of books is endangered.

Attaining the overall goal of enjoyment of books, as well as the more specific objectives, requires the use of several steps or phases in the presentation of books to the preschooler. His first introduction to books should be to picture books. The pictures should be large, in bright but real-life colors, and of whole objects, usually one to a page. Because at this early age the toddler does not yet function on an abstract level, the pictures should be realistic and present accurate concepts, without too much detail, of people, animals, objects, and places that the child has already experienced. In other words, in this first phase, books should be used to reinforce the child's already acquired concepts and experiences rather than to introduce the child to new concepts and experiences. To use the abstract and the unfamiliar may well result in disinterest on the part of the child and in rejection of the book and the activity.

The youngster's first books should be of a kind that he can handle and easily manage. The pages should be heavy cardboard or cloth so that the child can learn to turn single pages without tearing them. Pictures of common animals which the child has seen and of people that the child can relate to are good for beginners. Sensory books with pictures to feel and smell are also good because they permit the child to involve more than one sense in the learning.

The technique in presenting the first books includes pointing to and naming the object pictured, helping the child recall any firsthand experience with the real thing, and involving the child in the learning by such things as asking the child to repeat the name of the pictured object, imitating sounds made by a pictured animal, feeling/smelling objects in a sensory book, and pointing to the pictured object when its name is spoken. For example, most children will have seen a dog or cat in their neighborhood. In presenting a picture of a dog, then, you might say: "See the dog? (Point.) Can you say *dog?* / Do you remember the little dog you saw yesterday? / Dogs say 'Arf! Arf!' don't they? / Can you say 'Arf! Arf!' like a dog? / Oh, that was a good loud bark. What are some other things that a dog can do? / Can you point to the dog in the book?"

Another way to involve the beginner in a book activity is to use the real object along with a picture of it. An important learning objective in this approach is for the youngster to realize that a two-dimensional picture represents a three-dimensional, real object. Show the child, for instance, a real key. Let him feel and play with the key; talk about its use. Then show him the picture of a key. At this point you might say: "This is a picture of a key. This is a real key. Feel it. / Feel the key in the picture. / The picture key doesn't feel like the real key, does it?" Through such language and activities, the child learns the relationship between pictures and reality. At the same time the pictures become more meaningful to him.

Books with pictures of people who can be equated with family members and friends or schoolmates can also be effective in keeping the child's interest. "Look," you might say as you point, "Here's a picture of Mommy," or "Here's Granddad," or "Here is a picture of Judy" (child's name). Later, the child can name the various people with you, and then on his own. Not only does this game maintain the child's interest but it is fun for him, and that, of course, is your main objective.

As the child becomes familiar with a book and is able to talk more, ask if he can find various objects. To do this on his own, the child must be able to turn the pages of the book. So start working on this skill from the beginning. At first you will have to assist because the youngster will probably turn more than one page at a time. After a few sessions, he should be able to do better and, with additional time, manage the job by himself. But if the youngster continues to have problems with this skill, continue to assist him, thus providing opportunities to practice the skill without frustration.

When the child masters the one-object phase, he is ready for the second phase. Begin using books that have pictures which are somewhat more complex, showing some kind of action or relationship between two or more objects. A picture of a cat playing with a ball of yarn is an example. Start by having the youngster identify any objects in the picture that he can. If he misses a key object (one directly involved in the action, such as the cat or the yarn, in the example), point it out and talk about it so that the child can put it into focus: "That's a ball of yarn, pretty red yarn. Remember the little ball of yarn we felt the other day to see how soft it was?" And finally, ask the child what is happening in the picture by using a leading question, such as: "What is the cat doing with the yarn?" If the child is unable to respond to this question, supply the answer and talk briefly about it, pointing out an important clue or two to the answer. In the cat-yarn example, you might say, "That cat is playing with the yarn. See the cat's foot? (Point.) The cat is hitting the ball of yarn with its foot. Cats like to play like that, you know."

This action phase is important for the young child. Not only is it part of his language development but he also learns to interpret or "read" simple pictures, to find and understand relationships that exist between two or more objects in a picture. He needs to work with many pictures—pictures that are simple, realistic, colorful, and about objects and actions that are part of his own experiences. Use pictures more than once, as familiarity increases the enjoyment for most children. In repeating pictures, however, your last question should probably become less leading. Instead of asking "What is the cat doing with the yarn?" you might ask "What is the cat doing?" or even "What is happening in this picture?"

The child is ready for simple stories when he feels comfortable talking about pictures and is able to identify actions shown in pictures. Simple, brief stories told in your own words and illustrated by a picture or two are a good introduction to the story phase. ("Things To Do Another Time" in Activity 95 provides an example of such a story.) Story books with one picture and one sentence on each page are also recommended at this stage. The pictures should continue to be realistic, colorful, and related, for the most part, to concepts and experiences that are already familiar to the youngster. In a series of pictures illustrating a story, one of the story characters should appear in at least several of the pictures so that the child becomes aware of a sequence of events happening to the particular character.

To introduce a story to a youngster, take a few minutes first to look at the story pictures. Explain who each character is, the setting if important to the story, and any other important information provided by the pictures. Encourage the child to ask questions and to talk about the picture content as it relates to his own experiences. (See Activity 96 for an example.) With such an introduction, the child should be able to follow and comprehend the simple story sequence which you then present immediately. But keep the introductory part of your activity brief, or you may use up the youngster's attention span before you ever begin the story.

The story can be told in your own words or it can be read from the book. In the former instance, be sure you are thoroughly familiar with the story and tell it in a conversational tone. If you read the story, read slowly to give the child the time he needs to assimilate the meaning of the words and to translate the pictures he sees into the words he hears.

In both techniques, use words that the child will understand. Often, unfamiliar words can be replaced by familiar words without damage to the story. But if you must use a word which is new to the child, always explain its meaning in words with which he is familiar. (Activity 96 provides an example when the adult explains that the word *crown* means *head*.) If the new word is a name of an unfamiliar object or action, it may be important to introduce the concept and the concept-word to the child prior to the reading activity. (In preparation for Activity 98, for example, a visit to a pet store to see fish and watch them swim will greatly enhance the youngster's understanding of what is happening in the story *The Runaway Bunny* when the baby bunny threatens to become a fish and swim away.) Taking time, in the introduction to the story activity or at some appropriate point in the reading of the story, to look at a picture of a new object and to explain its use is another way to give some meaning to a new word. (Activity 98 uses this technique to introduce the child to the concept *fishing rod*.)

Another good rule of thumb in telling or reading a story is to let your own enthusiasm for the story come through. Use enough inflection, gestures, and sound effects to keep the story interesting and enjoyable for yourself and the youngster. But don't overdo it to the point that what you do distracts from the story.

As the story progresses, view the pictures in proper sequence with the child. Pointing to the pictures as you read or talk is often all the child will need. But if you sense that the child needs more help, pause for a moment to point out a picture clue the youngster may have missed and to say, for example, in the "Jack and Jill" story rhyme, "See, Jack hit his head when he fell down. That's what *crown* means: *head*. 'Jack fell down and broke his crown. . . .' "

After the story, talk about the characters, the event, and any tie-ins the story may have with the youngster's own experiences. Take your leads from the child so that his interests and ideas play a dominant role in the follow-up.

Read and reread a variety of stories to the child, but avoid stories and pictures which may be frightening to him. Remember that the young child has difficulty distinguishing between what is real and what is unreal. Books about witches and wolves and other disturbing elements are best left until the child is older when he can distinguish between reality and fantasy.

Let the child choose books for himself, perhaps from two or three books on hand. Reread stories, especially the child's favorites, until he can "read" them to others and can do such things as act out a story or use puppets to tell the story or a flannel board to illustrate it. Above all, have many appropriate books around: picture books, sensory books, books of nursery rhymes, story books with pictures, records with picture books, and home-made books that can often be personalized for a child. (See Activity 90 for information on making a book.) And use books often. In every way you can think of, help the child grow in his love for them.

The public library is not only an excellent source of books but also often a source of special story hours conducted by professionals. Books taken from the public and school libraries should be used by the child at first only under supervision, but later, when he learns to treat them carefully, let him use the books on his own. Another good practice is to remove the cards from the back pockets so that they will not be lost.

The book activities in this text suggest a variety of ways to interest preschoolers in books. They follow the three phases described above to introduce the very young child to books and to help him grow in love and understanding of them. In using these activities and in planning your own book activities for a particular child, remember these points:

1. *Always present books to the preschooler as something special.* Make enjoyment of books your primary goal in all your book activities.

2. *Select books that are appropriate for the young child.* Pictures, the most important element, should be large, clear, and colorful. They should present concepts realistically and accurately. Picture and story content should be understandable by the child in that he can relate it to his own experiences. The selected list of titles of children's books which follows on pages 234–236 may be helpful in applying this guideline.

3. *Present books when the child is relaxed and able to pay attention.* If necessary, create a mood for reading through introductory quiet conversation and other transitional activities which are calming and conducive to attending to books.

4. *Prepare a physical setting that also promotes interest in and attending to books.* Have the child sit close to you. Be sure he has a comfortable view of the book and its pictures. If you are working with a small group of children, limit the reading group to two or three children so that closeness and comfortable viewing are provided each child.

5. *Keep your book activities short,* especially until the youngster is "hooked" on books. A few minutes of enjoyment with books each day is more apt to result in a love of books than are longer, tiring sessions.

6. *Work always to keep the child's interest in the book activity.* It is important to read slowly and clearly, substituting known words for unknown words or explaining new things to the child, using inflections and gestures to provide variety without distracting from the story, having the child follow the story through pictures, and encouraging his direct participation whenever possible.

7. *Involve the child in the activity.* Let him turn the pages. Let him ask questions and talk about the picture or the story. Ask questions to encourage participation and to check understanding of the picture or the story content. Plan follow-up activities which call for increased participation by the child as soon as he becomes familiar with the story.

SELECTED CHILDREN'S BOOKS

Listed below are titles of children's books, many of which relate to learning experiences suggested by the activities. They have been grouped according to the manual's three developmental levels—A, B, and C. Titles preceded by an asterisk have been found to be particularly useful with small children.

The list is by no means exclusive. Many additional, often inexpensive, books on the market can also be used successfully with the toddler. In fact, children's books which have been written and designed for somewhat older children are frequently excellent sources of clear, uncluttered pictures and simple stories that will interest the young child if related to his special world and experiences.

Level A

Baby's First A B C: Words to Say (Platt & Munk)—also useful at Level C to teach the alphabet
Baby's First Book (Platt & Munk)
Baby's First Mother Goose (Platt & Munk)
Baby's First Toys (Platt & Munk)
Baby's Things (Platt & Munk)
Kittens (Platt & Munk)
Little Bunny Follows His Nose, by Katherine Howard (Golden Press)—sensory book
Pat the Bunny, by Doroty Kunhardt (Golden Press)—sensory book
Puppies (Platt & Munk)
Things to See (Platt & Munk)
Touch-Me Book, by Eve and Pat Witte (Golden Press)—sensory book

Level B

All by Himself, by Kay Clark (Plakie Products)
The Apple, by Dick Bruna (Bruna Books)
Baby Farm Animals, by Garth Williams (Golden Press)
Best Book Ever, by Richard Scarry (Golden Press)

The Boy with a Drum, by David L. Harrison (Golden Press)—introduction
   to rhythm
Colors Are Nice, by Adelaide Holl (Golden Press)
The Fish, by Dick Bruna (Bruna Books)
From 1 to 10 and Back Again, by Ken Wagner (Golden Press)—a counting
   book
Golden Shape Books (Golden Press)—entire series, each shaped to book's
   subject
The Horse Book, by Virginia Parsons (Golden Press)
I Am a Bunny, by Richard Scarry (Golden Press)
Is This the House of Mistress Mouse, by Richard Scarry (Golden Press)—
   sensory book.
Goodnight Moon, by Margaret Wise (Harper and Bros.)
The Me Book (Golden Press)—parts of the body
Mother Goose in the City (Golden Press)—in a modern setting
My Big Golden Counting Book, by Lilian Moore (Golden Press)
Papa Small, by Lois Lenski (Henry Z. Walck)
Rainbow Rhymes, by Virginia Parsons (Golden Press)—colors
Shopping Book, by Jan Sukus (Golden Press)
Teddy's Book of 1-2-3, by Betty Ren Wright (Golden Press)—counting
   book
10 Little Animals, by Carl Memling (Golden Press)—counting book
Truck and Bus Book, by William Dugan (Golden Press)

Level C

A Fly Went By, by Mike McClintock (Random House)
Are You My Mother? by Philip D. Eastman (Random House)
Bears' Picnic, by Stanley and Janice Berenstain (Random House)
Big Beds and Little Beds (Wonder Books)
The Big Golden Animal A B C, by Garth Williams (Golden Press)
The Bike Lesson, by Stanley and Janice Berenstain (Random House)
The Carrot Seed, by Ruth Krauss (Harper & Row)—book and record
Cat in the Hat, by Dr. Seuss (Random House)
Dr. Seuss's A B C, by Dr. Seuss (Random House)
Fast and Slow, by John Ciardi (Platt & Munk)
The Fire House Book, by Colin Bailey (Golden Press)
Four Puppies, by Anne Heathers (Golden Press)—four seasons
Giant Nursery Book of Things That Go, by George Zaffo (Doubleday)
Giant Nursery Book of Things That Work, by George Zaffo (Doubleday)
Golden A B C Book (Golden Press)
Hop on Pop, by Dr. Seuss (Random House)
Katie and the Big Snow, by Virginia Burton (Houghton Mifflin)

The Noisy Baby Animals (Winston)—pictures and record of "Old Mac-
   Donald Had a Farm" with sound effects
One Fish, Two Fish, Red Fish, Blue Fish, by Dr. Seuss (Random House)
Put Me in the Zoo, by Robert Lopshire (Random House)
*The Runaway Bunny, by Margaret Wise Brown (Harper & Row)
Saturday Walk, by Ethel Wright (William R. Scott)
The Snowy Day, by Ezra Keats (Viking)
*The Very Little Boy, by Phyllis Krasilovsky (Doubleday)
*The Very Little Girl, by Phyllis Krasilovsky (Doubleday)
What Am I? by Ruth Leon (Golden Press)—picture quiz book
Whistle for Willie, by Ezra Jack Keats (Viking)
The Zoo Book, by Jan Pfloog (Golden Press)

ACTIVITY 90:   Naming Pictured Objects

WHY

To name the animal pictured.
To turn single page.

WHAT YOU NEED

Picture book of common animals.

TALK ABOUT WHAT YOU DO

(Use your own language. This is an example.)

"Look at the nice picture book I have. It's all about animals. Sit right here beside me and we'll see if we can find some animals you know."

(Open book to a picture of an animal the child has seen.) "Oh, what is that? / Yes, it is a dog. Did you ever play with a dog? / What did the dog say? / He said 'Arf! Arf!' Can you say 'Arf! Arf!' like a dog? / Oh, you sounded just like a little dog."

"What is this? (Point to tail in picture.) / It is the dog's tail. Can you find the dog's eyes? / Very good! The dog has two eyes, just like we have. One eye / two eyes. / Where is the dog's nose?" (Continue pointing out and talking about other features of the dog which are clearly shown in the picture.)

"Would you like to pet the dog in the picture? / It doesn't feel like a real dog, does it? / Remember how soft the dog feels when you pet it?"

"Do you want to see what is on the next page of the book? / We have to turn the page. You help me turn the page. Put your finger under the page here. (Lift page slightly for child.) That's right. Now turn it over carefully. / Oh my, look what's on this page!"

(If child is interested, look at and talk about another animal.)

HELPFUL HINTS

Before you introduce a picture book, try to give the child experiences with the real things pictured in the book.

At first the youngster will not be able to turn single pages of the book by himself. Continue providing practice in turning pages each time you present a book, always helping if necessary so the child will turn the page successfully.

The child's attention span may permit you to present only one picture in the activity. Or you may even have to reduce time spent on the one picture. Do not extend the activity beyond the child's interest and enjoyment.

THINGS TO DO ANOTHER TIME

Present other books which picture objects with which the child is already familiar. Talk about and point out the most important characteristics of the object and its uses. Help the child relate the picture to his own experiences with the object.

Make a book by pasting appropriate pictures of common animals, objects, and foods on heavy cardboard or cloth. You can starch the cloth to stiffen the pages for easier turning. Punch or cut holes in one side of the pages and insert loops of heavy twine or loose-leaf rings (available at stationery counters in drug or dime stores). Magazines, newspapers, and catalogs are sources of simple, single-object pictures, but you can also use pictures in coloring books to which color may be added with crayons or paint.

ACTIVITY 91:   A Sensory Book

BOOKS
A

WHY

To use more than one of the senses
 to enjoy books.

WHAT YOU NEED

A sensory picture book.

TALK ABOUT WHAT YOU DO

(Use your own language. This is an example.)

"I have a picture book we can look at today. It is a very special book because we can feel and smell some of the pictures as well as look at them. Sit right here beside me on the rug so we can use the book together."

"Look at that! What is it? / Teddy, that's right. It is a picture of a teddy bear. It looks just like your teddy bear, doesn't it? / See its ears? / Where is its nose? / Right. Feel the teddy bear's fur. / Does it feel like your teddy bear? / It does feel smooth and sort of soft like a teddy bear."

"Let's turn the page. You help me. (Lift the page slightly for the child if help is needed.) Say, you're getting good at turning pages."

"What's on this page? / It is a flower, a pretty red flower. I wonder if the picture flower smells like a real flower. Smell the flower and tell me how it smells. / Bring the book close to your nose and then smell. / Did the flower smell nice and sweet?"

"Wasn't that a good book? / What did you see in the book? / What felt nice and soft in the book? / What did you smell?"

HELPFUL HINTS

If you do not have a sensory book, make several pages of one. See directions below under "Things To Do Another Time."

If you have available the real objects pictured in the book, you may wish to incorporate them in the activity. You might, for example, have the child feel a teddy bear and then the pictured teddy bear and smell a real flower and then the pictured flower to help the child become aware of the relationship between real objects and their pictures.

Continue having the child practice turning a single page of the book to master the skill.

THINGS TO DO ANOTHER TIME

Repeat the activity for other pictures in the sensory book or for pictures in other sensory books. Add the real objects if available to help the child learn the relationship between pictures and reality.

Make a sensory page or two in a homemade book (see Activity 90) or in a scrapbook. Add, for example, a fluffy bit of cotton for a bunny's tail by glueing the cotton to a picture or outline of a bunny. Or cut a simple outline of a flower from colored felt, paste it on a page, and add a sprinkle of perfume.

ACTIVITY 92:   Comparing Real and Picture Objects

BOOKS
A

WHY

To be aware of the relationship between real objects and picture objects.

WHAT YOU NEED

Picture book with large, realistic picture of a familiar object (apple) and a sample of the real object.

TALK ABOUT WHAT YOU DO

(Use your own language. This is an example.)

"Sit right here beside me and look at what I have. What is this? / Right. And what is this? (Hold up apple.) / Yes, it's a real apple. Can you eat an apple? / You bet you can. Apples taste good, don't they?"

"See if you can find a picture of an apple in the book. / Remember, turn the pages carefully so they won't tear. The book is made of paper and paper tears. / What have you found? / Yes, you found the apple. Does it look like our real apple? (Hold up real apple.) See, the real apple is round (make circular motion around apple) and so is the apple in the picture (circle pictured apple). What color are the apples? / Red. They are both red. Very good!"

"Let's see if the apples feel alike. (Have the child feel the apple in the book and then handle the real apple.) They feel differently, don't they? / Can we eat both apples? / Which one would you rather eat? / Okay, let's eat this apple. I'll cut it up so we can each have a piece."

"Did you like the apple? / Would you like to eat the picture apple now? / No, neither would I. It's only paper and paper doesn't taste very good. Real apples are for eating, but apples in books are just for looking at."

HELPFUL HINTS

If you do not have a book with a picture of an apple, substitute another object (picture and real object) or use a magazine picture of an apple pasted in a homemade book (see "Things To Do Another Time").

Try to match the general shape and color of the real apple with the pictured apple.

Introduce and talk about the real object first so that you are sure the child has formed the concept before introducing the task of finding the picture.

THINGS TO DO ANOTHER TIME

Repeat the activity for other objects such as a key, a cup or glass, or any object already familiar to the child. Each time, talk about the object and its use. Let the child use the object if he has learned how, and then contrast it with the picture which can only be looked at.

Find pictures of familiar objects in magazines or catalogs and paste them in a homemade book (see Activity 90) or a scrapbook. Ask the child to identify an object pictured and then to find a sample of the object in the room (set up the room so that the object can be found easily). Have the youngster show or tell you how the object is used. Then ask him to use the pictured object the same way. Most youngsters will find the last question very amusing.

ACTIVITY 93:   Personalizing Pictures

BOOKS
B

WHY

To identify pictures of people as family members and friends.
To be aware of some detail in pictures.

WHAT YOU NEED

Picture of a group of people, among them small boys and girls.

TALK ABOUT WHAT YOU DO

(Use your own language. This is an example.)

"We have something very special to look at in this book today. Here it is on this page. Just look at that picture! / Who are those people? / It's a family just like your family: a mommy and a daddy and a little boy and a big sister." (Point to each pictured person as you talk.)

"Can you point to Mommy? / That's right. She has on a pretty pink dress, doesn't she? (Point to dress.) Where is Daddy? / Yes, see his blue shirt. (Point.) Which one could be you? / Yes, sir, there's Timmy. What do you have in your hand? / I think it's a toy car. Look real close. Do you see the car? / And who do you suppose this is? (Point to girl in picture.) Of course, that could be Karen, your big sister. What is Karen playing with? / Oh, that's very good. Karen has a ball.''

"Tell me all about the people in the picture. I'd like to hear about each one again.''

HELPFUL HINTS

If you are unable to locate a picture of a family group in a book, find one in a magazine or newspaper and paste it in a homemade book (see Activity 90) or in a scrapbook.

The picture need correspond to a child's immediate family only in a general way. If extra people are in the picture, identify them as other relatives or friends with whom the child is acquainted.

This activity works best with a single child. Try to find out a little about the size and members of the child's family and plan the activity for the individual child.

THINGS TO DO ANOTHER TIME

Adapt the activity to pictures of people the child can identify with as aunts, uncles, grandparents, or friends. Begin making up very brief stories about the pictures. An example of a story, using a picture of a family birthday party, might be: "Look, it's a picture of Timmy's birthday party. See the pretty birthday cake (point) with candles on it? Granddad and Grandmom (point to each in picture) came to the party. Everyone sang 'Happy Birthday to Timmy.' Then Timmy blew out the candles and everyone ate a piece of the birthday cake.''

Make a small album or a page in your homemade book (see Activity 90) of snapshots of the child's family and friends. Let the child identify each person. Help him recall where and when the pictures were taken and any other events related to the picture-taking.

ACTIVITY 94:   Identifying Multiple Pictured Objects

BOOKS
B

WHY

To identify multiple objects in a picture.

WHAT YOU NEED

Book entitled *Goodnight Moon* or a picture of a room (see "Helpful Hints").

TALK ABOUT WHAT YOU DO

(Use your own language. This is an example.)

"Oh, look at this book. It's called *Goodnight Moon.* It's all about a beautiful room. See, here is a picture of the room. What are some of the things you can see in the room?" (Let the child point out and identify the things he recognizes.)

"Let's play a game. I'll read the book to you and you point to each thing I read about. Okay?" (Read slowly.)

In the great green room
There was a telephone

(Pause to give the child time to locate the telephone. You may have to remind him of what he is to do and help him find the object in the picture.) Can you find the telephone? / Keep looking. It's there. / Look over on this side. (Point.) Oh, you found it! Very good!" (Continue reading.)

And a red balloon

(Pause for child to locate the balloon.)

And a picture of—

"Oh, we have to turn the page. Help me turn the page."

And a picture of
A cow jumping over the moon.

"Do you see the cow? (Point if necessary.) Where is the moon? / Isn't that a silly cow jumping over the moon?"

(Continue reading and helping the child identify objects as they are mentioned in the script.)

"My, that was a good book. We had lots of fun, didn't we? / We'll have to read that book and play that game again, won't we?"

HELPFUL HINTS

Goodnight Moon (by Margaret Wise Brown. New York: Harper and Bros., 1947) is a delightful book in verse that lends itself to the task of identifying multiple objects in a picture of a child's room. After the first picture of the entire room, it takes the child through a series of pictures of the individual objects. In a second reading of it, the child will probably be able to identify most of the objects in the room.

If you cannot locate the book, substitute a picture of a room from a magazine or book. Adapt the activity by making up a simple "script" that calls attention to particular familiar objects in the picture: "I see a green chair in the room. Can you find the green chair? / Oh, there is a pretty yellow rug on the floor. Where is the yellow rug?"

THINGS TO DO ANOTHER TIME

Adapt the activity to other pictures of multiple objects that will interest the youngster.

Some ideas for pages in a homemade book (see Activity 90) which lend themselves to adaptations of this activity are:

A picture of a boy or girl surrounded by pictures of familiar toys.
A picture of a kitchen surrounded by pictures of familiar kitchen equipment, dishes, and foods.
A picture of a park-like area with pictures of things the child associates with a park: tree, swings, slide, sandbox, picnic table.

ACTIVITY 95: Interpreting Action Pictures

BOOKS
B

WHY

To identify key persons or objects in action pictures.
To tell what is happening in simple action pictures.

WHAT YOU NEED

A picture book showing people or animals in action (mother and children cleaning house).

TALK ABOUT WHAT YOU DO

(Use your own language. This is an example.)

"It's story time. Let's look at this new book. I like to look at books, don't you? / Look at this picture. What do you see? / Yes, that's a boy. His name is Paul. Who else is in the picture? / That's a girl named Polly. / Yes, that's the mother."

"What is this (point) that Paul has? / It is a vacuum cleaner. It looks just like our vacuum cleaner, doesn't it? / What is Paul doing with the vacuum cleaner? / Right. He is cleaning the rug."

"What does the mother have? (Point.) What is she doing with the broom? / Yes. She is sweeping. See all the things she has swept up?" (Point.)

"What do you think Polly is doing? (Point.) She has a dustpan. See it there? (Point.) I think she is going to help her mother put all the trash she swept up in the dustpan. Do you think that is what she is doing?"

"Let's do what Paul and Polly are doing in the picture. We'll clean up the room. We'll sweep and vacuum and we'll use the dustpan to pick up all the trash." (Follow up the activity with a few minutes of dramatic play, using toy or real props.)

HELPFUL HINTS

This activity is based on a picture in *Papa Small* (by Lois Lenski. New York: Henry Z. Walck, Inc., 1951), which includes a series of illustrations of various family members doing such things as setting the table, eating dinner, going to a super market, cutting the grass. But any uncluttered picture of people and animals engaged in familiar actions is suitable for this activity.

Start the activity by giving the child time to study the picture and name people and objects he sees. Then ask questions to help the child identify any person or object directly involved in the action which the child has overlooked. Only after these identification tasks are completed should you ask the key question, what is happening in the picture? or what is an individual in the picture doing?

If the youngster cannot answer the key question, tell what is happening and point out an important clue or two to what is happening ("See the dustpan Polly has?"). Come back to the same picture in a day or two and ask "What is happening?" again.

THINGS TO DO ANOTHER TIME

Repeat the activity with a variety of pictures showing people and animals doing things the child is familiar with. Your goal is to help the child learn how to interpret a simple picture and tell you what is happening in the picture.

Begin making up and telling the child brief stories about the pictures as follow-ups to the activity above, stories that may help to spark the child's imagination. For example, using a picture of a little boy who is helping set the table, you might add: "I know a story about a little boy who helps his teacher set the table. His name is David. David had a favorite green cup. See it there on the table. (Point.) He always put the green cup at his place at the table so he could drink his milk from the pretty green cup. One day his mother came to visit the school. She liked the green cup, too, and told David how pretty it was. And do you know what David did because he loved his mother? / Well, when he set the table, he put the green cup at his mother's place so she could drink her tea from it. Wasn't that a nice thing for David to do?''

ACTIVITY 96: Nursery Rhymes

WHY

To follow the story in pictures.
To remember the story sequence.

WHAT YOU NEED

Book of nursery rhymes with several pictures illustrating a rhyme (Jack and Jill).

TALK ABOUT WHAT YOU DO

(Use your own language. This is an example.)

''You know what I have? / It's a nursery rhyme all about a boy named Jack and a girl named Jill. I'll read it to you. But first, let's look at these pictures of Jack and Jill.''

''See, there's Jack (point) and here's Jill (point). What are Jack and Jill carrying? (Point to pail.) It's a pail. Remember the pails we play with in the sandbox? / Oh, look at this big hill (point). The hill goes way up high, into the sky. / Do you know what this is at the top of the hill? (Point to well.) It is a well. A well has water in it. You can get water in a pail from a well.''

(Point to the next picture.) "Here are Jack and Jill again. Oh my! What is happening to Jack and Jill? / Yes, they fell down. Look at the pail. / The water in the pail is all spilled, isn't it?"

(Point to the next picture.) "Who is this in this picture? / Right. It's Jack. Where is he? / Yes, Jack is in bed. See, his head (point) is all bandaged. He must have hurt his crown. Crown is another word for head. Poor Jack hurt his head."

"Let's read what happened to Jack and Jill. You listen and watch the pictures so you can tell me what is happening in each picture." (Read rhyme slowly.)

"Poor Jack. Poor Jill. Can you tell me the story about Jack and Jill? / Yes, they fell down. But what did they do first? What is happening in this first picture? / Then what happened?"

(Point to the pictures and ask questions as needed to help the child recall the sequence of the story.)

"Let's look at some more pictures in the book. I'll read you another nursery rhyme if you find some pictures you would like to hear a story about."

HELPFUL HINTS

This activity can be adapted to any simple story or story verse which has several pictures illustrating the story sequence.

Focus the child's attention on the pictures throughout the activity so that he becomes aware of the relationship of the pictures to the story sequence.

Read the rhyme slowly so that the youngster can absorb the words and make sense out of them. Answer questions the child may ask, but don't overdo the explanation of the story to a point that it becomes tedious. Let the pictures explain the story whenever possible.

THINGS TO DO ANOTHER TIME

Adapt the activity to present many nursery rhymes and children's verses to the child.

When the child is familiar with the rhyme, recite the rhyme but omit key words for the child to fill in. For example, omit the last word of each line or omit the rhyming words (Jill/hill; down/crown).

Encourage the youngster to "read" the nursery rhyme to you, either from memory or by telling you the story with the use of the pictures to help recall the story sequence.

ACTIVITY 97:   Informational Books

BOOKS
C

WHY

To prepare for a trip by naming people and objects seen in pictures relating to the trip.

WHAT YOU NEED

Book with pictures showing a bus, bus driver, people getting on and off a bus, and so forth.

TALK ABOUT WHAT YOU DO

(Use your own language. This is an example.)

"Do you know what we are going to do tomorrow? / We are going to take a ride on the bus. I have a book all about a bus. Sit here and we'll look at it together."

(Point to picture of a bus.) "What is that? / Yes. It is a big bus like the one we will ride on. See the door. (Point.) That's where the people get on the bus. They walk right up those steps. I'll help you up the steps when we get on the bus."

(Point to picture of the bus driver.) "Do you know who this is? / Yes, it's a man. He drives the bus. He stops the bus to let people get on. Then he drives the bus to where the people want to get off the bus. You'll see the driver of our bus tomorrow. But it may be a lady bus driver. Women as well as men can drive a bus.''

(If additional appropriate pictures are available, present them also, talking about and relating each to what the child will experience the next day.)

''Oh, we are going to have fun on our bus ride tomorrow. Can you show me where we will get on the bus? / What are some other things we will do when we ride the bus? / What do you think we'll see on our bus trip?''

HELPFUL HINTS

If you cannot locate a book about buses, find pictures in a magazine or newspaper. Paste the pictures in a homemade book (see Activity 90) to use in this activity.

In preparing the youngster for the trip, be careful to avoid creating any apprehension or fears in the child. Stress the fun you will have.

THINGS TO DO ANOTHER TIME

Adapt the activity to prepare the child for other experiences: present and talk about pictures of animals before a visit to a farm or zoo or other places which house animals; pictures of a fire truck and fire fighters before a visit to a firehouse; pictures of fish before a visit to a tropical fish store, pictures of various kinds of food to be explored in a grocery store.

ACTIVITY 98:   Reading a Story

WHY

To tell what happened in the story.
To become aware of the protective
nature of the family.

WHAT YOU NEED

The Runaway Bunny (by Margaret
Wise Brown. New York: Harper
& Row, 1942) or a simple illustrated story about family love
and protection.

TALK ABOUT WHAT YOU DO

(Use your own language. This is an example.)

"Come and sit here beside me so I can read you a story. / Good. Now we
can look at the pictures together and you can help me turn the pages."

"Have you ever seen a bunny? / Well, this story is all about a baby
bunny and his mother. (Open the book to first page of story.) Can you find
the little baby bunny in the picture? / Where is the mother bunny? / Let's find
out what happened to them."

(Read first page.)
"See (point), there goes the little baby bunny hopping away. Is the
mother bunny running after her baby? / Oh, let's find out what happens
next. Turn the page."

(Read second page.)
"Look, there's the same baby bunny. (Point.) Where's the fish that lives
in the water? / Would you like to become a fish and swim in the water?
/ Let's see what the mother bunny will do if her baby becomes a fish. Turn
the page for me, please."

(Read third page.)

"Where is the mother bunny? / What is this? (Point to fishing rod.) That's a fishing rod. When you want to catch a fish, you put something a fish likes to eat at the end of this line (point). You put the line in the water and when the fish nibbles on it, you pull in the line. And you have a nice fish. / Are you ready to turn the page now so we can find out what the mother bunny does?"

"Oh, look at this big picture! What's the mother bunny doing now? / Right. She's fishing for her baby bunny. Can you find the baby bunny? / He's swimming in the water just like a little fish, isn't he? / What do you suppose the mother bunny has on the end of her fishing line? (Point.) By golly, it is a carrot. Bunnies like to eat carrots. That's why the mother bunny is using a carrot to catch the baby bunny. Would you nibble on a carrot? / You would make a good baby bunny then. Are you ready to turn the page?"

(Continue reading the story and looking at the pictures. Continue also having the child point out the story characters and tell what is happening in each picture. Identify and explain briefly any pictured objects with which the child is not familiar and which are important to understanding the story and the pictures.)

"Wasn't that a good story? / What did the baby bunny want to do? / Did the mother bunny let the baby bunny run away? / That's the way most mothers and fathers are. They love their babies and want to look after them."

HELPFUL HINTS

This activity is a model for reading any simple story the first time to a young child. Note the techniques used: (1) involve the youngster by having him turn pages and answer questions about the pictures; (2) use questions to determine if the youngster understands the pictures and the story; (3) identify objects and explaining concepts (words) with which the child is not familiar and which are important for understanding the picture or story; (4) encourage the child to talk about his own experiences and feelings as they relate to the story; and (5) build up the child's interest in finding out what happens next in the story.

To prepare yourself for the activity, read the story at least once so that you are familiar with what comes next and can anticipate any difficulties the child may have. Decide in advance on any adaptations needed for the youngster's understanding of the story: words to be substituted for those with which the child is not familiar, concepts to be experienced by the child prior to the reading (seeing a real fish swim, for example), or words to be explained as they appear in the story (such as fishing rod). But remain alert also during the reading to the need for additional adaptations you did not foresee; and, of course, answer any questions the child may ask.

Read slowly to give the child time to assimilate the words and to translate the pictures into meaningful and correct concepts. Read with sufficient in- flection and add gestures and sound effects when appropriate to convey your own enthusiasm for the story without overdoing it and distracting from the story.

Do not let your explanations of story content and pictures become so complicated they interfere with the forward movement of the story, because the child may lose interest. But do give the child all the time he wants to look at and talk about each picture and the story events, and relate them to his own experiences and feelings.

Do not expect the child to retell the entire sequence of the story on its first reading. The objective is rather that he grasps the main idea of the story and enjoys the reading experience. Note, too, that another specific objective in reading *The Runaway Bunny* is to give the youngster a feeling of security in his relationship with his own mother and father or with a mother or father figure.

THINGS TO DO ANOTHER TIME

Reread the story to the child. After several readings the child will proba- bly be able to retell the story in his own words, using the pictures to guide him through the sequence of events. In such follow-up activities, ask ques- tions to help the child recall what is happening in each picture and to relate the story to his own experiences and feelings.

When the youngster is familiar with the story, encourage him to act out parts of the story as you reread it. In *The Runaway Bunny,* for example, he might pretend to swim like a fish or to be a mother bunny fishing, to fly like a bird or to be a big wind blowing the bunny–sailboat.

Some simple stories will lend themselves to using a flannel board to illus- trate the story when it is reread or is retold by you or by the child. (See Activity 56 for directions for making a flannel board.) Story characters and objects are cut out of felt, or pictures can be used by attaching strips of sandpaper or masking tape to the back of the pictures so that they will adhere to the flannel board. As a character or object appears in the story, the child places the proper figure on the flannel board. This technique also develops listening skills. The child must listen carefully to know when the characters and objects appear in the story.

ACTIVITY 99: Listening to Stories on Records

BOOKS
C

WHY

To listen attentively to a story on a record.
To follow story sequence in illustrated book.

WHAT YOU NEED

Record and book *The Carrot Seed* (by Ruth Krauss. New York: Harper & Row, 1945) or any simple story in record and book form; record player.

TALK ABOUT WHAT YOU DO

(Use your own language. This is an example.)

"We are going to listen to a story that is on this record. (Point to or hold up record.) We'll play the record while we look at the pictures in this book. (Point or hold up.) The name of the story is the *The Carrot Seed*. Do you remember the seeds we planted? / What did we do with the seeds? / Yes, we put the seeds in the ground and watered them. That's what you have to do with a carrot seed to make it grow. Let's find out what happened to the carrot seed in the story."

"Can you find the first picture in the book? / Good. That's the little boy (point) who plants the little carrot seed. (Point to seed.) I'll put the record on now. We'll find out what happened to the little boy and his carrot seed. Are you ready to listen? / Okay, we have to be quiet and listen now.''

(Sit next to the child as you listen to the story. As persons and objects are mentioned in the story, silently point out those you think the child may be overlooking or not recognizing. Help the child turn the pages if he runs into difficulty keeping up with the record.)

"Say, that was a good story, wasn't it? / Can you tell me what happened in the story? / Let's go back and look at the pictures again. You can tell me about all the things you see and what the little boy is doing.''

HELPFUL HINTS

Prepare yourself for the activity by listening to the record while following the story in the picture book. If there are any objects or words (concepts) in the story which are likely to be difficult, introduce the child to these concepts prior to the activity. For instance, in order to follow the carrot seed story, the youngster should be acquainted with the objects carrot, seed, and weed, with the process of planting a seed, and watering it to make it grow.

In looking at the pictures a second time (after listening to the story), check on the youngster's understanding of the story. Have him identify key objects in each picture and encourage him to talk about each picture. Provide information on objects missed and ask leading questions when necessary to help the youngster interpret a picture correctly.

THINGS TO DO ANOTHER TIME

Replay the story record. Have the child point to people and objects in the pictures as they are mentioned in the story.

When the story and pictures are familiar to the child, have him use only the picture book to tell you the story.

Act out the story using a few simple props: a seed, a watering can (without water), a leafy twig, and a carrot. You be the stage manager, furnishing props when needed. If several children participate, let each child have a turn at being the little boy.

See Activity 156. This activity planting a seed and growing a plant is not only a good preparation activity but also a good follow-up for *The Carrot Seed* activity.

Adapt the activity and suggested follow-up activities to other stories in record and book form.

ACTIVITY 100:   A B C Books: 1

BOOKS
C

WHY

To point to the identifying characteristics of the letter *A*.

WHAT YOU NEED

A B C picture book; paper; pencil.

TALK ABOUT WHAT YOU DO

(Use your own language. This is an example.)

"Let's look at the A B C book. See, it says right here (point to each letter as you continue) *A / B / C. / A* and *B* and *C* are letters of the alphabet.
We use letters to make words, like *apple* and *animal* and the magic word
abracadabra. We are going to learn all about the letter *A* today.

"What's this? (Point to picture of apple.) Right. It's an apple. And this
(point to large capital *A*) is a letter. It's name is *A*. Can you say *A*? / Good."

"Let's trace this big letter *A*. Give me your finger (index finger) and I'll
help you. (Trace each leg from the bottom up to the point at the top. Talk as
you trace.) The letter *A* has two legs. Leg number one comes up on this
side and leg number two comes up on this other side. They make a point at

the top. (Touch.) Then there is this little line (trace) that goes from one leg to the other leg.''

"Look at all these letters. (Point to sentence *"A* IS FOR APPLE" or similar sentence in your book.) Can you find a letter *A?* / Remember, *A* stands on two legs. It has a point on the top and a little line in the middle between the legs. / Here is an *A*. (Use a pencil to point to letter and then to each of its distinguishing characteristics as you talk about them.) See the two legs? One / two. / There is the point at the top / and there is the line in the middle. / See if you can find another *A* in all those letters. / Very good! You found an *A!''*

"I am going to make a letter on this paper. Watch. (Talk as you make the letter *A*.) One leg goes up on this side. Another leg goes up on this side so there is a point at the top. And a little line goes from this leg to the other leg, like that.

"What letter did I make? / Can you show me the two legs? / Where is the point at the top? / Where is the little line in the middle / That's very good. The letter *A* is your friend now. You know all about the letter *A*.''

HELPFUL HINTS

Before you use an A B C book for this activity, let the child become familiar with the objects pictured in it. If he has already learned to identify the objects pictured, it will be easier for you to focus his attention on the letters of the alphabet.

Do not expect too much from the child in these first alphabet activities. When you ask the child to locate the letter *A* in the sentence, "A is for apple," do not be upset if he cannot do so. Simply locate the letter for him and go over the characteristics of *A* again. Your objective in this activity is to acquaint the youngster with the characteristics; locating and naming the letter is the child's task in the next activity.

Avoid actually saying, "*A* is for apple," or similar sentences. The child should not be given the impression that *A* stands for apple or any other single object since it is is used in many words.

THINGS TO DO ANOTHER TIME

Repeat the activity for each letter of the alphabet. The following characteristics of each letter may be helpful, or you may find your own better way to describe each letter:

B: one leg with two bumps on the side
C: a rounded line with a hole
D: one leg with one big bump on the side
E: one leg with a line at the top, one at the bottom, and a little line in the middle
F: one leg with a line at the top and a little line in the middle
G: a rounded line with a hole and a little line at the bottom of the rounded line
H: two legs straight up (no point) with a line in the middle
I: one leg
J: one leg with a hook at the bottom
K: one leg with two leaning lines on the side
L: one leg with a line at the bottom
M: two legs with two small lines at the top that make a point in the middle; point is down
N: two legs with a leaning line in between the legs
O: a rounded line, no hole in the line
P: one leg with a bump at the top
Q: a rounded line, no hole but with a tail at the bottom
R: one big leg with a bump at the top and a small leg at the bottom
S: a crooked line with a round at the top and a round at the bottom
T: one leg with a line across the top
U: two legs with a rounded bottom
V: two legs with a pointed bottom
W: two legs with two small lines at the bottom which make a point in the middle; the point is up
X: two legs that cross
Y: one short leg which becomes two
Z: one leaning leg with a line at top and bottom

ACTIVITY 101:   A B C Books: 2

WHY

To locate the letters *A* and *B*.
To name the letters *A* and *B*.

WHAT YOU NEED

A B C book; 5″ x 8″ cards or paper; crayons.

TALK ABOUT WHAT YOU DO

(Use your own language. This is an example.)

"Let's look at your A B C book again. Can you find the page that has a picture of an apple? / There is a great big letter on this page. Can you point to the big letter for me? / Very good. Do you remember the name of the letter? / Oh, you remembered. Good, good, good!"

"Where are the two legs on the big *A?* / Where is the point at the top? / Can you find the line in the middle that goes from one leg to the other leg? / Very good! You really know your friend, Mr. *A.*"

"Look at all these letters. (Point to the sentence on the page or to a printed word.) See if you can find the letter *A* in these words. / It looks just like the big *A,* only it will be smaller. / Oh, you found another *A!* You are so smart!"

"Turn the page now. / What is this? / Yes, it's a ball. Is there a big letter on this page, too? / Very good. Can you remember the name of the letter? / It's *B.* (Trace the letter as you talk.) The letter *B* has one leg and two bumps on the side: one bump, two bumps. Now you trace the *B* the way I did."

"Look at these words. (Point to sentence on page.) See if you can find a *B* in all those letters. / Keep looking. / That's right. That's a *B*."

"I am going to make some letters on these cards. (Make a large *A* and *B* on separate cards.) Can you tell me their names? / Good. That's an *A*. What is this letter? (Point to *B*.) Right-o! It's Mr. B."

"We'll put both of these letters up on the board because you know their names. Each time you learn the name of a new letter, we'll add the new letter to your alphabet friends."

HELPFUL HINTS

This activity assumes that you have already worked with the child on the characteristics of the letters being taught. But at the beginning of the activity, always review with the child both the letters' names and their characteristics, checking on what he remembers and repeating what he has forgotten. Then move on to the new task of locating the letters.

Reinforce the learning by asking the child at odd moments to identify the posted *A* and *B* letters. This is important to make the learning permanent and to help the child avoid confusion, which may come with the learning of additional letters. Also, expect the child to make mistakes. When he does, supply the correct answer and review the characteristics of the letter with the youngster.

THINGS TO DO ANOTHER TIME

Have the youngster identify capital letters *A* and *B*, in large print, in newspapers and magazine titles. It is important to keep each of the letters fresh in his mind as you continue to teach him new ones.

If the child's name contains the letters *A* or *B*, print the name in all capitals. Tell the child it is his name and ask him to locate these letters in it. Use the child's name when you teach the other letters in it.

Adapt the activity to the other letters of the alphabet, one or two letters at a time. As the child learns to locate and name a new letter, add the letter to those posted on the board.

Include new and old letters in reinforcement activities. For example, have the child distinguish between *A* and *B* as well as the more newly learned *C* and *D* after teaching *C* and *D*. It is a good idea also in reinforcement activities to get away from the A B C book used in the original learning activities. The child may be using the picture clues (*A* is on the "apple page") rather than the characteristics of the letter to identify it.

ACTIVITY 102: Number Books

BOOKS
C

WHY

To recognize numerical symbols 1 and 2.
To count one and two pictured objects.

WHAT YOU NEED

A number book.

TALK ABOUT WHAT YOU DO

(Use your own language. This is an example.)

"Look at this book all about numbers. Can you count to five? / Say, that's good. You counted all the way up to seven."

"Now open the book at the beginning. / See if you can find a picture of just *one* apple. / Yes, there's one apple, one big red apple. Can you point to the apple and say *one apple?* / Good."

(Point to the numeral 1.) "See, this is the number 1. This straight up-and-down line (trace it with finger) is number 1. Can you use your finger to trace the number 1 as I did? / The number 1 looks like my finger (hold index finger up) when I stick it straight up. Can you make a number 1 with your finger? / Oh, that's a dandy number 1."

"See if you can find a picture of *one* car? / Can you find a number 1 too on this page? / Keep looking. Remember that a number 1 looks like one skinny finger. / That's right. That's a number 1."

"Turn the page and see what is next. / Oh, look! / Yes, little dogs. How many little dogs are there? / Let's count the dogs. Count with me. (Point as you count.) One dog / two dogs. There are two dogs on this page. Can you say *two dogs?* / Good."

"Here is the number 2. (Point.) A 2 isn't straight like a number 1, is it? / Give me your finger and we'll trace the 2. (Talk as you guide the child's finger.) The 2 is round at the top and straight and flat at the bottom."

"Can you find two of something else? / Oh, you're so smart. Two balls. Count them for me. / Good. Now can you find the number 2? / Here it is. (Point.) Remember how we traced the 2? / Can you trace the 2 all by yourself? / Start with the round part at the top. / It's flat at the bottom, isn't it?"

"What were some things you saw in the book? / How many apples were there? / How many balls did you see?"

HELPFUL HINTS

If you do not have a number book (or wish additional materials on numbers), make your own number pages in a homemade book (see Activity 90). Make two or more pages with a picture of a single familiar object and the number 1 on each page. Make two or more pages of two identical objects and the number 2 on each page.

Do not expect the youngster to master these number tasks in a single session. You may have to repeat the activity several times.

THINGS TO DO ANOTHER TIME

Use other number books (or homemade number pages) to count one and two objects and to identify the symbols 1 and 2.

When the child has mastered counting one and two objects and the identification of the right number symbols, use number books to work on three objects and the number 3. Describe the number 3 as having two bumps. Most children at the C developmental level will not be able to go beyond the number 3 symbol, but if the child masters 3, you may wish to continue with other number symbols in sequence.

See also the Mathematics section of this text for activities involving counting objects.

Acting out fledgling concepts and feelings helps the child to clarify and verbalize his ideas and feelings. A make-believe telephone call provides such an experience.

Part 6

Dramatic Play and Games

DRAMATIC PLAY AND GAMES

Dramatic play is the acting out of a concept as perceived by the young performer. In dramatic play the child plays a role without written lines and often with few props. He may be the only actor or he may share the stage with others. Being a mommy or a daddy, a barking dog, a flying bird, or a car that chugs is all part of the child's dramatic play.

Play in general is the most important learning tool of young children. Through play they discover new things they can do. They practice and develop new skills. They use play to extend their experiences with objects and people, often working out patterns and solving problems to help them cope with the physical world and the ways of their culture. Through play they express themselves creatively and emotionally.

Dramatic play can stimulate all these kinds of learning. Through an active role in dramatic play, youngsters are able to expand and deepen concepts and make them their own. They express ideas, thus practicing and extending language skills. They are often original and creative in what they say and do. They develop motor skills when making vigorous use of muscles or concentrating on fine muscular coordination in the performance of make-believe tasks. Feelings and frustrations are acted out, providing an outlet for the emotions and giving the actors additional understandings about themselves. Social development, too, is stimulated as children try out a variety of social roles, interact, and cooperate with others in small-group role playing.

Older children tend to use dramatic play naturally. They love to pretend. They play "house" or "cowboy" or "dress-up," sometimes giving attention to elaborate detail which they have seen first-hand or on television. Younger children may also use dramatic play naturally, but for much briefer periods of time and with far less detail. Before the child is two years old, for example, he may, after seeing and hearing a dog, mimic the dog by saying, "Woof! Woof!" Or he may, drawing from his own experiences, hug a doll and say, "Nice baby." After the age of two, the child's dramatic play may begin to combine several ideas. To play "doggie," he may get down on his hands and knees, barking and moving his body like a playful puppy. He may hold a doll and pretend to feed the "baby" his cookie, perhaps saying, "Eat, baby. Eat, nice baby." Or he may decide to put the baby to bed, covering the doll with a blanket because it is time for "baby to take a nap." This process of imitating what has been observed is called modeling.

In these early stages of dramatic play, the child is apt to need fairly realistic props. He experiences the world as it is. Whereas an older, more experienced child might simply use "pretend food" to feed the "baby," the younger child usually needs the real object to spark the imagination. To distinguish between real and pretend may also be difficult for the young child.

Early first experiences with pretend cookies made from Play Dough may include actually trying to eat them.

Even though dramatic play is basically unstructured play in which the child is free to express his own ideas and be creative, it can be encouraged and promoted by planned activities. The activities, however, must be planned and used in such a way that the child does sense, and will use, his freedom to play a role as he sees it. An important part of the planning, then, is to select a theme or simple idea *from the child's past experiences,* and to provide a few fairly realistic props which will help the child enter into the role-playing situation. Ordinary life experience is the best source of ideas for the preschooler's dramatic play: "what Mother (Father) does" in everyday home life.

Essential to the successful use of *planned* dramatic play to bring about *spontaneous* dramatic play are two key factors: (1) The teacher becomes one of the role-players. Thus any suggestions contributed to the pretending come from a fellow actor and are simply suggestions which the youngster is free to follow or reject as he sees fit. (2) The teacher remains flexible. If the child begins to move the pretending in a direction different from that which has been planned, the original plan is put aside in favor of the child's own ideas of what and how to pretend. These two conditions, freedom and flexibility, must be present in all structured dramatic play if spontaneous dramatic play is to result and contribute to the total development of the child.

Games differ from dramatic play in several ways. They are more organized than dramatic play since they involve specific rules which the players must follow. Acting out or pretending is not essential to a game. Games usually are a group activity whereas dramatic play can be carried on by one child. The most important learning value of game playing rests in the socialization of the child: understanding the importance of rules and complying with them, cooperating with others for a common purpose, interacting with and enjoying other people.

Games, as defined here, may be too difficult for the young child. He has trouble remembering and following specific rules and is unprepared for the idea of competition and the give-and-take of group participation in organized games. Dramatic play, on the other hand, can be readily adapted to the child's maturity level to grow in complexity as he becomes able to handle more complex concepts and roles. It serves, too, as a useful forerunner to organized games, introducing the child to some of the social requirements of game playing.

For these reasons, dramatic·play predominates in the sample activities of this section of the book. In the few games which are included, the rules are very simple and the idea of winning has been eliminated. The preschooler can play and enjoy these games with only minimum attention to the rules. Or if he makes up his own rules, which he is apt to do, the games can be

played on his terms. In other words, these first games for the young child
are primarily for enjoyment, but will serve at the same time as a bridge from
the youngster's dramatic play activities to the more organized games he will
enjoy when he is older.

The use of dramatic play and simple games to promote desired kinds of
learning by the child calls for the awareness on the part of the teacher of
several important guidelines:

1. *Select a simple idea for the dramatic play of a particular child from the
child's past experiences.* To pretend to do something, the child must have
already experienced first hand (or on television or through stories and pictures) the concepts and roles used in dramatic play. His *everyday life* is the
best source of such ideas.

2. *Do not allow too much time to elapse between the original experience
and the follow-up dramatic play.* If the experience is not one repeated often
in the child's everyday life, help the child recall the original experience
before introducing the activity. Appropriate pictures or a story are often
helpful in refreshing the child's memory not only of an experience but also
of his original interest in and enjoyment of it.

3. *Set the stage with a few simple but fairly realistic props.* Elaborate, expensive toys are not the key to success. Their charm is usually lost on the
young child. A box with a homemade doll's pillow and a piece of terry cloth
will do just as well as a fancy toy crib and bedclothing.

4. *Do not overplan.* Remember the key words are *flexibility* and *freedom*.
The child must have freedom to introduce his own ideas into the role playing. You must be flexible enough to follow his leads. Moreover, spontaneous ideas often work better than rehearsed ones. And don't be afraid to
humor things you might find ridiculous. In other words, relax, enjoy the activity yourself, and help the child to enjoy it, also.

5. *Start the role playing by taking part in it.* Keep your part simple so that
the child can at least imitate your ideas. It is even more important for him to
use your ideas as stepping stones to spontaneous role playing. Try to avoid
telling the child directly and specifically what he should pretend to do, but
use the role playing to make suggestions. For example, in playing family
roles, as the "daddy" you might say: "Should Daddy put the baby to bed
now?" or "It is time for baby's nap. Mommy, do you have time to put baby
to bed?"

6. *Once the role playing gets going, try to reduce your participation.* The
more the child takes over and the more you can stand back, supplying adult
support and an appreciative audience for the child, the more effective is the
activity in promoting the values of spontaneous dramatic play for the child.
If the child runs out of ideas, you may then want to step back into your role
and come up with another idea.

7. *In general, keep the dramatic play and game activities short,* especially at first when the child's attention may last for only a few minutes. If the child shows considerable interest, continue the activity longer, but always cut it off at the first sign of disinterest or fatigue. If the child shows no interest in a proposed activity or becomes simply your audience, stop and try the same idea or another idea at a later time.

8. *In both dramatic play and game playing, do not force a child to participate.* If you are working with a small group of children, let an unwilling child watch from the sidelines. He may change his mind when he sees the fun or builds up his own confidence. So after a few minutes of play, invite him again to join the group or tell him he can join the group whenever he is ready.

9. *In game playing, do not insist upon following the rules.* Young children will fall out of line or peek when their eyes are supposed to be closed. Permit the child to play on his own terms as long as he is not completely disruptive to the game. The freedom the child enjoys does not include disregard for his safety or the safety of other children.

As in other sections of this book, these activities have been classified by general levels of maturity: Levels A, B, and C (see pages 16–18 for an explanation of these levels). Note too that other activities in the book often provide the skill and concept learning or the first-hand experiences the child will need to successfully undertake a dramatic play or game activity. Keep these factors, as well as the interests of the child, in mind in selecting an activity for a particular child. The "Helpful Hints" in each activity provide additional specific guidelines which will be helpful to you in making your selections and in using the activity with maximum learning and enjoyment by the child.

ACTIVITY 103: Pretending To Be Animals

DRAMATIC PLAY
A

WHY

To imitate sounds and actions of a dog.

WHAT YOU NEED

Two pictures of a dog—one of a little dog, one of a big dog.

TALK ABOUT WHAT YOU DO

(Use your own language. This is an example.)

"Look at this picture. / What is that? / Yes, it is a little dog, like Speckles next door. What does a dog say? / That's right. A little dog says 'Arf! Arf!' (Use a small, high voice.) A big dog like this one (show picture of big dog) says 'Woof! Woof!' " (Use a loud, deep voice.)

"Let's play 'Dogs.' I am a little dog like Speckles. Arf! Arf! (Get down on your hands and knees and nuzzle the child gently with your head.) Arf! Arf! I'd like to be petted. Can you pet me on the head? / Arf! That means that I like being petted."

"What kind of dog are you? / Are you Speckles? / Come here, Speckles. I'll pet you. / Nice dog."

"Woof! Woof! Now I am a big dog. I like being petted too. / Woof! Woof! That means, 'Thank you very much for petting me.' / Oh, you are a big dog too. Let me pet the big dog. / Your fur is so nice and soft. / Do you have a name, big dog?"

"That was fun, playing dogs, wasn't it?"

HELPFUL HINTS

Be sure the child is already familiar with whatever it is you want him to pretend to be. He needs to know, for instance, what a dog looks like, what sounds it makes, and other things it can do if he is going to pretend to be a dog. Looking at pictures and talking about a dog at the beginning of the activity helps him remember these things and prepares him for the role-playing task. Helping him recall stories or TV programs about an object or event is another way to prepare him for eventual role playing.

Encourage the child to add his own ideas in dramatic play. Even if the ideas are not realistic, do not discourage them but allow him to express his imagination.

THINGS TO DO ANOTHER TIME

Play at being other animals familiar to the child and act out what each does: for example, cat (meow, purr, wash your face with a "paw"); duck (quack and waddle like a duck); bird (chirp and flap your arms as if flying); goat (baa and gently butt the child). Introduce the activity by using pictures to reacquaint the child with the animal or help him recall any first-hand experiences he has had with the animal, or any TV acquaintance he has had: what the animal looks like, the sounds it makes, and other things it can do.

ACTIVITY 104: Peek-a-Boo

GAMES
A

WHY

To participate in a game.
To interact with another person in game playing.

WHAT YOU NEED

Small, light-weight scarf.

TALK ABOUT WHAT YOU DO

(Use your own language. This is an example.)

(Hold up scarf.) "Look at the pretty scarf. / See, I can wear the scarf on my head. (Demonstrate.) Or I can wear the scarf around my neck like this. (Demonstrate.) Would you like to put the scarf around your neck?" (If the answer is "no," do not insist. Instead, let the child feel and examine the scarf if he is interested.)

"Let's play a game with the scarf. I am going to hide behind the scarf and peek around to see if I can find you. Watch. (Hold scarf in front of your face and peek around one side of it.) Peek-a-boo. I see you." (Repeat several times.)

"Would you like to hold the scarf and 'peek-a-boo' at me? / Here is the scarf. Hold it up the way I did. / Oh where, oh where is Tony? / There he is! / Can you say *peek?* / Very good. Play 'Peek-a-Boo' again with me. Remember, say *peek* when you find me. / Oh, I see you. Did you say *peek?*" (Continue playing the game as long as the child enjoys it.)

"Did you have fun playing the game?"

HELPFUL HINTS

A small, square scarf will be easier for the child to hold in front of his face. If you do not have one, use a large handkerchief, and demonstrate such uses as mopping your forehead and pretending to blow your nose.

If the child does not wish to take a turn at peeking from behind the scarf, do not insist. Continue "peek-a-booing" at him as long as he enjoys the game. He may be willing to take a more active part in the game the next time you play it.

Nor is it important that the youngster say *peek* when it is his turn with the scarf. This, too, may come with additional playing of the game.

THINGS TO DO ANOTHER TIME

Play other simple "Hide and Seek" games. For example, use a larger scarf or light cloth to throw over your head; then ask the child to find you.

Let the child take a turn at hiding beneath the cloth while you try to find him. Or use a large, open box or wastebasket and hold it over your head, saying something like: "Where are you? Where can you be? I can't see Susie. Can you find me? / Oh, you found me! You're so smart. / Now you hide under the box and I'll try to find you."

Play "Hide and Seek" in one room. Use chairs, curtains, and other obvious places to hide while the child closes his eyes. Then have the child take his turn hiding while you close your eyes.

ACTIVITY 105:   Playing Family Roles

DRAMATIC PLAY
A

WHY

To model family roles.

WHAT YOU NEED

A doll or teddy bear; a box large enough to hold the toy; small towel.

TALK ABOUT WHAT YOU DO

(Use your own language. This is an example.)

"Can you find the doll? / Is the doll a good baby? / What do real babies do? / Yes, they cry. Babies sleep a lot too. Let's play we are a mommy and a daddy. The doll can be our baby. This box can be the baby's bed. This towel can be the baby's blanket. Okay? / You be the mommy and I'll be the daddy."

"Mommy, it's time for the baby's nap. Do you want to put the baby in the bed or do you want Daddy to put the baby to bed? / Maybe you'd better tuck the blanket in so she won't get cold. / Good night, Baby. Sleep tight, Baby."

"Mommy, do you think it is time for the baby to wake up? / Wake up, Baby. / Oh, is the baby crying? / Why is she crying? / Maybe the baby just wants to be held and loved. / Oh, you are a good mommy. I think the baby has stopped crying. Let Daddy hold the baby now."

"What did we do? / Right. We put the baby to bed. Where is the baby's bed? / Were you the mommy or the daddy? / You are a good mommy. You took good care of the baby."

HELPFUL HINTS

If you have toys to use as props in the activity, do so, but any kind of a doll or figure will do, with a box for a crib and a towel for a blanket.

If the child is a boy, let him first play the role of "Daddy" and make the baby a boy to help him relate to his own sex role. But also let him sometimes play the role of the mother to help him develop his understanding of the mother's role. The same holds for little girls playing the role of the father.

If the child catches on readily to the idea of role playing and carries a family role off in a direction different from your plan, go along with it. Always let the child express his own concept of a role and put it in action.

THINGS TO DO ANOTHER TIME

Use other simple family situations involving the roles of the mother, father, and baby: feeding the baby (use a small, empty bottle, or a bowl and spoon with a little dry cereal); dressing the baby (use a scarf or something similar to wrap around the baby); giving the baby a bath (use a small basin and washcloth); taking the baby for a ride in the car or bus (use several chairs for car or bus and wrap Baby in a blanket to keep him warm). Let the child play alternate roles.

Extend the activity to include two (or more) of the situations above.

ACTIVITY 106: Dressing Up

DRAMATIC PLAY
B

WHY

To model male and female roles.

WHAT YOU NEED

Large box; male and female cloth-ing and accessories; mirror (large).

TALK ABOUT WHAT YOU DO

(Use your own language. This is an example.)

"Look at this big box. What do you think is in it? / Let's see what is in the box. / Oh, what is that? / Right. It is a hat. Who wears a hat like that? / What else is in the box?" (Continue identifying articles of clothing and who might wear them.)

"Let's play dress-up. What would you like to try on? / Oh, you look just like a grown-up daddy in that hat. Look at yourself in the mirror. / I'm going to wear this hat. I'll be a fancy lady. / Let's go to a party. What else should we wear to the party?"

"Now I am all ready for the party. Are you ready? / You look very ele-gant, Daddy. See in the mirror how elegant you look. / Do you like my party clothes?"

"The party is over now. Did you have a good time at the party? / It's time to take off our party clothes. / We'll put them in the box and save them for another party."

HELPFUL HINTS

Any old clothes can be used in this activity, but it is best to keep it simple: a hat with a big flower, a long skirt or piece of curtain for a wrap-around skirt, and a necklace or some other piece of costume jewelry for a little girl; a man's hat, coat or jacket, and a necktie or bowtie for a little boy. Older children's clothes will fit the young child better than adult clothing, but quick adjustments can also be made, often with safety pins. Hats can be adjusted by stuffing the crown with tissue paper. Other articles of clothing popular with children are shoes, vests, belts, suspenders, frilly blouses, purses, scarfs, and anything made of velvet or trimmed with fur.

THINGS TO DO ANOTHER TIME

Repeat the activity using varied articles of clothing and accessories.

Extend the activity to include the event for which you are dressed up: a dancing party at which there is music and a few minutes of free dancing; a birthday party with imaginary presents and cake; a "grown-up" visit to a friend or relative during which you "chat" and have a snack.

ACTIVITY 107: Playing House

DRAMATIC PLAY
B

WHY

To extend modeling of family roles.
To reinforce the concept *setting the table*.

WHAT YOU NEED

Low table or large cardboard box; tablecloth; non-breakable dishes; spoons.

TALK ABOUT WHAT YOU DO

(Use your own language. This is an example.)

"Let's play 'Setting the Table.' We are getting ready for dinner. / This can be our table (point to or touch) and these are our dishes (point to or touch). Do you want to be the mommy? / I'll be your little girl and I'll help you set the table."

"Mommy, is it almost time for dinner? / Would you like me to help you set the table? / Here is the tablecloth. You have to help me put it on the table because that is hard to do. / Which dishes should we use? / These are pretty dishes. Can you show me how to set the table with them?"

"There, the table is all set. Is Daddy coming home for dinner? / Should we let Teddy be Daddy? / Good. Now we can eat. I'm so hungry. (Imitate eating.) These potatoes are so good. Can I have some more, Mommy? / My, that was a good dinner. Did you cook it all by yourself?"

"Wash up time. Let's pick up the dishes now. / Help me put the dishes away so that we can use them when we play house again."

HELPFUL HINTS

Use a small low table or an overturned cardboard box as a table. Dishes may be plastic or small cardboard circles for pretend plates. A dishtowel makes a good tablecloth.

You may want to add a plastic serving bowl or a paper plate with a picture of some food pasted on it to make the pretend dinner more realistic. The bowl or plate can be passed around for serving everyone at the table.

Do not insist that the table setting be done properly if the child in the role of "Mommy" gives wild directions to her "little girl." Go along with the directions and later adjust things as needed for the dinner scene.

If the child remains interested, you might extend the activity to pretend to wash and wipe the dinner dishes.

THINGS TO DO ANOTHER TIME

Play that company (perhaps Grandma or Aunt Jane) is coming to visit and you have to clean the house (a small area of the room). Provide a broom, dustcloth, some artificial flowers, and a vase. After a few minutes of sweeping, dusting, and straightening, suggest putting the flowers in the vase (helping as needed) and setting the flowers where the company will see and enjoy them.

Pretend you have visitors. Dolls may be used as visitors or children may alternate roles. Serve imaginary refreshments. Use a few cookies or crackers on a plate which the child can pass around. Or cut out a picture of cookies and paste it on a paper plate for serving. Exchange polite news with your visitors and thank them for coming.

Play "Laundry Work." Wash the clothes (a washcloth or two), hang them up to dry (on a line or towel rack), and, when they are dry, "iron" them (use a toy iron or a rectangular block as a make-believe iron). If you wash the "clothes" in real soap and water (which the child will enjoy), let them dry overnight and role-play the ironing the next day.

ACTIVITY 108: Follow the Little White Road

GAMES
B

WHY

To be aware that games have rules.
To follow a simple direction.

WHAT YOU NEED

Ball of string; a surprise package.

TALK ABOUT WHAT YOU DO

(Use your own language. This is an example.)

"See this long piece of string on the floor? / We are going to play a game. We have to pretend the string is a little, white road. We have to follow the road wherever it goes. When you come to the end of the road, you'll find a big surprise. Are you ready to play the game? / Remember the rule of the game: walk along the little white road until you find the surprise.''

"That's right. Follow the road. You are playing the game just right. / No, you have to go around the chair. The road goes around the chair. / Where does the road go from here? / Then we have to go into the hall too. Can you see where the road ends? / Oh, you found the surprise! / Do you want me to help you open it?''

"It is a pretty balloon. I'll blow it up for you. / Let's tie a piece of string on the balloon so that it will stay nice and fat and the air won't get out.''

"Did you have fun playing the game? / What rule did you have to follow in the game? / Yes, you had to walk along the string until you found the surprise. You did just what the rule said you should do.''

HELPFUL HINTS

Before beginning the game, unwind the string so that one end is where you want to start the game and the other end is where you want to hide the surprise. Tie the surprise to the end of the string and use a wastebasket or box to conceal it. Make the road wind from one side of the room to the other and into a second room or hall if the string is long enough.

Remind the child of the game rule if he fails to follow it. But don't overdo it. A few mistakes won't matter.

The game can be played with a small group of children. Just be sure that you have a surprise for each child at the end of the road.

THINGS TO DO ANOTHER TIME

Play the game in different rooms. Or unwind the string so that it goes up or down a small flight of steps.

Play the game outdoors. Change the rule to ''run along the little white road.''

ACTIVITY 109: Simon Says

GAMES
B

WHY

To join with others in game playing.
To follow one-step directions.

WHAT YOU NEED

No materials needed.

TALK ABOUT WHAT YOU DO

(Use your own language. This is an example.)

"Let's sit here on the rug and play a game. / We are going to play
'Simon Says.' I am going to be Simon. Simon will tell you things to do.
You have to do what Simon says. Watch Simon now and listen to what he
says."

"Simon says, 'Put your hands on your head.' (Put your hand on your
head.) Where is your head? / Very good! You are doing just what Simon
says."

"Simon says, 'Put your hands on your knees.' (Put your hands on your
knees.) Where is your other knee? / Simon says, 'Put your other hand on
that knee, too.' "

"Simon says, 'Close your eyes.' / Simon says, 'Open your eyes.' "

"Simon says, 'Touch your nose.' / Where is your other nose? / Oh,
Simon forgot. You have only one nose."

(Continue with other parts of the body or directions that require using part of the body: wave a hand, pull an ear.)

"Would you like to be Simon? / Well, maybe the next time we play 'Simon Says' you would like to be Simon."

HELPFUL HINTS

Have the child sit facing you. Simon should also *do* whatever he says to do. A child will be able to mimic Simon even though he does not know the name of a part of the body, and thus he will still have fun.

A young child may not be ready to be Simon the first, second, or even the third time he plays the game. Continue being Simon until he is willing to take a short turn at being Simon.

THINGS TO DO ANOTHER TIME

Play a more active game of "Simon Says" by having the child do such things as jumping, taking three little or big steps, dancing, turning around, swinging arms.

"Simon Says" can be used to reinforce other learning. In the lesson above, it is reinforcing learning the parts of the body. It can be used, for example, to reinforce learning colors (Simon says to find something that is yellow), shapes (Simon says to touch something that is round), or positional relationships (Simon says to sit *on* a pillow; Simon says to get *under* the table). Make up your own games of "Simon Says" to reinforce particular kinds of learning suggested by other activities in this book.

ACTIVITY 110:   Talking on the Telephone

DRAMATIC PLAY
C

WHY

To act out talking on the telephone.

WHAT YOU NEED

A toy telephone.

TALK ABOUT WHAT YOU DO

(Use your own language. This is an example.)

"Let's play 'Telephone.' Where is the telephone? / Show me what part
of the telephone you hold to your ear to listen when someone calls you. /
That's right. It's called a receiver. Show me how you hold the receiver to
your ear. / Very good! What do you talk into when you talk on the telephone? / You have to talk into this part. (Point to or touch.) Watch. (Demonstrate.) I hold the receiver like this and then I say 'Hello' into this end. /
Can you do that? / Very good!"

"I'll be your friend Charlie and I'll call you on the telephone. Okay?
(Pretend you have a telephone and go through the motions of picking up the
receiver and talking into the mouthpiece.) Ding-a-ling. Ding-a-ling. That's
the telephone ringing. You have to answer it. / No, turn the receiver around
the other way. / Right. Hello. Is that you, Susie? / This is Charlie. Would
you like to come to my birthday party? / We are going to have ice cream.
Do you like ice cream? / I'll call you again sometime. Goodbye, Susie."

"Oh, you answered the telephone very well. Would you like to call
someone on the telephone? / All right. I'll be Charlie and you call me."

HELPFUL HINTS

If you do not have a toy telephone, use a real one to identify the receiver and the mouthpiece and to demonstrate how to hold the receiver and talk into the mouthpiece. For props in the role playing, use empty tubes such as come in rolls of paper towels. The child can hold one end of tube to his ear and talk into the other end.

Young children often become tongue-tied in front of a telephone, so don't expect the child to carry on a lengthy conversation. Encourage him to say "hello" and "goodbye," and be prepared to ask questions to which you think the child will respond.

Pretending to receive a call may be easier for the child than pretending to make one. If the child does not want to make a call, do not insist. He may, however, be willing to pretend again that someone is calling him and respond to such a call.

If you are working with a small group of children, and have two toy telephones, encourage the children to call each other and carry a on a brief conversation, even if it is only "hello" and "goodbye." It may take time, however, for the children to reach this stage in telephone play.

THINGS TO DO ANOTHER TIME

Play "Talking on the Telephone," receiving calls from and making calls to different people the child knows. Talk about particular things that are of interest to the child and always have questions to ask if the child cannot think of anything to say.

ACTIVITY 111:   Baking "Cookies"

DRAMATIC PLAY
C

WHY

To develop and deepen concepts of housekeeping tasks.

WHAT YOU NEED

Hard-surfaced table; clay or Play Dough; rolling pin; cookie sheet; large box; aprons.

TALK ABOUT WHAT YOU DO

(Use your own language. This is an example.)

"Let's play we are going to have a party and need to make some cookies for the party. We can make our cookies from the Play Dough. This big box will be our stove. We can bake the cookies in it."

"Bakers always wear big white aprons. So let's put our baking aprons on. / There, now you look just like a baker."

"I'll be your helper and roll out this little piece of dough with the rolling pin. (Demonstrate.) Okay, Mr. Baker, it's time for you to get busy so that we have the cookies ready for the party."

"Here is a cookie cutter, Mr. Baker. Would you like your helper to cut out one cookie? (Demonstrate.) I'll help you by putting the cookie on this cookie sheet. / There! What else would you like your helper to do?"

"Are these cookies all ready to be baked in the oven? / Pop them in the oven then, Mr. Baker. / I'll turn the heat up in the oven so the cookies will bake." (Make motion of turning heat up.)

"Do you think the cookies are baked? / Maybe we should peek in the oven and see if they are done. / Are they done? / Good, let's take them out. / Say, they look good enough to eat! We are all ready for the party."

"We can't really eat these Play Dough cookies, can we? / No, these cookies would taste awful. They are made from Play Dough. But I have some real cookies. We can eat them at our party."

HELPFUL HINTS

It is important that you introduce the child to the ideas of *baker* and *baking* before you use this activity.

Substitute props can be used instead of the real thing. An empty bottle can be a rolling pin; a piece of heavy cardboard, a cookie sheet; and dishtowels or pieces of sheet, baker's aprons. You can use a real oven (no heat on), but a large cardboard box also makes a good stove. If you wish, you can cut an oven door in one side of the box (cut the oven door on three sides and bend the fourth side so the door will open). Also you can paint stove grills on the top of the box for more realism (and use the stove in other play cooking activities).

THINGS TO DO ANOTHER TIME

Play baker and make a loaf of bread or rolls in a muffin pan from Play Dough or clay. Add a baker's hat to your props by turning over the open end of a paper bag several times to make a cuff which will fit the child's head.

After the child has learned how to use an egg beater, mix a pretend cake in a mixing bowl, pour the batter into a cake pan, and pretend to bake it in the oven. One cup of soap flakes and one–fourth cup of water make an interesting sudsy batter.

Perform other pretend cooking tasks on your cardboard stove: frying chicken, cooking vegetables, making pudding.

ACTIVITY 112:   Playing Grocery Store

DRAMATIC PLAY
C

WHY

To develop/deepen the concepts *grocery store* and *buying*.

WHAT YOU NEED

Several large cardboard boxes stacked one on top of the other to make "shelves," empty food boxes and cans, large box or table for checkout counter, paper bags.

TALK ABOUT WHAT YOU DO

(Use your own language. This is an example.)

"Remember our trip to the grocery store? / What did you see at the grocery store? (Help the child recall such things as the food on shelves, the checkout counter where you paid for the food, and the bagging of the groceries.) Let's play going to the store. Where will we have our store? / What things can we put on the shelves?"

"Good! Now we have some food we can buy. (Point to "food" on shelves.) This box (table) will be where we pay for the things we buy. Remember the lady (man) at the cash register who took the money? / Well, this is where she (he) works. And we'll use these bags to put our food in and take it back to school."

"Do you want to be a mommy (daddy) who comes to the store to buy food? / Good. I'll be the lady (man) at the cash register."

"Good morning, ma'am. Are you shopping for your little children today? / Just pick out the food you want from the shelf and pay me here. / Is that all you need today? / It comes to one dollar. / Thank you, ma'am. Here is your change. / I'll put the food in a bag so you can carry it home. / Come again when you need more food. Goodbye. Have a nice day.''

"Would you like to be the lady (man) at the cash register? / All right. I'll be the shopper this time. / I've come to buy food for my little boy (girl).'' (Continue playing the shopper's role but follow any leads of what to do or say that may be suggested by the child.)

"That was fun, wasn't it? / Help me put the food and boxes away so that we can use them again when we pretend to go to the grocery store.''

HELPFUL HINTS

Be sure that the child has visited a grocery store before trying this activity (see Activity 165).

Keep the activity simple at first. Later you may wish to add such things as a toy cash register (or a box for a pretend cash register) and play money (small pieces of paper and coins made from cardboard).

As in all dramatic play, take your leads from the child. If he has ideas of what to do and say, go along with them.

This activity works well with a small group of children. Let the children be shoppers first while you play the role of the checker. Then give the children turns at being the checker also if they are interested.

THINGS TO DO ANOTHER TIME

Adapt the activity to a department store. Fill the shelves with such things as toys, an old clock, hats, and any other objects which the child especially noted on his visit to a department store (see Activity 168).

. After the child has had the experience of shopping at a shoe store, adapt the activity to a shoe store. Reuse the store shelves and provide props of shoes (in boxes if possible) and a low stool or chair for the customer to sit on when he tries on the shoes. Play the roles of shoe clerk and the shopper trying on shoes, deciding on the pair to buy, and paying for them. Let the child alternate roles.

ACTIVITY 113:   Playing Mail Carrier

DRAMATIC PLAY
C

WHY

To develop and deepen the concept *mail carrier.*

WHAT YOU NEED

Old letters in envelopes; shoulder bag; several chairs.

TALK ABOUT WHAT YOU DO

(Use your own language. This is an example.)

"Let's play 'Mail Carrier.' This can be your mailbag. Hang it over your shoulder like your mail carrier does. / Here are some letters to put in your mailbag. / You can pretend to deliver the letters to the houses along a street. What can we use for pretend houses? (Use what the child suggests if feasible. If not, continue.) How about these chairs? We can line them up like houses along a street. Okay?"

"You pretend to be the mail carrier. I'll be someone who lives in this house. You deliver the mail to my house like your mail carrier does."

"Good morning, Mr. Mail Carrier. Aren't you early this morning? / Do you have any mail for me? / Oh, you have lots of mail for me. Thank you. / I see you brought me a letter from Johnny's grandmother. She probably wants to know how Johnny is. / Do you have any mail for Mr. Schultz who lives next door? / That's good. Goodbye. I hope you come back with mail tomorrow."

"You did a good job delivering all the mail. Do you want to pretend now that you live in one of the houses and I'll be the mail carrier?"

HELPFUL HINTS

Save some of your junk mail for this activity. Or use cheap envelopes and have the child help you write letters to put in the envelopes, thus providing the child with the opportunity to practice scribbling with a pencil or a crayon.

A school bag can be used as a mailbag. Or cut down or fold back a large paper bag. Fasten a short shoulder strap to it by stapling or safety-pinning a strip of material to each side of the bag.

Remember that the child should have first-hand experience with a mail carrier (see Activity 167) or any other community worker before pretending to be such a worker. For the young child, do not be too elaborate either in your props or in the ideas you act out. You may, of course, want to repeat an activity to elaborate further on the worker's role. For example, in replaying "Mail Carrier" you could have a child deliver a package (a birthday present) or magazines.

In a group, alternate roles among the children. Ask those who receive mail such questions as "Who did you get a letter from?" and "What do you think he/she says in the letter?"

THINGS TO DO ANOTHER TIME

Pretend to be other workers in your community with whom the child has had a first-hand experience. Some examples are given below.

Pretend to be a policeman or policewoman directing traffic. Use a cap and a police badge (cardboard covered with foil) as props. You might be a mommy with a baby who wants to cross the street. Or use toy cars and have the child direct automobile traffic.

Pretend to be a bus driver and riders. Several chairs in rows become the bus and a chair in the front, the driver's seat. A pie tin or other circular object becomes the steering wheel. Be sure to stop at street corners to let riders off and on the bus. In a repeat of the activity, or if the child suggests it the first time, have a box for fares and have the driver collect fares (buttons) from riders.

Play newspaper delivery boy or girl. Use parts of old newspapers and reuse the mail carrier's bag to hold the newspapers.

Pretend to be house painters. Have the child use a real paintbrush and a bucket with some water to paint bricks outside or a tile wall.

ACTIVITY 114:   Playing with Boats

DRAMATIC PLAY
C

WHY

To develop and deepen the concept *boat*.

WHAT YOU NEED

Small toy boats or foil boats (see directions below); sink or large basin with water; a few small buttons.

TALK ABOUT WHAT YOU DO

(Use your own language. This is an example.)

"Look at these pretty boats. (Let the child examine them if he is interested.) What can you do with boats? / Right. You can put them in water. They float. Let's run some water in the sink so you can sail your boats. / There. Now put the boats in the water. See, they are floating on top of the water."

"Let's pretend we are captains of the boats. The captain has to make the boat go in the water. Which boat do you want to be the captain of? / All right. You be Captain Blue because you have a blue boat. I'll be Captain Green because my boat is green. The edge of the sink (touch) is the land where we live. Okay? / We have to get on our boats from the land. (Bring boat to edge of sink.) Are you on your boat, Captain Blue? / We are ready to steer our boats, then." (Let the child sail his boat for a few minutes.)

"Let's pretend these little buttons are people on the land who want to go for a boat ride. We have to bring our boats back to the land so they can get

on the boats. / Hold your boat still, Captain Blue. We have to help these
people get on the boat. (Put several buttons in the boat.) We don't want to
lose anybody in the water, do we? / Have a nice ride, Captain Blue.''

"Is the ride over? / Are you going to let the people off the boat? / They
have to get back on the land, you know.''

"What should we do now with our boats, Captain Blue?'' (Let Captain
Blue continue with boat play until he runs out of ideas or interest.)

HELPFUL HINTS

You can make your own boats out of aluminum foil. See the directions,
Fig. 114.1. If you do make foil boats, tie pieces of different colored yarn on
one end of toothpicks and insert the other end into the center of the foil
boats. Thus, you can dub the child "Captain Blue" if he picks a boat with a
blue flag or name him after whatever color of flag he chooses.

THINGS TO DO ANOTHER TIME

Adapt the activity to other kinds of boats: soap boats with a toothpick
sail, the rind of half an orange, small pieces of wood, or anything else that
floats. Use the sink or basin to make a pretend ocean, or put a partially filled
tub of water outdoors for boat play.

Pretend there is a big storm on the ocean or lake and the boats have to
sail through it. Create the storm by adding a mild detergent to the water and
whipping it to a froth with an egg beater. Show the child how to use the egg
beater; he will enjoy being a big storm that makes the boats go every which
way.

DIRECTIONS FOR MAKING A FOIL BOAT

STEP 1:   **Fig. 114.1**

Start with a rectangular sheet of foil,
about 8″ x 11″. Fold it in half.

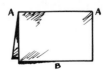

STEP 2:

Fold Corners A (at folded end) to
meet in center of double sheet. An
inch or two of foil will remain at un-
folded side B.

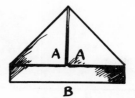

STEP 3:

Fold the B sides (each on its own
side) up toward the point. You should
now have a triangular "hat" that
opens at the B ends.

NOTE:

If you had started with a half-sheet of newspaper, you
would have a good hat for your little Captain to wear.

STEP 4:

Take hold of each of the B sides in
the center and pull all the way out
until the triangle becomes a double
square.

STEP 5:

Fold up point C on each side to meet
point D. You are now back to triangles. Crease firmly the folds at the
bottom of the triangles.

STEP 6:

Take hold of the triangles at their bottom centers (E) and pull all the way
out until you again have a square.
Press firmly all edges of the square.

STEP 7:

Hold the two points F of your square
and slowly pull apart—all the way.
And presto! You have a boat. Spread
out the opening at the bottom of the
boat for "smooth sailing."

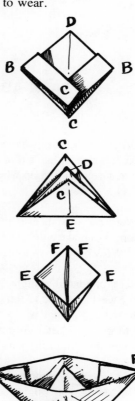

ACTIVITY 115: Camping Out

DRAMATIC PLAY.
C

WHY

To develop and deepen concepts of *tent* and *camping*.

WHAT YOU NEED

Card table (or four chairs); large sheet or blanket; picture of a tent.

TALK ABOUT WHAT YOU DO

(Use your own language. This is an example.)

"Do you remember what a tent is like? / Here is a picture of a tent. / See, it's like a house. It has a roof and a door. (Point to each.) A tent is a special house that you can live in when you go camping. You can sleep and eat in a tent. Let's make a tent and pretend that we are camping out in the park."

"We'll put this sheet over the card table. / There's our tent. I'll pin up this corner to make a door. / Let's go inside the tent. / See what a nice house it is? / We won't get wet even though it rains."

"Let's pretend it is night, and we are going to sleep in our tent. / Nighty night. Sweet dreams. (After a few moments make a chirping sound.) Did you hear that? / That was a little bird chirping. It is saying 'It's morning. Time to get up.' Let's go outside the tent. Maybe we can see a squirrel or find some flowers in the park."

"Did you like camping out? / Do you want to play in the tent some more? / Maybe you would like to take your doll or Teddy on a camping trip with you. / You can have a snack to eat in your tent if you like."

HELPFUL HINTS

TV programs will often introduce the child to "camping out" activities. Or you may be able to visit a campground where people are camping out in tents. Or cut out pictures of a tent (from catalog or newspaper ads), a campfire, someone fishing, and other similar activities, and make up a simple story about each picture to tell the child. With one or more of these kinds of experiences, the child will probably enjoy pretending to camp out.

To encourage the child to enter into dramatic play on his own, leave the tent up (in some out-of-the way corner) or set it up again another day for the child to use in his unstructured play. Encourage him further by asking such questions as "Is your tent in the park? / Did you sleep in the tent over-night?"

THINGS TO DO ANOTHER TIME

Put up the tent in the playground and pretend to gather wood and make a campfire. Tell the child a story or sing a song while sitting around the "campfire."

Pretend to go fishing while camping out. Use a stick with a line tied to one end as a fishing pole. Tie a small nail at the end of the line as a hook. Show the child how to "fish" in an imaginary lake or pond (an empty bucket or one partially filled with water). Then let the child pretend to fish and to catch fish for "supper."

Pretend to be Indians who live in a tepee in the woods. A real feather or a cardboard feather (painted or crayoned) can be attached to a ribbon or paper headband for an Indian headdress. You might pretend to look for nuts and berries to eat for supper or to paddle a canoe (a large cardboard box and a stick for a paddle).

ACTIVITY 116:   Follow the Leader

GAMES
C

WHY

To join with others in game playing.
To follow one-step directions.

WHAT YOU NEED

No materials needed.

TALK ABOUT WHAT YOU DO

(Use your own language. This is an example.)

"We are going to play a game called 'Follow the Leader.' I'll be the
leader and show you how to play the game. You have to do everything the
leader does. Ready? / Watch me now."

"Raise your hands over your head like this. / Remember, you have to do
whatever the leader does. Can you raise your hands over your head? / Good.
Now we'll clap our hands. / The leader will take two big steps. / Oh, your
steps were really big. Now let's bend over." (Continue with other simple
actions the child can copy, such as jump, walk on hands and knees, wave
arms as if flying, turn completely around.)

"It's your turn to be the leader now. This time I have to do everything
you do. / You can do anything you want. You can walk or jump or wave
your arms. / Oh, that's good. I hope I can do that, too."

"My, that was fun. You are a good leader and a good follower!"

HELPFUL HINTS

The game will probably work best with the young child if the leader stands facing the child or children. Also use verbal directions at first. Later, when the child or children have a better grasp of the game, you may line up with the leader in front. You can then drop the verbal directions and let the child or children simply imitate the leader's actions.

If the child has trouble doing exactly what you did, do not scold but ignore it. Come back to the same action later and see what he does the second time. Or omit the action if it is too difficult for him. Remember, a game is supposed to be fun.

Do not force children to play the game. If a child is reluctant to play, let him just watch. He may be willing to join the game later.

Stop the game as soon as there is any sign of disinterest and before the child or children become over-tired. Follow it by a quiet activity: looking at pictures in a book, listening to a story, listening to music for a few minutes.

THINGS TO DO ANOTHER TIME

If you are working with one child only, invite one or several other young children over and play "Follow the Leader" with them. The experience of playing games with other preschoolers is important for the young child.

Or ask a willing adult or older children to play "Follow the Leader" with you and the child. Warn them, however, to keep their actions simple so that the young child can imitate them.

Puzzles help children to recognize differences in shapes, colors, and sizes, and to develop hand-eye coordination.

Part 7

Puzzles

PUZZLES

Working with puzzles can and should be fun as well as a learning experience for the young child. Preschoolers learn many things from puzzles. They learn to recognize shapes and colors and sizes. They learn the names of objects. They become aware of positional relationships among objects and parts of objects: that heads are on top of bodies and feet are at the other end, that sky and clouds are over trees, that the sun is up in the sky and grass and flowers are down on the ground. They learn, too, the parts of an object and that the parts put together can make a whole. They experience problem solving, and they develop hand–eye coordination skills as they place pieces of a puzzle in a puzzle frame or fit them together to make a whole picture.

Children may be ready for puzzles some time between the ages of 18 and 24 months. Usually they will first have to learn to tower blocks, nest cans or cups, and place small objects in a jar or bottle. Part of the preparation for puzzle solving is also such initial experiences with a puzzle as looking at the pictures, learning the names of the pictured objects, dumping the pieces on the floor or table, and examining the pieces.

The child's first puzzle should be a simple whole-object puzzle, one in which a puzzle piece represents a complete object: an apple or a banana, a kitten or a baby chick. The large wooden puzzles with colorful picture pieces are especially good for the young child. The pieces are easy to handle, and they drop into the puzzle frame with an exciting and enjoyable "plop."

Presenting the first puzzle to a youngster in a structured activity calls for a series of steps:

1. Select a one-piece, whole-object puzzle (a single piece of a three- or four-piece whole-object puzzle) in which you think the child will be interested. Name the object and talk about it, relating the object pictured, whenever possible, to the child's past experiences with the real thing. Point out colors, parts, and other interesting and important details in the picture.
2. Demonstrate removing the piece. Then help the child explore its shape. Show him how to trace around the piece with a finger and have him trace it. Call attention to one or several key factors of its shape, to a part of the object which protrudes and is easily recognizable or to a particular rounded, pointed, or elongated shape. Let the youngster trace also the hole in the puzzle board which is the outline of the piece you are working with.

In using a fruit puzzle, for example, you might say in this step: "Watch me, John. I am going to take the big red apple out of the board. / There. See the apple piece? / Watch carefully how I run my finger all around the apple.

303

(Continue talking as you trace.) The apple feels round. Oh, here's a bump. That's the stem of the apple. See the stem? (Point.) Now you try that. / Oops! You found the bump. Look (point), the stem of the apple sticks out. / Now use your finger to trace the hole in the board where the apple was, like this. / Can you find the bump where the apple stem was? / There it is, right there. Feel it?''

3.   You are ready now for the next step, demonstrating how to replace the piece in the puzzle board and giving the child a try at it. Use exaggerated motions or ''slow motion'' in your demonstration. Talk again about the bump or some other easily recognized features of the shape of the object that you are using as your clue to replacing the piece correctly. A verbal ''Plop!'' as the piece falls in place will help to dramatize the achievement. See then what the child can do with the piece. If he has difficulty, remind him of the particular clue that will help to get started. But also guide his hand if necessary for him to experience some measure of success. Don't let him fail!

This third step might go something like this in the fruit puzzle: ''Now watch closely how I put the red apple back in its hole. / There's that bumpy stem. It fits right here in the hole. / Plop! Did you see that! The apple went right in! / Now you try it. / First find the stem. / Turn the piece a little more. / Let me help you. / That's right. Now push the apple in. / Oh, it went 'Plop!' for you too. You got the apple in the hole!''

4.   Have the child try to replace the piece again on his own. Success in this step, however, remains very important. So if the youngster has difficulty, again give whatever help is needed. Try verbal directions first (''Turn the piece until you find the stem''), but give more direct help (like turning the piece for the child or guiding his hand) if the child fails to respond correctly to the verbal directions.

These steps, or adaptations of them, should be repeated as needed in working with the same puzzle piece until the youngster learns to mount it without assistance. Continue then, in similar fashion, with each of the other whole-object pieces of the puzzle, one at a time. When the child is able to replace each of the pieces individually, remove two puzzle pieces at the same time and work on their replacement. With success in this task, increase the number of pieces removed to three and then to four or until the child is able to replace all the whole-object pieces of the puzzle at one time.

This achievement may well take a series of short sessions. Keep the sessions closely spaced, two or three times in a week, so that what the child learns in a previous session is carried over to the next one. Usually a preschooler's interest in a puzzle will increase with use. But if the child becomes bored or frustrated, put the puzzle away temporarily and move on to other activities. Or give the youngster a choice of puzzles to work on. By allowing him to choose the puzzle he prefers, the chances are that interest and enjoyment will follow.

When the youngster is able to complete easily many whole-object puzzles, he is probably ready for simple divided-object puzzles. These puzzles have several pieces that divide a picture into several parts: a dog, for example, that is made up of a head, body, legs, and tail pieces or a farm picture of which the pieces are a house, barn, haystack, cow. The divided puzzle adds to the preschooler's learning task in that the child in putting the pieces together must be aware of positional relationships between the parts of the picture (the head goes on top of the dog's body; the legs, at the bottom) as well as of matching shapes. The more complex divided-object puzzles may also require the child to match colors. ("That piece is blue like the sky. See if it goes at the top of the puzzle where the sky is.")

To introduce the child to these new tasks, you may want to start with a simple two-piece divided-object puzzle, such as a house with its roof and chimney on one piece and the rest of the house on a second piece. The steps in introducing the child to a two-piece puzzle are:

1. Present the puzzle first as a whole picture. Talk about the picture: name the object and, whenever possible, relate it to the child's past experience with the object; identify what he sees on each of the puzzle pieces; and point out important positional relationships that exist between the parts. For example: "See the red roof? / It is on top of the house. The roof has to be on the top so the people who live in the house won't get wet when it rains."
2. Demonstrate removing one piece. Name the piece. ("This piece is the roof. See, it is all red, and the chimney sticks out.") Let the child trace the piece with his finger and call attention to recognizable parts which protrude and to their positional relationship to the rest of the picture. ("Oh, there is a big bump. It is the chimney, isn't it? / The chimney sticks out of the roof at the top of the house."
3. Demonstrate replacing the piece in proper position to the other puzzle piece, and have the child try to do the same. ("Watch. I am going to put the roof and the chimney back on the house. / See. The roof is at the top of the house, and the chimney sticks out over the roof. / Now you try it.")
4. Repeat Steps 2 and 3 with the second piece of the puzzle.
5. Have the child try on his own to place the two pieces in their proper relationship. Help only if he needs help and, with or without your help, make him feel that he has been successful.

A simple three-piece divided-object puzzle is presented in the same way, with Steps 2 and 3 repeated for both the second and third pieces. Then, remove two pieces and try Step 5. Finally, scramble all three pieces and have the child try to reassemble them. And remember, don't let him fail in this final step.

When the youngster can do these very simple divided-object puzzles, move on to more complex ones, first to puzzles with four to eight pieces and then on to eight- to 12-piece puzzles. The first three teaching steps for the puzzles are the same as those given above for simple divided-object puzzles. The additional steps are:

4. Remove two pieces: one the same as before and one new piece. Name the new piece, have the child trace it, and talk about any of its distinguishing features (shape, positional relationship, color).
5. Demonstrate replacing both pieces. Talk about your clues to proper replacement (shape, positional relationships, color).
6. Continue in similar fashion, removing one new piece each time until the entire puzzle can be done at once.

More than one session probably will be needed to move the child through the entire puzzle, but make him feel successful each time by being able (with or without your help) to replace some of the puzzle pieces. After a few practice sessions, repeating steps whenever necessary, the youngster will probably be able to complete the entire puzzle "all by myself." Starting always with only one or two puzzle pieces, the preschooler usually experiences quick success, which often is needed to maintain his interest and convince him that he can do it.

The importance of the feeling of success can hardly be overemphasized in working with puzzles. Praise, applause, simple rewards, enjoyment—all help in bringing about success feelings. But even more important is providing the right kind of help at the right time to prevent frustration and failure. At first, direct help will be needed. You may have to turn over a piece or turn it to a better position for the child. You may have to guide his hand until the piece is in position for the final push into the board. As the youngster becomes more experienced in verbal communication and in working puzzles, your help should become more verbal: "Turn the piece around," or "Push it in now," or "Do you think that blue piece is part of the blue sky? / See if it fits up here at the top." At the same time, however, give the child a chance. *Don't be too quick to step in. A toddler may, with a little time, find his own clues and work out his own strategy for solving a puzzle. And that, of course, may be the most important kind of learning to come out of puzzle activities.*

The puzzle activities of this manual provide samples of structured lessons that will carry the child from an introduction to the concept *puzzle* to working with the more complex divided-object puzzles. Keep in mind in using them and in planning your own puzzle activities the steps suggested above for the various kinds of puzzles and the following general guidelines:

1. Present puzzles as enjoyable games.
2. Complete the puzzle or some part of it at each session so that the child has a feeling of "I can do it."
3. Master one series of the same kind of puzzle before beginning the next level.
4. Use verbal praise or applause when the child does any part of a puzzle correctly.
5. Let the youngster do a puzzle he likes over again (and again) for enjoyment and reinforcement.

YOU CAN MAKE YOUR OWN PUZZLES

As already mentioned, the large wooden puzzles with colorful pictures are especially good for preschool children. They may be purchased in most toy departments and stores. (See also pages 309–310 for additional titles of puzzles found to be appropriate for preschoolers.) However, to supplement your puzzle supply you may want to make some of your own puzzles. Suggestions and directions for making puzzles are given below.

Puzzle Pictures and Their Sources

Select simple, fairly large pictures of familiar objects for your puzzles. Pictures of objects with regular shapes (not too irregular and no fine-line protrusions) and with one or two distinguishing features are best. A few examples of such pictures for whole-object puzzles are: shoe or boot, mitten, hat, hammer, broom, shovel, cup and saucer, mug, jack-o'-lantern, leaf, flower, butterfly, fish, toy block (square), clock (circle), ice cream cone (triangle), heart, star, and a tracing of a child's hand or foot.

Pictures for the child's first divided-object puzzles should also be of familiar objects with fairly regular shapes. They should lend themselves to division into two or three easily recognized units or pieces. Some examples of such pictures (with parts or pieces indicated) are: simple house (roof/rest of house), animal (head/body or head/body/legs or tail), child or adult (divided at waist or head/body with arms/legs), tree (trunk/branches and leaves), flower (blossoms/stem and leaves), boat on water (boat/water), and car (body/wheel/wheel).

Keep an eye out for simple, colorful pictures in magazines. Mail-order catalogs are another source of such pictures. Inexpensive picture books often provide excellent pictures for puzzles, many of them stylized so that outlines are easy to cut out. Or color an object or simple scene in a child's coloring book and use it to make a puzzle.

Directions for Making Puzzles

1. You will need a picture, sharp-pointed scissors, paste, and cardboard somewhat larger than the picture. The cardboard will serve as the puzzle frame and should, therefore, be thick enough to give both the picture and its "hole" some depth for easy replacement but thin enough to cut with scissors. Corrugated cardboard, such as you find in cardboard boxes, works well.
2. Cut out the pictured objects carefully. Paste the picture in the center of the cardboard. Place a heavy book on top to keep the picture pressed against the cardboard while it dries.
3. When the picture is thoroughly dry, cut it out of the cardboard. You can usually start the cutting by puncturing the cardboard carefully at the edge of a straight part of the picture with sharp-pointed scissors. Or you may find it easier to make a cut from the edge of the cardboard to the picture at an angle that will permit you to continue cutting along the edge of the picture. Note in Figure A below that the dotted cutting line is directly lined up with a straight cutting edge of the object.

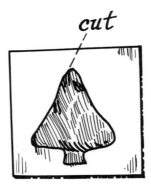

Fig. A

4. If you are making a divided-object puzzle, remove the picture from the cardboard frame and cut it again carefully to divide the picture into the desired two or three pieces.
5. Repaste any loose edges of the picture. If you cut through the cardboard frame, repair the slit with tape on the back of the frame.

(See also Activity 122 for directions for making paper plate puzzles.)

SELECTED PUZZLES

Simple puzzles for young children can often be purchased in toy stores. Those listed below have been found useful in working with the very young child. The list is not exclusive. By becoming familiar with some of the puzzles listed, you will be able to select others of similar simplicity and characteristics which appeal to the very young.

Whole Object Puzzles

Buildings We See (Sifo/Judy)—4 pieces
Carpenter's Tools (Sifo/Judy)—6 pieces
Cat and Kittens (Fisher–Price)—6 pieces
Children's Pets (Sifo/Judy)—5 pieces
Colors I See (Playskool)—4 pieces
Form Board (Playskool)—8 pieces (circle, square, triangle, curve)
Fruit (Judy)—5 pieces
Fruits I Like (Playskool)—4 pieces
I Set the Table (Playskool)—5 pieces
Leaves (Judy)—5 pieces
My Baby Pets (Playskool)—4 pieces
My Toys (Playskool)—4 pieces
Nature (Fisher–Price)—6 pieces
Pets (Judy)—5 pieces
Rain (Judy)—4 pieces
Tools (Judy)—6 pieces
Toys (Judy)—5 pieces
Transportation (Judy)—6 pieces
Vehicles (Fisher–Price)—8 pieces
Weather (Fisher–Price)—5 pieces
When It Rains (Playskool)—4 pieces

Divided Object Puzzles

Airplane (Judy)—12 pieces
Butterfly (Judy)—5 pieces
Cat and Kittens (Judy)—13 pieces
Cat and the Fiddle (Playskool)—13 pieces
Chickens (Playskool)—15 pieces
Children of the World (Creative Playthings)—set of 18 mini-puzzles, 4
    pieces each
Colors and Things (Playskool)—24 2-piece, interlocking puzzles

Dog and Puppies (Fisher–Price)—8 pieces
Ducks (Playskool)—12 pieces
Fire Engine (Fisher–Price)—12 pieces
Hippo (Playskool)—7 pieces
Humpty Dumpty (Playskool)—12 pieces
Kitten (Playskool)—9 pieces
Nursery Jigs (Condor)—6 puzzles, 3 interlocking pieces each
Puppy Love (Playskool)—9 pieces
Rocking Horse (Playskool)—12 pieces
Speedy Delivery (Child Guidance)—Wonder What's Under? puzzle, 3
    levels
Squirrel (Playskool)—6 pieces

ACTIVITY 117: One-Piece, Whole-Object Puzzle

WHY

To fit whole-object correctly in the frame.

WHAT YOU NEED

A simple whole-object (animal) puzzle.

TALK ABOUT WHAT YOU DO

(Use your own language. This is an example.)

(Place the puzzle on the floor or a flat surface in front of the child.) "Look at this pretty picture. Can you tell me what it is? / Yes, it is a cat. It is a baby cat. A baby cat is called a kitten."

"Where is the kitten's head? / Show me the kitten's ears. / Yes, that's one. Where is the kitten's other ear? / That's right. The kitten has two ears just like you have. (Point to each ear as you count.) One ear, two ears."

"Can you find the kitten's tail? / Look hard. / There is the tail. (Point.) Now, let's see if you can find the kitten's feet. / Oh, you found one. Where is another foot? / Let's count the kitten's feet. (Point to feet as you count.) One, two, three, four."

"You know what? This is a picture puzzle. A puzzle is something you can take apart. Watch. (Demonstrate.) I can take the picture of the kitten right out. / See the hole (point) where the kitten was?"

"Let's learn how to put the kitten back in the hole. That's what we do with puzzles. Can you run your finger around the kitten like this? (Demonstrate.) That's right. Find the kitten's head with your finger. / Oh, that bump is an ear, isn't it? / There is another ear." (Identify also *tail* and *feet*, which protrude, as the child continues to trace the kitten.)

"Now let's trace the hole where the kitten was. Start here where the kitten's head was. (Point to or demonstrate.) Oh, you found where the kitten's ear was." (Identify also outlines of the *tail* and *feet* as the child continues to trace the edge of the hole.)

"Can you find the kitten's head in the picture? / Show me again the hole where the kitten's head fits. / Very good! Watch me. I am going to put the kitten's head in the hole first. / There. Now the kitten will fit right back in the hole if you push it. Go ahead. Push the kitten in. / Oh, you did it! You put the puzzle together!"

"Do you want to take the kitten out again and try to put it back in the hole?" (Help the child as needed if he tries again. If he does not wish to try again, do not insist.)

HELPFUL HINTS

A one-piece puzzle refers to a single whole object in a frame. A simple three- or four-piece whole-object puzzle can be used if you focus the learning on only one of the objects. See also suggestions for making your own puzzles on pages 307–308.

For the child's first puzzle, select an object that has a distinctive shape, one the child is familiar with.

In tracing the object, help the child identify the parts of the object which protrude and can, therefore, be easily recognized when tracing the outline of the object in the frame (the "hole"). Use one of these distinctive features as the clue for replacing the object correctly in the frame.

THINGS TO DO ANOTHER TIME

Repeat the activity soon, using the same puzzle. It may take several sessions before the child is able to do the activity without assistance. Do *not* start a new puzzle until the first one is mastered.

Use other whole-object puzzles. Remember, if you have, for example, a four-piece whole-object puzzle, you have materials for four activities similar to the one suggested above. See also page 309 for list of simple whole-object puzzles.

ACTIVITY 118:   One-Piece, Whole-Object Puzzle

WHY

To recognize a particular shape or dimension of an object or part of an object.
To fit the object correctly in the frame.

WHAT YOU NEED

A simple whole-object puzzle which includes a particular, clearly defined shape (hammer).

TALK ABOUT WHAT YOU DO

(Use your own language. This is an example.)

(Place the puzzle on the floor or on a flat surface in front of the child.) "Look at the nice picture we have. / What is that a picture of? / It is a hammer. What can you do with a hammer? / We can pound pegs with a hammer, can't we? / Yes, we can also bang nails with a hammer."

"Help me take the hammer piece out of the puzzle. / There, it is out."

"Which part of the hammer do you use to bang the nails? / Right! It's called the head of the hammer. It's little, isn't it? / Where is the handle of the hammer? / This lo-ong (run finger along length of handle) part is the handle. You have to hold on to the handle when you pound nails, don't you? / Can you run your finger all along the handle like I did? / That's right. My, that's a lo-ong handle."

"Now let's find the long part of the hole in the board. Where is the long hole where the handle of the hammer was? / Can you trace it with your fingertips? / Does the hole feel long too?"

"Watch carefully. I am going to put the *long* handle of the hammer in the *long* hole. / I can push the whole hammer in, now. / See how easy that was?"

"Help me take the hammer out again and then you can try to put it back in the hole. / Remember, the long handle goes in the long hole. Turn it a little more like this. (Guide child's hand.) That's good. Now push it in. / Ka-plop! In it went! Oh, you're good at doing puzzles. Let's do it again."

HELPFUL HINTS

See pages 307–308 for suggestions for making your own whole-object puzzles.

This activity differs from Activity 117 in that the emphasis is on a particular shape or dimension of an object or part of an object (in the sample lesson, on the length of the handle). If the child recognizes the particular shape or dimension both in the puzzle piece and in the outline of the piece in the puzzle frame, he will have a clue to replacing the piece correctly in the frame. If he fails to recognize the similarity, repeat the tracing of the long handle in the picture and the outline of it in the frame. If additional help is needed, guide the child's hand. Remember, it is important for the child to have some success in solving the puzzle.

Do not expect the youngster to necessarily form the concept *long* (or other concepts of shape and size) through this activity. His task is simply to recognize similarity of size (or shape) and to replace the piece accordingly. The activity does, however, provide readiness learning for acquiring particular concepts of size and shape.

THINGS TO DO ANOTHER TIME

Use the same puzzle to repeat the activity, preferably within the week of the first session. It may take more than one session for the child to master the puzzle on his own.

Adapt the activity to other whole-object puzzles in which a particular shape or dimension (long, short, fat, skinny) are an integral part of the piece. Some examples which lend themselves to the approach are: star (points), lollipop (round top/long, skinny stick), car (rounded wheels), toy block (pointed corners), leaf or flower (long, skinny stem), ice cream cone (rounded top/pointed, triangular bottom), heart (two rounds at top/pointed bottom), open umbrella (fat, rounded top/long, skinny handle).

ACTIVITY 119: Two-Piece, Whole-Object Puzzle

PUZZLES
B

WHY

To distinguish between the shapes of two objects.
To fit the objects correctly into the frame.

WHAT YOU NEED

Two pieces of whole-object puzzle (fruit).

TALK ABOUT WHAT YOU DO

(Use your own language. This is an example.)

"Do you know what puzzle we have today? (Place puzzle on flat surface in front of child.) It is the fruit puzzle you like. Can you remember the names of the different fruit in the puzzle? / Apple. That's right. What color is the apple? / Red it is! The apple is round too. (Make a circling motion with finger around the apple.) Can you tell me the name of another fruit in the puzzle? / *Ba-na-na*. That's right. Is the banana red like the apple? / No, the banana is yellow. And the banana is long." (Run finger over length of banana.)

"What is this fruit called?" (Continue to identify the other fruit and review their colors and shapes.)

"Let's take out two of the pictures of fruit. Which ones would you like? / Okay, take out the apple. / Which other one do you want to take out? / Good. Now see if you can put both the apple and the banana back in the puzzle."

"Is that the round apple hole or the long banana hole? / Right. It's the apple hole. / Oh, won't the apple go in? / Trace the apple and see if you can find its stem. / Feel it? / Now see if you can find the place in the apple hole for the stem. / That's right. Push it in. / Wheee! You did it! You got the apple in all by yourself."

"Try the banana now. / Turn the banana around. / Keep trying. I know you can do it. Oh (clap), you got the banana in too!"

"Let's see if we can get the grapes and the pear back in the right place." (Repeat tracing and talking about distinguishing features of each piece if the child has difficulty.)

"That was very good. You really know how to work the fruit puzzle, don't you?"

HELPFUL HINTS

This activity calls for working with two whole-object puzzle pieces (which are probably part of a three- or four-piece whole-object puzzle). It assumes that the child has already worked with the puzzle pieces singly and has been successful in mounting each individually.

Mounting two puzzle pieces is more difficult than mounting a single piece in that the task requires distinguishing between the shapes of the two pieces to replace them correctly in the frame.

Try giving only verbal help in the activity. But if the child has difficulty and is in danger of failing or becoming frustrated, give additional direct help, such as turning a piece around or guiding his hand. Don't let the child fail.

Puzzles the child can do on his own are usually very enjoyable for the child. Encourage the child to use the puzzles also in unstructured play.

THINGS TO DO ANOTHER TIME

When the child has success with two puzzle pieces, gradually increase their number so that the child must distinguish between three, four, or five shapes. A review of the shapes of the objects or other key features of an object will be helpful to the child in each task.

Repeat the activity using other simple whole-object puzzles that the child is already familiar with and has successfully replaced the puzzle pieces individually in the puzzle frame.

ACTIVITY 120:   Two-Piece, Divided-Object Puzzle

PUZZLES
B

WHY

To recognize parts of a whole.
To put parts together to make a whole.

WHAT YOU NEED

A two-piece divided-object puzzle (animal).

TALK ABOUT WHAT YOU DO

(Use your own language. This is an example.)

"Look at the new puzzle we have today. What kind of animal is in the puzzle? / Yes, it is a pretty little dog. Where is the dog's head? / Can you find his ears? / That's one ear. See the other ear on this side of the little dog's head? (Point.) Now where is the dog's nose? / I hope he hasn't lost his nose. / Oh, yes, there is the nose. Does the little dog have a mouth? / Very good! The little dog can say 'Arf! Arf!' if he has a mouth."

"This is a little dog's body. (Make an encircling motion to indicate body area.) What is this over here? (Point to tail.) / Yes, it's a tail. Do you have a tail? / You would look pretty funny with a tail, wouldn't you?"

"What are these? (Point to legs.) / Right. The legs are under the little dog's body (point to legs again) so the little dog can run. And the head is on top of the little dog's body (move hand up to head) so he can see you and say 'Arf! Arf!'

"Look. I can take the little dog's head away from the rest of the little dog. (Remove top piece.) The little dog needs his head so we had better put it back. Watch. I'll put it back. (Continue talking as you slowly replace the piece.) The little dog's head has to go on top of the little dog's body. Right there!"

"Can you take the head piece out of the puzzle? / Oh, the poor little dog has lost his head again. You put it back. / Oops! His head is upside-down. Turn it around. / Good. Shove it down a little further. / See. The little dog has his head again."

"This time we'll take away the little dog's body. Oh, he has lost his tail and his legs too. Can you put the little dog back together again? / Whoops! Find the little dog's legs. They have to go at the bottom of the picture (indicate position below head of the dog) so the little dog can use his legs to run. / You've got it. I think you've got it! Yup! The little dog is saying 'Arf! Arf!' He is saying, 'Thank you, Jimmy, for putting me all together again.'"

HELPFUL HINTS

See pages 307–308 for suggestions for making your own two-piece divided puzzles.

If you use a three- or four-piece divided-object puzzle, simply limit the activity to removing and replacing two key pieces such as the head and body of the dog. Remove and replace one piece at a time.

If the child needs help in placing the pieces together, guide his hand the first time. But try verbal directions to help him the second time. And continue to stress the logic of the picture: legs at the bottom of the body (to run) and the head at the top (to see).

THINGS TO DO ANOTHER TIME

Make and use in similar activities other simple two-piece divided-object puzzles. Be sure the pieces are made up of whole units of the picture. For example, in a simple house puzzle, the roof is one piece and the rest of the house is the second piece. And stress the logic of where the pieces go: "The roof has to go on top of the house, you know. Otherwise the people in the house will get all wet when it rains."

See pages 309–310 for suggestions for simple divided-object puzzles.

ACTIVITY 121: Three-Piece, Divided-Object Puzzle

PUZZLES
C

WHY

To recognize positional relationships among puzzle pieces.
To replace each puzzle piece correctly.

WHAT YOU NEED

Two paper plates; crayons (see directions below).

TALK ABOUT WHAT YOU DO

(Use your own language. This is an example.)

"Meet Mr. Smiley, the happy face. He is smiling the way you smile when you are happy. Can you give me a big smile just like Mr. Smiley?"

"Where are Mr. Smiley's eyes? / Right. (Point and count.) One eye, two eyes. Both eyes (move finger in straight line from one eye to the other) are at the top (indicate top of face with hand) of Mr. Smiley's face."

"What is this (point to mouth) at the bottom of Mr. Smiley's face? / Yes, it is a big smiling mouth at the bottom (indicate bottom of face with hand) of Mr. Smiley's face."

"Can you find Mr. Smiley's nose? / That's right. The eyes are up here (indicate with hand) at the top of the face. And Mr. Smiley's nose is under (move hand down to nose) his eyes. And what is under his nose (move hand down to mouth) at the bottom of his face? / Very good."

"Now watch. I am going to take a piece of Mr. Smiley's face away. (Remove piece which has one eye.) Oh, Mr. Smiley lost an eye! Can you find his eye on this piece? (Give child the puzzle piece.) Let's give Mr. Smiley back his eye. Show me where the eye has to go on Mr. Smiley's face. / That's right. It has to go at the top of his face, next to the other eye. See, like this. / There. Mr. Smiley has two eyes now. Let's take the eye away again and then put it back." (Help as needed, guiding child's hand if necessary.)

(Repeat for piece with mouth. Talk about putting the mouth back at bottom of face and under Mr. Smiley's nose. Then repeat for piece with nose and eye, talking about the eye having to go at the top of the face and the nose under the eyes.)

"Now close your eyes and I'll take away one piece of Mr. Smiley's face. / What is missing from his face? / Here is the piece. Can you put it back?" (Continue removing other pieces in similar fashion.)

HELPFUL HINTS

Draw with crayons (or colored pens) a smiling face on the top side of one paper plate: Cut into three pieces as indicated by the dotted lines in Fig.

Fig. 121.1

121.1. Place the pieces in proper position in the second plate. The second plate serves as a frame to hold the pieces in their proper position, which will be helpful when replacing the single pieces.

THINGS TO DO ANOTHER TIME

Cut from another paper plate a puzzle piece that is identical in size and shape to the smiling mouth piece. Draw on the new piece a turned-down, unhappy mouth. Have the child alternate making Mr. Smiley and making Mr. Frown by using the two different mouth pieces.

When the child has mastered replacing each piece of the puzzle singly, take out all three pieces of the puzzle and let the child try to put them back to make Mr. Smiley or Mr. Frown. Help him with verbal directions ("I don't think the mouth piece goes at the top of the face, do you?" or "Turn the piece around. / Now put it in the plate like that"), but guide the child's hand if necessary for success.

Draw or paste other simple pictures on a paper plate and cut into three pieces, each of which has an easily recognized part of the total picture. Adapt the activity to the puzzle picture.

ACTIVITY 122: Four- or Five-Piece, Divided-Object Puzzle

PUZZLES
C

WHY

To recognize parts of a whole object.
To fit puzzle pieces together correctly.

WHAT YOU NEED

Puzzle which includes a whole object divided into several pieces (see "Helpful Hints").

TALK ABOUT WHAT YOU DO

(Use your own language. This is an example.)

"Oh, look at this pretty picture! What do you see? / Yes, dogs—a mother dog and two baby dogs. Baby dogs are called *puppies,* aren't they? / Can you point to one of the puppies? / Where is the other puppy? / Where is the mother dog? / Very good! The mother dog's name is Ginger. It says so right here (point) on the doghouse."

"What do you think the mother dog, Ginger, is doing? / She is watching the puppies play. She wants to be sure they don't get hurt or run away. Can you find Ginger's head? / Right! Can you find the pretty red bow around Ginger's neck? / Where is Ginger's body? / I'll give you a hint. Ginger's body is right under Ginger's head. / Oh, you found the body. Is your body under your head too? / Yes, heads (point to head piece) are always *on top* and the body (move finger from head to body to indicate *under*) is always *under* the head. Does Ginger have a tail? / What are these? (Point to legs.) Oh, you're so smart!"

"Do you know what! This picture is a puzzle! See, I can take out Ginger's body with this little yellow knob. (Demonstrate removing the body piece.) Where is the hole in the puzzle where the body piece goes? / Can you trace the hole like this? (Demonstrate.) That's right. Now use your finger to trace the body piece. (Help the child if necessary, and talk about one or two irregularities of the piece that will serve as clues.) Oh, that bumpy part is where Ginger's red bow goes. / O-o-oh, that's Ginger's stomach. It bulges, doesn't it?"

"Okay, let's put Ginger's body back under Ginger's head. Show me again where this piece goes. / Good. Watch now. See this bumpy place (point) on the piece? / It fits right here under Ginger's red bow. There! Ginger's body is back under Ginger's head."

"You take out the body now. / Very good! Can you put it back the way I did? / Find that bumpy place. /Where is the red bow on Ginger's neck? / Wiggle it a little. (Clap.) You got it in! Ginger is all together again."

HELPFUL HINTS

"Dog and Puppies," an eight-piece pick-up and peek puzzle by Fisher–Price, was used for this activity. It serves as a good introduction to a simple divided-object puzzle because the mother dog is made up of five pieces. Any puzzle with an object divided into three, four, or five pieces can be used for this activity.

If the child is curious about the knobs on some of the puzzle pieces, you may want to let the child see what is under each of these pieces and talk about what he sees when each piece is removed. But come back to the focus of the activity (the divided-object pieces) when the child's curiosity is satisfied.

The sequence used in this activity applies to any divided-object puzzle: (1) talk about and identify all major objects in the picture; (2) talk about and identify some important detail of the particular pieces which are part of the divided object (head, body, bow) and their positional relationship (over, under); (3) working with one piece at a time, demonstrate removing the piece, name the piece, trace it and its shape in the puzzle board, and talk about one or two easily recognized bumps or parts of the piece which will serve as clues in replacing the piece; (4) demonstrate replacing the piece; (5) have the child remove and replace the piece but give any help that may be needed for the child to be successful; and (6) repeat Step 5.

If the child remains interested in the puzzle, you may want to go on to a second piece of the puzzle, removing the original piece and a second piece and using Steps 3–6 above for the new piece. Each time the child replaces the new piece, have him replace also the first piece.

THINGS TO DO ANOTHER TIME

Repeat and adapt the activity to include the additional puzzle pieces of the divided-object puzzle, adding one piece at a time until the whole puzzle can be done at once by the child. Begin each activity by a review of the pieces already mastered by the child. Always be prepared to help the child as needed.

Select your new pieces in some logical fashion for easy mastery by the youngster. In the "Dog and Puppies" puzzle, for example, the logical second piece is Ginger's head. Talk about how it is on *top of* the body; identify the eyes, nose, tongue, and ears on the new piece; trace the rounded top of the head piece, the protruding right ear, and the bumpy red bow; demonstrate replacing the head piece at the very top of the puzzle ("Heads go on top, you know") and use the right ear as a clue for mounting the piece correctly; have the child remount the head piece, with help if needed, and then the body piece; and finally let him remove the two pieces and try again on his own to replace them. But don't let him fail.

On the next round, after reviewing the replacement of the first two pieces, remove a third piece and repeat the key procedures suggested above. Continue in similar fashion until all pieces are removed and the child is able to complete the whole puzzle.

Work with other simple divided-object puzzles in the same way (using steps given in "Helpful Hints" and procedures given above for additional pieces). If the child loses interest or becomes fatigued or frustrated, stop the activity and come back to the puzzle on another day.

See pages 309–310 for a list of divided-object puzzles for young children.

Internalizing abstract concepts such as *little* and *big* may require many firsthand experiences in sorting objects by size. Buttons and other small household objects can be used in sorting tasks.

Part 8

Sorting and Ordering

SORTING AND ORDERING

The ability to sort or classify things by shared characteristics is an important part of concept development and an important part of learning. The human mind is able to recognize similarities and differences between specific things and to group those things which share important characteristics into categories or classes of things. *When the mind forms a mental or generalized picture of the important characteristics of a class of things, we say that a concept has been formed.* Once we have formed a concept, we are able to recognize, on our own, other new specific examples of the concept group without relearning each time what each new specific thing is. And when we have learned the concept word or phrase which is commonly used to designate the particular class of objects, qualities, or actions (such as *cat, house, chair, animal, big, red, jumping, getting dressed*), we are able to communicate the generalized idea of the concept to others who have formed the same concept, without use of a specific example of it. Our learned concepts, then, organize and give order to our world of millions of specifics and make it possible for us to function in it.

Because concepts are internalized, abstract mental pictures of a group or class of objects, qualities, or actions (not merely the learned concept word), no one can form a concept for another person. Concepts are formed as the result of the individual's own experiences. One can only help another develop concepts by providing many of the right kind of experiences and by supplying the proper concept words to communicate the concepts. But keep in mind that the mere repeating of a concept word is of itself no indication that the concept has been formed by the learner.

For young children the right kind of experiences are those which involve specific, concrete objects they can see, feel, taste, hear, smell, and/or manipulate and first-hand experiences in actions and events. Young children do not think at an abstract level. Their world is full of only specific, concrete things. They must use their first-hand sensory experiences and their involvement in using and manipulating objects to form their first concepts. From many such experiences, they begin to perceive relationships of similarities and differences that exist between objects and between actions and of relationships of time and space that exist between them and objects. And from these awarenesses they are able to form simple concepts.

For example, to form the concept *car*, the youngster must experience many specific examples of *car*. The more he is directly involved in these experiences (riding in a car as well as seeing, hearing, smelling, and feeling cars), the more learning will probably take place. From these experiences, he becomes aware of common characteristics of cars: they all have wheels, they can move, and they make a certain kind of noise when they move. By hearing and repeating the word *car* as part of his encounters with the specific cars, he learns too that the name applies to each of the cars he has seen. Thus when the youngster at some point sees a car not seen or experienced by him before and says, without coaching, *car*, one can assume that he has formed at least a rudimentary mental picture (concept) of the group of objects called *car*.

Preschoolers are able to develop concepts of many kinds of objects (*car*, *house*, *chair*, *cat*, *apple*) because the abstract concepts are closely related to concrete objects which the youngster can see and feel or use his other senses to experience the objects. But above these low-level concepts are others, somewhat more complex and abstract, which the preschooler is also capable of forming through first-hand sensory experiences. Concepts like *toy*, *animal*, *fruit*, *furniture*, *dishes*, and *clothes* are some of these. They are one step further removed from the concrete object than are low-level concepts since each includes and is applicable to several similar kinds of low-level concepts.

Take, for example, the concept *toy*. It includes within its meaning the (low-level) concepts of any number of concrete objects (such as *doll*, *ball*, *block*) which have as a primary purpose play. Figure B below illustrates this relationship between the concept *toy* and its subconcepts as well as its relationship to specific, concrete objects experienced by the child.

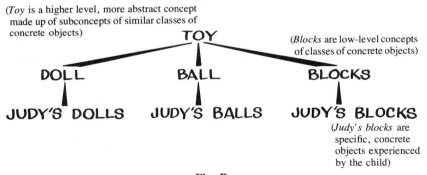

(*Toy* is a higher level, more abstract concept made up of subconcepts of similar classes of concrete objects)

TOY

(*Blocks* are low-level concepts of classes of concrete objects)

DOLL   BALL   BLOCKS

JUDY'S DOLLS   JUDY'S BALLS   JUDY'S BLOCKS

(*Judy's blocks* are specific, concrete objects experienced by the child)

Fig. B

As the diagram indicates, Judy must first experience through her senses an adequate sampling of specific dolls to form a generalized mental picture (concept) of what a doll is. When Judy has so formed the concepts of *doll*, *ball*, *block*, or other kinds of playthings, she is then ready to begin conceptualizing at the next, more abstract level. She does so by becoming aware of a larger group of objects all of which share the common purpose of play and all of which are called *toy*. But until the appropriate low-level concepts are formed by Judy, she will not be able to perform the more difficult task involved in conceptualizing at the next level. This necessary sequence which the mind uses naturally to form concepts is also the sequence which must be followed in structured learning activities to help the child form concepts: starting with first-hand experiences with specific, concrete objects to form low-level concepts and then using these already learned low-level concepts to help the youngster develop appropriate higher-level concepts.

The young child is also able to form concepts of various kinds of actions or activities if he experiences them. He begins to understand what is meant by jumping or running or climbing as he sees others doing these things. He deepens his understanding of these actions as he himself discovers what it feels like to jump, run, or climb. The abstract concepts of basic colors, simple shapes and sizes and such qualities as *hard/soft* and *smooth/rough* are also within the preschooler's grasp if his first-hand experiences are properly focused on these qualities as they exist in specific, concrete objects.

As the young child, through his senses and first-hand experiences, stores up many impressions of specific objects and events, he begins to associate particular characteristics with these specifics. When he perceives basic characteristics which are shared by like or similar objects, he is ready to organize the specific items into groups on the basis of these characteristics. The grouping task of this latter process is called classification. It is one way to promote concept development.

Children begin to classify objects first by gross differences. They learn, for example, some of the overall characteristics of specific blocks and balls. They are able to select a block or a ball when named and to match a block with another block, a ball with another ball. And finally, they are able to sort or classify blocks and balls on the basis of their overall or gross differences. A demonstration of such sorting skill by the youngster indicates some elemental understanding of the distinguishing characteristics of blocks and balls or, in other words, of the concepts *block* and *ball*.

Young children are able also to classify objects by use. They often perceive functional relationships between and among things they use or see used in everyday life. Through these experiences they become aware that certain objects go together because they are used for the same purpose (fork and spoon, plate and bowl) or at the same time (cup and saucer, washcloth and towel, hammer and nail). Grouping items by their use is another form of classification which can be used to promote such higher-level concepts as *food, toys, clothes,* and *dishes.*

As the child's experiences with objects grow, the youngster begins to use finer differences as a basis for grouping. Size, shapes, and colors become distinguishing characteristics of objects. He learns grouping within a class of objects: to put all the red cars in one pile and all the blue cars in another pile; to separate all the little cars from all the big cars. He learns to recognize other abstract qualities which he can use to group items; *soft/hard, smooth/rough, round/square.* A comb and a key go into a *hard* pile, a ball of cotton and a marshmallow go into a *soft* pile; round objects are separated from square objects.

With still further enlargement of experiences, the youngster begins to perceive gradations between two extremes of a quality, becoming aware, for example, that between *little* and *big* are other sizes, and that between *soft* and *hard* are other degrees of softness and hardness. The task of ordering or arranging objects on the basis of size or some other quality that lends itself to gradation is called seriation. Its primary purpose is to refine and extend the dimensional or quality concept involved in the ordering.

Other ordering or seriation tasks for young children include patterning: arranging objects in some kind of a color or shape pattern such as first a red bead, next a blue bead, and last a yellow bead; or first a round block, then a square block, and last a triangular block. Sequencing events is also an ordering task which youngsters can learn to handle in a very simple form: what happens first, what happens next, what happens last. Note, however, that *first, next,* and *last* denote different meanings in patterning and in sequencing. In the former, they denote a relationship in the position of objects in space; in the latter, they denote the relationship of events or things done in time.

The samples of sorting and ordering activities which follow in this section are directly focused on helping the child build concepts through the processes of classification and seriation. They are arranged in keeping with the general development of the child so that they progress from simple to more complex and from more concrete to more abstract concept levels. The codes A, B, and C designate the general level of child development for which each activity is recommended. (See pages 16–18 for a detailed description of these levels.) However, because tasks of classifying and ordering are usually too difficult for children at the A level, the simplest tasks in this section begin at the B level and progress in difficulty through the C level.

Other general principles to be kept in mind in using these activities and in planning your own sorting and ordering activities for a particular child are:

1. *Select the specific objects to be used and the kind of sorting/ordering task to be performed by the child on the basis of his previous learning.* Learning that involves recognizing and naming objects or qualities of objects should precede the tasks of sorting and ordering objects. To combine the two kinds of learning in a single activity is usually too much for the child to absorb at one time. As the youngster becomes adept at identifying common objects by name or by basic color, shapes, and sizes, he is probably ready to begin simple matching and sorting tasks involving the already learned objects and qualities.

2. *Make the focus of learning clear in each activity.* If the learning task calls for sorting by size, keep color and shape of objects constant. To use,

for example, all little blue buttons and all big red buttons will permit the child to sort by color as well as by size without your knowing which characterisitic he is using. The same holds true in sorting by shape if all the circles are blue and all the squares are red. The child may also become confused if, in sorting by size, the difference in sizes of objects is not great enough to be easily recognized or if, in sorting by kinds of objects, the objects to be sorted are too similar (beads and ball-shaped buttons, or balls and round blocks). These finer distinctions are appropriate only when the child's experiences include the perception of finer differences between objects.

3. *Introduce your sorting/ordering activities by reviewing the child's previous related learning:* names of the objects, colors, sizes, shapes. Include also a demonstration of the sorting task and the use of guiding language ("Where is the round basket?" or "Is that the little or big box?") to help the child remember the sorting directions. This is especially important when the task is new to the youngster.

4. *Involve the child actively throughout the activity.* Let him do as much of the arranging and rearranging of the materials as he can. Let him also help you prepare sorting materials: making Play Dough balls and small flat "pancakes" or painting objects to be sorted.

5. *Keep the activity fun.* Make it play for the youngster. Praise him often. If he is unable to perform a sorting/ordering task, adjust the task to one he can do. For instance, if the task is one of sorting *soft* and *hard* objects and the youngster is failing, quickly sort the objects yourself. Give him the soft objects. Have him squeeze each object, say "soft," and then place it on, say, the soft pillow. Follow the same procedure with the hard objects. Try him on the original sorting task another time, after providing him with additional "touching" experiences.

Other more specific helpful hints are provided with each of the activities. Remember, too, that concept development is a slow, gradual process. Do not expect immediate and certainly not complete mastery by the child. He needs time and repetition. In fact, his education during preschool and elementary school years is largely devoted to building concepts, including extending and refining the concepts he learns in his first years.

ACTIVITY 123: Matching Like Objects

SORTING
B

WHY

To match objects that are alike.
To identify objects that are different.

WHAT YOU NEED

Two balls and two toy cars (identical or very similar in size and color); a single block; box.

TALK ABOUT WHAT YOU DO

(Use your own language. This is an example.)

(Place one ball and one car and your single object in the box and set the box aside. Use the other ball and the other car to start the activity.)

"Look at what I have! (Hold up ball.) What is it? / That's right. It is a red ball. What can we do with the ball? / Okay, let's roll it. I'll roll it to you and then you roll it back to me. / Roll the ball back to me. / Oh, that was a good roll. Let's roll the ball some more."

"I have something else. (Hold up car.) Right, it is a car. Can you show me where the wheels of the car are? / Where does the driver of the car sit? / Can you show me how the car goes when you drive it? / Say, that is a fast car."

"Look in this box now. See if you can find another car like the car you have. / Look carefully. / Oh, you found it! Put the cars right in front of you. / Like this. Are the cars alike? / Well, let's see. Show me the wheels on each car. / Do both cars have a place for the driver to sit? / Do both cars move when you push them? / The cars are alike, aren't they?"

"See if you can find a ball in the box that is just like this ball. / That's right. Put the balls together. / Are the two balls alike? Do they look alike? / Yes, they are alike. Both are red, and they both are round. Do they both roll? / You roll one of the balls to me. / I'll roll the other ball to you. / Yes, they both roll. They must be alike."

(Place one ball and one car together in front of child.) "Are these two things alike? / Are they both balls? / Are they both cars? / No, they are not alike. One is a ball and one is a car. Can you fix them so that they are alike? / I'll take the car away. Now can you find a ball that is just like this ball? / Good. Now you have two things that are just alike. / Here is one car. Can you find the other car like it? / Right. Now you have two cars that are alike."

HELPFUL HINTS

Use only objects with which the child is familiar.

Lead up to the matching task by reviewing important characteristics of each object to be matched. Involve the child actively in these introductory strategies.

The youngster probably will not use the words *alike* (*same*) or *different,* but accept any other way he is able to communicate to you that the objects are matched or mismatched.

If the child gives no indication of understanding what is meant by *alike* and is unable to respond to the question "Are they alike?" continue using the words always supported by words he understands: "They are alike. They are both cars." Or "They are different. One is a car and the other is a ball." He may need several sessions to grasp these abstract ideas.

THINGS TO DO ANOTHER TIME

Repeat the activity using other paired familiar objects for the child to match: combs, clothespins, buttons, spoons, cups.

When the child becomes adept at matching two paired objects, increase the difficulty of the task by (a) using pairs of objects that are similar in some way but not the same (forks / spoons, crayons / pencils) or (b) adding a third pair of like objects so that the child must match and differentiate between three sets of objects.

Play a game in which the child must find an object in the room which matches an object which you present or identify: chairs, lamps, books, pictures. You may have to set up the room for the game by bringing in matching objects and placing them within the child's line of vision.

Play a game with a variety of matched and mismatched objects. Have the child close his eyes or turn the other way while you put two objects side by side. The child's task each time is to tell whether the objects are alike or different.

ACTIVITY 124:   Sorting Objects

SORTING
B

WHY

To identify objects that are alike.
To identify objects that are different.

WHAT YOU NEED

Three to five cars and three to five blocks; two shallow containers (lids of boxes or platic bowls).

TALK ABOUT WHAT YOU DO

(Use your own language. This is an example.)

(Place all the toys in one box lid.) "Let's see what is in the box. Can you dump all the things in the box on the rug? / Oh, look! What do we have? / Right, that's a car. Is there something else? / Yes, that's another car. See if you can find something that is not a car. / That's good! You found a block. A block is *different* from a car."

"Let's play a sorting game with all these things. We'll put all the cars in this box (point) because the cars are all *alike*. And we'll put all the blocks in this other box (point) because blocks are *different* from cars. Okay? / Show me a car. / The car goes in this box (point). / Good. Now can you find a block? / Right. It goes in this other box (point). / No, that box is just for cars. This box (point) is for blocks because blocks are *different* from cars. / Very good!"

'What is that? / Where is your car box? / Oh, now you have two cars in the box. (Count and point.) One car, two cars. See if you can get all the cars in this box (point) and all the blocks in that box.''

"Say, you sorted all the cars and blocks into the right boxes. (Clap.) What did you put in this box? (Point.) Yes, all the things in this box are *alike*. They are all cars. Is there something *different* in the other box? / No, there are no cars in this box. These are all blocks. The blocks are all *alike,* but blocks are *different* from cars, aren't they?''

"Let's dump both boxes on the rug and play the game again.''

HELPFUL HINTS

Any two sets of small objects familiar to the child can be used in this activity. Each set, however, should not be all the same color. Your focus is on gross differences between objects. If the objects in a set are all one color, you will not know if the child is differentiating between objects or color. If both sets of objects are the same color or objects are all different colors, the distinguishing feature will have to be the objects themselves.

The first time you use this activity, be prepared to spend time on the nature of the sorting task: how to put the objects in two different groups. Keeping the containers straight may also be a problem. Demonstrate the sorting task and help the child as needed to find the right containers. The youngster will probably need less and less help of this kind as he repeats the activity.

Remember that concept development is a slow, gradual process, so repeat the activity and be patient. If the child errs, the key questions are: "Is that *like* the things already in the box or is it different? / Can you find the box that has things *like* the one in your hand?''

THINGS TO DO ANOTHER TIME

Repeat the activity for many other easily handled objects with which the child is familiar: buttons/jar lids, spoons/forks, mittens/socks, plastic cups/plastic bowls, balls/blocks.

Play a game of "Find the Buttons.'' Collect several small but different objects and add about ten very similar buttons (in size and shape but varied in color). Place the objects in scattered fashion in front of the child. Tell the youngster that the game is to find all the buttons and put them into a box or wide-mouth container. Then say something like this: "Can you find a button? / Good. Now drop it into the box because that is where all the buttons go. / Is that a button? (Point.) No, that is a bottle cap. It is different from a button. Only buttons go into the box. Find all the buttons and put them in the box." Use the words *alike* and *different* often in talking about the task and especially in providing verbal help to the child.

ACTIVITY 125:   Sorting by Color

SORTING
B

WHY

To identify different colors of objects.

To sort objects by color.

WHAT YOU NEED

Red and blue poker chips; red and blue boxes.

TALK ABOUT WHAT YOU DO

(Use your own language. This is an example.)

"Look at the two boxes I have. Do you know what color this box (point) is? / Yes, it's red. What color is this other box (point)? / That's right. It's blue."

"I think there is something inside these boxes. Do you want to shake the red box? / Hear that? I wonder what it is. Let's find out. (Let the child open box, helping him if necessary, and empty contents on floor or table.) Oh my, look at all those chips! What color are they? / Yes, the red box was full of red chips. Shake the blue box now. / Is there something in it? / Oh, more chips! What color are they? / Blue, just like the box they are in." (Let child examine and manipulate chips if interested.)

"Let's mix the chips all up. / Now you have to pick out a chip and put it in the right box. The red chips have to go back in the red box and the blue chips go in the blue box. Okay? / Pick out a chip and tell me what color it is. / Which box does it go in? / Very good! Put all the chips back in the right boxes. Remember, red chips in red box, blue chips in blue box."

"How did that red chip get in this blue box with all the blue chips? / It must have sneaked in when we weren't looking. Can you take the red chip out and put it with the other red chips? / Good! What color are all the chips in this box? / What color are all the chips in this other box? / Very good!"

"Would you like to play with the chips for a while?"

HELPFUL HINTS

Paint (or crayon) boxes red and blue or cover them with red and blue paper. If you do not have poker chips, color thin cardboard red and blue and cut out circles or squares that you can use as chips. Six chips of each color are sufficient but you can use more, especially if the child enjoys the task.

The child should be able to identify the colors red and blue before tackling this sorting task. (See Activity 18.) Be sure also to review the colors and take the youngster through the sorting task before putting him on his own to complete the task. Help and correct mistakes pleasantly, either as they are made or after the chips are sorted.

THINGS TO DO ANOTHER TIME

Make and use chips of other colors to repeat the activity as the child learns to identify other colors. Also repeat the colors red and blue in combination with other colors: red and yellow, blue and orange, and so on.

Use various objects, some of which are red and others of which are blue: red toy car, red crayon, red mitten, red book, blue boat, blue pencil, blue crayon. Place sheets of blue and red construction paper (or cloth) on the floor or table and have the child sort the objects by color onto the proper colored paper. Repeat the activity for other pairs of colors to which the child has already been introduced.

For variation, sort into an egg carton. Color the inside of each cup a different color. Start with two colors, but continue to add other colors as the child's skill in identifying them grows. Bits of colored construction paper or cardboard (colored) or colored buttons or beads can be used for the sorting task.

ACTIVITY 126:   Sorting by Size: *Little/Big*

SORTING
B

WHY

To identify *little/big* objects.
To sort objects by size.

WHAT YOU NEED

A little and a big can; several little buttons (all one size, varied colors); several big buttons (all one size, varied colors).

TALK ABOUT WHAT YOU DO

(Use your own language. This is an example.)

(Spread all the buttons out in front of child.) "Look at what we have. What are they? / Right. Lots of buttons. (Let the child examine them if he likes.) What are these? (Point to cans.) They are pretty cans. See? (Hold one can so child can see into it.) You can put things in the can. / Which can is little? / Which can is big? / Very good!"

"Can you find a *little* button? / That's right. Drop it in the *little* can. / Good. Now find a *big* button? / The *big* button has to go in the *big* can. / Oh–oh, is that the *big* can? / Good, you found the big can. Put the big button in the big can."

"You have to put all the *little* buttons in the *little* can and all the *big* buttons in the *big* can. Can you do that? / Of course you can. Find another *little* button and put it in the *little* can. / See, I knew you could do it. Put some more buttons in the can. Just remember that *little* buttons go in the *little* can and *big* buttons in the *big* can.''

(If the child has difficulty, continue asking questions to remind him to use the concepts *little/big* in the sorting task.) ''My, that's a pretty blue button. Is it a *little* or *big* button? / If it is a *big* button, then which can does it go in? / Right! It goes in the *big* can.''

''All the little buttons are in the little can. Shake the little can to see if the buttons are there. / They are there, all right. Now shake the big can. / Are the big buttons still in the big can? / Yes, you put the big buttons in the can all by yourself.''

HELPFUL HINTS

This activity assumes that the child has already been introduced to the concepts *little* and *big*. (See Activity 29.)

At this stage of the child's development the youngster must work with gross differences in size to be successful. Select the cans and buttons so that their differences in size can be readily seen by the child.

You may wish to paint the cans or cover them with Contact paper to make them more attractive.

The child may be able to complete the task without a great deal of coaching, but if not, provide him with the verbal help he needs. If he continues to have trouble, have him first sort the buttons into groups of little and big buttons and then put them in the proper cans.

If you are working with a small group of children, have them take turns selecting buttons and putting them in the proper cans. Or provide each child with his own set of materials to work with after you have introduced the task as suggested in the first two paragraphs above.

THINGS TO DO ANOTHER TIME

Vary the kind of sorting material and repeat the activity: little/big pebbles, little/big washers, little/big crayons, little/big pieces of drinking straws.

Use little/big boxes for similar sorting tasks which involve somewhat bigger objects: balls, blocks, spoons, plastic jars. Limit the task to finding differences of little and big within a single class of objects until the child shows mastery of this skill. Then you may want to move the child into ordering by size (see Activity 132).

ACTIVITY 127:   Sorting by Function

SORTING
B

WHY

To identify functions of objects.
To sort objects by function.

WHAT YOU NEED

Banana; carrot; cookie; block; ball; doll; tray.

TALK ABOUT WHAT YOU DO

(Use your own language. This is an example.)

"Let's see if we know what all these things are on this tray. Can you tell me their names? / Yes, that's a banana. Do you like to eat bananas? / Yes, I like them, too. They are nice and sweet, aren't they? / What else is on the tray? / A doll. What do we do with a doll? / Right, we play with it. Do you like to play house with a doll? / Can you eat a doll? / Oh, I wouldn't like to try to eat a doll. It would be too hard to chew and it would taste awful." (Continue identifying the other items and talk about whether they are something to eat or to play with.)

"Can you take all the things off the tray that we can eat? / Put them here (point) beside the tray. / Oh . . . what's that? / Yes, it's a ball. Can you eat the ball? / No, the ball stays on the tray because it is not something you can eat. / What else on the tray can we eat?"

"Oh, you did just fine! All these things are things we can eat. They are called *foods*. Anything that we can eat is a food. Can you say *food?* / Good."

"What's still on the tray? / They are all things you play with, aren't they? / They are *toys*. Toys are things that are made to be played with. Can you say *toys?* / Very good."

"Help me put the food back on the tray with the toys. / Thank you. Now you can take all the toys off the tray. / Take off all the things that you can play with."

"How about a snack for doing such a good job? / Which of the foods left on the tray would you like to eat? / The cookie? Okay. It's yours to eat."

HELPFUL HINTS

Use foods and toys for this activity that the child is familiar with.

Sort out one group of items at a time as suggested in the sample activity. When you repeat the activity, you may want to vary it by having the youngster sort both kinds of items into two groups.

If you are working with a small group of children, be sure to have at least as many of each kind of item as there are children so that each child can have a turn sorting a food and a toy.

THINGS TO DO ANOTHER TIME

Repeat the activity with other foods and toys the child is familiar with. For variation, have the child sort all the items into two groups rather than remove one kind of item from the tray at a time or have him sort the items into containers (food onto a plate and toys into a toy box).

Adapt the activity to sorting other kinds of objects by their common function. Be sure the child has already experienced each particular object you use and has learned its name. For example, you might use a shoe, sock, and shirt to teach the higher level concept *clothes* or a bowl, plate, and cup to teach the concept *dishes*. Some other concepts based on function of objects that you might teach are *furniture, tools, things for cleaning the house* (cleaning equipment), and *things used in cooking* (cooking utensils). Note that you will probably use such concept phrases as *things for cleaning* and *things used to cook with* rather than the more precise and more difficult terms of *cleaning equipment* and *cooking utensils.* The child will learn the more precise language later when he is older and more mature.

ACTIVITY 128:   Sorting By Soft/Hard Qualities

SORTING
C

WHY

To identify soft and hard objects.
To sort objects by *soft/hard.*

WHAT YOU NEED

Three or four soft objects (cotton ball, marshmallow, yarn, sponge); three or four hard objects (small mirror, pebble, spoon, pencil); soft pillow; tray.

TALK ABOUT WHAT YOU DO

(Use your own language. This is an example.)

"We are going to have fun feeling some things today. Are you ready to have some fun? / Remember how we squeezed different things to tell if they felt soft or hard? / Well, let's try that again. You have to close your eyes and hold out your hand. I'll put something in your hand and you squeeze it. / Eyes closed? / Don't peek. (Put cotton ball in child's hand.) There. Now squeeze it. / Does it feel soft or hard? / Open your eyes and see what it is. / You were right. It is a *soft* cotton ball."

"Close your eyes again, and I'll put something different in your hand. (Place pebble in child's hand.) Okay, squeeze it good. / Is it soft or hard? / Look and see what it is. / It is a little hard stone, isn't it?"

"Let's look at the things on the table. Can you tell me their names? / Yes, that's a marshmallow. Poke it with your finger. / Is it hard or soft?"

(Continue in similar fashion until all items are identified. Be sure to supply names if the child cannot remember them.)

"See the pillow and the tray on the floor? / Touch them and tell me which one is soft and which is hard. / Very good. We'll play a game now."

"You have to feel one of the things on the table. If it feels soft, take it and put it on top of the soft pillow. If something feels hard, then put it on the hard tray. Okay? / Soft things on the soft pillow and hard things on the hard tray."

"What are you going to begin with? / Does it feel soft or hard? / Where are you going to put it? / Oh, that's very good! Feel something else on the table now." (Continue until all the items are sorted. If the child errs, have him feel the object again and ask him if it feels soft like the cotton ball or hard like the little stone.)

"That was a fun game, wasn't it? / Would you like to eat something soft—like a marshmallow? That's your prize for playing the game so well."

HELPFUL HINTS

Before the child attempts this sorting task, he should have had many experiences with the qualities *soft* and *hard*. (See Activities 12 and 19.)

In first reviewing the qualities soft and hard (first two paragraphs above), have the child feel objects most easily recognized as soft (cotton) and as hard (pebble). His success in properly identifying each as soft or hard will encourage him to continue the activity. If the child makes a mistake, do not scold. Have him feel the object again, talk about its softness or hardness, and have him place it on the pillow or tray accordingly. If the game proves too difficult, change over to a game of feeling each object and identifying it as *soft* or *hard* (see Activity 12). Provide additional experiences with the concepts *soft* and *hard* before trying the sorting task again.

THINGS TO DO ANOTHER TIME

If the child is making a book (see book Activity 90), have him make (with your help) pages of soft and hard things. Use such things as cotton, yarn, a bit of sponge, and a small piece of fake fur for the soft page and small twigs, small washers, paperclips, and small flat pebbles for the hard page. Make it a sorting activity by having him decide which items go on which pages. Use plenty of Elmer's glue for the hard items and let dry until the glue is completely hardened. Adapt the sample activity and the book activity to sorting *smooth* and *rough* objects: smooth pieces of cardboard and material (silk or satin), smooth stone or shell; and pieces of rough textured material, sandpaper, corrugated paper, rough uneven stones or shells.

ACTIVITY 129:   Sorting Multiple Objects

SORTING
C

WHY

To identify differences among objects.
To sort objects into like groups.

WHAT YOU NEED

Egg carton; three or more of each: acorns, pebbles, small leaves, twigs.

TALK ABOUT WHAT YOU DO

(Use your own language. This is an example.)

"Look at all these things we found in the park yesterday. Let's see if we can name them. / Right. That's a stone. What else can you see that you can name? / Good. That is a leaf. / Do you remember what this is called? (Point to acorn.) It's an acorn. Can you say *acorn?* / Very good! If you planted an acorn it would grow into a big tree like those we saw in the park."

"There is something else in our pile that we haven't named. Can you find it? / It is this. (Pick out twig.) It is a twig from a tree. Remember all the twigs we found on the ground in the park? / The twigs we found had fallen off the trees. Help me break this twig into little pieces so we can use it in the game we are going to play."

"We are going to play 'Fill the Egg Carton.' See all the little cups in this box that eggs come in? (Let the child feel the cups.) The eggs fit right in those little cups so they won't get broken when we bring them home from the store."

"We have to put all these things we found in the park in these cups. But we can only put things that are alike into one of the cups. Which of these things do you want to put in a cup? / Okay. Put the acorn in one of the cups. / Right. Now only acorns can go in that cup. Pick out something else to go in the egg carton. / What is that? / Put it in a different cup. It can't go with the acorn because it is not an acorn. / Now that cup (point) is just for stones. Nothing but stones can go in that cup."

"What are you going to put in the egg carton next? / An acorn. Do you have a cup for acorns? / Look in all the cups. Can you find one that is just for acorns? / Oh, you found it! That acorn can go in with the other acorn because that cup is for acorns."

(Continue the game until all items are sorted.)

"See how nice and neat you made all the things we found in the park. Now if you want an acorn or a stone you know just where to find it in the egg carton."

HELPFUL HINTS

This activity assumes a recent activity in which the youngster has helped to collect the objects used and has been introduced to their names and where each object came from. If this is not possible, be sure to precede the activity with one in which you introduce the objects, naming and talking about each so that the child can relate it to his own experiences with the object.

Or substitute small household objects with which the child is familiar. See "Things To Do Another Time" for suggestions.

You will have to use small twigs or small pieces of twigs if they are to fit in the egg carton box. Start with a brittle twig that is large enough for the child to recognize as a twig. Have him help you break it into small pieces so that he is fully aware of where the pieces came from and what they are.

If the child finds the activity difficult, continue helping the child to iden- tify each object he picks from the pile and to find the right cup for it in the egg carton. Do not let him fail or become frustrated. He may need this kind of guidance before he can attempt the task more on his own.

THINGS TO DO ANOTHER TIME

Adapt the activity to sorting small household items: buttons, paperclips, plastic bottle caps, rubber bands, small pieces of crayon, thimbles, beads, dried beans, macaroni.

Cut small hearts, stars, circles, triangles, and squares out of construction paper and have the child sort them into the egg carton by shapes.

Cut small pictures of animals, flowers, and other familiar objects out of greeting cards and adapt the activity to sorting the pictures into the egg carton. Be sure that you and the child talk about the pictures first. Christmas cards, for example, are good sources of small pictures of houses, trees, Santa faces, wreaths, ornaments, and other things.

ACTIVITY 130:   Sorting Multiple Kinds of Objects by Size: *Little/Big*

SORTING
C

WHY

To identify little and big objects.
To sort objects by size.

WHAT YOU NEED

Pairs of objects, one little and one big: boxes, balls, toy cars or dolls, plastic bottles, buttons.

TALK ABOUT WHAT YOU DO

(Use your own language. This is an example.)

"We are going to play a game today. These are the things we will use in the game. Can you tell me their names? / Right, that's a ball. What is this? (Point to other ball.) Yes, it is a ball too. Does this have a name? (Point to box.) Very good. Can you find another box?" (Continue in similar fashion until all objects are identified by name. Supply the name of any objects the child does not recognize and talk about the object briefly to help the youngster recall any experience he has had with it.)

(Place the two balls in front of the child.) "Which of these balls is a little ball? / Which is the big ball? / Good! Can you find the box that is little? / Where is the big box? / Very good! Let's put the boxes on these chairs." (Boxes should be slightly separated.)

"We are ready to play the game now. You have to put the little ball in the little box and the big ball in the big box. Can you do that? / Remember, little things go in the little box and big things go in the big box. / Oh, that was very good."

"Find the two toy cars. / Which is the little car? / Which box does it go in? / Where does the big car go? / You really know how to play this game, don't you?"

"What do you want to put in the boxes next? / A button? Okay. There are two buttons. Can you find them? / Is that the little or the big button? / Big. Good! / Oh–oh, is that the little or big box? / That's right. The big button has to go in the big box."

"What's left to put in the boxes? / Yes, the bottles. Which box does each of the bottles go in?"

"Wasn't that game fun? / Let's dump out everything in the boxes and play it again."

HELPFUL HINTS

Select your objects so that difference in size within each pair is easily recognized. The boxes must also be large enough to hold the little and big objects, respectively.

In your introduction to the activity and prior to introducing the game, review the names of the objects. Also line up one pair of objects in front of the child to check his concepts of *little/big*, since concepts of size are given meaning only by comparing the size of objects. For the same reason, have the child line up the pairs of objects as he plays the game.

THINGS TO DO ANOTHER TIME

Repeat the activity using other little and big paired objects which are familiar to the youngster: toys, plastic dishes, cans, spoons, shoes, books.

ACTIVITY 131:   Ordering Objects by a Pattern

ORDERING
C

WHY

To identify objects by colors.
To order objects by a color pattern.

WHAT YOU NEED

Three red cardboard circles; three blue cardboard circles.

TALK ABOUT WHAT YOU DO

(Use your own language. This is an example.)

"Look at all these pretty circles. Tell me what colors the circles are. / Yes, that one is red. / Right, blue. Can you put the circles in a red pile and a blue pile? / Good! Now we are going to play a game. Do you want to play the game with the red circles or the blue ones? / I'll play with the blue, then."

"I'll start the game by putting a blue circle here. / Now you put a red circle on this side (point) of the blue circle. / Good. It's my turn again. My blue circle goes after your red circle. / Your turn again. / That's right. Now it's my turn. / Your turn. / Look at our pretty design. (Point to each circle as you continue.) Blue. / Red. / Blue. / Red. / Blue. / Red.''

"Let's put the circles back in red and blue piles again. / This time you can play with the blue circles and I'll use the red ones. You have to start with a blue circle. (Repeat ordering by color pattern blue–red.)

"We have to put the circles in the two piles again. / Guess what! This time you can play with both piles. Remember to start with a blue circle the way we did before. / What color comes next?'' (Continue reminding the child only if he needs help to complete the pattern.)

"Oh, you did it all by yourself! Can you tell me the color of each circle? Start here.'' (Point to first circle and continue down the line so that the child says ''blue–red–blue–red.'')

HELPFUL HINTS

Use two colors the child already knows. Blocks, large buttons, or large beads can also be used if they are all alike except for the color variation.

If you are working with a small group of children, double the number of circles of each color and have the children take turns in positioning one color of circles in the first two games. When they are familiar with the rules of the game, let each pair of children play the game together (with half of the circles) or provide each child with his own circles to make the pattern.

THINGS TO DO ANOTHER TIME

Repeat the activity, using the reverse color pattern of red–blue.

Adapt the activity for making other two-color patterns: blue–orange, yellow–orange, and so on, as the child learns the various colors.

String beads to make a two-color pattern.

When the child is adept at making two-color patterns, add a third color for a three-color pattern. Play the game first with the child handling only the middle color of the pattern. Then repeat the game with the child handling the first and third colors of the pattern. Finally, let him complete the pattern on his own.

Adapt the activity to ordering shapes in a variety of two-shape patterns: circle–square–circle–square; square–triangle–square–triangle; little circle–big circle–little circle–big circle. When the youngster masters these and other two-shape patterns, try a pattern involving three shapes: circle–square–triangle–circle–square–triangle.

Colored tiles, blocks, or pieces of paper can be used for more complex patterns, as in Fig. 131.1. In the pattern below four small squares are used to make a large square with a particular color pattern. Make up your own patterns, but don't make them too difficult for the youngster.

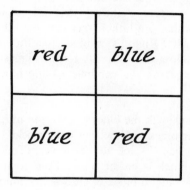

Fig. 131.1

ACTIVITY 132:   Ordering Objects by Size

ORDERING
C

WHY

To compare three different sizes of an object.
To order objects from littlest to biggest.

WHAT YOU NEED

Three blocks or boxes (lids sealed on) of different sizes: little, medium, and big.

TALK ABOUT WHAT YOU DO

(Use your own language. This is an example.)

(Place the smallest and the next bigger block in front of child. Keep largest block out of child's direct line of vision.) "What are these? / Which is the little block? / Which is the big block? / I have another block. (Place it next in line so blocks are in order from little to biggest.) This block is bigger than the other blocks. It is the biggest block of all. (Touch each block as you continue.) This is a *little* block. / This block is *bigger* than the little block. / And this block is the *biggest* block."

"Let's mix the blocks up. / Let's see now if we can put them back the way we had them. First comes the little block. / That's right. Put the little block here. (Indicate a space slightly to one side of the child.) Now you have to find the block that is a little bigger than the little block. / No, that's the biggest block of all. / Right. That block is a little bigger than the little block. It goes next. / Now you are ready for the biggest block of all. / Very good! (Touch each block as you continue.) Little block. / Bigger block. / Biggest block of all."

"Let's build a tower with the blocks. Take the little block and put it on top of the next bigger block. / Now, put both blocks on top of the biggest block of all. I'll help you. / Look at your tower! (Touch each block as you continue.) The little block is on the top. / Then comes the block that is a little bigger. / And the biggest block of all is at the bottom of your tower."

"Let's see if we can put the blocks back on the floor again the way they were. Which block comes first? / That's right. Which block is next? / Very good! Where does the biggest block of all go? / Say, the blocks are all lined up again. (Touch or point to each block as you continue.) Little block. / Bigger block. / Biggest block."

"Can you build another tower with the blocks? / Oh, that's another fine tower. Show me where the little block is in your tower. / Where is the next bigger block? / Where is the biggest block of all? / Oh, you're so smart!"

HELPFUL HINTS

Be sure the differences in size of the objects used are easily recognized. For example, their diameters might range from two or three inches to about six inches to about 12 inches.

Your focus should be on the task of ordering the objects by size, from littlest to biggest (later in reverse order), not on the word labels (little, bigger, biggest). The use of the words will come with repeated experiences of ordering which involve the use of the words.

Young children can usually imitate or model your arrangement of objects. If a youngster has difficulty, continue ordering the objects or help the child order them by size, and later see if he can do it on his own.

THINGS TO DO ANOTHER TIME

Adapt the activity to ordering many other objects by three sizes: plastic bottles, balls, buttons, nesting cans (inverted), toy cars. Those which cannot be stacked should be placed in order from little to biggest and the child encouraged to order them in the same fashion. Later, order them from biggest to littlest.

Use three sizes of paper plates (cut large plates to the smaller sizes) and paste a picture of a toddler on the smallest size, picture of an older child on the middle size, and a "mommy" or "daddy" on the largest size. Line up and stack the plates by size, have the child identify the pictures (personalize) and talk about sizes: "Little Billy (child's name) is on the little plate. Bigger Judy (older child's name) is on the next bigger plate. And Mommy is on the biggest plate."

Increase the number of objects to four distinguishable sizes and gradually add more as the youngster masters each task of ordering.

ACTIVITY 133:   Sorting by Shape: *Round/ Square*

WHY

To identify square and round objects.
To sort objects by shapes.

WHAT YOU NEED

Five cardboard squares and five
cardboard circles (all same
color); square box; round basket
(circular at top).

TALK ABOUT WHAT YOU DO

(Use your own language. This is an example.)

"Come and look at all these shapes. What color are they? / Right! They
are all red. Do you remember the names of these shapes? / Yes, that's a
circle. (Hold up a square.) What is this shape called? / It's a square. Can you
say *square?* / Good!"

"Can you show me a corner on the square? / Right! That's a corner. Now
trace the square like this. (Demonstrate.) We'll count the corners when you
come to them. Okay? / One corner / two corners / three corners / four corners. / The square has four corners and four sides, and they are all alike."

"See if you can find a corner on the circle. (Have the child trace a
circle.) Did you find a corner? / No, a circle has no corners. It's round."

(Hold up box so a square side or square opening is facing child.) "Is the
box square or round? (Have the child trace the edge of square if he cannot
respond and repeat the question.) Very good! The box is square, too."

"Do you know what this is? (Hold up basket.) It is a basket. Feel the basket. / The basket feels rough, doesn't it? / That's because it is made of straw. (Hold the basket so the round opening at the top is facing child.) Is the top of the basket round or square? / Yes, it is round."

"We are going to sort the shapes now. The circles go into the round basket and the squares go into the square box. Go ahead. Pick one of the shapes. / What is that shape called? / Where do the round shapes go? / No, the box is square. It is for the square shapes. / Good! The circle goes in the round basket. / Can you find a square? / Oh, very good! (Clap.) You put it in the square box. You know exactly what to do. You sort all the shapes, and I'll watch."

"You did a good job of sorting. What are the shapes in the box called? / What are the shapes in the basket called?"

HELPFUL HINTS

Make your circles and squares about three inches across for easy handling by the youngster. They should all be of one color so that you will know the child is sorting by shapes and not by color.

Note, too, that balls and blocks will not do for this sorting task. The child could sort them by objects (balls/blocks) rather than by a recognition of their shapes. Be sure the child has had some success in recognizing the shapes to be sorted before he is asked to sort by shapes. (See Activities 140, 141, and 143.)

If the child has difficulty recognizing the shapes as he sorts, continue asking him to find corners on each shape. And repeat: "A circle is round and has no corners," or "A square has four corners and the sides are all the same."

THINGS TO DO ANOTHER TIME

Precut small circles and squares from one color or various colors of construction paper. The child may be able to help you cut the squares from outlines. Cut also a large circle and a large square out of white paper. Have the youngster paste the circles on the large circle and the squares on the large square.

If you have blocks (styrofoam) that are round (like checkers, not balls) and square (flat, square on top, not cubes), have the chiid sort them into the box and basket.

Let the child help you make flat "cookies" from Play Dough or clay that are approximate circles and squares. Let them dry. Use these for sorting by shape.

ACTIVITY 134:   Sorting by Shape: *Round/ Triangle*

SORTING
C

WHY

To identify round and triangular objects.
To sort objects by shapes.

WHAT YOU NEED

Five cardboard circles; five cardboard triangles (all same color); large round paper circle; large paper triangle.

TALK ABOUT WHAT YOU DO

(Use your own language. This is an example.)

(Place the large paper circle and triangle on a flat surface and place the smaller circles on the large circle and the smaller triangles on the large triangle.) "Look at all these pretty red shapes. What are these shapes called? (Point to circles.) Good! Can you point to a circle that is big? / Very good!"

"What are these shapes called? (Point to triangles.) Good! You remembered. (If child does not remember, continue as follows.) It is called a *triangle*. Here, you take a triangle, and I'll take one. Let's count the sides.

Watch. (Trace and count.) One side / two sides / three sides. Now you do that and count. / Good. A triangle has three sides. Now let's count the corners on the triangle. Each time we find a new corner, we'll count it. Okay? / One corner / two corners / three corners. The triangle has three corners too. / Can you find a big triangle? / Oh, very good!''

"Let's play a game. The game is to put all the shapes in a big pile right here (point) in front of you. I'll tell you whether to pick up a circle or a triangle and put it in the pile. Ready? / A circle. / A triangle. / Another triangle.'' (Continue until all the smaller shapes are in the pile.)

"Now we'll play a different game. This time you have to sort all the shapes back to where they were. All the circles go back on the big circle and all the triangles go back on the big triangle. / Oh–oh, what shape was that? / Yes, a triangle. Can it go on the big circle then? / That's right. It has to go on the big triangle.''

"Say, you played that game very well. All the shapes are back where they belong.''

HELPFUL HINTS

Make your circles and triangles of a size that the child can handle easily, about three inches across. Be sure they are all one color so that the child is not able to sort by colors rather than by shapes.

Be sure the child has had some success in recognizing shapes to be sorted before he is asked to sort by shapes. (See Activities 140, 142, 143.)

Circles are usually easier for the child to recognize, so start with them (identifying, sorting) to ensure some degree of success. And don't let the child fail in the sorting task. Give whatever help is needed.

If the child has difficulty, repeat tracing tasks. Several sessions may be needed before the youngster can sort by shapes without error.

THINGS TO DO ANOTHER TIME

Precut colored, small circles and triangles to paste on a large circle and a large triangle, respectively. This makes a good sorting activity.

Make Play Dough circles and triangles and sort them by shape.

Adapt the suggested activities to sorting tasks involving squares and triangles.

When the youngster has mastered the various tasks involving two shapes, introduce the task of sorting all three shapes: circles, squares, and triangles.

ACTIVITY 135:   Matching Pictures

SORTING
C

WHY

To identify pictured objects and colors.
To match identical pictures.

WHAT YOU NEED

Lotto game of object pictures.

TALK ABOUT WHAT YOU DO

(Use your own language. This is an example.)

"Look at all the pictures on this board. See if you can find a picture of something that you can name. / Yes, that's a boat. What color is the boat? / You're right. It is yellow. Some of the boat is also white. See (point), this part of the boat is white. / What is this? (Point to water.) / Oh, you're so smart. Of course, the boat is in the blue water."

"See these little wooden blocks? / They have pictures on them, too. The pictures are just like the ones on the board. (Place two blocks in front of the child, including the block with the picture of a boat.) Look at the pictures on the block and see if you can find a picture of a yellow and white boat on blue water. / Keep looking. You'll find it. / Hey! You found it!"

"Is the boat the same color as the boat on the board? / Is the water blue just like the water in the picture on the board? / The two pictures are just alike, aren't they? / You can put the block on the board on top of the picture that is just like it. / Which picture are you going to put it on top of? / Very good!''

(Let the child select another picture on the board and repeat the process: talk about the object pictured and its key elements; then let him look for the same picture on two or three of the blocks. Point out and talk about how the two pictures are alike before he places the block on the identical picture on the board.)

"We found a lot of pictures that were just alike, didn't we? / The picture game is called 'Lotto.' We'll play Lotto again soon so that you can find some more pictures that are just alike.''

HELPFUL HINTS

You can make your own Lotto game if you can find identical pictures of objects that will fit on, say, a four-inch square background. Duplicate copies of catalogs are good sources for such pictures. Choose objects that are familiar to the child and not too complex in design. For your board, use a piece of construction paper or cardboard 8" x 12" for a six-picture Lotto (8" x 8" piece for a four-picture Lotto) and rule it off into six four-inch squares. See Fig. 135.1.

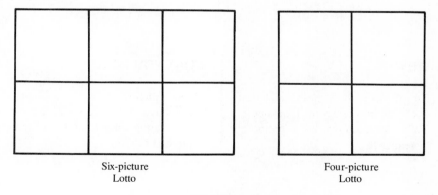

Six-picture
Lotto

Four-picture
Lotto

Fig. 135.1

If you wish to vary the color of the background of each picture (which is a good idea), cut four-inch squares of different colored paper and paste one of these in each of the board's squares. Then paste one set of the pictures on top of the colored squares. Cut four-inch squares in colors to match those used on the board squares and paste identical pictures on the same colored paper as was used for its match on the board.

Work gradually through the pictures of the Lotto. Trying to do them all at one time may be too much for a toddler. And continue to use the step-by-step process used above in the sample as long as the child needs it.

THINGS TO DO ANOTHER TIME

Make other sets of matching pictures (in Lotto form or simply by pasting identical pictures on matching background paper or cardboard) and repeat the activity. Keep the pictures simple and the objects familiar. Continue to use the step-by-step process used in the sample above as long as the child seems to need it: looking at and talking about one picture of the first set of pictures, finding its identical match in the second set, talking about the sameness of key features of the pictures, and placing the second picture on top of or beside its match.

ACTIVITY 136: Ordering Pictures in a Temporal Sequence

ORDERING
C

WHY

To identify first, next, and last events in a temporal sequence.
To order pictures in a temporal sequence.

WHAT YOU NEED

Three pictures of a simple sequence of events: cooking dinner, eating dinner, and washing the dishes.

TALK ABOUT WHAT YOU DO

(Use your own language. This is an example.)

"Come sit beside me here on the floor and we'll look at some pretty pictures together. / Oh, look at this first picture! Who is in the picture? / Yes, a mommy. What is the mommy doing? / Well, let's see if we can figure out what she is doing. Can you find a stove? / Is there something cooking on the stove? / Can you point to it so I can see it too? / Say, you're right. The mommy is cooking. I think the mommy is cooking dinner. What do you think? / Yes, she is probably cooking dinner for her little girl (boy). Do you think the little girl's (boy's) name is Susie (child's name)?''

(Show second picture.) "Look at this next picture. Who are all those people? / Yes, there is the mommy again. / And daddy. / And where is Susie? / What do you think the family is doing? / Very good! They are eating the nice dinner that the mommy was cooking in the first picture. (Point to each picture as you continue.) *First,* the mommy cooks the dinner. *Next,* the whole family eats the dinner.''

"Let's see what is happening in this last picture. Can you find the mommy? / What is she doing? / What are these? (Point to dishes.) Right, dishes. Everyone has finished eating dinner, so the dirty dishes have to be washed. Is Susie helping? / What is Daddy doing? / Yes, both Daddy and Susie are helping Mommy wash the dishes.''

(Place the pictures on the floor so that all three are visible to the child.)

"Do you know that every time you eat dinner someone has to cook the food first? / Which of these pictures shows what happens *first?* / Next, after the dinner is all cooked, the whole family eats the dinner. Which picture shows what happens *next* after the mommy cooks the dinner? / And last, after everyone is through eating dinner, someone has to clean up the dirty dishes. Can you find the picture that shows what happens *last?* / Say, you did that just fine!''

"Can you tell me the story about the pictures? / Find the first picture and tell me about what happens first. (Continue in similar fashion with the second and third pictures, prompting or pointing out clues in the pictures if the child has difficulty retelling the story.) My, that was a good story. And you got the pictures just right, too.''

HELPFUL HINTS

Pictures that treat in three parts everyday experiences familiar to the child are good for this activity.

The concepts you are teaching in this activity are the temporal concepts of *first, next,* and *last* applied to events, the order of things done in *time.*

They should not be confused with the spatial concepts of *first, next,* and *last,* the ordering of objects in space. To avoid confusing the child, talk about what is happening or what is being done in the pictures.

Be sure to talk about each picture first to assure that the child is perceiving correctly what is happening in each picture and to help him relate the events to his own life.

THINGS TO DO ANOTHER TIME

Adapt the activity to other three-part picture sequences of events with which the youngster is familiar: getting ready for bed, getting into bed, asleep in bed; getting up, dressing, eating breakfast; shopping at a grocery store, checking out the groceries, bringing them home.

Have the child role play simple sequences of events which he experiences in real life. You might start with acting out some of the picture sequences you have used, but also let him move on into other familiar sequences such as Daddy or Mommy going to work or visiting a friend. Whenever possible, let the child choose his own particular events within a particular sequence and use his own ideas in acting them out.

Learning about geometric shapes is challenging to the toddler. Fitting a square block into a square hole is part of the learning process.

Part 9

Mathematics

MATHEMATICS

Numbers are an important part of everyday life. They are all around us. We use numbers in telling time and dates, in shopping and making change, in telephoning and turning on TV channels, in following recipes, in measuring distance and size and volume, and in a great many other daily activities.

Long before the child learns to use numbers, he begins to grasp concepts that he will later express numerically. He becomes aware of sequences in events before he can talk about what is first, second, or third. He is able to distinguish between differences in sizes of people, animals, and toys before he has any notion of measurement. He recognizes, too, distinctions between *one* and *many* and between *few* and *lots* before he acquires precise number concepts. And he develops a sense of time long before he can tell time by a clock. His ideas of time grow out of hearing us say such things as "It is time for lunch," "It is time to go to bed," We are going for a walk today," and "We went to the park yesterday."

Before the child is three years old, he often can count to ten in proper sequence. Such recitation, however, may have little meaning for the youngster. The words may be only sounds to him, sounds repeated in a particular sequence. Quite different from and much more difficult than rote counting is the understanding of the numbers as they apply to a sequence of objects: that each number represents the position of an object in the sequence (button 1, button 2, button 3, and so on). Equally or more difficult to understand is the idea that the last number counted in a sequence of objects represents *all* the objects in the sequence, the total number of objects counted. For example, in counting six buttons the child must grasp the idea that six, the last number counted, tells him how many buttons he has—that he has six buttons in all.

These higher-level numerical understandings develop slowly for most children. But they can be taught to most preschoolers through carefully structured activities that take one idea and present it to the child one step at a time. Through such a process, the preschool youngster will probably learn to count by rote from one to ten, and perhaps beyond ten. He may also learn to count ten objects in sequence, understanding that each object's position in the sequence determines its number. And, on request, the youngster may be able to count out three or four objects from a pile of objects and bring them to you, a sign that he has some idea that the last number counted tells how many objects he has.

Young children who have reached the C level of development (as defined for this book) may also be able to learn to recognize the geometric shapes of round, triangle, and square and then to distinguish among them. To accomplish these tasks, the youngster must be taught one shape at a time, with a new shape being introduced only after the mastery of the previous one.

Sensory experiences of tracing (with finger) objects that are round, triangular, or square are an important part of learning shapes as is also the use of a variety of different objects of a given shape. The child will probably also require many repeated experiences with each shape to grasp the concept and to assimilate or internalize it, making it part of his thinking processes.

The sample activities related to mathematical concepts in this book provide simple ways to introduce the child to numbers, to counting skills, to basic numerical understandings, and to geometric shapes. They should be used generally in the order given, moving the child on to the next kind of activity only when he has mastered the tasks of the previous activity. The following general guidelines will also be helpful to you in using the activities and in planning other similar activities for a particular child or small group of children.

1. *Keep the activities brief and repeat them often.* Five minutes a day (or every other day) is much better than longer sessions held less frequently.
2. *Always relate counting to real objects.* Count fingers and toes, buttons and blocks, balls and spoons, or what-have-you. By counting and touching simultaneously each object in a sequence, the child is helped to realize that he is giving a number name to an object because it is in a particular position in the sequence. Rearranging the objects between counts strongly reinforces that idea, since, for example, what was button number 1 now becomes button number 3. The exception to the rule of touching objects while counting is in teaching rote counting. This memory task can be done without any props and at odd moments by simply having the child repeat the numbers after you or by chanting number sequences with the child.
3. *Always count objects from left to right or from top to bottom.*
4. *Work on number conepts and skills gradually.* Start with numbers 1–3, increase to numbers 1–5, and add higher numbers in sequence as you perceive that the child is ready for them. But in any number sequence always start the counting with number 1.
5. *Like all learning activities for preschoolers, make your math activities enjoyable for the child.* Try to start your activities with questions that the child will be able to answer so that he has feelings of success and a sense of "I can do it." And praise each small achievement to encourage sustained and renewed effort.

Above all, be patient. If number learning comes slowly to the child, repeat the activities over and over again. Look for new twists to keep the child's interest and your own. No matter how small the progress, your efforts will be well worthwhile, for a sound and pleasant beginning in understanding numbers and geometric shapes will be valuable to the child not only in later mathematical learning but also in language development.

ACTIVITY 137:   Numbers One and Two

MATHEMATICS
B

WHY

To count one and two like objects.
To relate quantities of one and two
   to parts of the body.

WHAT YOU NEED

No materials needed.

TALK ABOUT WHAT YOU DO

(Use your own language. This is an example.)

"We are going to have fun counting today. Can you say *one?* / Can you
say *two?* / Very good! One and two are numbers. They tell us how many
things we have. Let's see if we can find out how many noses and ears and
other things we have. Okay?"

(Demonstrate each direction given, keeping your fingers on your nose,
mouth, or chin while you say "one nose," etc.) "Touch your nose. / We
have one nose. Can you say *one nose?* / Touch your mouth. / Say *one
mouth.* / Touch your chinney-chin-chin. / Say *one chin.* / Very good! You
counted one nose, one mouth, one chin."

"Now let's count some things we have two of. (Follow your own directions. Be sure to touch an ear on each count. Do the same for eyes and feet.)
Touch one ear. / Touch your other ear. / Let's count and touch our ears. One
ear / two ears. / Point to one of your eyes. / Now point to your other eye. /
Let's count our eyes. One eye / two eyes. / Where are your feet? / Touch
one foot. / Touch the other foot. / Let's count our feet. One foot / two feet. /
Say, that's good. You counted two ears, two eyes, and two feet."

"Let's play a counting game. I'll play it with you. So watch me and listen to what I say."

"Touch your nose and say *one nose.*" (Touch nose and repeat *one nose*
   with child.)

"Touch your feet and say *one foot, two feet.*" (Touch a foot as you repeat each count.)

"Touch your chin and say *one chin.*" (Touch chin and repeat *one chin.*)

"Touch your ears and say *one ear, two ears.*" (Touch an ear as you repeat each count.)

"Touch your mouth and say *one mouth.*" (Touch mouth and repeat *one mouth.*)

"Point to your eyes and say *one eye, two eyes.*" (Point to an eye as you repeat each count.)

"Do you want to try the game all by yourself? / Okay. Listen carefully to what I say."

(Repeat game. If child gets stuck, repeat and follow directions yourself. Then continue as before.)

"Oh, you can really play the counting game. We'll play it again tomorrow."

HELPFUL HINTS

Your focus in this activity is on counting (one, two) parts of the body. The child must already be able to identify the parts of the body to follow this activity. If he cannot do this, review the parts of the body before trying this activity again.

Note that in the lesson, the child first repeats the counting–touching task after or along with you. If he is unable later to do these tasks by himself, continue your participation in the game. He may need more practice before he can do the tasks on his own.

THINGS TO DO ANOTHER TIME

Repeat the activity, coordinating the counting with touching other parts of the body: head, neck, chest, stomach, legs, knees, arms, hands.

Count two of many different kinds of objects: buttons, balls, blocks, books, nails, combs. Use paired objects that are different in some way (a red and a black button). Always insist that the child touch each object as he counts, that he move from left to right, that he touch each object only once.

Then switch the position of the two objects and repeat the tasks. This will help him realize that the numbers apply to the object in a particular position and not to some other characteristic of the object.

ACTIVITY 138:   Rote Counting (One to Ten)

MATHEMATICS
B

WHY

To count from one to four.

WHAT YOU NEED

No materials needed.

TALK ABOUT WHAT YOU DO

(Use your own language. This is an example.)

"Listen! I've got a very special rhyme for you."

> One, two. Buckle my shoe.
> Three, four. Shut the door.
> One, two, three, four.
> Annie (use child's name) can count to four or more.

"Let's learn to count to four so you can say the rhyme with me. You can already count *one, two,* can't you? / Let me hear you count *one, two.* / Good! Do you know what comes after two? / Three comes after two. Can you say *three?* / Great! Listen. One, two, three, four. After three comes four. Can you say *four?* / Very good."

"Let's count all the way to four. I'll say a number and then you say it. One. / Two. / Three. / Four. / Oh, that's good. (Chant.) Annie can count all the way up to four. Let's do it again. Let's count some more."

(Repeat as before, the child saying the numbers after you. Repeat the chant lines also to encourage the child to one or more additional repetitions of the task.)

"I am going to say the rhyme I said before. Listen carefully and say the numbers after me. Ready?"

"One, two." (Allow time for child to repeat and prompt if necessary.)
  "Buckle my shoe."
"Three, four." (Allow time for child to repeat.) "Shut the door."
"One, two, three, four." (Allow time for the child to repeat.)
"Annie can count to four or more."

"That was very good. Oh, you're so smart!"

HELPFUL HINTS

Do not confuse rote counting with counting objects. The former is simply to recite the number words in their proper order. The latter is a more complex and more important learning task: to understand that each number represents the position of an object in a given sequence. Rote counting is usually mastered relatively easily through repetition. Acquiring the basic concept of each number (its representation of a particular number of objects in a sequence) will take more time and many experiences in counting many different kinds of objects.

The major thrust of this rote counting activity is the child's repetition of each number in sequence as often as his attention will allow. Use odd moments during the day to repeat the number sequence and the rhyme. Do not go on to additional numbers in sequence until the child can count from one to four on his own.

In any counting sequence, always start with the number one and have the child do likewise. If you are working with a small group of children, insert a different name in the rhyme each time you use it. And do not leave anyone out.

THINGS TO DO ANOTHER TIME

March or clap to the numbers one, two, three, four. Have the child say the numbers with you.

When the child has mastered counting one to four, add the number five. Say something like this: "I have a new number for you. It is five. Can you say *five?* / Five comes after four. Listen. One, two, three, four, five. Count with me all the way to five. / Let's do that again.'' Also use the rhyme as you used it in the activity above, but add these lines:

> One, two, three, four, five.
> Fiddle-de-de and sakes alive!
> Annie can count all the way to five.

Continue in similar fashion until the child can count to ten (or beyond). Additional rhyming lines you might use are:

> Five, six. Pick up sticks.
> One, two, three, four, five, six.
> Annie has a lot of tricks.
> She can count up to six.

> Seven, eight. Don't be late.
> One, two, three, four, five, six, seven, eight.
> Annie doesn't want to wait
> 'Cause she can count up to eight.

> Nine, ten. A big fat hen.
> One, two, three, four, five, six, seven, eight, nine, ten.
> Annie knows some big fat men,
> And she can count up to ten.

ACTIVITY 139: Counting Objects in Sequence

MATHEMATICS
B

WHY

To count three objects in sequence.

WHAT YOU NEED

Three buttons of different colors and/or sizes (not too small).

TALK ABOUT WHAT YOU DO

(Use your own language. This is an example.)

"Look at the pretty buttons. / How many buttons do we have? / We can find out how many we have if we count them. Help me put the buttons in a row and then we'll count them." (Space the buttons so they are at least six inches apart.)

"Watch now. I am going to count each button, and I am going to touch each button as I count it. (Count and move hand from left to right.) One / two / three. Why, we have three buttons!"

"Can you count the buttons the way I did? / Use this finger. (Point to child's index finger.) Remember, you have to touch each button as you count it. / Start with this button. (Point to button at the far left.) I'll help you get started. (Guide the child's hand to each button and count with him if he needs help.)

(Rearrange the buttons so that button 3 becomes button 1.) "Count the buttons again. Do you want me to help you or do you want to do it all by yourself? / Okay. I won't help unless you want me to. / That's right. Go on. You are doing great. / You counted one, two, three buttons. We have three buttons in all."

(If the child is willing to repeat the counting and touching task, rearrange the buttons again and have him repeat it.)

"That was very good. You counted the buttons and found out we had three buttons in all."

HELPFUL HINTS

The learning task of this activity is focused primarily on counting objects in sequence to understand that each number represents the object's position in the sequence. To promote this understanding, be sure that you and the child count from left to right, and that the child touches each button, and one only, at the same time as he gives it a number. Correct the youngster gently if he fails to follow these basic rules.

If, in lining up the buttons, you leave at least six inches between them, the child will be less apt to touch a button more than once as he counts.

The rearrangement of the buttons for each recount will help the child realize that you are not giving a particular number to a particular button but rather that you are giving a number to a particular position in a sequence. As the order of the buttons is changed, the new positions determine the numbers given the button.

If the child is able to perform the task without your help, by all means let him. Help him only if he has difficulty.

THINGS TO DO ANOTHER TIME

Plan similar activities for counting a variety of objects in groups of three. Use objects that you can line up in a row (spoons, cups, blocks, books, boxes, shoes). Be sure the child follows your basic rules in counting (see "Helpful Hints").

When the child is able to count sets of three objects, plan similar activities for counting four objects in sequence. Continue increasing the number of objects to be counted (to ten or more) as the child masters each counting task.

ACTIVITY 140:   Recognizing Shapes That Are Round

MATHEMATICS
C

WHY

To identify an object that is round.

WHAT YOU NEED

A circular (cylindrical block; a round metal or plastic lid; a square block.

TALK ABOUT WHAT YOU DO

(Use your own language. This is an example.)

"Look at what I have! It is a block. It's a *round* block. Can you say *round?* / Good." (Let the child examine the block if interested.)

"See this end of the block? / It has a round shape. (Trace outer edge as you continue.) My finger can go round and round the block. Round and round it goes. / You make your finger go round and round the block like I did." (If necessary, guide the child's hand.)

"Let's go round and round the other end of the block. / Oh, your finger went round and round."

"Can you roll the block like this? (Demonstrate.) It rolls just like a ball, doesn't it? / That's because the block is round. Roll it again. / Wheee! Look at it go!"

"Here is a lid. (Place lid, top up, in front of child.) The lid was on a peanut butter jar. (Let the child examine it if interested.) The lid is round too. Watch. My finger can go round and round the lid. (Trace outside edge of lid.) That feels round. See if you can feel that the lid is round. / It feels round just like the block, doesn't it?"

(Place the square block beside the circular block.) "Can you show me the block that is round? / Very good! Let's play with the round block and roll it some more. / You can roll the lid too."

HELPFUL HINTS

Various shaped blocks can be found in toy departments and stores. The block used in this activity is not a completely rounded, ball-like block (orb) but a circular one or a cylinder ⊖ . You may wish, however, to purchase or make a shape sorting toy which consists of varied shaped blocks (usually a cylinder, square, triangle, and rectangle) and a box with correspondingly shaped holes through which the blocks can be inserted. The shape sorter blocks can be used in this and other shape identification lessons and, along with the box, in shape matching lessons as well as in the child's free play. If you are interested in making your own shape sorter or the circular block for this activity, see Activity 143 for directions.

Important steps in this activity include (a) identifying the objects (blocks, lid) to help the child realize that *round* is something other than the object itself, (b) tracing and rolling the objects to feel and see *roundness,* and (c) checking the child's perception of roundness by introducing a square (non-round) block at the end of the activity.

It may take several experiences with circular objects before the youngster will be able to identify a round object. If he is unable to point out the circular block in the last task of the activity, point to it and say, "This is the round one." Then encourage continued tracing and rolling of the block and lid if the child's attention span permits. Repeat the activity once or oftener within the next week.

You should be aware of and alert to the strong possibility that a child may be able to identify the cylinder block as round through its color rather than by its shape. So at some point use a different circular object, one not used in your lessons, to check his understanding of the concept *round.* You might use a cardboard tube (as found in toilet tissue) or a lid that is different in size and color.

THINGS TO DO ANOTHER TIME

When the child is fairly good at identifying circular objects, focus a lesson on round holes through which the cylinder block and a lid will easily go. If you have a shape sorting toy, use its round hole and the cylinder block. A second round hole through which the lid can be inserted can be made by outlining the lid on one side of a box and cutting out a circle that is a little larger than the lid. In the lesson, review the concept *round* as it applies to the cylinder block by having the child trace one end of the cylinder. Then have him trace the rim of the hole "to feel how round it is, just like the round block." Demonstrate putting the block through the round hole and let the child do the same, helping only if necessary. Repeat task, also using the lid and its corresponding hole. And finally, ask the child to show you a hole that is round.

Reinforce and extend the learning by using round objects that are not cylinders: plates, wheels of toy vehicles, large buttons, a clock. Repeat the tracing task and roll or rotate the object when possible. Use a non-round object (square, triangle) and a new round object to check on the child's ability to identify roundness in objects.

Find pictures of things that make use of circles in their design (wallpaper, print materials, windows in houses, large letter *Os* in signs). Or cut out or draw circles of different sizes and colors. Include in your materials a few shapes that are not circles (squares, triangles). Introduce the youngster to the word *circle*. Have him trace the circles with a finger and talk about their being round like a wheel on a toy car or another familiar toy. Make an approximate circle with a crayon and help the child to do the same.

Extend the concept *round* to orbs. Use balls and round blocks (not cylinders) or large round beads. Explain that these also are round, trace their circumference, and roll them. Have the child repeat these actions and have him find other similar round objects (orange, apple, balloon) from among a few non-round objects (box, block, book).

ACTIVITY 141: Recognizing Shapes That Are Square

MATHEMATICS
C

WHY

To recognize an object that is square.

WHAT YOU NEED

A square block (cube); a small square box (cube) with lid taped on; and a cylinder block.

TALK ABOUT WHAT YOU DO

(Use your own language. This is an example.)

(Place the square block on floor in front of child.) "What is that? / It sure is a block. It is a block in the shape of a square. Can you say *square?* / Say it again: *square.* / That's pretty good."

"See this side of the block? (Point to top side.) Watch. I'll trace it. (Continue talking as you trace all four sides.) I'll start here and go along this side. Oops! My finger has to turn here and go around this corner. Then it goes along this side. Oh, it has to turn again. Now along this side. Here comes another corner. And here we come back to where my fingers started. A square has a lot of corners, doesn't it? / Now you use your finger to go around the square. (Help only if needed. Talk about the turns the child's finger makes.) That was good. Your finger turned every corner."

"Look. (Turn block on another side.) Now another side is on top. It looks just like the side you traced, doesn't it? / You turn the block so another side is on top. / Oh, that side looks just like the other sides. See if you can find more sides that look just the same."

"Let's roll the block. / Oh, it went sort of bumpty-bump-bump, didn't it? / You know what? No matter which side the block lands on, it always looks the same. Roll it again and see if the block always looks the same."

(Hold up box.) "What is this? / The box is in the shape of a square too. See if you can find corners to turn when your finger goes along the side of the box. / Oops! Your finger forgot to turn. That's all right. Start again. / The box has corners just like the block. That's because the block and the box are both squares."

"See if you can find other sides of the box that look square. / Very good. Can you roll the box. / Does it look the same? / Squares always look the same no matter which side is up."

"Let's put the block, the box, and this other block (cylinder) in a row. / There. Can you find a square now? / Can you find another square thing? / Very good. (Point to cylinder block.) This is not a square. Do you know what shape it is? / It's round. (Trace one end.) See, your finger goes round and round. It has no corners to turn. / Do you want to play with the round and square blocks for a while?"

HELPFUL HINTS

This activity should be used after the child has had some success in identifying round objects. To help the child recognize differences between *square* and *round,* place a major emphasis on tracing one side of the block and on the need to turn corners. The emphasis on the block looking the same no matter which side is up is the beginning of the idea that all sides of a square are of equal length. A rectangular block (a shape which you may teach later when the child is more mature) will not always look the same: sometimes it will be short and sometimes it will be tall, depending on which side it is on. Do not in this activity stress that a square has four sides. Only when the child has mastered counting four objects should this quality be added by having the child count the sides of a square.

The child may require several repetitions of this activity to identify an object that is square. If he identifies the cylinder as a square, use the tracing tasks to help him feel the difference between the round and square shapes. Then repeat the activity soon and as often as needed for success in the identification task.

Remember, too, that the child may in this activity identify the block and box as squares through color or some coding system other than shape. At some point, then, use an object not used previously in your activities to check on the understanding of *square*—a new square box, a photo cube, cube made from Play Dough.

THINGS TO DO ANOTHER TIME

When the child has had some success in identifying square objects (cubes), focus a lesson on square holes through which a square block and a small square box will easily go. If you have a shape sorting toy, use only its square hole and the square block. A second square hole through which your small box will pass can be made by drawing an outline of the box on one side of a larger box and cutting out a square that is a little larger than your small box. In the lesson, review the concept *square* as it applies to the block by having the youngster trace one of the sides. Then have him trace the rim of the corresponding square hole, noting especially all the corners (finger turns). Demonstrate lining up the block with the sides and corners of the hole and putting the block through it. Have the child do the same but help him as needed. Repeat the task, using also the box and its hole. Your final question should be a check on the child's ability to point to one or both of the holes that are square when asked to do so.

Reinforce and extend the learning by using square objects which are not cubes: a picture frame, napkin, pillow, checkerboard. Continue the tracing of the square and looking for corners or turns.

Play a game of "Find the Squares." Set up the room with several square objects, including cubes. Use some objects you have used in previous activities. Ask the youngster to find the square objects. Check on his understanding of *square* by pointing to a non-square (for example, a round pillow) and ask if it is a square.

Enlarge the game to one of "Rounds and Squares." Set up the room with objects of both shapes. Alternate asking the child to find a square object and a round object. If he becomes confused, repeat the tracing tasks and talk again about each shape.

Use pictures of things that are square or have squares in their design. Or cut out or draw outlines of squares in different sizes and colors. Include in your materials one or more shapes that are not square (circle, triangle). Have the child trace the squares and talk about their corners or turns. Make an approximate square with a crayon and help the child to do the same.

ACTIVITY 142: Recognizing Shapes That Are Triangular

MATHEMATICS
C

WHY

To recognize an object that is triangular.

WHAT YOU NEED

Two blocks in shape of triangle (see "Helpful Hints" below); a cylinder or square block.

TALK ABOUT WHAT YOU DO

(Use your own language. This is an example.)

(Place the smaller triangular block on floor in front of child.) "Do you know what this is? / It's a block. It's a special block in the shape of a triangle. Can you say *triangle?* / Good!"

(Let the child examine the block if interested. Then turn it on end so that the triangle is visible at the top of the block.) "Watch. I'm going to trace the shape of the triangle. (Talk as you trace.) My finger goes along this side to this point. Now it has to turn. Then it comes along this side and—by golly!—it has to turn again. And when the finger goes along this side and turns once more, it is back where it started. Can you trace the triangle the way I did? / Start here. / Your finger has to turn now. / Good. Keep going. / Turn again. / Turn once more, and your finger is back where it started."

(Place the block on one of its sides so that the triangle is visible to child at one end. The point of the triangle should be at the top.) "Look at the bottom of the triangle (point). (Run your finger across bottom as you continue.) See, the triangle has a big, flat bottom. (Pick up block and hold in same position.) Feel the big, flat bottom. (Replace block on floor in same position.) Look at the top now (point). It has a little, tiny top. It has a point at the top. Feel the point at the top of the triangle."

"I'm going to turn the triangle over. (Turn it slowly to one of its other sides.) Well, how about that! The triangle still has a big, flat bototom (point) and a pointed top (point). Feel the point at the top. / It feels just like the other point, doesn't it?"

"You turn the triangle like I did and see what happens to the big bottom and the point of the triangle. / Where is the big flat bottom? / Where is the point? / Yes, siree! No matter how you turn the triangle it always has a big bottom and a point at the top."

"Let's look at this other block. It's a triangle, too." (Have child repeat the tracing task, turning the triangle on several sides to check the bottom and top after each turn.)

"Now put this block (cylinder or square) beside your other blocks. / Does it have a point at the top? / You're right! It doesn't because it is not a triangle. Can you find the blocks that are triangles? / Do they have a point at the top? / Oh, you're so smart!"

HELPFUL HINTS

Objects in triangular shape are scarce so you will probably have to use two triangular blocks in this activity. One of the blocks can be part of your shape sorting box. The other block should be somewhat larger (three-inch side). It can be cut from styrofoam. See page 388 for directions.

This activity should be introduced after the child has mastered reasonably well the identification of circular and square objects. The emphasis is on the large flat bottom and the pointed top of the triangle. The three sides of a triangle should be introduced later, when the child is able to count three objects. The tracing and turning tasks remain important elements of the lesson.

Repeat the activity soon if the child has difficulty identifying the triangular blocks. But remember, too, that when he is successful he may well be using something other than shape (color, perhaps) to accomplish the task. So introduce at some later point a triangular block not seen before (different size and color, one made from Play Dough, for example) to check on his recognition of the triangular shape.

THINGS TO DO ANOTHER TIME

When the youngster has had some success in identifying triangular blocks, focus a lesson on triangular holes through which the triangular blocks will easily go. If you are using a shape sorter, use only its triangular hole and block. A second triangular hole through which your larger block will pass can be made by drawing an outline of the block on one side of a box and cutting out a triangle that is a little larger than your block. In the lesson, review the concept *triangle* by having the child trace the smaller block and check that the point is always at the top no matter which side of the triangle is at the bottom. Next have the child trace the corresponding hole, noting especially the turns and the top point. Demonstrate lining up the block with the sides and top point of the hole and putting the block through it. Have the child do the same, but help him as needed. Repeat the task using the other triangular block and its hole. Your final question should be a check on the child's ability to point to one or both of the holes that are triangular when asked to do so.

Cut out of construction paper or cardboard triangles of various sizes and colors. Include a circle and a square in your materials. Ask the child to find and trace a triangle. Turn the triangle so that each side is at the bottom and check that a point is always at the top. Have the youngster find other triangles as well as the non-triangles.

Play a game of "Find the Triangle." Place your triangular blocks and cut-outs around the room and have the youngster find as many as he can. Pin a triangular badge on him as a reward for finding triangles.

Play a game of "Triangles and Squares" by placing square objects and triangular blocks around a room. Each time the child brings you one of the objects, have him identify it as a square or a triangle.

Use drinking straws or pipe cleaners to make triangles by laying three straws or cleaners in proper position to form a triangle. Or if it is easier for the child, have him bend a pipe cleaner to form a triangle.

ACTIVITY 143: Matching Shapes

MATHEMATICS
C

WHY

To distinguish between shapes.
To match shapes with holes in box.

WHAT YOU NEED

Sorting box with a circular, a square, and a triangular block (see "Helpful Hints" below).

TALK ABOUT WHAT YOU DO

(Use your own language. This is an example.)

"Look. We have the sorting box to play with today. (Point to holes in box.) See all the holes. / Here are the blocks."

"See if you can find the round block. / Which is the square block? / Which block is in the shape of a triangle? / Remember, look for the block with the big flat bottom and a point at the top. / Oh, you found it. Good!"

"Now let's look at the holes. Can you find a round hole? / Right! Which block will go through the round hole? / Try it and see if it goes through. /

Kaplunk! It went right through.'' (Repeat in similar fashion for the square and triangular holes and blocks. Help child line up blocks with holes if he has difficulty doing so.)

"We'll take the blocks out again. / This time you pick any block you like and put it through the right hole. / It won't go through the round hole, will it? Try another hole. / There, it went! That block was a square. It went through the square hole.''

"Which block do you have this time? / Yes, it's a triangle. Which hole will it go through? / No, don't push. If the block doesn't go through, try another hole. / I think it will go through that hole if you turn the block a little more. / Like this. Now try it. (Clap.) You did it! You found the hole that is a triangle and put the block through it.''

(Let the child continue fitting the blocks into the holes with as little help from you as possible. But don't let him become frustrated or fail. Give verbal and direct help when needed.)

"You found all the right holes, didn't you? / I'll leave the shape sorter out. You may want to play with it later.''

HELPFUL HINTS

Start with the round block and the round hole. The round block will be less difficult to manipulate through its hole.

Don't stop the child from using a trial-and-error method in finding the right hole if he is inclined to do so. But do try to prevent frustration from developing and make sure some success results from the method. For example, if a child has found the right hole for a block but has difficulty lining up a block properly with the hole, help him.

Let the youngster use the shape sorter in his free play to reinforce the learning.

Making a Shape Sorter

MATERIALS:
1. A sturdy box with a lid that measures about 9" x 12" or 12" x 12" (see also Step 6 of the directions below to determine lid size).
2. A sheet of one- or two-inch styrofoam for the blocks. Styrofoam (available in hobby and craft stores) usually comes in 1" x 12" x 36"

and 2″ x 12″ x 36″ sheets. The advantage of using the two-inch sheet is that the blocks are correspondingly larger and the need for gluing is eliminated (see Step 2 below).

3.   A heavy white glue (such as Tacky). *The glue is needed only if you are working with the one-inch sheet of styrofoam.*

4.   A sharp, narrow knife (or a coping or hack saw) for cutting the styrofoam.

5.   Spray paint (optional).

Directions

1.   Cut block patterns to size and shape out of cardboard or heavy paper. The square block must be smaller than the other blocks so that only the square will be able to pass through its corresponding hole in the box. See Fig. 143.1 for suggested dimensions:

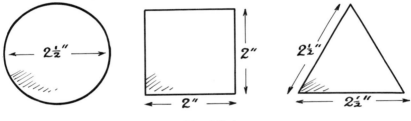

Fig. 143.1

2.   Trace your patterns on the styrofoam. If the styrofoam sheet is one inch thick, make two squares. You will need to glue the two one-inch thick squares together to make a two-inch cube. To elongate the cylinder and triangular blocks in similar fashion, make two of these shapes, also.

3.   Cut out the shapes with the knife or saw. Sand any rough edges with another piece of styrofoam.

4.   If you are using the one-inch thick styrofoam, glue the two squares together to form a two-inch cube. Do the same with other shapes if you wish to elongate the blocks. Let dry thoroughly.

5.   If you wish to add color to the blocks, spray paint them and let dry. Your finished block should look like this:

Fig. 143.2

6. Select a sturdy box with a removable lid. The lid should be large enough to take the three shapes and allow enough room between the holes to minimize the danger of tearing. If the box lid is sufficiently large, you may wish to make blocks and add holes in the shape of a rectangle ☐ and an oval ⬭ in order to teach these shapes later. Suggested layouts for the lid are given in Fig. 143.3.

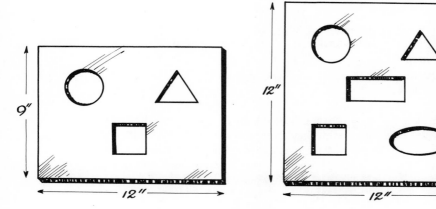

Fig. 143.3

7. Trace the shapes on the lid.
8. With a sharp knife or pair of scissors cut out each shape so that it is slightly larger than its corresponding block.
9. To add color, spray the box with spray paint.

THINGS TO DO ANOTHER TIME

Outline each of your blocks with crayons on heavy paper. Have the child place each block within its proper outline.

Cut out pictures of objects that are round, square, and triangular. Have the youngster help you paste each picture on a piece of construction paper. Help him to identify each object and its shape. Then have him place the block that is similar in shape on or beside each picture. If necessary, have him trace the block and the picture to help him recognize similarities in shape.

When the child has a fairly good mastery of round, square, and triangular shapes, plan lessons to introduce the rectangle ☐ and the oval ⬭. Start with identification tasks involving rectangular and oval blocks.

Activities 140, 141, and 142 can be used as models. For the rectangle, use the tracing technique and show the child how a rectangular block looks different depending on which of its sides it is on: sometimes it is short, sometimes it is tall. Have him trace a long side and a short side. Help him compare the rectangular block with the square block by setting them side by side and noting that the former is longer. Use a small box that is long and narrow as your second rectangle.

To teach the oval, have the youngster trace the block to feel that it is not completely round like a circle. Let him roll it to see that it does not roll the same way a round block rolls. Help the child compare the oval block with the round block by setting them side by side and noting that the oval is longer. Talk about the oval looking like an egg, and use a plastic Easter egg as your second oval.

Plan a matching lesson in which the task is to match the rectangular block and the oval block with their corresponding holes in a shape sorting box. The activity above will serve as a model for your lesson. See also the directions above for making a shape sorter for information on making blocks and their matching holes. The rectangle and the widest parts of the oval should measure about 1½" x 2¾".

See also Activities 133 and 134 for tasks of sorting by shape.

ACTIVITY 144: Finger Play with Numbers

MATHEMATICS
C

WHY

To perform motions a specified number of times.

WHAT YOU NEED

No materials needed.

TALK ABOUT WHAT YOU DO

(Use your own language. This is an example.)

"I know how we'll have some fun! We'll use numbers and sing a song. Listen and watch what I do." Chant, counting slowly:

Clap your hands: 1, 2, 3.	*(Clap on each count)*
Clap your hands, just like me.	*(Clap three times)*
Roll your hands: 1, 2, 3.	*(Make quick, short rolling*
Roll your hands, just like me.	*motion with hand on each*
	count and repeat three
	times on last line)

"I know you can clap your hands. Show me how you can clap. / Can you roll your hands like this? / Good. I'll sing the song again, and you clap and roll your hands when I count."

(Repeat chant, allowing time when you count for the child to clap and roll his hands.)

"That was lots of fun. Let's do it one more time. You count along with me when we clap and roll our hands. Okay?" (Repeat.)

"How many times did we clap each time in the song? / We clapped three times, like this: one, two, three."

HELPFUL HINTS

The child's finger play with numbers should be limited at first to a few numbers. Increase the numbers gradually only as the child becomes more adept at counting.

Repeat the activity often so that the child will learn the chant and be able to say it with you or on his own.

Do not be concerned with perfect timing of clapping and rolling of hands. By all means, keep the finger play fun.

THINGS TO DO ANOTHER TIME

After the child has learned the words of the chant, increase the tempo of the counting. The hand-rolling may get all jumbled up, but that is part of the fun. And remember, having fun with numbers is one of your basic objectives.

Plan activities around other finger-play chants and songs which include counting. Here are two examples:

> Hickory dickory dock.
> The mouse ran up the clocR.   *(Swing one arm up)*
> The clock struck one.   *(Count one, clap at same time)*
> The mouse ran down.   *(Swing one arm down)*
> Hickory dickory dock.

Repeat, changing third line: The clock struck two. (Count *one, two,* clap on each count.) Continue increasing number, counting and clapping, as the child's skill in counting grows.

> A great big ball,   *(Use both arms to form circle)*
> A little, tiny ball,   *(Use index finger and thumb on one hand to form circle)*
>
> A middle-sized ball I see.   *(Use index fingers and thumbs on both hands to form circle)*
>
> Let's see if we can count them,
> One, two, three.   *(Make each of the three circles as it is counted)*

ACTIVITY 145:   Counting Song

MATHEMATICS
C

WHY

To count fingers.
To count and sing to ten.

WHAT YOU NEED

Picture of an Indian.

TALK ABOUT WHAT YOU DO

(Use your own language. This is an example.)

"Do you remember the story we read about a little Indian boy? / Well, here's his picture. Remember now? / What kind of a house did the little Indian boy live in? / Yes. He lived in a tepee with his mother and father."

"I know a song about Indians. I'll sing it and pretend my fingers are little Indians. Okay?"

> One little, two little, three little Indians   *(Touch a finger*
> Four little, five little, six little Indians,   *at each count)*
> Seven little, eight little, nine little Indians,
> Ten little Indian boys.

"Let's do it again. Pretend your fingers are little Indians and count them along with me. Ready?"

(Sing the song a third time if the child is interested. Encourage him to begin singing along with you.)

HELPFUL HINTS

The song "Ten Little Indians" is included in many children's song books. If you cannot locate it, chant the lines.

Use exaggerated, quick motions in counting the fingers on both hands.

Sing the song as often as the child is willing to listen to it. He will learn the words by hearing it over and over again. Alternate Indians girls for Indian boys from time to time.

If the child is not ready for counting to ten, start with two lines:

> One little, two little, three little Indians,
> Three little Indian boys.

When the child has mastered these, increase the song to three lines, using the first two lines as given in the activity and adding:

> Six little Indian boys.

And finally, use the entire song as given in the activity above.

THINGS TO DO ANOTHER TIME

Repeat the song, varying the action by counting toes or other objects lined up in front of the child: "Let's pretend these blocks are little Indian boys and girls. Use this stick to tap each block as we count the little Indians. See, like this."

Vary the verse of the song by substituting for *Indian* such words as *farmer, sailor,* or *drummer.* For drummer, you might use a drum and have the child tap the drum at each count.

Make up your own counting chants and finger action. Here is an example:

One little doggy barking at the moon.
Along came another dog and then there were two.

Two little doggies barking at the moon.
Along came another dog and then there were three.

Three little doggies barking at the moon.
Arf! Arf! Woof! Woof! Bow-wow! Bow-wow!

Extend one finger on first line of chant, two on second line, and three on fourth line.

ACTIVITY 146:   Counting To Find Total Number of Objects

MATHEMATICS
C

WHY

To be aware that the last number counted tells the total number of objects.

WHAT YOU NEED

Three fairly large buttons.

TALK ABOUT WHAT YOU DO

(Use your own language. This is an example.)

(Put three buttons in your hand. Hold out closed hand.) "Guess what I have in my hand! (Open hand after a moment.) What are those? / Right. Let's find out how many buttons we have. I'll put the buttons on the rug one at a time. You count them as I put them down."

(Place one button in front and to left of the child). "Start counting. (Place second button in line with first, about six inches to the right of it.) What number is that button? (Line up third button in similar fashion.) That's right, three. What comes after three? / Yes, four. But I don't have any more buttons. (Show child empty hand.) See, all our buttons are on the floor. We have just three buttons in all. (Touch and count.) One / two / three."

"Watch. I am going to move all the buttons to over here. (Point to spot well away from the row of buttons.) Each time I move a button I am going to count it. / One / two / three. / Oh, there are no more buttons to move. I moved three buttons and that is all we have. You count the buttons again and see if we have just three buttons in all. / See. You had to stop at three, because we don't have any more buttons."

"Now you move the buttons back the way we had them. Each time you move a button, I'll count it. / One / two / three. / Are there any more buttons to move? / No, there are no more buttons to move. That's because we have just three buttons in all."

"This time you move and count the buttons. Don't forget to count each time you move a button. (Give help as needed, especially if the child forgets the number he is on.) You moved and counted three buttons. Are there more buttons to move? / How many buttons do we have then? / Three. You counted three buttons and that's all we have."

(Repeat the moving–counting task if the child remains interested.)

HELPFUL HINTS

Each time you position the buttons keep them in a row and about six inches apart. Always move the buttons a sufficient distance away from the original row of buttons so that the child will see readily that there are no buttons left.

The child's main problem in the counting–moving task may well be to remember the last number he counted. Always supply him with the number when this happens, and be patient. It may take preschoolers several sessions to grasp the numerical understanding of totals.

If the child continues to have difficulty, try the activity using only two buttons and then progress to three. This may help him.

THINGS TO DO ANOTHER TIME

Plan similar activities, varying the objects (spoons, blocks, shoes) and the number of objects (between two and five). Begin asking the child after each moving–counting task how many objects he has in all. But supply the answer yourself whenever he cannot.

Play the game "How Many?" Select objects of which there are three or less in the room: chairs, lamps, books, windows. Ask the child, for example, "How many chairs can you find?" The child must touch and count each chair (only once) and tell you how many he found. Clap when he is right, or pin bits of colored ribbons on him as awards for right answers. Be sure to have plenty of snippets of ribbon on hand, especially if you are working with a small group of youngsters. And by hook or by crook, be sure each child gets an award.

ACTIVITY 147: Counting to a Specified Number

MATHEMATICS
C

WHY

To stop counting at a specified number.

WHAT YOU NEED

No materials needed.

TALK ABOUT WHAT YOU DO

(Use your own language. This is an example.)

"Let's play 'Magic Numbers.' I will count to a magic number and then stop. Then you have to count to the same magic number and stop. Ready? / One, *two*. What is the magic number I stopped at? / Right. Now it is your turn to count to the magic number. / Good!"

"It is my turn again. Listen for the magic number this time. One, two, three, *four*. Now it is your turn. Don't forget the magic number. / That's good! You stopped counting on the magic number."

"It's my turn again. One, two, *three*. / Go ahead. It is your turn. / Whoops! You went past the magic number. Let's do that one again. Listen for that magic number now. One, two, *three*. / Oh, you got the magic number that time."

(Continue the game, counting numbers within one to five. When the child catches on, go on to numbers beyond five.)

HELPFUL HINTS

For the preschooler, remembering the specific number on which to stop counting is not always easy. It is, however, part of the task of counting out a specific number of objects from a pile of objects (rather than all the objects in the pile). The game focuses on the memory task to prepare the child for the larger task of counting out a specified number of objects from a pile.

When you count, always stress the magic number. And at first, include in the game (after you count and before the child counts) the question "What is the magic number?" or some other reminder. When the child becomes aware of the importance of remembering the magic number, then simply take turns counting, with reminders as needed of whose turn it is. Of course, if the child forgets the magic number, don't scold. Just repeat your turn and ask again, "What is the magic number?" for a turn or two.

THINGS TO DO ANOTHER TIME

Play the game reversing roles: have the child go first, counting to a number of his choice (or to one suggested by you); you repeat the count.

Pretend once or twice to forget the magic number and ask him what it is. Or count past the magic number and say, for example: "Oops! I didn't stop at the magic number. I counted to four and your magic number was three. Oh, you're better at magic numbers than I am."

Play a game of "Secret Numbers." Introduce the child to the game by saying, for example: "I have a secret number. I'll whisper the number in your ear. Then you have to count up to the secret number. Okay? (Whisper.) Two. Did you hear the secret number? / Don't say it. Just remember it and count up to the secret number. / Oh, your secret number must have been *two*. Was that the secret number?" This is a good game to play with a small group. Give each child a turn with a secret number (from one to five) and have the others tell what the secret number is from the number at which the counting stops.

ACTIVITY 148:   Counting Objects to a Specified Number

MATHEMATICS
C

WHY

To count out a specified number of objects (one to three).

WHAT YOU NEED

An abacus (see directions under "Helpful Hints").

TALK ABOUT WHAT YOU DO

(Use your own language. This is an example.)

"Look at what I have. (Hold up abacus.) It is an abacus. That's a funny name, isn't it? Abacus. / See the spools here? / They can move." (Demonstrate moving the spools with your fingers from one side to the other. Let the child examine the abacus and move the spools.)

"Let's find out how many spools are on our abacus. We have to count them to find out. Count with me. (Demonstrate moving one spool at each count to the other side of the abacus.) I'll hold the abacus and you count and move all the spools the way I did. / How many spools do we have in all on the abacus? / Very good. We have five whole spools."

"Now let's move only some of the spools. We'll count out and move just two spools. You count with me to the magic number two, and watch how I move the spools. Ready? One / two. (Move one spool to other side on each count.) Count how many spools we have on this side. (Point to the side with two spools.) How many spools did we count out? / Right, two spools. That's because we stopped at the magic number two."

(Return all spools to one side.) "This time I'll count to the magic number two, and you move the spools. When I stop counting, remember that you have to stop moving spools. One / two. / Very good. Now count the spools you moved (point) and see how many spools you moved. / Two, that's right."

(Return all spools to one side.) "This time you count out two spools all by yourself. Don't forget to count to the magic number two and then stop. / Oh, you're so smart! You counted out two spools all by yourself."

"Do you think you could do that again all by yourself?" (Repeat with two spools.)

HELPFUL HINTS

You need a wire coat hanger and five small spools to make an abacus. Cut the coat hanger with a wire-cutting pliers at points shown in Fig. 148.1.

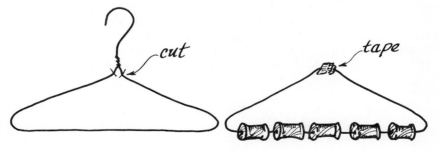

Fig. 148.1

Straighten one side of the triangle so that you can thread the spools easily on the bottom of the triangle. Form the triangle once more. Bring the cut ends of the wire as close together as you can, and tape them well with adhesive or plastic tape so that the sharp ends are of no danger to the child.

Since the child will have difficulty holding the abacus and moving the spools at the same time, hold the abacus when he performs the tasks.

Counting out a specified number of objects from a larger group of objects (not all in the group) can be a difficult task for the toddler. If there is danger of frustration, change the task to one of counting all the spools on the abacus, and try the activity again when the child is older.

THINGS TO DO ANOTHER TIME

Increase the number of spools to be counted to three and then to four, each time working with the child as suggested above. You may have to start by demonstrating both the counting and moving of the spools; then count and let the child move the spools; and finally, have the child do the task all by himself.

Plan similar activities using blocks or other objects (spoons, buttons, shoes). Vary the number of objects to be counted (from one to five). Always have the child move objects on each count from one pile to another pile. The new pile should contain the specified number of objects to be counted *without using up all the objects in the old pile*.

Place a pile of buttons (15–20) on the floor or on a low table. Ask the youngster to count out a particular number of buttons and bring them to you. Start with one or two buttons and gradually increase to five buttons but stop if he has trouble with the larger numbers. When he makes a mistake, re-count aloud the buttons given you and ask him to return the extra buttons to the pile. Then have the child return buttons in small numbers to the pile, saying, for example: "Here are some buttons you can put back in the pile of buttons. / How many buttons do you have to put with the other buttons? / Good! Put them in the big pile of buttons. / Come back and I'll give you some more buttons."

A slinky is a fascinating toy for this child as he learns what a spring is like and what he can do with it.

Part 10

Science

SCIENCE

Science experiences are an important part of the preschooler's efforts to make sense out of his world. Science education starts when the child begins to form simple concepts related to people and his own body, to plants and animals, to weather and common physical features of the earth, to tools and vehicles. It expands and deepens as the youngster discovers new wonders around him and perceives relationships which exist within our natural and man-made environment. By exploring and experimenting within the bounds of safety, he begins to learn ways of coping with this environment.

Most young children try hard to make sense out of the world. Thus, the world becomes their laboratory, and everyday experiences become their science textbook. This, then, is the setting that the adult must capitalize on to further the child's interest in science and to promote the development of a scientific attitude: the immediate observable surroundings, the objects within it, and the child's everyday experiences.

Within this setting, questions become an important tool. When a young-ster, out of a natural curiosity, begins to ask questions—"What is it?" "What can it do?" "Why?" "How does it work?"—brief but accurate an-swers should be given in language the child will understand. The adult's asking questions, too, about things observed, leading the child to take a closer look, to extend his observations beyond what he might do on his own, is equally important in developing an inquiring mind. "It's a squirrel," you might say when Jimmy excitedly discovers an animal busily eating on some-thing. "See its long bushy tail? / Let's be very quiet and watch for a minute. We don't want to frighten it away. / What do you think the squirrel is doing? / What do you suppose it is eating? / Maybe it is eating an acorn. Can you see how the squirrel uses its paws when it eats? / Oh, there it goes! My, can't squirrels run fast?"

Developing an interest in science and a questioning, probing mind about the environment are important goals of early science education. Two ave-nues lead to these ends. The first is acting on a child's spontaneous interest in science phenomena, taking time to share, for instance, a few moments of excitement over a crawling caterpillar or a ripened feathery dandelion. Together, you can see if the caterpillar will crawl onto a green leaf or what happens to a ripened dandelion if you blow on it. If, on the other hand, your response is "Not, now, Jimmy. We're doing something else now," the youngster's interest and curiosity is easily dampened, and he soon learns that a lack of interest is the more accepted pattern.

More than this kind of spontaneous, incidental learning can be provided. Helping the child develop his powers of observation and fill in information gaps, which are bound to occur when learning is left to happenstance, call for a more systematic approach. The second avenue to the ends of early science education, then, is the planned short lesson. These lessons include questions to spark the child's curiosity and to guide him to more extensive observation, to observe first gross distinguishing characteristics of an object and then its finer, more detailed quantitative and qualitative characteristics. From these perceptions, often after many repetitions, the youngster begins not only to find relationships that explain scientific phenomena but also to use his powers of observation to answer some of his own questions.

You might, for example, plan a short activity around a flower. "Look," you might say, pointing to a particular flower, "here's a pretty flower. What color is it? / Does the flower smell sweet?" Then you would gently separate a petal of the flower so that it is distinguishable from the other petals. "See the flower leaf? / It's called a *petal*. How many petals does the flower have? / Oh, there are so many petals, I don't think we can count them all. This flower has lots of petals. / Look, here's another flower. (Point to a bud.) Where are its petals? / That's right. But the petals are all tight together. (Make a fist to demonstrate tightness.) That's because this is a baby flower. It is a flower *bud*. (Hold the two flowers so that the child can see both.) Which flower is smaller? / Yes, the bud needs more sun before it will open all its petals and look like this other big flower. / We'll look at the bud again tomorrow to see if the sun has opened some of its petals."

Note in the example that bits of information are supplied in addition to the questions which encourage the child's extended observation. The language used is kept simple for the youngster's understanding, but a new word or two (*bud, petal*) are introduced to keep the information accurate. Both the information given and the new words are considered incidental learning. The focus of the lesson is on encouraging the child to make comparisons and to find relationships between the bud and the flower in full bloom. For the young child to be successful in this, it is important that both objects to be compared are visible. Later, when the child is older and more experienced, he may be able to recall an object seen within the recent past and make comparisons, but at first both objects must be concrete and visible.

Becoming aware of relationships that exist among objects is a natural outgrowth of repeated observations. In the example above, the adult encourages the child to find relationships of size and position of petals. The adult, however, also explains to the child a relationship that exists between the sun and flower growth. To make this relationship more concrete for the youngster, they will check on the bud after another day of sun (or several days of sun, if needed), at which time the relationship will be restated by the adult: "Oh, look! The bud's petals are opening up. The sun helps the flower open up all its petals." Many more experiences with flowers and plants, of course, may be required before the youngster grasps the idea and demonstrates that he has made it his own (internalizes it). And when he does, he may say something like this: "I'm going to put this plant in the sun so it gets big flowers."

Science education starts early for children in that much of their early learning can be applied to science phenomena. They become aware of and learn the names of different kinds of animals and plants, of foods and clothing, of rain and clouds and sunshine, of tools and machines and other man-made structures and objects. They learn also to distinguish among shapes and colors and sizes of objects and to recognize other quantitative and qualitative differences such as *few* and *many, hard* and *soft, hot* and *cold, wet* and *dry*. A youngster learns that mirrors reflect his image, that water cleanses and soap helps to do the job, that electric bulbs can be turned on to make a dark room light. He learns that people live in houses and go to work, that there is a red tree on the corner and that Freckles, the cat, lives next door. He sees chemistry at work in the kitchen when he watches water boil, sugar dissolve in water, or ice cream melt. He becomes aware of tools and machines and what they do, the noises they make. He sees and feels rocks and leaves and flowers, feels rain and wind and sun, watches a bird fly and listens to its chirp, and, if he is around animals and pets, learns what they eat and the noises they make. He discovers that objects can be manipulated, that beads can be dropped into a bottle, that puzzle pieces can be put together to make a picture, that there are different colors and that you can make them with paint and crayons.

All of these kinds of learning, and more, are the building blocks of science education. In a very real sense, then, many of the learning activity samples throughout this book make contributions to a young child's science education. The activities which follow in this section are focused more directly on simple scientific concepts, processes, and relationships. They assume that the child has already acquired the general concepts and skills he is expected to use. For this reason, most of the science activities are classified at Level C. (See pages 16–18 for an explanation of the A, B, and C levels of child development as used in this text.)

To determine the readiness of a particular child for a particular science activity, check carefully what concepts and skills a youngster is expected to be able to use in the activity. If a concept or skill has not yet been learned by the child, fill in the gap first by other appropriate activities; then only use the science activity. The child's chances of success are greatly enhanced by following this simple rule.

In summary and for quick reference, the following guidelines relate to effective science education, both in using these sample activities and in planning your own activities:

1. *Center science activities on the familiar*. The youngster's everyday life is the best source of science content.

2. *Build the child's science learning on concepts and skills already acquired by him.* Expecting too much learning in a single lesson usually spells disaster.

3. *Make the activity relevant and concrete.* Having a youngster watch what happens to shortening, sugar, and an egg when mixed together is more meaningful to him if the end product is cookies that he can eat.

4. *Be sure your science information is accurate.* Don't promote myths or incorrect information. A children's encyclopedia and beginner's science books are good sources with which to check your information. But don't be afraid to say, "I don't know. Let's see if we can find a book (or person) that will tell us."

5. *Use questions often, rather than simply supply the child with ready-made answers.* Remember that your long-range goals are to help the youngster develop an inquiring mind and observation skills.

6. *The information or explanations given should be short and simple.* Introduce a new word as needed to keep the information accurate but demonstrate the meaning of the word by concrete examples. And consider these kinds of learning (information, new words) as incidental learning rather than the main focus of the lesson. Over time and with repetition, an interested child will gradually absorb such incidental learning.

7. *Repeat!* The preschooler often enjoys doing again what he has enjoyed before. Or repeat with variations to regain the youngster's interest. Developing science concepts and finding existing relationships are gradual processes growing out of many perceptions and experiences.

8. *Don't forget to praise! Don't forget to make it fun!* Be enthusiastic yourself and enjoy, for your pleasure will most likely rub off on the child.

ACTIVITY 149: Kinds of Weather

SCIENCE
B

WHY

To relate dark clouds to rain.
To feel that rain is wet.

WHAT YOU NEED

Rain clothes and umbrella.

TALK ABOUT WHAT YOU DO

(Use your own language. This is an example.)

"Let's look out this window and see what is happening outside today. / Oh, what are these drops on the window? / Yes, it's raining outside. These are drops of rain water. Watch them run down the window."

"Can you see the sun? / What do you see up in the sky? / Right, lots of clouds. Are the clouds nice white, fluffy clouds? / The clouds are dark, aren't they? / That's because they are rain clouds. The raindrops fall out of those dark clouds."

"Look at the street now. What do you see that the rain has made all wet? / Do you think the grass is wet too? / Oh, look! There is a woman with an umbrella. Why does she have an umbrella? / That's right. The umbrella keeps the rain off so that she doesn't get all wet like the sidewalk."

"Let's open the window and feel the rain. Put your hand out like this so the rain hits it. / Oh, the rain made my hand all wet. Did the rain make your hand wet, too?"

"Would you like to go outside and see how it feels when it rains? / We'll have to put our raincoats on and take an umbrella to help keep us dry. / When we get outdoors we'll look at all those dark clouds again. We'll feel the grass, too, to see if it is wet from the rain. What else would you like to feel to see if the rain has made it wet?"

HELPFUL HINTS

The rainy day you pick for this activity should be one of pleasant, gentle showers. If it is raining hard, you will want to omit the walk in the rain.

The activity assumes that the child is already familiar with the concepts and words used in the language above (*sun, clouds, wet, dry*). If not, teach the concepts before using the activity.

When you are outdoors in the rain, provide firsthand experiences which are related to the information already given in your indoor conversation. For example, look again at the clouds, feel the grass and other objects noted before as wet from the rain, remove the umbrella for a minute to feel the wetness of the rain on your face.

THINGS TO DO ANOTHER TIME

Plan similar activities for other kinds of weather in your locale:

Watch a thunder storm from a window. Talk calmly and with no trace of fear about the loudness of the thunder and the brightness of the lightning. Be very careful not to cause fear of the storm in the child.

On a warm, sunny day call attention to the sun, how warm it feels, and touch some things that have been warmed by the sun. Find a spot of shade to sit or stand in and talk about how it feels cooler out of the sun. Look for things that sparkle in the sun (leaves, water, metals, glass). Talk about the kinds of clothes you are wearing and that you don't need heavy clothing as you do on a cold day or rain clothes as you do on a rainy day.

On a windy day, watch and talk about the wind blowing the leaves or clothes. Give the child a pinwheel and watch it spin in the wind. Walk into the wind to feel the wind in your face and then away from the wind to feel the wind push you along. Fly a kite and let the child hold the string; explain that the wind keeps the kite in the air.

On a cold day, bundle up well and talk about the need for wearing warm clothing because it is cold outside. Talk about how cold your nose and ears feel after you are out for a bit. Feel something that is very cold (bench, sidewalk, ground) and explain that you can't sit outside when it is cold the way you can when it is warm.

On a snowy day, wear snow clothes and talk about needing them on a cold, snowy day: that the snow is wet and that the boots and mittens will help keep you dry as well as warm. Feel the snow with your hands and on your face. Try to catch a snowflake on your tongue. Catch a snowflake on your gloves or sleeve and let the child observe it. Walk in the snow and then on a cleared area to feel the difference in walking through deep snow. Help the child make a snowball or build a small snowman. Bring some snow back into the school and watch it melt and become water.

ACTIVITY 150: Air

SCIENCE
B

WHY

To see and feel balloons filled with air.
To feel air escaping from a balloon.

WHAT YOU NEED

Two balloons of different colors; string or small rubber bands.

TALK ABOUT WHAT YOU DO

(Use your own language. This is an example.)

"Look at what I have. (Hold up an uninflated balloon.) It's a red balloon. See how the balloon stretches. (Demonstrate.) Here, you feel the balloon. / Stretch it the way I did. / Oh, it went 'snap!', didn't it?"

"Let's blow up the balloon. I'll blow air into it and you watch it get bigger and bigger as more air goes into it. (Inflate the balloon only partially so that it remains soft.) There, I'll fasten this end so that the air can't get out. (Twist mouth of balloon and tie.) Feel the balloon now. Does it feel soft? / That's because I put only a little air in it."

"Let's blow up the yellow balloon with air too. This time I will put lots of air in it. Watch now. (Inflate the balloon so that it is distinctly larger and tauter than the red balloon. Hold out for child to feel.) Feel the yellow balloon. / Now feel the red balloon again. / Which one is soft? / All the air I blew in the yellow balloon makes the balloon feel harder."

"Do you know something funny about air? / You can feel air but you can't see it. Watch carefully while I let the air out of the yellow balloon. (Hold hand over mouth of balloon and slowly release the air.) Did you see anything? / I didn't either. But I felt it on my hand. I'll blow up the balloon again so you can feel the air. / Hold out your hand and keep your eyes on it just in case you see some air. / Ready? (Release air slowly.) Did that feel good? / Did you see anything? / You want to do it again? Okay. (Repeat.) Did you hear the air that time? / Did you feel it? / Did you see the air?"

"I'll blow up the balloon again and fasten it so that the air can't come out. Then you can play with both balloons. / Now you've got two balloons full of air."

HELPFUL HINTS

Use two colors to make the identification of the soft and hard balloons clearer.

Releasing the air the first time on your own hand demonstrates to the child that it is a pleasant experience and dispels any fears he may have. If the child is eager for the experience, however, you may omit the demonstration. Also, after feeling the air on his hand, he may enjoy feeling the air blow against his cheek or the back of his neck.

If the youngster wishes to try to blow up a balloon, let him try one that has already been blown up several times. Show him how to hold it in his mouth, lips rounded. But it may well be too difficult a task. Explain that it takes "a lot of air" and that he will be able to blow up balloons when he is a little older.

THINGS TO DO ANOTHER TIME

To help the child develop a concept of *air,* tell him air is all around us, even though we can't see it. Use a hand fan to move air so that he feels it on his face, arms, and legs, repeating, "Feel the air?"

On a windy day, go outdoors and watch the wind blow the leaves on trees. Talk about the wind being "lots of air blowing everywhere." Ask, "Can you feel the air blowing on your face?" And explain, "When the air blows like this we call it *wind*."

Have the child breathe deeply to feel the air in his nose or mouth. Have him exhale to feel the warm air on his hand.

Have the youngster blow on a pinwheel to make it spin or on the sail of a toy boat to make it move in water. Say, "That was a good blow. The air made the pinwheel spin (boat move)."

ACTIVITY 151:   Using a Flashlight

SCIENCE
B

WHY

To use a flashlight.
To observe the effects of light.

WHAT YOU NEED

A flashlight that is easy to manipulate.

TALK ABOUT WHAT YOU DO

(Use your own language. This is an example.)

"We are going to have lots of fun with a flashlight today. This is a flashlight. (Let child examine it if interested.) I'll show you what a flashlight can do. (Switch the flashlight on and shine it on a particular object.) Look at that circle of light."

"I'll show you how to work the flashlight. See that button. (Point to switch, holding flashlight so child has a good view of it while you talk.) I push the button forward, like this. / On goes the flashlight! I push the button back like this. / Off goes the flashlight!"

"Now you turn the flashlight on. / Push the other way. / Push hard. / There it goes! Can you turn it off too? / Very good!"

"Let's darken the room a little. I'll close the shades. / Now we can see better the light the flashlight makes. Turn on the flashlight and see what you can find with the light. / Oh, there's a chair. / Now the light is on the table. / Move the flashlight some more and see where the light goes."

"Let's shine the light on this wall. If you move your arm in a circle, the light goes in a circle too. / Here, I'll help you. (Move child's arm in circle if he needs help.) See what else you can do with the light."

"That was fun! / Can you turn the flashlight off now? / See this round glass part at the front of the flashlight? (Trace circle with finger.) That's where the light shines out when you turn the flashlight on. / What's this? (Point to switch.) / Yes, you turn the flashlight on and off there."

HELPFUL HINTS

Use a flashlight that switches on and off easily. But if necessary, help the child manipulate the switch.

If the child takes the initiative in exploring objects and walls with the flashlight, let the activity follow these leads. But if the youngster shines the light in your face or the faces of other youngsters, tell him that "we do not shine the flashlight in other people's eyes."

If the youngster is curious about how the flashlight works, take it apart and show him the batteries, telling him they make the light.

THINGS TO DO ANOTHER TIME

Explore a dark closet or any other dark room with a flashlight. Be careful not to frighten the child. Open the door first and flash the light all around the dark room as the child watches. Then, with flashlight on, let the child enter. Encourage him to use the flashlight to look at the ceiling, floor, walls, and objects in the room. Talk about the contrasts between light and dark ("What can you see in the dark? / What can you see when the flashlight is on?") and emphasize that the child can control light and darkness by using a flashlight ("See, you made it light. Can you make the room dark again?").

Beam a strong flashlight or a projector on a wall or screen for the child to observe shadows. Have the youngster stand so that he can see his shadow on the wall. Call his attention to the fact that the shape of the shadow is the same as his own shape. Have him walk toward the wall and away from it to see what happens to his shadow. Have him raise an arm, hold up an object, dance, and so on, as he observes his shadow.

ACTIVITY 152: Water Properties

SCIENCE
B

WHY

To discover things that float in water and things that do not float.

WHAT YOU NEED

Shallow basin; water; newspapers; small objects that float (piece of wood, plastic bottle with tight cap, leaf, ball of aluminum foil, acorn); non-floating objects (stone, nail, paperclip, washer).

TALK ABOUT WHAT YOU DO

(Use your own language. This is an example.)

"Help me fill this basin with water so we can have some fun with water today. Where can we get the water? / Right. Can you turn on the faucet? / See the water running into the basin? / The basin is getting fuller . . . and fuller . . . and fuller. / You can turn off the water now. The basin is full enough. / Let's spread these newspapers on the floor. We'll put the basin of water on the newspaper so that if we spill a little water it won't hurt. / I'll put the basin of water on the newspaper."

"See the box of things on the table? Please bring the box over here. / You may empty all the things in the box onto the newspapers. / Oh, look at all those things. Can you tell me some of their names?"

"Remember how your toy boat floats on the water? / Let's see which of these things will float on the water like a boat. Pick one thing at a time and put it in the water. We'll watch and see what it does."

"Oh, the piece of wood floats. It makes a good boat, doesn't it? / Ka-plunk! What happened to the stone? / Yes, it sank right to the bottom. / Look at that leaf boat! What is it doing? / It's floating on top of the water." (Continue until all objects have been used.)

"Look, I am going to push the piece of wood down so that it goes under the water. / Watch what happens when I let go. / Swish! Up it came again. / You try that with the bottle. / Hold it all the way under. / Now let go quick. / It popped right up, didn't it?"

"Take out all the things that float first. / Now take out all the things that did not float, all the things that sank to the bottom because they were too heavy to float. / Very good! That was a lot of fun."

HELPFUL HINTS

Use a basin or a pail that's deep enough to hold sufficient water to cover the wood and the bottle in the experiment on releasing these objects under water.

In this same experiment, hold the object with both hands cupped around the object. Release the object quickly under water by opening the thumbs. The object, especially the bottle, will pop to the top of the water in a delightful way.

If you are working with several children, you may wish to use a larger basin or a small tub and a set of objects for each child.

THINGS TO DO ANOTHER TIME

Repeat the activity with other small floating and non-floating objects.

Have the youngster float a small plastic bowl in a basin of water. Then slowly pour water into the bowl until it sinks. Talk about how heavy the water was in the bowl; it made the bowl sink. Experiment with a plastic bottle: first float an empty bottle with the cap on; then fill the bottle with water and see if it floats.

ACTIVITY 153:   Nature Collections

SCIENCE
C

WHY

To identify nature objects.
To distinguish differences within classes of nature objects.

WHAT YOU NEED

Leaves, stones, and other nature objects in a paper bag (collected by the child); several boxes; paste; scotch tape; crayons.

TALK ABOUT WHAT YOU DO

(Use your own language. This is an example.)

"When we were outdoors yesterday, we found lots of things and put them in this bag. Remember? / Let's look at the things we found. You can spread them out here on the table."

"What are all these things? / Yes, that's a leaf. Are there other leaves? / Let's put all the leaves at this end of the table. / That is a twig off a tree. But you can put it with the leaves because leaves and twigs are parts of a tree. / Look at all those leaves! Did you find a great big leaf? / Say, that *is* a big one. Which leaf do you like best? / I like that one too. It is a pretty color."

"What else do you have here? (Point to remaining objects.) Yes, that's a pretty white stone. Did you find any other stones? / Let's look at each of the stones. / What color is that one? / It is sort of gray. / Oh, that stone is almost round. (Make a circling motion with finger.) Can you make a little pile of stones here on the table? / Very good!'' (Continue sorting out and talking about each object in the collection.)

"I have some boxes. We can put the leaves in one box and the stones in another box. Then when you find some more leaves and some more stones, you can put them in the same boxes. / Good. Let's paste one of the leaves on the lid of this box so you know where your leaves are. / I'll tape this little, flat stone on top of this box so you know it is a box for stones. / What should we do with these other things? / Okay. We'll put them in another box. / This can be your special box for other things you want to save. I'll print a big 'S' on top. / That means *special.''*

HELPFUL HINTS

Have the child, if possible, collect his own nature specimens for the activity. There may be times, of course, when you find interesting nature objects (shells, feathers) around which you plan similar activities.

The activity above encourages the youngster to become a collector. This is a long range goal which should be promoted throughout early years.

Instead of or in addition to organizing the materials by boxes, you may prefer to set up a science table or corner. The collections may then be made readily available to the child or children for their self-directed play, involving such things as feeling, observing, and sorting.

THINGS TO DO ANOTHER TIME

Encourage the child to seek out and collect other nature specimens: seeds, nuts, shells, dried grasses, small growing plants in pots. Encourage, too, adding to collections every chance the child gets.

Renew interest in a collection by providing a magnifying glass to observe detail and find finer differences among objects of a particular collection.

Encourage the youngster to use the collected items on his own and plan some of your activities around them: sort by colors or sizes, make a nature collage, use the materials as props in dramatic play.

ACTIVITY 154: Color Changes

SCIENCE
B

WHY

To observe effect of food coloring added to water.
To observe color changes by mixing colors in water.

WHAT YOU NEED

Six clear plastic glasses; red, yellow, and blue food coloring in plastic squeeze bottles; aprons.

TALK ABOUT WHAT YOU DO

(Use your own language. This is an example.)

"We are going to have lots of fun with colors today. First we have to get into these aprons so our clothes won't get full of colors."

"These little bottles are full of different colors. Let's find out what colors they are. Which one should we try first? / Okay. Watch, and I'll show you what to do. First you hold the bottle upside down over a glass of water, like this. / Then you squeeze the plastic bottle hard. / There's a drop of color. Oh, look at what it is doing! / What color is the water now?"

"You try one of the other colors. Use this other glass of water. / Squeeze the bottle harder. / Oh, that's beautiful! See the funny swirls. / What color is it?" (Continue with the third color.)

"Let's try putting two colors in the same water. Which color do you want to start with? / Now try another color. / No, put it in the red water this time. / What is happening to the red water? / Yes, it is changing color. Put another drop of the yellow in it. / What color is the water now? (Continue to make all three secondary colors: orange, purple, and green.) How many colors do we have? / Let's count them to find out.''

"What do you want to do with the colors now? / Okay, you do that and see what happens.''

HELPFUL HINTS

Plastic aprons provide good protection of clothes in this activity. But you might also use an old shirt, towel, or sheet to cover the child.

The plastic squeeze bottles of food coloring are especially good for younger children. If you must use the glass bottles and eye droppers, teach the child how to manipulate an eye dropper first, before the activity, using just water. Place the glass bottles in small boxes to avoid spilling.

The activity above guides the child through making the three secondary colors (red and yellow for orange, red and blue for purple, blue and yellow for green). You may prefer, however, to let the child experiment with the colors on his own (after demonstrating the squeeze-bottle technique) and let him discover the various colors as they happen.

In both approaches, be prepared for the child to mix all the colors to come out with drab brown. This, too, is important learning for the child.

If you are working with several children, it is a good idea to divide the materials so that every two children have their own colors and water for the activity.

THINGS TO DO ANOTHER TIME

Have the youngster experiment with different shades of one color: one drop of color in one glass of water, two drops of the same color in a second glass, and three drops of color in a third glass. Set the glasses side by side for the child to observe the lighter and darker shades.

After making glasses of different colored water, have the child set the glasses in the sun to see how the colors become more intense. Or, better yet, find a spot where you can set one glass of colored water in the sun and a second glass—same color—out of the sun. Let the child observe the difference in brightness.

After the child has prepared glasses of colored water, show him how to dip the corners of white paper napkins or paper towels (folded) in the various colors. Talk about how the paper absorbs the colored water. Let dry and see how the color remains in the napkin or towel. Then have a party at which you use the decorated napkins.

See also Art section for other activities involving colors.

ACTIVITY 155:   Mechanics

SCIENCE
C

WHY

To discover that a wheel goes around.
To discover that wheeled objects move when their wheels go around.

WHAT YOU NEED

Two toys with wheels (large toy car, pull toy).

TALK ABOUT WHAT YOU DO

(Use your own language. This is an example.)

"Let's play with the car today. What is this? (Point to a wheel.) Yes, it's a wheel. (Turn car over so that the wheels are on top. Spin one wheel.) Oh, look at the wheel go around and around. It spins. Can you make the wheel spin? / Say, you really made the wheel spin." (If the child is interested, let him continue to spin the wheels.)

"Now, turn the car over so that it is on its wheels. / That's right. You watch what the wheels do when I push the car. (Push it slowly with your hand.) What are the wheels doing? / Yes, they went around and around. Did the car move? / The car moved when the wheels went around and around."

"It is your turn to push the car and make the wheels go around. I'll watch the wheels. / Oh, that's good! The wheels are going around and around when the car moves."

"Let's give the car a big shove and watch what the wheels do. Ready? / What did the wheels do? / The wheels went around very fast and the car moved very fast. / Do it again and watch those wheels."

"Does your Moo Cow (a pull toy) have wheels? / Let's see if its wheels go around when you pull it. / Did the wheels go around?"

HELPFUL HINTS

The larger the wheels on the toys you use, the easier it will be for the child to observe them moving."

Do not hurry the youngster through this activity. Let him take all the time he wants to spin the wheels and to pull and push the toys to make the wheels go around.

Reinforce the learning by calling attention to other objects on wheels that move when the wheels go around: a slow-moving car, grocery cart, bicycle, truck.

THINGS TO DO ANOTHER TIME

Repeat the activity with other wheel toys.

Put a load of blocks or a heavy object in a large box. Talk about how heavy it is and that you want to move the load to the other side of the room. Let the child feel how heavy the box is. Then get a "brilliant" idea: if you can put the box on a wagon (a toy wheelbarrow, large toy truck), you can easily pull or push the heavy load to the other side of the room. Help the youngster load the box on the vehicle and let him see if your idea works. Talk about how the wheels made the job easier.

Explore with the child what springs can do. Walk a Slinky down a flight of stairs. Show the youngster how springs can get big (expand) and little (retract). Wind up a mechanical toy and make it perform. Explain that a spring inside the toy makes it go. Show how a spring in a flashlight holds the batteries in place.

With a third person, explore what a teeter–totter can do. While one person holds the child on one end of the teeter–totter, the other person slowly pushes down on the other end and "Janie goes up . . . up . . . up! Wheee!" When the other person slowly releases the other end of the teeter–totter, "Janie comes down . . . down . . . down."

ACTIVITY 156: Growing Plants

SCIENCE
C

WHY

To observe that plants grow from seeds.

WHAT YOU NEED

Two or three navy beans; flower pot with drainage dish; soil; large spoon; water in a sprinkling can (see "Helpful Hints" below).

TALK ABOUT WHAT YOU DO

(Use your own language. This is an example.)

"You will never guess what I have in my hand. (Hold out hand to show beans.) / They are seeds, bean seeds. If you put the seeds in the ground and water them, they grow into bean plants." (Let the child feel and examine the seeds closely.)

"Look at these other things. / Yes, that's dirt. Flowers and trees grow in dirt. What is this? (Point to flower pot.) It is a flower pot. We are going to use it to plant our bean seeds. I bet you know what this is in this bottle. / Right. It is water. See the little holes (point) in the top of the bottle? / Watch what happens when I turn the bottle upside-down. (Sprinkle a little water on your hand and/or the child's hand.) The water comes right out of the little holes, doesn't it?"

"The first thing we have to do to plant our bean seeds is to put some of the dirt in this flower pot. You can use this big spoon as a shovel. Scoop the dirt into the pot. / That's right. Put a lot more dirt in the pot. / That's good. Can you pat the dirt down a little now with your hand?"

"We are ready for the next step now. Make a little hole in the dirt with your finger, like this. (Make hole about ¼ inch deep.) There, see the little hole? / Put one of the bean seeds right in the hole. / Can you make a little hole in the dirt the way I did? / Now put another bean seed in your hole. / Oh, you're a good little planter!"

"Now you have to cover up the seeds with a little dirt. Take just a little dirt with your spoon and pour the dirt right over your two bean seeds. / Not too much. / Yes, that's good. See, the beans are all covered."

"Our bean seeds are going to need water to grow. You will have to use the sprinkling bottle to water the seeds. / A little more. / I think that is enough water. See how wet the dirt looks. Does it feel wet?"

"Where can we put the pot so that it will get some sun? Sun helps plants to grow, you know. / That's a good place. We'll check the pot every day to see if it needs more water. And very soon, we'll see the little bean plant shoot right out of the dirt."

HELPFUL HINTS

A can, paper cup, or a milk carton can be used instead of a flower pot if you punch several holes in the bottom for drainage. An egg carton, too, is good for planting multiple seeds. Make a sprinkling can by punching small holes in the metal cap of a plastic bottle.

Cover your work area with newspapers so that any spillage of dirt or water is not a problem and the final clean-up is easy.

Following this activity by having the child watch for the bean to sprout is important for his understanding of the relationship between the seed and the growing plant. For this reason, fast growing seeds should be used so that the child's interest does not wane. In addition to beans, pumpkin and tomato seeds sprout quickly.

If you are working with a small group of children, color coding the pots is a good idea so that each child knows which is his.

THINGS TO DO ANOTHER TIME

Follow up this activity with a daily check of the pot by the child. Point out when the soil looks dry and remind the child to water it to make the seeds grow. When a shoot appears, react excitedly and talk about how it is pushing itself right through the dirt. And note changes in the plant as it grows.

At some point, the child may want to see what the original bean seed looks like after a plant has formed. If so, pull out one of the bean plants and examine it carefully together. Or place several beans in a shallow dish of water for the child to watch from day to day as they sprout.

Because children usually enjoy watching what happens to a plant as it grows, growing an onion top or a sweet potato in water allows the youngster to observe actual growth. Cut off the top of an onion (a good inch or more) and place it in a shallow container of water, such as a jar lid. Keep it wet by daily watering. When the onion begins to grow at the bottom, insert three toothpicks into the sides of the onion and rest the toothpicks on the top of a clear plastic tumbler filled with water. The bottom of the onion should be immersed in the water (see Fig. 156.1). The youngster will be able to watch the "tail" that grows from the bottom of the onion.

Fig. 156.1

To grow a sweet potato, insert toothpicks (as described above) in the sides of the potato. Immerse half of the potato in a clear plastic tumbler so that the bottom half of the potato is in water to grow roots. Vines will also grow from the top of the potato.

Both the onion and the sweet potato can be transplanted to a garden or a pot of soil for the child to continue to watch the growth of the plant.

With the child, plant a few radishes or carrots in the playground. Talk about each step: loosening the soil with a shovel or hoe, removing weeds, making holes and putting the seeds in, covering with dirt, and watering. Make daily checks on the plants, watering and weeding. Be prepared to pull up a plant from time to time to let the child see how big the radishes or carrots have grown.

ACTIVITY 157:   Seasons of the Year

SCIENCE
C

WHY

To relate changes in color of leaves to the autumn season.

WHAT YOU NEED

A tree with leaves that are turning color; pictures of a tree in winter (no leaves), spring (budding), and summer (full-grown leaves); blanket to sit on.

TALK ABOUT WHAT YOU DO

(Use your own language. This is an example.)

(Take the child to a tree with leaves which have turned red or yellow and are beginning to fall.) "Oh, look at all these pretty leaves! See if you can find a red leaf. / Now look for a yellow leaf. / What color do you like best? / I like that one, too." (Continue collecting leaves as long as the child remains interested in doing so.)

(Hold up a leaf that is still green.) "What color is this leaf? / Yes, it's green. In summer all the tree's leaves were green like this one. I'll tell you a story about this green leaf. But first, help me spread out the blanket so we can sit on it. / Now sit here beside me. We'll look at these pictures and I'll tell you the story."

"When it was cold in the winter, this tree had no leaves, just big empty branches. It looked like the tree in this picture. (Show the picture of the tree in winter. Answer any questions the child may ask. Point out that the tree has no leaves. Encourage the child to talk about what he sees.)

"But after the cold winter, springtime came. The sun began to make the ground and the air nice and warm. The tree, too, began to feel nice and warm. And do you know what happened? / All kinds of little green leaves began to grow all over the tree. (Show picture of tree in spring.) Can you see the little green leaves on the tree? / That's the way this tree (point to real tree) looked last spring."

"Well, the warmer it got, the bigger and bigger grew the little green leaves. When summer came and it was really warm, the tree was covered with big green leaves, like this tree in this picture." (Show picture of tree in summer. Call child's attention to the green leafiness of the tree.)

"When the warm summer was over, it began to get colder again. That meant that autumn was here. It is autumn now. That's why we have sweaters on today, to keep nice and warm. In autumn, too, all the green leaves of the tree begin to turn red and yellow. They begin to fall off the tree. See all the red and yellow leaves that have fallen from this tree onto the ground? / And as it gets colder each day now, more of the leaves will fall. When it is really cold again and winter comes back, all the leaves of this tree will be on the ground. The tree will be ready for a nice long winter nap."

"Can you guess what will happen when it begins to warm up again in the spring? / Why, this tree will get busy growing all kinds of new green, baby leaves. We'll come back next spring so you can see all the new green leaves on the tree. Would you like to do that?"

'Let's see now if we can find some red and yellow autumn leaves to take home with us. / When we get home, you can tell me all about what happens to the tree and its leaves in the autumn."

HELPFUL HINTS

Choose a cool, crisp day for this activity so that the child will experience the coolness of an autumn day.

If you are unable to take the child to a tree with leaves that are turning color, collect several green, red, and yellow leaves. Include in your picture collection a picture of a brightly colored tree in autumn. Adapt the activity to telling the story of the tree in the four seasons, using the four pictures in doing so.

Be sure to ask the child to tell you the story about the tree when you are back inside at school. Ask questions to help him remember. Or tell the story again if he has difficulty with it. In either case, ask the key question: "What happens to the leaves of the tree when it gets cooler in autumn?"

THINGS TO DO ANOTHER TIME

Post pictures of trees that show their change over the four seasons of the year. Tell the story of how a tree and its leaves change, and have the child tell it to you.

Paste colored leaves on construction paper. Call the collage the child's autumn picture.

Rake and pile up leaves in the fall. Let the youngster run and jump and play in the leaves. Talk about what fun leaves are in the autumn.

Make a jack-o'-lantern for Halloween. Talk about how the pumpkin grows all summer when it is warm to be ready in time for Halloween in the autumn.

Relate the leaf cycle and seasonal events to the other seasons of the year as the child experiences them. Some ideas are given below.

WINTER: View and talk about the leafless trees that are taking a winter's nap; experience snow, ice, fog, frost on windows, or other characteristics of your winter season; freeze water in the refrigerator to make ice and watch the ice melt again; watch and talk about things people do in winter (ice skating, sledding, wearing heavier clothing).

SPRING: View and talk about newly sprouting plants and the trees waking up to grow new leaves; grow a bulb that produces an early spring flower; watch for other signs of spring such as birds returning, early spring flowers blooming, soft spring rains, people planting gardens.

SUMMER: View and talk about trees with heavy green foliage; water and talk about the need for watering plants and lawns; demonstrate the use of fans to keep cool; have fun with water play on hot days; view and talk about flowers and vegetables and fruit as they mature.

ACTIVITY 158:   Magnets

WHY

To see how magnets attract some metal objects.

WHAT YOU NEED

A magnet; small metal objects (safety pin, nail, paper clip); toothpick; two small pieces of paper; a metal and a non-metal button.

TALK ABOUT WHAT YOU DO

(Use your own language. This is an example.)

"Look what I have! (Hold magnet in open hand in front of child.) It's a special piece of metal called a *magnet*. Feel how hard the magnet is. / Let's see what a magnet can do."

(Put the safety pin, small nail, and paper clip on the table in front of child.) "These things are all made of metal like the magnet. Can you tell me their names? / Right! That's a safety pin and that's a nail. This is a paper clip. See how you can use it to clip paper together." (Demonstrate with your two small pieces of paper.)

"Watch carefully now. I'm going to hold the magnet *over* the pin—but not touch the pin. / Oops! Did you see that? / The magnet lifted the pin right off the table and held on to it. I'll put the pin back on the table and you try it now. / Oh, it lifted the pin for you too!"

"See if the magnet will pick up the nail too. / Do you think it will pick up the paper clip? / It sure did. The magnet picked up all the metal things."

"Here is a toothpick. (Put it on the table.) It's not metal. It is made of wood. Try the magnet on it. / Oh, the magnet won't pick up the wooden toothpick. Try it on this little piece of paper. / No, it won't pick up the paper, either."

"Try all the metal things again and see what the magnet does. / Did it pick up all the metal things?"

"Can you think of some other small things to try the magnet on? / Let's try it on these buttons. / What happened?"

HELPFUL HINTS

Supervise this activity closely since you are using small metal objects. Be sure that the child does not put any of the objects in his mouth or in a pocket.

You will want to demonstrate the use of a paper clip only if the child is being introduced to a paper clip for the first time. If you use other objects the child does not recognize, explain and demonstrate their purposes also.

THINGS TO DO ANOTHER TIME

Let the child use the magnet to try to pick up other objects (small metal/plastic bottle caps, metal/plastic thimbles, metal/glass buttons, rubber band, cork, screw, small key). Talk about what each object is made of.

Play a game to see which objects in the school a small magnet will adhere to. Try objects made of different kinds of materials and talk casually about what each is made of.

Make a fishing pole by tying a small magnet to the end of a line that is fastened to a stick or rod. Cut outlines of fish from construction paper and clip two outlines together with a paper clip or two. Put the "fish" in an empty pail and let the child catch them with his magnetic line. When the youngster catches a "fish," remind the child that the magnet and the paper clip are attracted to each other. Other surprise objects that the magnet will attract can be added to the pail.

ACTIVITY 159:   Ice

SCIENCE
C

WHY

To observe that water changes to ice in a refrigerator.

WHAT YOU NEED

Ice cubes; clear plastic tumbler; ice tray; pitcher; water. For second day, ingredients for a soft drink; glasses.

TALK ABOUT WHAT YOU DO

(Use your own language. This is an example.)

(Place several ice cubes in clear plastic tumbler.) "I have something here that is very, very cold. (Hold up tumbler.) Do you know what it is? / Yes, it is ice. Feel the ice with your finger. / Is it cold? / Hold the glass in your hand and see if the glass feels cold like the ice. / Hold it a little longer. / Can you feel the cold now? / The cold ice is making the glass feel cold, too."

"Let's make some ice. Ice is frozen water. Our refrigerator can change water into ice. It makes the water so cold that it freezes and changes into ice."

"We need this ice tray and a pitcher of water. Help me fill this pitcher with water. / Now you pour the water into the ice tray. (Set the tray where the child can pour comfortably and where any spillage will go into the sink.) There, the tray is full. I'll carry the tray carefully to the refrigerator and put it where the water will freeze."

"This is the place where the refrigerator is very cold. (Point.) See, the tray fits right in there. / Now, we'll close the door and by tomorrow the water will be changed into ice."

(Continue on next day.) "Let's see what happened to our tray of water that we put in the refrigerator yesterday. / Here is the tray. What has happened? / Feel the ice. / Is it hard? / Is it very cold? / Say, you made a big tray of ice. Let's use the ice in some nice lemonade, shall we? / Okay, help me make some lemonade."

"Let's taste the lemonade before we add the ice. (Put a little lemonade in a glass for tasting.) Is it very cold? / All right, let's put in some of your ice then and see what happens. / I'll stir it. / Here is your lemonade. Is it colder now from the ice? / The ice makes it taste nice and cold, doesn't it?"

HELPFUL HINTS

Any soft drink the child or children enjoy may be used in the second part of the activity.

If the school has no kitchen facilities, bring ice cubes in a cooler. Adapt and use only the second part of the activity.

THINGS TO DO ANOTHER TIME

Adapt the activity to making colored ice cubes by adding food coloring to the water. Let the child observe what the coloring does when you add it to the water and what it does to the ice.

Let the child help you make popsicles from orange juice or other fruit juices. Insert sticks (tongue compressors work well) in each cube after the liquid is partially frozen.

Let the youngster observe ice melting. Put several cubes of ice in a clear plastic glass, noting that there is no water in the glass, only ice. Have the child check the ice at intervals to note how the ice is changing back to water because it is getting warm.

ACTIVITY 160:   Changing Ingredients in Cooking

SCIENCE
C

WHY

To observe changes in ingredients when mixed together.

WHAT YOU NEED

Pudding mix ingredients; large bowl; measuring cup; mixing spoon; egg beater; pudding dishes.

TALK ABOUT WHAT YOU DO

(Use your own language. This is an example.)

(Place all ingredients and utensils on a table or counter where the child can see them.) "We are going to make some real, honest-to-goodness chocolate pudding today. Then we'll eat our honest-to-goodness pudding for lunch. How about that? / Here are all the things we need to make our pudding. Can you tell me what they are?" (Help the child identify each item.)

"First we have to measure out two cups of milk for the pudding. I'll pour some milk carefully into the measuring cup. / Now you pour the cup of milk carefully into the bowl. / Now I'll pour out a second cup of milk. / You pour cup two into the bowl. / There, that's two cups of milk in the bowl. See how white the milk is?"

"You can empty this pudding mix into the bowl now. / Oh, look! The pudding mix is getting wet from the milk. It is beginning to disappear. / Stir the milk and the mix carefully with the spoon. See if the mix all disappears. / Can you see the white milk any more? / The milk has turned brown, hasn't it? / That's because the pudding mix was brown. The mix had brown cocoa in it. It made the milk all brown.''

It's time to beat the pudding with this egg beater. Can you do that? / Start slowly. / Is the pudding getting thick? / I think the pudding is almost ready. (Hold egg beater up to test thickness of pudding.) See, the pudding sticks to the egg beater. That means it is getting thick. I'll beat it a little more just to be sure that it is done.''

"Let's pour the pudding into the dishes now. / Would you like to taste the pudding? / You can lick this spoon. / Help me put the pudding dishes in the refrigerator so the pudding gets nice and cold. / We'll have some of our pudding for lunch. / You know, you are a good cook.''

HELPFUL HINTS

Pudding of any flavor will do. But chocolate or butterscotch provide a very definite change in color of the milk for the youngster to observe.

Let the child help you in any way he can. An apron will reduce worry about getting clothes messy. But don't expect too much of the child. He may, for instance, be able to operate the egg beater only very slowly. Be diplomatic and complete the job yourself without calling attention to any inability to complete the job.

If you are working with several children, divide the tasks among them and give each child a chance to pour, stir, beat, and dish up the pudding.

THINGS TO DO ANOTHER TIME

If the school has cooking facilities, provide other simple cooking experiences for the youngster: making cookies, fixing jello, baking cupcakes, making hot chocolate (adding a marshmallow). Call attention to the way butter melts, how jello thickens as it cools and fluffs when you beat it, how the marshmallow melts in the hot chocolate, how raw cookie or cake batter tastes.

Pop corn. Let the child feel the popcorn before and after it is popped. Listen to the corn pop and explain that heat makes the kernel burst open with a loud "pop" as it does so. Place a kernel of popped and unpopped corn side by side for the youngster to compare color and size. Let the child watch the butter melt and help to salt and serve and eat the popcorn.

ACTIVITY 161:   Insects

WHY

To observe an insect.

WHAT YOU NEED

An insect (caterpillar) in a glass jar with holes punched in lid; a small green leaf or two.

TALK ABOUT WHAT YOU DO

(Use your own language. This is an example.)

"Look! There is something alive in this jar. Do you see it? / It's a caterpillar. It looks like a fuzzy worm, doesn't it? / What color is the caterpillar? / Yes, it's green, but can you find some brown on the caterpillar too?"

"Let's put this green leaf in the jar and watch what the caterpillar does. / Do you think it will eat the leaf? / Watch how it moves. / I think it may crawl on the leaf. / When a caterpillar is on a green leaf, it is hard for a hungry bird to see it. Birds like to eat caterpillars. But because this caterpillar is the same color as a leaf, it would be hard to find."

"Remember that pretty orange butterfly we saw in the park? / Well, believe it or not, this little caterpillar will become a pretty butterfly. You know how it does that? / After the caterpillar has been a caterpillar for a while, it covers itself all up with silk and then takes a long nap. While it is sleeping, it turns into a pretty colored butterfly. And when it wakes up, it flies away."

"We better let the little caterpillar go. It needs green leaves to eat so that it can turn into a butterfly. Let's take the jar outdoors. / We can watch the caterpillar crawl away home."

HELPFUL HINTS

The main purpose of this activity is to expose the preschooler to the world of insects by letting him examine closely some of the common insects in your locale. Any insect you can capture (or watch closely uncaptured) will do. In fact, the child may capture one himself to prompt the activity.

Do not supply too much information about the insect, but whatever information you supply should be accurate. A child's book on insects is a good source to go to in planning your lesson. If the child asks questions that you cannot answer, just say you don't know but "let's find out." Refer then to a child's book on insects or a children's encyclopedia.

Be sure to put your information about insects into words the youngster will understand.

THINGS TO DO ANOTHER TIME

Adapt the activity to other insects. Some common specimens and their characteristics are given below.

BUTTERFLY: A butterfly is like a pretty flying flower. It has two pairs of wings which are often brightly colored. It feeds on the nectar of flowers but doesn't hurt the flowers. The butterfly comes from the caterpillar, growing to its full size in its silk cocoon.

ANT: Ants live in large families. Each ant has a job to do. Ants often live in tunnels they build underground. Some ants eat grasses or other insects. An ant can carry a load much larger than itself.

FIREFLY: This insect is often called a lightning bug and is a kind of beetle (six legs) that can glow like a spark in the dark. Its light is on its abdomen, under its wings. It feeds during the day on pollen and other foods and it flies at night, flashing its light on and off.

LADYBUG: A ladybug is a small beetle. Its coloring is often red with black spots on its wings. It can fly. The ladybug is considered a good insect because it eats other insects which are harmful. It also eats green leaves.

Short trips introduce preschoolers to the wider world around them. A trip to the park
provided these youngsters with an opportunity to try out a new swing and an experience in sharing.

Part II

Trips

TRIPS

Trips are a way to introduce children to the wider world around them through firsthand experiences that cannot be brought into the nursery school. On trips they come in contact with new, real objects and events and with people in new and interesting roles. Trips can also be used to reinforce and extend concepts already learned: colors, shapes, sizes, smells, sounds, textures, objects, and concepts of movement and relational positions. They often provide ideas for dramatic play and make pictures, stories, and songs more meaningful to youngsters. A child, for example, who has experienced a bus trip may later enjoy pretending to be a bus driver or showing you in a picture of a bus just where the driver sits. He may take greater pleasure in listening to and participating in the song "The Wheels of the Bus Go Round and Round."

For children, and especially for the young child, the learning which takes place through firsthand experiences provided by a trip will be greatly enhanced if you follow a few general rules.

1. *Keep the trip simple.* Keep it close to the school. Do not search for the exotic. Young children will probably be more excited and interested in a kitten or a rabbit that they can hold and pet than in an elephant or a museum's dinosaur.

2. *Select a few "close-ups" for the child's particular attention on the trip and plan your learning activity around them.* Although the total trip experience is of importance to the child (who may see and remember things not included in your plans), maximum learning is more apt to take place if you limit your goals to a few concepts. On a trip to a department store, for instance, the largeness and bustle of the store may well overwhelm and confuse the child. But by pointing out and talking about a clown-faced clock and by looking at and touching one or two stuffed animal toys, you will give the youngster something he will remember, something that can be used and built on in developing an accurate understanding of what department stores are all about.

3. *Prepare the child for the trip by giving him some idea of what to expect.* Pictures, stories with pictures, toy replicas, and talking about what you will see and do, as well as the kind of behavior you expect of the child, are all ways to prepare for a trip. Before a bus trip you might show a picture of a bus (or use a toy bus) and point out the doors and windows. Talk about how you will get on the bus at the door and will look for a window seat so that you can see all the things the bus passes on the street. Or before a trip to a department store, you might talk about the moving stairs called an escalator and how you must stand very still on the steps while the escalator moves all the way to the top where you can get off.

4. *Timing the trip is another consideration.* Keep it short so as not to over-tire the child (or you). Pick a day of the week when the place to be visited is not too crowded. Arrange in advance for trips that need the cooperation of others: a visit to a friend's home to play with a puppy or to a firehouse to examine some of the fire fighting equipment. Plan to alternate your activity on the day of the trip with contrasting activities: quiet play or a nap prior to an active romping trip to the park, or romping, active play before a quiet trip to the library for a story hour.

5. *Give some thought to the dangers that may be involved in a trip and the kinds of fears the young child may have in coping with new people and new surroundings.* Make and stick to safety rules. Transmit a feeling of security by holding the child's hand, putting an arm around him when there is noise and confusion, and lifting him up in crowds so that he can see what is going on. If you are taking a small group of children on a trip, keep the group small enough for you to handle effectively, or secure the help of another adult. One adult for every two young children is a good rule of thumb to follow.

6. *But don't be overprotective of the child.* Encourage trying new experiences, responding to a friendly bus driver or clerk, playing with another child. These, too, are important kinds of learning for the youngster.

7. *After each trip, provide follow-up activities that help to reinforce and deepen the learning.* Read stories, or make them up, and look at picture books that relate to the child's trip experiences. Make a scrapbook of pictures and drawings or construct replicas of something seen on the trip. Encourage the child to act out trip experiences in dramatic play. Most important, let him tell you or someone else all about the trip, what he liked best and would like to do again.

The trip activities of this section suggest visits to places that are found in most neighborhoods. The number of trips, however, can be greatly increased, their nature depending on the community in which you live. Children are often interested in watching workmen at a construction project or a large machine at work. Some youngsters are interested in what goes on at a gas station or a car wash or a dairy. They may enjoy a visit to a nature museum, an amusement park, a camp ground, a zoo, or a marina. A wading pool or a shallow creek, lake, or river may provide them with an experience long remembered.

The structured trip activities found in this section follow the general rules given above. They often suggest simple ways to prepare the child for the trip and follow-up activities for after the trip. But be flexible. Pick up cues from the child. Let him do some exploring, discovering perhaps some of the very things built into the planned activity. And if you find that the child's interest takes an entirely different bent, adjust the activity to go along with his immediate interests. You can always try your planned activity another time.

ACTIVITY 162: Exploring the Immediate Neighborhood

TRIPS
B

WHY

To be aware of objects and people in the neighborhood.

WHAT YOU NEED

No materials needed.

TALK ABOUT WHAT YOU DO

(Use your own language. This is an example.)

"We are going for a walk today. You will be able to see and hear a lot of things. But remember you can't run into the road. The road is only for cars and trucks."

"Let's walk down this street. Where is the sidewalk? / Right. We have to walk on the sidewalk, don't we? / We can't walk in the road because that's where the cars are. You can hold my hand if you like."

"Can you tell me something you see on this street? / Yes, that's a car. What color is the car? / It is blue. Do you see a red car? / Very good."

"Look at the boy over there. (Point.) What is the boy doing? / He is riding a bike. See how fast he can ride. Oh, there he goes! His bike goes much faster than we can walk. What was the boy riding? / A bike. Very good."

"There is a pretty white house. (Point.) Who do you think lives in it? / Does the house have windows? / Where is the door? / Are there steps going up to the house?"

"I see some red flowers in that yard. Do you see them over there? (Point.) I bet the flowers smell nice. / No, we can't go over to see them. We can't walk on the grass. You can feel the grass though if you like. / How does the grass feel?"

"Shhh, listen. I hear something. Do you hear it? / What is it? / Yes, it's a dog barking. Can you see the dog? / Oh, there are two dogs, a big dog and a little dog. Can you bark like a dog? / Say, you sound just like the little dog!"

"Here we are at the end of the sidewalk. Let's turn around and go back."

"What did we do this morning? / Tell me about some of the things you saw on our walk."

HELPFUL HINTS

Make the trip as multi-sensory an experience as you can by calling attention to sounds, smells, and textures as well as to things to see.

Follow any cues to the child's interest in particular objects. But also focus attention on a few particular objects and sounds that might otherwise be missed.

Hold the child's hand if he shows any fear of new surroundings, and be alert to any possible dangers (bicycle rider, curbs). If you have a small group of children, have them hold each other's hands. Be strict about your rule to walk on the sidewalk.

THINGS TO DO ANOTHER TIME

Repeat the activity, walking on different streets in your neighborhood. Call the child's attention to a few new objects and talk about them. Ask him to name "old" objects and tell you about them. Stop and let him examine objects whenever possible: a mail box, a stop sign, a fence, a gate, a flower, or whatever attracts his attention.

Take a neighborhood walk on a rainy day so that the child experiences firsthand the feel of the rain and the sounds and smells that are part of a rainy day. Have him wear boots and a raincoat and use an umbrella. Show him how the umbrella opens and closes and how to carry it. Talk about the things that are associated with rain: puddles, streams, clouds, wet soil, raindrops on the grass and dripping from branches or roofs.

ACTIVITY 163:   Visiting a Pet

TRIPS
C

WHY

To become acquainted with animals and their ways.
To learn how to play with animals.

WHAT YOU NEED

No materials needed.

TALK ABOUT WHAT YOU DO

(Use your own language. This is an example.)

"You'll never guess what we are going to do today! We are going to pay a visit to Fluffy. Do you know who Fluffy is? / She's a little white dog that lives across the street."

"This is Fluffy. Listen to her bark. She's saying 'Hello' to you. / Let's pet her. Fluffy likes to be petted very gently. (Demonstrate.) Would you like to pet her? / She feels very soft, doesn't she? / Oh, Fluffy likes you. See, she's wagging her tail. That means she likes you."

"Where are Fluffy's ears? / Where is her nose? / This is one of Fluffy's paws. (Touch or hold the paw in your hand.) Dogs' feet are called *paws*. Some dogs shake hands with their paws, like this." (Demonstrate if dog is gentle.)

"This is Fluffy's dish. She can drink water out of it. There, see how she laps up the water. My, she must have been thirsty."

"Where do you think Fluffy sleeps? / Does she have a bed like yours? / This is her bed. She likes to sleep on the rug in the box when she is tired."

(Let the child watch and play with the dog if he is interested in doing so.)

"Say good-bye to Fluffy now. / Did you have fun playing with Fluffy? / Tell me all the things Fluffy can do."

HELPFUL HINTS

Arrange ahead of time for the visit with a friend or neighbor who owns a pet. Be sure that the pet is friendly with children.

Give a timid child time to become acquainted with the pet. A child who at first is reluctant to pet a dog (or handle any animal) should not be forced to do so. With a little time the child may well lose his fear and find himself enjoying playing with and petting the dog.

As a follow-up to the visit, look at pictures of dogs and read or tell simple stories about dogs.

THINGS TO DO ANOTHER TIME

Arrange to visit other pets in your neighborhood: a kitten or cat, fish, bird, hamster, turtle, or any other small, tame animal. Let the child watch and, when feasible, touch and pet the animal. If the child asks questions about the pet, the owner may be able to answer them. Talk about what the pet eats, its shelter, how it sleeps, and the sounds it makes. Always emphasize gentleness in handling the animal.

Visit an available park or farm that has animals. Children usually enjoy seeing rabbits, ducks, lambs, ponies, and other animals that can be petted and played with.

Visit a zoo or a pet shop to extend the child's experiences with animals. Prepare for the visit by looking at pictures of animals, and help the child select several to see at the zoo or petshop. Do not try to see too many at one time. Allowing the child to spend time watching a few animals and talking about them will be more profitable.

ACTIVITY 164:   Exploring the Neighborhood by Bus

TRIPS
C

WHY

To take a bus ride.
To extend the child's world.

WHAT YOU NEED

Picture of a bus; bus fare.

TALK ABOUT WHAT YOU DO

(Use your own language. This is an example.)

"We are going to take a bus trip today. Do you know what a bus looks like? (Show a picture of a bus.) We'll get on the bus right here. (Point to door.) I'll hold your hand and help you up. Then we'll sit down on a seat by the window so that you'll be able to see all kinds of things as we ride. What would you like to see?"

"This is our bus stop. See, it says *Bus* on this pole so people know the bus will stop here and they can get on. / Here comes our bus now. / Give me your hand. Up you go!"

"What can you see out of your window? / What is that? Right! It's a house. Look at all the houses on this street. Who do you think lives in them? / What else do you see?"

"Here's another bus stop. The bus has to stop so those people can get on the bus. Where do you think they are all going? / Some are probably going to work or to the store. Maybe some are just taking a ride the way we are."

"Oh, look at this big building. See the tall steeple? It goes up, up, up, into the sky. / The building is a church where people go to talk to God. Can you say *church?* / Very good!"

"Look. There is a school. See all the children playing in the playground. / Those children go to school to learn to do lots of things just like you."

"We are going to get off at the next bus stop. Then we'll get on another bus to take us back to school again."

"Did you have fun riding on the bus? / What did you like most about the bus trip?"

HELPFUL HINTS

Do not make the trip too long or the child's interest will wane. Remember you have to cover the same distance to get back again.

Try to pick a route that will interest the child. A stop for a snack or a closer look at something interesting (a playground or a fire engine) may give the trip the variation the child needs.

If the child seems concerned in any way, hold him on your lap in the bus. It will reassure him.

If you do not have a bus system, plan the trip around a car ride or a school bus ride. Be sure the driver drives slowly to give the child the time he needs to see particular things.

THINGS TO DO ANOTHER TIME

Repeat the activity, taking a trip through other parts of your community that will allow the child to see stores, garages, a firehouse, and other places of interest.

Extend the learning on later bus trips by focusing for a little while on the driver and the fares. Sit in the front of the bus and watch other people pay their fares, and notice what the driver does when driving the bus.

Encourage the child or children to pretend to take a bus ride. A few chairs will serve as bus seats with a chair in front for the driver. Play money and a box for fares are other props which will help the child act out getting on the bus, paying fares, finding seats, and imagining things seen out the window. And don't forget the role of the bus driver. The child will enjoy it, too.

ACTIVITY 165: Exploring the Grocery Store

TRIPS
C

WHY

To be aware of a grocery store and buying food.
To see and name various kinds of fruit.

WHAT YOU NEED

No materials needed.

TALK ABOUT WHAT YOU DO

(Use your own language. This is an example.)

"Today we are going to a grocery store. What can you buy at a grocery store? / Yes, cookies. You can buy many other kinds of food, all kinds of good things to eat. Do you like oranges? / You can buy oranges at the grocery store. What other kinds of fruit do you think you will see at the grocery store?"

"Here's our grocery store. My, it's big, isn't it? / Let's look at the fruit and see if you can find some of the kinds you told me about."

"Look at all the different kinds of fruit! Can you find an orange? / That's right. The orange juice you drink comes from oranges like this."

"What other kinds of fruit do you see? / What is that called? (Point.) It's a banana. Bananas are yellow. Can you say *banana?* / Good! Remember how sweet a banana tastes when you eat it?"

"Is an apple a fruit? / Yes, it is. Can you see any apples? / Very good! Those are red apples. What's this? (Point to or hold up a green apple.) It's an apple too, but it's a green apple. Green apples are good for apple pie."

"What are these? (Point to or hold up a bunch of grapes.) They are grapes. Grapes are fruit, too. See all the little grapes."

"Let's buy some fruit. What would you like? / Okay, we'll get some bananas."

"We have to give the bananas to the lady at the counter and pay her for them. I'll give you the money and you can pay the lady."

"When we get home, we'll have a banana party. You can peel a banana and we'll eat it. And you can tell all about your visit to the grocery store."

HELPFUL HINTS

Select a time for your visit when the grocery store has relatively few customers.

Be sure the child understands the food is *for sale*. Take precautions against overhandling the produce or otherwise damaging store items.

Keep the focus of the trip on a particular category of food and use it to extend the child's concept of the category by seeing and identifying items belonging to the category (fruit).

Encourage the child to talk about what he sees. Use questions and give information as needed to broaden the experience and the concepts.

THINGS TO DO ANOTHER TIME

Repeat the activity, visiting other sections of the store: fresh vegetables, dairy products, bakery goods, canned goods. Let the child help you shop for a few items each time.

Cut out pictures of goods and people seen at the grocery store. Help the child make a scrapbook. Encourage the child to talk about each picture and his trips to the grocery store.

Set up a grocery store for dramatic play. See Activity 112 for suggestions.

ACTIVITY 166: A Trip to the Park

TRIPS
C

WHY

To be aware of a park and some of its uses.
To examine and collect nature objects.

WHAT YOU NEED

A bag or box for items collected; a picnic snack.

TALK ABOUT WHAT YOU DO

(Use your own language. This is an example.)

"We are going to a park today. Do you know what a park is? / It's a place with lots of trees and grass. People go to the park to play and have picnics. Would you like to visit a park? / Well, we are going to the park. Maybe you can find things like pretty stones and leaves to bring home with us. We can have a picnic in the park, too."

"Here we are at the park. See all the grass and trees? / Let's walk down this path to see what you can find to put in your bag. Look for anything you would like to save and take home with you."

"Oh, that's a pretty leaf you found. What color is it? / Your leaf is pointed here at the top. (Touch or point.) Feel the point? / See the stem of the leaf? Look at this tree. (Pull down branch so child can see the leaves closely.) See how each leaf is attached to the tree by its stem? / Would you like to put the leaf in your bag?"

"Look at these pretty little stones. Can you find a white one? / That's a pretty white stone. It is round too. Can you roll it? / See if you can find a stone that isn't round, a flat one. / That's sort of flat, but it has bumps. Can you feel the bumps? / Here is a stone that is flat. Try to roll it. / No, it won't roll. The stone is flat."

(If the child is still interested, have him look for other nature objects and talk about them.)

"It is time for our picnic now. Let's sit here in the shade and eat our picnic lunch."

"We have to pick up all our trash. We want to keep the park clean. / Let's put our wrappers in the picnic bag so that we can throw them in a trash container."

"When we get home, you can look at all the things you found and tell me about them."

HELPFUL HINTS

Use a park in your neighborhood for this activity. It can be very small or even just open space.

Let the child enjoy any aspect of the park that he likes, but set aside the first 10–20 minutes for the directed learning experience, the collecting of nature objects. Use the activity to reinforce sensory learning by encouraging the use of all the senses in examining his collection.

Give the child freedom to find and select items on his own. But if you spot such things as an acorn, a pine cone, a dandelion, a feather, or some other collector's item, call attention to it and let the youngster take it from there.

THINGS TO DO ANOTHER TIME

Repeat the activity to add to the child's collection. Or vary the learning focus: watch and listen to birds and squirrels; find things of different colors or shapes; find things that are *long/short, soft/hard, smooth/rough;* look for insects such as ants, bees, and butterflies.

Visit a park to introduce the child to swings and slides and to the idea of taking turns when other children are using the same equipment.

Use the park for running, jumping, and hopping for motor skill development. If the park has a sandbox or the equivalent, use it also to introduce the child to the skills of digging and shoveling.

ACTIVITY 167:   A Trip to the Mailbox

TRIPS
C

WHY

To mail a card.
To introduce, reinforce, and extend concepts *mail carrier, card,* and *mailbox.*

WHAT YOU NEED

Note card (see "Helpful Hints" below); pen; envelope; and stamp.

TALK ABOUT WHAT YOU DO

(Use your own language. This is an example.)

"Look at this pretty card. See the picture? / Yes, it's a kitten. Open the card. / There (point) is a place for writing. I'm going to write a note to you and send you this card. Won't that be nice? / Remember the mail carrier we saw yesterday? / Well, we will take this card to a special mailbox and mail it. Then after a while the mail carrier will bring the card and put it in our mailbox just for you."

"First, I have to write inside the card. (Say each word as you write it.) 'Dear—John, I—love—you.' I'll add some hugs and kisses. / These little round circles (point) mean a big hug for you. These crosses (point) mean a big kiss. / I have to write my name so you will know who sent you this card."

"We have to tell the mail carrier where you go to school so he will know where to bring the card. (Address envelope.) Now we can put the card in the envelope. / You know what? / When I wet the edge of the envelope it gets all sticky. There is glue on it. / Feel the glue? / Help me close up the envelope. / Press hard so the glue will stick. / We have to put a stamp on the envelope. This is a stamp. (Point.) The stamp has glue on the back too. / Help me stick it on this corner of the envelope. / Now we are all ready for our trip to the special mailbox."

"Here is the mailbox. What color is it? / See this little door? (Open mail slot.) We have to put the card in that little door. I'll lift you up and you put the card in the door. (Hold door open, too.) You mailed the card. Terrific! Now the mail carrier will pick up the card, read where you go to school, and put it in our mailbox for you."

"We can go back to school now. / Let's look in our mailbox and see if the mail carrier left us any mail today. / No, your card won't be there yet. Maybe it will come tomorrow or the next day."

HELPFUL HINTS

The note card can be made by folding a piece of paper and pasting a picture on the top side of the paper.

Before the activity, be sure to point out the local mail carrier to the child and explain in simple language what he or she does: brings mail to your house and school and puts it in the mailbox. Show him the mailbox and a letter or card which the mail carrier delivered.

Follow up the activity by watching for the mail carrier and checking the mailbox to see if the card was delivered. Let the child open the envelope and talk again about the card, mailing it, and its delivery.

THINGS TO DO ANOTHER TIME

Help the child make a card and send it to someone. Repeat the trip to the mailbox for this purpose. See Activity 65 for suggestions for making a card.

Be outdoors when your mail carrier comes. Talk about what he does. Walk with the child down the street to watch the delivery of mail to several mailboxes along the way. Let the child open some letters (junk mail) delivered in your mailbox.

Take short walks to see and watch other workers in your neighborhood: a crossing guard directing traffic, men repairing a road or painting a house, sanitation workers doing their jobs. Talk about any tools they use as well as what they are doing.

ACTIVITY 168:   Exploring a Department Store

TRIPS
C

WHY

To be aware of a department store and some things it sells.
To ride on an escalator.

WHAT YOU NEED

No materials needed.

TALK ABOUT WHAT YOU DO

(Use your own language. This is an example.)

"I bet you can't guess where we are going today! We are going to a department store. A department store is a big, big store that sells a lot of different things: shoes and socks and TVs and blankets and clocks and toys and ever so many other things. What would you like to see at the store?"

"Here we are at the big store. Hold my hand. / First we will look at the clocks. That was one of the things you wanted to see, wasn't it?"

"Look at all those clocks. / See the big clock (point) that looks like a frying pan? / Oh, there is a blue one that looks like a cat. (Point.) See its long tail? / Do you remember what a clock says? / It says 'tick, tick, tick,' doesn't it? / That clock cat says 'tick, tick, tick,' but a real cat says 'meow.' "

"See those steps? (Point.) They are moving. Watch the lady get on the steps. The steps are taking her up to the next floor. The steps are called an *escalator*. Let's ride on the escalator. I'll hold your hand. Remember, you have to stand still on these steps."

"Here we go! / Stand still. We are going up, up, up. / We are almost at the top. / We have to get off now. / That was fun, wasn't it?"

"We are going to look at some stuffed animal toys now. / Oh, my goodness, look at that big giraffe! (Point.) See the long neck it has? / What color is the giraffe? / Yes, it's yellow and it has black spots. / Here is a little puppy. Would you like to hold it? / Feel how soft the puppy's fur feels. / The puppy belongs to the store, so we have to put it back carefully. / Would you like to touch another one of the animals?"

"It is time to go back now. / We can come back again and look at some more toys."

"What did you like best in the department store? / Yes, the ride on the escalator was fun. Tell me about some of the other things you saw in the store."

HELPFUL HINTS

Select only a few things for the child to view and, when possible, to touch and manipulate. Those merely viewed should be large objects that can be seen well from a distance and will hold the child's attention for a short time.

If the youngster is frightened by the escalator or you feel it is safer, hold him during the ride on the escalator. If you have more than one child on the trip, ride an elevator rather than the escalator.

Limit time spent in the store and leave before the child becomes fatigued or disinterested. Do *not* make the trip an extended shopping trip, although the purchase of one item that the child can help pick out may interest the youngster.

THINGS TO DO ANOTHER TIME

Repeat the activity, exploring other departments of the store. Other toys and a tropical fish section will probably be of special interest to a young child. If the store has an elevator, ride it also.

Visit other kinds of stores: shoe stores, drugstores, and hardware stores are often of interest to children.

Help the child put together a store for dramatic play. See Activity 112 for some suggestions.

ACTIVITY 169:   Exploring a Library

TRIPS
C

WHY

To be aware of a library.
To take out a book.

WHAT YOU NEED

A library card; picture of a library (inside view) or of shelves of books.

TALK ABOUT WHAT YOU DO

(Use your own language. This is an example.)

"Look at this picture. What do you see? / Yes, lots and lots of books. A place that has lots and lots of books is called a *library*. Can you say *library?* / Try again: *li-bra-ry?* / Good! We are going to visit a library and see all kinds of books. You can bring a book back from the library, too."

"Here we are at the library. See all the books? / Some are about animals, like puppies and baby horses. Some are about little boys and girls like you. You can pick out a book and look at it. Which book would you like to look at? / Oh, that is a nice book. Sit here and turn the pages carefully."

(Allow the child to look at several books if he remains interested. Help him turn the pages if he has difficulty. Talk about the pictures.)

"Which of these books should we take with us? / That's a good book. Let's take it to the lady at the desk. She is called a *librarian*. The librarian will check the book out for us. Then we can take it back to school for a while."

"Can you tell me where we went today? / What did you do at the library? / What did the lady at the desk do? / Let's read the book you took out of the library."

HELPFUL HINTS

Be sure to obtain a library card before the visit so you can take out a book.

The child is ready for this activity when he has learned to turn individual pages of a book and not to tear pages. If the child has not reached this stage, you may want to visit a library but without the child's handling the books by himself. Turn the pages for him so that he can look at the pictures.

Supervise the child's use of the library book which you bring home or back to school. It may be a good idea to let him handle it only when you are present. Remind him to turn the pages carefully so as not to tear the pages because the book belongs to the library and must be returned to the library in good condition. Remove the date-due card so it isn't lost.

THINGS TO DO ANOTHER TIME

If the child enjoyed the visit to the library, repeat it to help him develop an interest in books.

Check the schedule of story hours at the library and take the child to the library for a story hour.

Play "Librarian" at home after one or several trips to the library. Place some books on a shelf (cardboard boxes) and make a library card. Let the child act out a visit to the library, taking out a book, and being the librarian. If you are working with a small group of children, have them take turns in both the role of the visitor and of the librarian.

ACTIVITY 170:   A Trip to the Firehouse

TRIPS
C

WHY

To see a real fire truck.
To name some fire equipment.

WHAT YOU NEED

Picture of a fire truck or a toy fire
truck.

TALK ABOUT WHAT YOU DO

(Use your own language. This is an example.)

"We are going on a trip in the neighborhood. Bet you can't guess where. / We are going to visit a firehouse. What do you think you will see there? / Right! A fire truck and maybe some of the people who are fire fighters."

"Look at this picture of a fire truck. See the man (point) who drives the truck? / Where is his hat? / What is this? (Point to ladder.) Right! The fire fighters use a ladder to climb up a burning building, don't they? / Can you find the fire hose? / There it is. (Point.) They use a hose to spray water on the fire to put out the fire. What is this? (Point to bell.) Very good! We are going to see all these things at the firehouse."

"Oh, do you see what I see? It is a big, big fire truck! What color is it? / Let's see if we can find some of the things we saw in the picture of the fire truck."

(If anyone is available, ask to be shown the fire truck and equipment at close range. If this is not possible, point to various pieces of equipment from a short distance and talk about how each is used.)

"We can look at the picture of the fire truck again when we get home, and you can tell me all about the real fire truck and the other things you saw."

HELPFUL HINTS

The closer a child can get to the fire truck and equipment, the more interesting the experience will be for him. If someone at the firehouse is willing to spend a few minutes with you and the child, by all means have him do so.

If you take a group of children on the trip, it is a good idea to stop at the firehouse or call in advance and arrange for the visit.

Don't go into great detail on the equipment or get too technical. The fire fighter's hat, ladder, hose, bell, and siren are probably the items the child will understand most easily.

THINGS TO DO ANOTHER TIME

Make a firehouse from a good sized box. Cut doors at one end for the fire truck to go in and out of. Cover the box with red Contact paper or paint it red. Encourage the child to pretend to be a fire fighter going to a fire and putting it out. If a toy fire engine is not available, use a toy truck or some other vehicle. A rope makes a good hose. Have the youngster make his own sound effects (bell, siren).

Make a fireman's hat for the child to wear: (1) Use a double sheet of newspaper. Start from the folded top and fold corners to center (Fig. 170.1). About two inches will be left at the bottom.

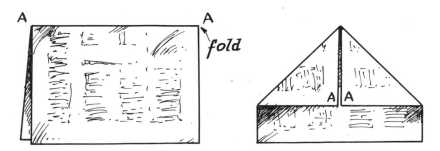

Fig. 170.1

(2) Fold up bottom of each sheet to make the brim of a three-cornered hat (Fig. 170.2). Staple the brim in place on each side of the hat.

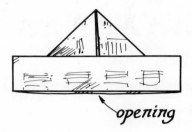

Fig. 170.2

(3) Fold one end under to make the front of the hat (Fig. 170.3). Staple in place. The hat may also be painted red.

Fig. 170.3

Index

Up 96–97, 131
Unzipping *See* Zipping and unzipping

Visual memory 133–135

Walking, running, jumping 129–131
Water properties 415–417

Wavy *See* Straight/wavy
Weather 409–411
What You Need 18
Whole-object puzzles 311–312, 313–315, 315–317

Zipping and unzipping 97–99